Leo Durocher

Leo Durocher

Baseball's Prodigal Son

PAUL DICKSON

BLOOMSBURY
NEW YORK · LONDON · OXFORD · NEW DELHI · SYDNEY

Bloomsbury USA
An imprint of Bloomsbury Publishing Plc

1385 Broadway	50 Bedford Square
New York	London
NY 10018	WC1B 3DP
USA	UK

www.bloomsbury.com

ISBN: HB: 978-1-63286-311-9
       ePub: 978-1-63286-312-6

LIBRARY OF CONGRESS CATALOGING-IN-PUBLICATION DATA

Names: Dickson, Paul, author.
Title: Leo Durocher: baseball's prodigal son / Paul Dickson.
Description: New York: Bloomsbury USA, An imprint of Bloomsbury Publishing
Plc, 2017. | Includes bibliographical references.
Identifiers: LCCN 2016031064 (print) | LCCN 2016033019 (ebook) | ISBN 9781632863119
(Hardcover) | ISBN 9781632863133 (Paperback) | ISBN 9781632863126
(ePub) | ISBN 9781632863126 (e-book)
Subjects: LCSH: Durocher, Leo, 1906-1991. | Baseball managers—United
States—Biography. | Baseball—United States—History.
Classification: LCC GV865.D83 A3 2017 (print) | LCC GV865.D83 (ebook) | DDC
796.357092 [B]—dc23
LC record available at https://lccn.loc.gov/2016031064

2 4 6 8 10 9 7 5 3 1

Typeset by RefineCatch Limited, Bungay, Suffolk
Printed and bound in the U.S.A. by Berryville Graphics, Inc., Berryville, Virginia

Paul Dickson can be reached through his webpage: pauldicksonbooks.com

To our grandchildren, Pearl, Everett, and James

A restless Leo prowls and growls. Photo credit: Library of Congress, *Look* Magazine Photograph Collection, James Hansen photographer, 1966

Fate is a rat.

Enormous charm, but back him into a corner and he is still that kid in a pool room in Springfield, wearing a leather jacket, with a sawed-off cue in his hands.

Leo Durocher is more of an American institution than Colonel Sanders. Before this country ever heard of Kennedy, Nixon, Gable, Disney, Earhart, DiMaggio, Presley, Flash Gordon or Dr. Spock, people knew about Leo Durocher.

After a time you will gradually forget all about the other world of Republicans and Democrats, Communists and Capitalists, Hemingway, the D. and D. of Windsor and Leo Durocher.

Contents

1. Pregame   1
2. Enfant Terrible   9
3. Damned Yankee   25
4. The Red Menace   46
5. Gashouse Tough   61
6. The Artful Dodger   75
7. Mutiny in Flatbush   102
8. Game Changer   131
9. Exiled   155
10. Over the River   181
11. Miracle Man   202
12. Hollywood Dodger   224
13. The Contentious Cub   247
14. Endgame   269
15. The Rocky Road to Cooperstown   288
   Acknowledgments   *309*
   Bibliography   *313*
   Notes   *323*
   Index   *351*

CHAPTER 1

Pregame

L EO DUROCHER (1905–1991) was baseball's all-time leading character—cocky, flamboyant, and galvanizing, casting a shadow across several baseball eras, from the time of Babe Ruth to the space-age Astrodome, from Prohibition through the Vietnam War. For more than forty years, he was a dominant figure in the game, with a Zelig-like ability to be present as a player or manager for some of the greatest teams and defining baseball moments of the twentieth century.

Unlike the passive Leonard Zelig, however, Durocher was an actor in all of it. He performed on three main stages: New York, Chicago, and Hollywood. He entered from the wings, strode to where the lights were brightest, and then took a poke at anyone who tried to upstage him. He shared the limelight on occasion, but only with Hollywood stars such as Spencer Tracy, whom he called his "lucky coin"; movie tough guy and sometime roommate George Raft; "best friend" Frank Sinatra; and his third wife, movie star Laraine Day.

He had the right script. Durocher played shortstop for four major league teams, including two that were given nicknames that still resonate today—the 1928 "Murderers' Row" New York Yankees and the 1934 "Gashouse Gang" St. Louis Cardinals. Both of these great teams won the World Series with Durocher playing shortstop. He also appeared as a player on three National League All-Star teams: in 1936 (as a Cardinal) and in 1938 and 1940 (as a Brooklyn Dodger). Although he had a lackluster lifetime batting average of .247—teammate Babe Ruth nicknamed him "the All-American Out" because of his anemic

1

offense—he earned a reputation as the best defensive shortstop of the era before World War II.

DUROCHER WENT ON to become manager of four major league teams for a total of twenty-four seasons. He managed 2,008 wins in 3,739 games, winning three National League pennants (in 1941, 1951, and 1954) and the World Series in 1954. He was named Manager of the Year three times by *The Sporting News*. His lifetime winning percentage with the Dodgers, Giants, Cubs, and Astros was .540. At the time of his death, only five managers in major league history had won more games than Durocher's 2,008.

Two of the teams he managed—the New York Giants and the Chicago Cubs—played in pennant races considered to be two of the most exciting of the twentieth century. One was in 1951, when Durocher's Giants overcame a 13½ game deficit, going 37–7 down the stretch to catch the runaway Brooklyn Dodgers and beat them in a playoff series that ended with Bobby Thomson's epic home run, the "Shot Heard 'Round the World." That final game, called the "Miracle of Coogan's Bluff," is still regarded as among the greatest single games in baseball history. The other pennant race involved Durocher's 1969 Cubs, who had a nine-game lead in August, only to lose to the underdog New York Mets, who came out of the pack to win the pennant and ultimately the World Series.

These two pennant drives are the only two in baseball history routinely described with the word *miracle*, and controversy followed Durocher after each of them. Did his elaborate system of sign stealing and cheating contribute to the come-from-behind wins and Thomson's home run? Did the 1969 Cubs lose in part because Leo so demoralized his players, treating them unevenly down the stretch, deserting them during two key moments, creating turmoil in the clubhouse, and callously degrading them in defeat? "Our offense went down the toilet, the defense went down the drain, and I'm still looking for a pitching staff," he said of his 1969 team after they lost the pennant. "I could have dressed nine broads as ballplayers and they would have beaten the Cubs."

Durocher had a profound impact on managing, with disciples who are now among the handful of managers in the National Baseball Hall of Fame. "When I was a coach, my number was 52," Tommy Lasorda said at the time of Durocher's death. "When I became manager, I wanted to carry Leo's number because of my respect and my admiration for him. He was an outstanding manager. In wearing his number, I hoped some of him would wear off on me. He was brilliant, by far one of the greats. He was a gambling, aggressive manager. He didn't worry about people second-guessing him. He had an electrifying personality with an ability to motivate men."

Durocher was also one of the most hated men in the game, a distinction he did little to shed and much to cultivate. Called "baseball's problem child," he routinely attracted adjectives for aggressiveness: *combative, fierce, fiery, feisty, bellicose, pugnacious, cheeky, contentious, truculent,* and *scrappy.* He was one of the fiercest bench jockeys of all time. As a manager, he unapologetically used the brush-back and beanball as weapons of intimidation, and his victims knew who to blame when they got drilled. In September 1953, when Durocher was managing the New York Giants, he told his pitcher to hit star outfielder Carl Furillo of the Brooklyn Dodgers. As Furillo made his way to first base after being hit, Durocher wagged his finger at him. Furillo charged the Giants' dugout, got Durocher in a head-lock, and began choking him. In the melee, Furillo's hand was broken, and he was shelved for the rest of the season. At the time, Furillo led the National League in batting. Durocher could also intimidate his own players when it suited him. Ralph Cannon of the *Chicago Herald-American* wrote in 1947, "He could infuriate his men to superhuman effort out of sheer hatred of him personally."[1]

Ty Cobb hated Leo because he constantly baited him with insults. Leo also played the bully to Babe Ruth, whom he called "Dummy" when they were Yankee teammates. Ruth accused Durocher of stealing his wrist-watch. Years later, when Ruth's playing days were over, he was hired by the Brooklyn Dodgers as a first-base coach. Durocher went out of his way to humiliate Ruth. The relationship ended in a fistfight that began when Durocher slapped Ruth in the face because of confusion over a signal. Manager Burleigh Grimes had to pull them apart.

In December 1948, after Durocher became manager of the New York Giants, Dan Desmond, who wrote for the Hearst newspaper chain, began a series on Durocher that opened with: "No man in baseball history has been so consistent at provoking antagonisms, developing hatreds and setting up situations of violence. There is no temporizing for him. Once he has started an argument—he fights down to the finish. For him it's all out or nothing." Less than a year later, the legendary columnist Shirley Povich, writing in *The Washington Post,* called Durocher "the most hated man in his profession."[2]

Yet for all of the hatred he generated, he was a genius at turning it to his favor and making himself the center of attention. He thrived on bad press and the use of incivility as a means to getting his way. "No matter where you are," said one of his friends, an advertising executive named Corny Jackson, "you can stock a room with twenty people with better minds and better looks, and Leo will stand out like a neon light." As Harold Parrott, a former newsman and an official of the Brooklyn Dodgers during Durocher's years with the club, put it: "If he wanted to he could walk into a room full of atomic scientists with some kind of information he had picked up in the men's room, and hold them spellbound."[3]

Durocher hogged headlines for decades, and not just atop the sports pages. He was an icon of popular culture, appearing regularly in the gossip columns and being heard on radio comedies and then seen on popular television sitcoms of the black-and-white era.

Durocher also garnered headlines for his four weddings and four divorces. Three of his wives were strong women with their own careers who divorced him either because of his serial infidelities or his inability to give up gambling, or both. For all of his on-field reputation as a hothead, his main offense against these women was indifference and inattention. Durocher's most famous ex-wife, Laraine Day, remarked about their post-divorce relationship: "There was no bitterness. We had just become interested in different things and different people. But we always stayed friends." Leo's public savagery, she said, was a "self-created thing." She insisted that he was a nice guy, even if he lived by the motto "Nice guys finish last," sliding into *Bartlett's Famous Quotations* on the strength of that line.[4]

Durocher gained notoriety for several odd tiffs and snits, such as when he sued actress Zsa Zsa Gabor and the advertising agency that hired her for a cool million because she invoked his name in a television commercial for the AAMCO chain of transmission shops. "Tell 'em Leo sent you" was the offending line, and it worked because there was only one Leo out there who mattered. Gabor and the advertising agency settled out of court, but in typical Durocher style, the matter was hashed out on Johnny Carson's *Tonight Show*, where both Leo and Zsa Zsa were regular guests.

Durocher was a fan favorite, not because the fans liked him, but because they loved to bait him, even when he was winning. The writers knew this and gave him ink by the barrelful. They loved to watch him crash and burn and then rise from the ashes more arrogant and confident than ever.

In New York, he dominated the sports pages from the time of Damon Runyon and Grantland Rice up to that of Pete Hamill and Jimmy Breslin. When Durocher died in 1991, the sportswriter Dave Anderson wrote a piece about him in *The New York Times* entitled "Leo the Lip Was Baseball in New York," and when he was finally elected to the National Baseball Hall of Fame in 1994, Steve Jacobson of *Newsday* wrote "Durocher was one of the things the world disliked about New York."[5]

Durocher's appeal came in part because he chose to live and operate outside the lines—literally and figuratively outside the box. Unlike other managers, when his team was at bat he ran the offense from the third-base coach's box, but only after he had erased the chalked rectangle forming the box. Friend and baseball historian David Hubler, who grew up in the Bronx as a devoted Giants fan, recalls the ritual. "The first thing we did was find Laraine Day in her special box and then we waited for the Giants to bat and for Durocher to come running out of the dugout and use his spikes to kick away all the chalk lines on the third base. He always stayed in the box but it had no lines."[6]

Durocher's words, like baseball shoes, came with sharpened spikes. "How you play the game is for college boys," he said. "When you're playing for money, winning is the only thing that matters." When he was a manager, opposing batters moving close to the plate often heard him bellow to his pitcher, "Stick it in his ear." He scoffed at the concept of good sportsmanship: "Show me a good loser in professional sports, and I'll show you an idiot." Or: "If I was playing third base and my mother was rounding third with the run that was going to beat us, I'd trip her. Oh, I'd pick her up and brush her off and say, 'Sorry, Mom,' but nobody beats me." In his 1975 autobiography *Nice Guys Finish Last*, Leo recalls how hurt his mother was when she heard this. "She looked at me, and her eyes bugged out. 'Then you *would* have tripped me,' she screamed. 'You would have *tripped* me. You *would*! You *would*!' For the rest of my visit she walked around with an injured air. And I guess she had a right to. God rest your soul, Mom, I'm afraid I would."[7]

At his worst Durocher was a cologne-soaked bully with a talent for creating bad situations and, as Brooklyn Dodgers general manager Branch Rickey once said, "then making them worse." At his best, Durocher was a brilliant manager with a comic timing that allowed him to play straight man to a talking horse in a 1963 episode of the sitcom *Mister Ed.* He also played a key role in baseball's racial integration, gaining acceptance for

Jackie Robinson and nurturing a scared, slumping rookie named Willie Mays into becoming one of the game's all-time greatest players.

For all of his shortcomings, Durocher was generous and generally kind when it came to his dealings with children and with batboys, who occupied the lowest rung on the clubhouse ladder. Stan Strull, who knew him on a regular basis at Ebbets Field, later said, "He was aces in the clubhouse and always a big tipper." Another batboy who worked under him recalled him as somewhat distant from the clubhouse kids but as someone who would put the arm on the players to kick in for their expense money.[8]

As a manager, he integrated the New York Giants. Outfielder Monte Irvin and infielder Hank Thompson were called up late in the 1949 season and were welcomed by Durocher. Irvin remembered, "Manager Leo Durocher called a team meeting and said, 'I want to introduce these two fellows. I think they can help us. Let me say this about race—I don't care if you're black, white or green, if you can play baseball, you're welcome. That's all I'm going to say about it.' So he paved the way for us."[9]

Willie Mays and Irvin always maintained their respect for Durocher, and Mays was the only baseball player to speak at his funeral. Other black players chimed in over time. "In terms of kindness to younger players, the compassion he gave to black players," wrote Maury Wills, who had encountered him as a coach for the Los Angeles Dodgers, "Leo Durocher was surely one of the nice guys."

Durocher himself would claim that his umpire baiting was just an act, carefully choreographed for the fans in the stands and the television cameras. "Sometimes I would be shaking my fist at [umpire Babe] Pinelli when actually we would be screaming about where we were going for dinner." Pinelli was known for occasionally turning a Durocher tirade into a smile. On one occasion in Brooklyn, Durocher charged onto the field to furiously question one of Pinelli's calls that Leo knew was good. As he talked, he caught a whiff of the lotion Leo used liberally after shaving, and leaned closer. "Leo," he said, "that stuff you use sure smells wonderful. What is it?" According to Pinelli, "Leo looked pained for a second, then broke into a grin and walked away."[10]

Durocher was posthumously voted into the National Baseball Hall of Fame in 1994 as a manager, despite some opposition. For years after his death, his friends and those who wrote about him were still trying to put him into context. Broadcaster Lindsey Nelson, who worked with Durocher as a broadcaster for NBC, said in his autobiography, *Hello Everybody*, that Durocher would be the manager he would choose if he had to win only one game. "He might steal it, or whatever, but somehow, he would figure out how to win it."

This book is a biography of an American original set in sports rather than a sports biography. Its draws heavily on time and place, exploring the rough-and-tumble world of New York baseball before, during, and after World War II; Rat Pack Hollywood; the radicalized Chicago of the Vietnam era and the 1968 Democratic Convention; and finally Houston, still basking in the light of the Apollo moon landing.

At the heart of Durocher's story is the conflict between reality and stagecraft, drama and dramatics—and this provides a way of looking at who he really was.

One of the difficulties of writing about Durocher is the fact that he periodically reinvented elements of his past to give them greater drama and give himself a more confrontational or heroic presence. It was as if he were a playwright constantly revamping the early acts of a play to make the work all the more melodramatic. A case in point is Durocher's alternative childhood—a childhood he manufactured over the years and portrayed in *Nice Guys Finish Last*—which is loaded with exaggeration and falsehood. His faux childhood was not without charm.

"There was no organized activity for kids," he wrote with the aid of collaborator Ed Linn: "We were on our own and we did everything. Crazy things. As soon as the Connecticut River would freeze over, eight or ten of us would put on a racing skates and skate all the way to Boston—100 miles back and forth. We'd start out early in the morning and when we'd get to the Harvard rowing club, we'd just turn around and come back." Durocher had, in the words of the *Springfield Journal*, contrived to make the Connecticut River run east to west rather than north to south. There was no way on earth, the *Journal* explained, that one could ice skate between Springfield and Boston and end up on the Charles River in Cambridge. The Charles runs south to north in eastern Massachusetts.

"There are few personalities in baseball history about which more has been written and less truly known than that of Leo Ernest Durocher," wrote author David Claerbaut in 2000 in his book *Durocher's Cubs: The Greatest Team That Didn't Win*. "Most of the writing about Leo is far more descriptive than analytical, driven by either the writer's admiration or more likely contempt for him, rather than by an effort to understand."[11]

Was he a nasty man or merely someone who sought celebrity by playing the bad guy? Was his gambling a debilitating addiction or was it simply part of the rough-and-tumble image that he created for himself? What kind of man would brag about winning money in a fixed horse race with a tip from a syndicate criminal named "Sleepout" Louie Levinson, as Durocher did, and not expect to raise other red flags and suspicions?

Even those who knew him for many years couldn't decide. The late Bob Broeg of the *St. Louis Post-Dispatch*, one of the most easygoing, likable sportswriters ever to peck at a typewriter, wrote the day following Leo's death: "Losing Leo Durocher is like losing—take your choice—an old friend or enemy."[12]

CHAPTER 2

Enfant Terrible

L EO DUROCHER WAS BORN at home in West Springfield, Massachusetts, on July 27, 1905, the youngest of four sons of a French-Canadian couple, George J. and Clara M. Durocher. A religious woman, Clara was pleased that Leo had arrived on the day after Saint Anne Day, as Saint Anne is patron saint of women in labor. Until two weeks before Leo's birth, Clara had been stitching baseballs at home for A. G. Spalding & Bros., the sporting goods manufacturer located in nearby Chicopee. She worked on a piecework basis, paid for each baseball that she finished and returned to the factory. So it was with a real sense of irony that she heard the attending physician say:

"Look at those hands! He's not a baby. He's more like a—baseball player."

The story sounds apocryphal and may be just that, but it was what Clara Durocher told interviewers when asked about the birth of her youngest son as he rose to fame.

George and Clara Durocher left Montreal when they were quite young and moved first to Cohoes, New York, and then to an apartment in a triple-decker building at 10 School Street in West Springfield, Massachusetts, a stone's throw from the Connecticut River, which ran south past their home from Quebec to the Long Island Sound.

The dream of the Durochers was to someday return to Quebec, so Leo and his brothers grew up in an atmosphere of impermanence as their mother strove to keep French culture and language alive, anticipating a day when they would need it "back home." Clara's devotion to the church and to Quebec would continue for many years. In 1951, Arthur Mann, a writer

9

who had gotten to know Clara in his role as Durocher's Boswell, learned that part of the allowance she received from Leo, and unknown to him at the time, was used to keep a candle lit at Ste. Anne de Beaupre in Quebec for her beloved son.[1]

Durocher's father was employed intermittently by the Boston and Albany Railroad, and the family eked out a living. Durocher's mother took in boarders and cleaned other people's houses—in the parlance of the time she was called a scrubwoman. His older brothers in order of their ages were Clarence, Raymond, and Armand.

Leo's religious instruction was given in French at the St. Louis Catholic Church, but by age seven he was unable to master the catechism in French, so he was barred from the classes that would lead to Holy Communion at the St. Louis Church. "That's all right," he told the priest, "I can go to Father O'Donnell's church. They have the same God down there."

Leo quickly became a boy of the streets and sandlots, interacting with other boys who mostly spoke English. He also attended Main Street and Park Avenue grammar schools in West Springfield, where English was spoken.

Leo always had a baseball glove with him wherever he went—even on the days he went to school, as he was given to truancy. Young Leo loved baseball and got to play on the baseball team of the Immaculate Conception Church of the Catholic Junior League. He played pickup ball around the neighborhood as well as with any team looking for a nimble infielder. Durocher also played basketball and football, and to each sport he brought a determined desire to win. He learned early that winning meant everything, and he had the gift of speed, agility, and extraordinary eye-hand coordination. Growing to five foot ten, he was the tallest of the Durocher brothers and best suited for athletics.

HE STOPPED ATTENDING school regularly when he was around age twelve. He worked at a local pool hall and became a consummate pool player and local pool hall hustler. One of his early jobs was as an office boy at Gilbert and Barker, manufacturers of pumps and oil burners. His restless nature didn't allow him to stay there for long (incidentally, his oldest brother, Clarence, eventually became the firm's chief accountant).

Little else is known about Leo's younger years. Those few writers who got close to him in the decades ahead found that he refused to discuss this period of his life. Reporter Tom Meany, who spent several months traveling and living with Durocher over the winter of 1944–45 while Leo was entertaining troops overseas, wrote that during that period Durocher never spoke of his family or his boyhood. "On at least two occasions over in Italy, I was with Leo when he ran across men who had known him in his youth, which apparently was as normal as that of the average American of modest means in a town the size of West Springfield."[2]

Harold Flavin, a local historian and reference librarian who wrote about Durocher for the *Springfield Journal*, noted that everyone who knew Leo Durocher, or knew of him when he lived in West Springfield, had at least one favorite story to tell about him. Flavin said that his own father never tired of telling about Leo getting caught switching dice in a big crap game and being chased all the way across the North End Bridge. Flavin added that Leo's agility, both mental and physical, as usual stood him in good stead.[3]

Durocher had a second, false childhood, which he fabricated as he became famous and more notorious. The bogus claims were added one at a time, but the primary source of this misinformation is *Nice Guys Finish Last*, which is awash in things that are totally exaggerated or demonstrably false.

Leo did such a good job hoodwinking his readers that there are constant retellings of these tales today not only online but in footnoted books on baseball history.[4]

In his book Durocher claimed he was born in 1906 and that his father was an engineer for the Boston and Albany Railroad before he had a heart attack. As Flavin pointed out in his article in the *Springfield Journal*, Leo was born in 1905. His father had a drinking problem, and when he worked, if at all, he had a lowlier job than engineer with the B&A.[5]

Leo claimed to have idolized Springfield neighbor Walter "Rabbit" Maranville, the first future Hall of Famer to enter his life, and to have watched Maranville play in the 1914 World Series in Boston. By his own account at the time, Leo had never seen a major league game until he was a member of the 1925 Yankee squad at the tail end of the season.[6]

According to the fabricated Durocher created for *Nice Guys Finish Last*, his formal education ended when he was suspended for getting into a fight with a high school math teacher, and he never went back. The teacher, according to this fable long repeated in print, slapped Durocher, and Durocher hit the teacher in the back with a long-hooked pole used to open and close windows.

Durocher also claimed in *Nice Guys Finish Last* that he forfeited a college scholarship to Holy Cross because of the violent incident with the high school teacher. In an earlier version of the Holy Cross story, he said that he was offered a baseball scholarship to the college but turned it down to pursue a professional career. Harold Flavin found no evidence in local school records that Durocher had ever attended a single day of high school. Durocher was alternatively telling interviewers from his earliest days in the majors that he was a high school graduate or that he had never gone to high school.[7]

Although Leo presented himself as the Durocher kid who got into trouble, the reality was that his brother Armand was the one whose transgressions made the newspapers. In July 1922, he was shot in the back while in a car with four companions in an incident that police suspected was part of a bootleggers' war. Later that year, Armand was found guilty of disturbing the peace, and vagrancy, and given a suspended sentence at a state prison farm.[8]

LEO FAST BECAME a star in the youth baseball leagues and sandlots of West Springfield. At age fourteen, he was recruited to play shortstop on the semipro team of the Merrick Athletic Association. He also played football for the Merricks and was the team's star halfback and its outstanding kicker. While playing for Merrick, he also played baseball for semipro teams outside the league as far afield as Turners Falls and Millers Falls, which were both about forty miles from Springfield.

In 1921, at age sixteen, Durocher went to work for Wico Electric of West Springfield in a factory that manufactured batteries for motorcycles and magnetos for small stationary engines. Many of the motorcycle batteries were installed in new Indian motorcycles rolling off an assembly line in a large brick factory in downtown Springfield. Wico fielded a first-rate industrial league baseball team for which Leo played as a quid pro quo for his job with the company. While working at Wico, Leo became a fan of the Hampdens, a short-lived Eastern League team that played regularly in Springfield at League Park. When Leo asked for an opportunity to play for the Hampdens, he was told he was not even good enough to merit a tryout. According to later accounts, at this point the teenage boy began boasting, "Someday I will be paid for playing baseball and you will pay to see me play."[9]

In March 1922, Durocher was fined $50 on two charges of illegally operating a "jitney bus." Time has obscured the nature of this crime and the reason it carried such a hefty fine, but he was likely operating an unlicensed taxicab or omnibus in a jurisdiction where licenses were a major source of revenue. This is the only record of his running afoul of the law recorded in the *Springfield Republican*.[10]

For the better part of the next two years, Leo kept his job at Wico, where he worked alongside a black man named David Redd who was a welder at the factory. Born in Georgetown, Georgia, Redd had come north to make a better living for himself and his family. Redd genuinely liked Durocher and argued that Leo was wasting his time in the factory and that it was time for him to go out and make some of that "good money" in baseball.[11]

In early 1925, Harry Nunn, a railroad foreman who coached boys' baseball teams, took an interest in Leo and arranged to get him a tryout with the Eastern League Hartford Senators, then a top-rung A-level team.* Through Nunn, Leo came to the attention of Jack O'Hara, an independent scout who wanted Leo to leave his job and come to Hartford, then managed by Paddy O'Connor, who had helped the New York Yankees develop their star first baseman Lou Gehrig. But Leo had uncharacteristically lost his confidence. He told Redd that it was a fast league and that two of the best ballplayers he had ever seen, brothers Bunny and Eddie Trauschke, had been unable to make it in the Eastern League. Leo was happy at Wico and did not want to lose his job, which paid $58.50 a week, a princely sum for a young man in those days.[12]

With renewed vigor David Redd convinced him to go to Hartford for a tryout. "I told him not to worry about getting a leave," Redd recalled to a reporter from *Sports Illustrated* in 1955. "You can always get a job, you're a brilliant young fellow, and you're a better ball player than all the others around here. You're different."[13]

Leo then went to his bosses, who granted him a two-week unpaid leave of absence. In Hartford, as the Senators prepared for the season ahead, he employed his customary hustle; but it was not enough, and on the morning of April 15, Leo and eleven other hopefuls were informed that they had not made the second cut. The *Hartford Courant* noted, "Some of these fellows showed good form and might turn out well if there was enough time to work with and redevelop their faults."[14]

On the following Monday, April 20, Leo arrived at the Wico plant gate planning to go back to work and was met by Jack O'Hara, who told him that a spot had opened for him on the Hartford team and that he had with him a

---

* At this time the minor league levels were A, AA, B, C, and D.

contract and the car fare Durocher needed to get back to Hartford and that he would travel with the team to Bridgeport for Opening Day on April 23.*

According to the *Hartford Courant,* the actual reason Durocher got his second chance was that O'Connor suddenly gave up on a temperamental and talented infielder with the surname Rose because of his negative attitude. He called on Durocher, whom he then penciled in as his starting shortstop.[15]

In Bridgeport, the Hartford Senators won their first game of the 1925 season by a score of 2 to 1. In his first professional game, Durocher, batting eighth, had one hit in four at-bats, scored a run, and had four putouts and two assists, garnering some nice press in the next morning's newspapers. The *Bridgeport Post* credited Durocher with "life-saving play," the *Bridgeport Times* (which referred to him as Deroiser) cited his two-out single to right field, and the *Hartford Courant* not only reported that he "performed like a veteran" but gave him his first headline, which read in part: DUROCHER'S HIT WITH TWO OUT, STARTS SUCCESSFUL RALLY. The *Hartford Times* said Leo had played "a sensational game."[16]

In the next game, Leo had two hits, an error, and his first double play. The next day he was part of two double plays and the day after that, against the Albany Senators, he got his first triple along with a note in the *Courant* that he had a "great and accurate arm."[17]

Leo was on his way. On May 20, Hartford played the Springfield Ponies in Springfield in a game that was designated as "Durocher's Day," and he was presented with a gold watch from his former shop mates from the Wico factory. He then appropriated much of the limelight through spectacular infield play in a game lost by Hartford. Durocher seemed to outdo himself when Hartford played Springfield; his first home run came on June 19 in Springfield, where it was reported that he was egged on by his old friends from West Springfield.[18]

Like all leagues, the eight teams of the 1925 Eastern League looked for players who could bring the less-than-rabid fan to the ballpark and increase

---

* When he handed back the signed contract to O'Hara, Durocher listed his date of birth as 1906, making him a year younger than he actually was. For reasons unknown, Leo clung to this erroneous date despite evidence to the contrary, including birth records and the unimpeachable testimony of his mother. He even listed the erroneous date of birth in his autobiography. In *Nice Guys Finish Last,* Durocher claimed that O'Hara picked him up and drove him to the game at the last minute and that Leo changed into his Hartford uniform just in time to take the field (42–43). This tale is at odds with all other versions of the signing.

the team's income. In 1924 it had been Lou Gehrig and increasingly in 1925 it was Leo Durocher who got fans to board a trolley car and head to the ball-park. The *Hartford Courant* described Durocher as a "find," a player who had risen from obscurity to fame in a matter of weeks and could draw people to the ballpark.[19]

Soon he was being scouted by major league clubs. The first wave came at the end of June from Brooklyn, Pittsburgh, and Cincinnati and was followed by Jack Doyle scouting for the Chicago Cubs. Doyle followed Durocher for several weeks and witnessed some sensational work in the field beginning with a July 12 triple play that began as Leo fielded a low line drive.[20]

On July 17, in Pittsfield with the bases loaded, a Pittsfield batter hit a low line drive that looked like it would be good for two runs. Durocher dove to his right and bare-handed the sharply hit ball. The runners held as Durocher doubled over in agony and the game had to be held up so he could recover. Hartford won the game and the headline in the next morning's *Springfield Republican* was the stuff of dreams for a young player:

DUROCHER'S GREAT CATCH HALTS PITTSFIELD'S ATTACK

West Springfield Boy Saves Game for Hartford by Making Sensational Nab with Bases Loaded. Hartford Wins 8 to 5.

The *Hartford Courant* described Durocher's catch as "sensational," "bril-liant," and "one of the best we have seen here all season."[21]

Doyle was not the only scout following Durocher from game to game. Paul Krichell of the New York Yankees, who was regarded as a top judge of talent and had previously scouted and signed Lou Gehrig while he was still a student at Columbia University, also had an eye on him. In another season, Durocher might not have even gotten a second glance from the Yankees, but 1925 was different. Expected to win the pennant and reclaim their 1923 World Series championship, they were mired in the second divi-sion on their way to a seventh-place finish. One problem was Babe Ruth's ailing stomach and relatively poor season. The other major problem was the infield. On the eve of the season, James Harrison of *The New York Times* wrote that veteran shortstop Everett Scott was a "great weakness." Scott had shown signs of age during the 1924 season. However, there was confidence that rookie shortstop Pee-Wee Wanninger, who one Yankees scout called "the best young fielding shortstop since Maranville," could take over if Scott continued to struggle in the field. But while most were high on Wanninger, Yankee manager Miller Huggins was not. During the Yankees' first visit to St. Louis, Huggins left his team and traveled to St. Paul to scout Mark Koenig of the St. Paul Saints.

Huggins made no bones about his dilemma. "It has been a shame the way balls have traveled through our infield," Huggins said in reference to his struggling middle infield. With this need in mind, the Yankee scouts hit the trail in hopes of finding the best young shortstops in the field. No big league teams had direct affiliations with minor league teams then; rather, they looked upon them as an open pool of talent.[22]

The top-rated shortstop in the minor leagues was Buddy Myer of the New Orleans Pelicans. However, Washington Senators superscout Joe Engel beat the Yankees to the punch by arranging for the purchase of Myer. Aware of Myer's reputation, the Yankees offered to pay $50,000 to Washington and $50,000 to New Orleans for him. Senators owner Clark Griffith balked at the offer.

With Myer gone, Krichell got Yankees chief executive Ed Barrow on the telephone.

"Durocher," Barrow barked into the phone. "He's hardly hitting his weight."

Krichell was adamant. "He'll be great, he's got moxie."*

Barrow relented.[23]

On July 20, Doyle made an offer of $10,000 to the Hartford Senators, but this was almost immediately topped by Krichell, who announced that he had purchased Durocher for a down payment of $5,000 and $7,000 to be paid later. Under the terms of the deal, Durocher was to stay in Hartford until the end of the minor league season and then report to the Yankees. He reported on September 20, 1925.[†24]

An article in his hometown *Springfield Republican* lauded Leo for the jump from the obscurity of the sandlots to signing with a major league club in a half season, but was quick to point out there were better shortstops in

---

* Barrow was variously termed secretary, general manager, and chief executive of the Yankees during his years with the team. All three terms were synonymous, so, to avoid confusion, I have termed him chief executive, which was the term used by the National Baseball Hall of Fame and Museum when he was inducted in 1953.

† Hours before Durocher was purchased by the Yankees, Casey Stengel, in his first role as player-manager of the Eastern League Worcester Panthers, made a trade offer for Durocher. Casey was willing to swap three of his players for Leo.

the Eastern League and named several of them. Durocher was picked not because he was the best but because he showed the most promise.*25

Like everything that the Yankees did in those days, the sale of Durocher made national news, and with it the kind of hyperbole that could only infuriate those minor leaguers—especially veterans—who felt they deserved the nod before Durocher. The *Los Angeles Times* reported that he "led the list" in both fielding and hitting and proclaimed: "He is fast and veteran players enthuse over his form, both afield and at bat." The same day, the *Hartford Courant* observed that Durocher had problems at the plate stemming from his proclivity to put his front foot "in the bucket"—which then, as now, alluded to a fearful batter who steps away from home plate with his leading foot in order to avoid getting hit by the ball.26

Sportswriter Bill Lee, who came to the *Courant* the same year Durocher broke into the Eastern League, later wrote that Durocher behaved so timidly that bench jockeys of rival clubs rode him unmercifully. Lee called Leo a "Mr. Milquetoast"—alluding to a comic-strip character of the time also known as "the Timid Soul"—alleging that players in the Eastern League said he didn't have the courage to dig in when rival pitchers were throwing close to keep him loosened up.27

Lee added, "They threw other accusations at Durocher too, and some of these continued to be directed at him when he progressed to the majors by way of the Yankees." Hartford manager Paddy O'Connor was reported to have caught him red-handed with marked bills. Reports of missing money from other ball players pointed toward Durocher. O'Connor held back the irate players from pounding Durocher by promising to get rid of him once the pennant race was over. Hartford won, and O'Connor kept his word by packing Durocher off to the Yankees.

Durocher was warmly received by the Hartford fans in his first game after signing with the Yankees, but one reporter noted in his game notes that the signing had not improved Durocher's ability as a batsman—he went 0 for 4 at the plate that day—but had, it seemed, given him added "dash" as an infielder.

Despite his lackluster plate appearances, writers who had never seen him somehow got the impression that he was much better than he really

---

* The three other Eastern League shortstops mentioned were Joe Benes, who played in ten games for the 1931 St. Louis Cardinals; Waddy MacPhee, who had played in two games for the New York Giants in 1922; and Johnny Wight, who never made it out of the minors.

was. On August 7 *The Boston Globe* called him a formidable hitter, even though he was below average for the league. However, he had a propensity for timely hits, such as at a game he won on July 23 with a bases-loaded game-winning single. His average on August 10 was .226.[28]

In mid-August the Yankees spent $75,000 acquiring another shortstop, Tony Lazzeri, from Salt Lake. The morning after the sale, the *Springfield Republican* ran a large photograph of Lazzeri under the banner RIVAL FOR LEO DUROCHER WITH YANKS NEXT SEASON. The Yankees' owner, Jacob Ruppert, had vowed to buy the players he needed to become a pennant winner—or in his words "to rebuild at any cost." During the course of the summer, he spent more than $350,000 on new players, including Mark Koenig, still another shortstop whom he had purchased from St. Paul for $60,000. One thing that Lazzeri, Koenig, and Durocher had in common was that all three had been scouted and signed by Paul Krichell.[29]

If Durocher had one bright shining moment with Hartford it came on August 11 against Casey Stengel's Worcester Panthers, in which he won the game with a slashing single. Paddy O'Connor was deliriously happy over the win and in his glee thumped and smashed Leo around, as did everyone else who could lay their hands on the youngster. He was then carried off the field on the shoulders of what the *Courant* termed "a maniacal horde." The goat of the 4–3 victory was player-manager Casey Stengel, who yanked a pitcher who was winning for a man who quickly loaded the bases.[30]

Stengel and Durocher were early and easy adversaries. One day when the two teams met, Stengel got to the ballpark early, and while the Senators were holding a meeting, Stengel went out to the shortstop position and scratched Durocher's batting average—.208 at the time—in the dirt in letters six feet tall. "And you ought to have seen his face when he came out and saw that," Stengel recalled later in his own memoir. "Of course, he knew then that I was a big smart aleck, the same as himself."[31]

The abuse heaped on Durocher increased as the season wore on. It came to a climax in a torrid series between the Senators and the Waterbury Brasscos at the end of the season to determine the championship. The Brasscos were riding the Senators hard but worked on Durocher in particular. They taunted him about his inability to stand up under fire and mocked him while he was in the batter's box.[32] The Brasscos secured the Eastern League championship after beating the Senators in a doubleheader on September 18. The final game of the season was in Bridgeport and therefore meaningless. Durocher arrived at the ballpark that afternoon without his uniform, and O'Connor was forced to replace him, thus allowing Durocher to depart Hartford with an act of bravado, as attested to by his last headline as a Senator—DUROCHER ARRIVES WITHOUT UNIFORM.[33]

But Durocher had acquitted himself well during the season. Casey Stengel learned that Leo was a formidable force on defense. "We might even have won the pennant that year if he hadn't thrown some of my men out at home on relays—and with me coaching at third and sending them in myself."[34]

Durocher's name would soon appear in *Spalding's Official Baseball Guide* along with his final statistics in the Eastern League for 1925. He appeared in 151 games with 536 at-bats and 118 hits for a batting average of .220 in the lower third of the league. His fielding percentage was .933, and he led the league with fifty-nine errors.[35]

Two days later, on September 22, Durocher left for New York to don the pin-striped Yankee uniform. The Yankees were 64–81, on their way to a seventh-place finish. Durocher's first game in the majors came on October 2, 1925, when, in the next-to-last game of the season, he pinch-hit for Garland Braxton in the eighth inning of a game the Yankees were losing to the Philadelphia Athletics. Durocher flied out, and the Yankees ended up losing the game 10–0. Durocher also got into the final game of the season for less than an inning with no at-bats.[36]

Durocher's inauspicious debut was captured by the great baseball photographer Charles M. Conlon, whose portraits of Leo as a 1925 Yankee suggest a quiet, shy young man seated at the end of the bench.*

In January, Durocher's contract was sold to the A-level Atlanta Crackers of the Southern Association for the 1926 season. Early letters home were shared and paraphrased in the local newspaper. He said he was feeling great and that there was a fine group of boys on the club. In exhibition play, he hit leadoff, but in late April he was yanked for his weakness at the plate and replaced by Grant Gilbert, also under contract to the Yankees. Gilbert was no equal to Durocher in the field, having committed three errors in his first game as shortstop for the Crackers. Gilbert was moved to third and Durocher put back at shortstop a few days later, leading the Crackers to an 8–7 victory over the Mobile Bears with two hits, a single, and a double, and what the *Atlanta Constitution* termed his "sensational fielding." On May 9, in three

---

* One of these images of Durocher is in the National Portrait Gallery in Washington.

times at bat, he had a triple, a single, and a sacrifice fly. In a game on May 12, he had a home run and a triple on which he scored on a wild throw.

Leo got into a jam on August 4 that landed him in police court. Crackers pitcher Hollis McLaughlin was being heckled by a man in the stands while he pitched during the first inning. When McLaughlin headed for the dugout, the man continued his heckling, and McLaughlin headed into the stands, where he punched the man repeatedly in the face and body. Durocher charged into the stands behind McLaughlin to give aid to his pitcher and took a couple extra swings at the man before police broke up the attack. "A general riot was averted," wrote Dick Hawkins, the sports editor of the *Atlanta Constitution*, the next day, "and peace was restored with everything much as before except the face of the fan, which alas, may never be the same again."[37]

In court, Leo was fined $11 for assault and battery, and McLaughlin did not appear in court, thereby forfeiting his bond. The man who had been beaten was a streetcar conductor named W. L. Lawrence who had come to the game with his young grandson and some friends and claimed he had been attacked for simply exercising the fan's right to "rag" a player. Lawrence sued the Atlanta Baseball Co., which owned the Crackers, for $20,000 in damages but lost when the court determined that McLaughlin was acting on his own and not as an employee of the team. The precedent set by this case was clear: if a fan was beaten or otherwise abused by an employee of a baseball team, the only way to recover damages was to sue the employee. Whether or not Leo understood this at that time, it would prove relevant to him in the years to come. Later in the season, after McLaughlin had been traded to the Birmingham team, he was jailed for getting into a fierce battle with a batter, which had to be broken up by the police.*[38]

Durocher's abilities as a shortstop seemed if anything to improve as the season went on. In the same afternoon that Leo was involved in the attack

---

* The case—*Atlanta Baseball Co. v. Lawrence*—became precedent and still shows up in most contemporary books on sports law. The court found: "The conduct of McLaughlin, the pitcher, in leaving his place upon the grounds and coming into the grandstand, and assaulting the plaintiff, was not within the scope of his employment, nor in the prosecution of his master's business, but was his own personal affair in resenting a real or fancied insult. 'If a servant steps aside from his master's business, for however short a time, to do an act entirely disconnected from it, and injury results to another from such independent voluntary act, the servant may be liable; but the master is not liable.' Under the circumstances described in the petition, McLaughlin's acts were not the acts of his master, and the latter cannot be held liable under the doctrine of *respondeat superior*, or the master and servant theory."

on the fan, the Crackers played a doubleheader with the Memphis Chicks in which he piled up sixteen assists without an error and figured in two double plays. Hawkins of the *Constitution* suggested that a bit of lightning hung suspended from Durocher's right shoulder. Earlier in the season, Hawkins had given Durocher the nickname "Leaping Leo" because of his extraordinary ability to leave the ground to make a play.

In all he played in 130 games and batted .238, but his eyes were always fixed on the Yankees, and he watched them stagger to the pennant and then lose to the Cardinals in the 1926 World Series. Durocher later claimed that he sat on the Yankee bench during this World Series and got to watch as old Grover Cleveland Alexander came shuffling in from the bullpen to strike out Tony Lazzeri with the bases loaded.[39]

He was particularly interested in the record of shortstop Mark Koenig, whom he hoped to replace. According to one report, he vowed that if he could get up to the big club, he would make Koenig look like an armless monkey.[40]

Returning home at the end of the 1926 season, Durocher once more received a slip of paper from the Yankee front office informing him that his contract had been sold to the St. Paul club of the American Association. However frustrating, it was a step up in leagues to AA.

Leo spent the winter in West Springfield, living with his parents. He played on a local semipro basketball team known as the West Siders. Basketball was enormously popular in western Massachusetts at the time, in part because it was invented at Springfield College and was regarded as the indigenous sport. Durocher lacked height but more than made up for it as a ball handler.

Leo left home for the St. Paul team's Spring Training camp in Texas on March 5, 1927, and the *Republican* soon carried stories to the effect that he was electrifying the fans of the Lone Star state with his sensational fielding—"In one game he made four consecutive banner plays," one report stated—but at bat he was still classified as fair.[41]

Durocher's manager at St. Paul was one Artemus Ward "Nick" Allen, who had played for the Cubs and the Reds and was now making a name for himself as a minor league skipper. Known as "Roarin' Nick" because of his umpire baiting on the field, Allen was directly responsible for turning Durocher from a tongue-tied youth into a first-rate bench jockey who excelled at riding the players on the opposing club.

Allen's confrontations with umpires were epic. On one occasion, five policemen were needed to complete an ejection. Later in his career he admitted to being an umpire baiter and "a wild bull," but the antics were just for show to increase attendance.[42]

Under Allen, the St. Paul Saints were the most aggressive club in all of professional baseball, and Durocher fit in nicely, especially when it came to unsettling the other players. Casey Stengel's Toledo Mud Hens were in St. Paul on Sunday, May 8, about the same time Durocher got his new voice. During the game, Durocher rode a rookie named Joe Kelly mercilessly. Finally Kelly challenged Durocher. Expecting a roundhouse right, Durocher was unprepared for a solid and powerful left. According to a later account in the *Toledo Blade*, Durocher went down "as if he had been dropped from the clouds, with his face badly disfigured and his front teeth down his throat." Then Allen rushed into the fray and Kelly decked him as well— again with a left hook. Back in Massachusetts, the *Springfield Republican* reported on the slugfest: "Reports from St. Paul state that Durocher is innocent of any blame in the rumpus." The *Blade* later claimed that for years to come the Mud Hens got an annual bill from the St. Paul club for $75 for Durocher's bridgework. It was never paid.[43]

Perhaps because of the Kelly fight Leo got a reputation of being all lip and no fist. Pitchers started throwing at Leo's head to provoke him and Leo learned how to get out of the way. "I became an expert bean-ball dodger," he later told Arthur Mann. "All it ever got them was Little Leo on first base. Those beanballs helped me get fifty-two trips to the bags."[44]

AFTER SWEEPING THE Browns in St. Louis in August, the Yankees planned to board a special train for St. Paul to play an exhibition game against the Saints. Just before they left St. Louis, manager Huggins and St. Paul president Bob Connery shared a taxi with Arthur Mann, who was traveling with the team for the *New York World*. As soon as the cab started, Connery spoke:

"Say, Hug, there's a shortstop on my team I want you to take a good look at tomorrow," he said. "He's really something in the field. Be sure and look him over."

"Okay," Huggins agreed. "What's his name?"

"Durocher," Connery said. "Leo Durocher. He might help you."

Mann was taken aback by what he considered to be an unwarranted display of presumptuousness at his expense. Durocher was ostensibly Yankee property, earmarked from the time he first played at Hartford and most certainly scrutinized during his year at Atlanta.

So Mann said: "I don't know what you guys are trying to do for me, but you're wasting your breath. Hug must know all about Durocher. Besides, he had the kid at Yankee Stadium for a short look late last September and the year before. Why do you pretend he's something new?"*

"There was no answer," Mann later recalled. "Indeed, there was no further conversation during the remainder of the cab ride to the Grand Avenue station."[45]

All of this was a puzzlement to Mann, but he later came to realize that it was part of a Huggins plan to shoehorn Durocher into an invincible Yankee team that was shaping up as the greatest ever seen in baseball—one whose lineup would soon be called Murderers' Row. Both on paper and in reality it was formidable. However, according to Arthur Mann, what the public didn't know was that Huggins felt Mark Koenig was not the fielder and play-maker he needed, and that the great Tony Lazzeri was epileptic, and though an attack had never happened on the field, he was subject to seizures.

"Being a young and supposedly green baseball writer," Mann later concluded, "I was counted on to assume from this phony conversation that Huggins had 'discovered' the phenom in a St. Paul exhibition game, and undoubtedly print it when the story of the actual player transfer broke. It is possible that the prime reason for the overnight St. Paul trip, made on a special train and augmented by the finest and largest meal ever served, was to show off Durocher to the itinerant New York writers."[46]

The Mud Hens under Stengel won the American Association pennant and Durocher left St. Paul at the end of the 1927 season with a metaphoric lip, a real set of dentures, a chip on his shoulder, and a genuine sparring partner in Stengel. By dint of a cab ride in St. Louis, he had piqued the initial curiosity of eventual friend and chronicler Arthur Mann. He had a new appreciation for umpire bashing as crowd-pleasing, attendance-building theatrics. He set an American Association record for 213 double plays, played in 171 games, batted a respectable .253, and hit seven home runs.

---

* Both Durocher himself and Mann claimed that Leo was in Yankee Stadium at the end of the 1926 season for a "cup of coffee," but there is no record of him actually taking an at-bat in a regulation game, nor does the *Springfield Republican*, which was hanging on Leo's every move, mention any 1926 visits to the stadium. On the other hand, Mann was covering the Yankees as a beat reporter in 1926 and was in a position to know. What may be true here is that Durocher was brought back to New York without ever being placed on the official roster of players.

The 1927 Yankees ended the season with a record of 110–44, finishing nineteen games in front of the Philadelphia Athletics and sweeping the Pittsburgh Pirates in the World Series. That winter, the Yankees bought Durocher's contract from St. Paul for an "undisclosed sum," although it was known to be in the range of $50,000. While he was being brought up to plug the hidden weaknesses in the middle of the Yankee infield, Huggins also believed that a "pepper pot" like Durocher was an asset.

During the winter of 1927–28, Durocher was determined to improve his hitting and make sure he was well positioned with the Yankees. Back home in West Springfield, he suspended a sandbag from the ceiling in the basement of his parents' house that he whacked away at with a bat every day. This, he said, would allow him to practice as a left-handed batter, which he felt gave him a "better cut" at the ball.[47]

Durocher now felt he was ready for the Yankees. He now had his own creation story, which was that his father had advised him that the best way to get along in professional baseball was to keep his mouth shut. He had followed this advice at first, but this went against Nick Allen, who had told him to "show 'em you're alive, talk it up, and make some noise. This is baseball, not a church."[48]

CHAPTER 3

Damned Yankee

O N FRIDAY, FEBRUARY 24, 1928, Leo Durocher arrived at Pennsylvania Station in Manhattan and boarded the *Orange Blossom Special*, the luxurious passenger train, southbound for St. Petersburg, Florida. His companions included four other New York Yankees, including Lou Gehrig and Babe Ruth, who would be vying for new home run records in the coming season. The Yankees Loyal Rooters Band played "Auld Lang Syne" as young fans darted up and down the station platform, peering in every window, attempting to get a peek at Ruth, who kept out of sight.

That night the train stopped at a whistle-stop in Georgia to pick up others headed for Yankee Spring Training, including sportswriter Tom Meany of the *New York Telegram*, who, upon boarding and hearing Ruth's booming voice coming from the next car, headed to Ruth and found him in a poker game with Eddie Bennett, the good-luck mascot of the team; Pee Wee Dougherty, the clubhouse attendant; and a dapper rookie Meany had never laid eyes on before.[1]

"And what's your name again, kid?" asked Ruth as he introduced the rookie.

"Durocher," he replied, "Leo Durocher."

Meany later recalled it was somehow prophetic that he would first glimpse Durocher in a poker game. "Here he was, bound for his first major-league training camp, sitting in at a card game with the greatest figure baseball had ever known, as cool, as at home, as though he had been a Yankee all his life."

Meany and writer Garry Schumacher of the *New York Evening Journal*, who boarded at the same stop, were dealt into the game, and before the first hand had been played, Leo had begun calling the writers by their first names, instructing them on when to bid and when to deal and announcing who had raised. Meany observed that Durocher had already taken charge.[2]

The Yankees trained at Crescent Lake Park in St. Petersburg and from the first day of exhibition play Durocher put on a dazzling defensive display as shortstop. The *St. Petersburg Times* reported that manager Miller Huggins and a few writers were looking on when Durocher charged forward for a slow grounder, stabbed the ball on the run, and whipped it to Lou Gehrig at first. "Huggins cracked a slight smile as his eyes softened, like a proud father watching his son."[3]

Huggins was immediately taken with Durocher's ability as an infielder and quickly declared that Durocher had made the roster as his substitute middle infielder, backing up Koenig at shortstop and Lazzeri at second base. Koenig and Lazzeri were both from San Francisco, had come up together, and had formed a close relationship off the field. Durocher posed a threat to both men.[4]

On the offensive side his new teammates were less impressed with the rookie they called "Frenchy." Babe Ruth advised him he could bat .400 by becoming a switch hitter. By doing that he could bat "two-hundred right-handed and two-hundred left-handed."[5]

As if to prove Ruth wrong, on the team's way north for Opening Day in Philadelphia, the Yankees stopped in Knoxville for a game against Gabby Street's Tennessee Smokies of the Sally League. Durocher played shortstop for Koenig, who was nursing an injured heel. The Yankees won 14–4. Durocher homered and Ruth did not—although the Babe did register a triple, a double, a single, and two walks.[6]

When the Yankees arrived at Shibe Park in Philadelphia to open the season against Connie Mack's Athletics on April 11, the temperature was 45 degrees and heavy wind blew newspapers and trash from nearby alleys around the stadium during the opening ceremonies. The moan of the wind was so loud that it drowned out the sound of the trombone duet, which Westbrook Pegler, covering the game for the *Chicago Tribune*, said was actually "a break for the customers, as their endurance was pretty well strained by other discomforts of the occasion."[7]

Durocher was in the starting lineup at second base because Lazzeri had torn a muscle when swinging at an outside pitch in an exhibition game a few days earlier. Koenig was back in the lineup at shortstop. In front of twenty thousand shivering fans, by his words and actions, Durocher asserted himself. He was, in the words of Arthur Mann, entering the big leagues with "a solid brass tongue," and his first target in the first inning of that Opening Day was Ty Cobb, at the beginning of his twenty-fourth and final year in the majors and playing this season for the Athletics. According to Frank Graham of the *New York Sun*, that day he taunted Cobb to "the verge of distraction."

The Yankees won 8–3 in a game that lasted for almost two and a half hours at a time when the average nine-inning game lasted one hour and fifty-five minutes. "Durocher drove in two runs in the third inning with a long single down the right field line, but far more notable was what had or had not transpired between Leo and Cobb on the basepaths. The question, still debated today, was whether Durocher had used his hip to impede Cobb's progress from first to third, throwing him off-stride so Cobb was thrown out at third. Passing Durocher on his way back to his post in the outfield Cobb snarled at him: 'The next time you try that I'll cut your legs off, you fresh busher.'"[8]

This was first recounted in Babe Ruth's *Babe Ruth's Own Book of Baseball*, ghostwritten by sportswriter and later Commissioner of Baseball Ford Frick and published later that same year. The story was later repeated by syndicated columnist Grantland Rice, then again with minor variation in many articles and at least a dozen books. The hip story had such strong legs attached to it that *Chicago Tribune* columnist Dave Condon retold it verbatim and in print on several occasions in the 1970s. Even veteran announcer Red Barber recalled "the hip" when he talked about Durocher.[9]

Cobb long denied the incident and explained in his 1961 autobiography: "Leo gets all kinds of credit for having slyly slammed a hip into me and put me flat on my face. He never saw the day he could do it. In 1928, when this play supposedly happened, I knew a few too many tricks to be caught by some skinny infielder's hip. What makes the lie all the more obvious is that the story has me out on the play. Had Durocher clipped me, I'd have been entitled to the next base on interference."[10]

Durocher himself never claimed the hip story was true. Later in the 1928 season, in an interview with Harold Burr of the *Brooklyn Eagle*, Durocher himself retold the story in his own words, asserting only that they had exchanged words and that Cobb threatened to "cut" him if he didn't stay out of his way when he was running the basepath.[11]

"Many stories have been written about the 'fight' I had with Ty Cobb the first time I ever played against him, and I always read them with great interest because no fight ever took place," he wrote many years later. "What happened was that Cobb was on first base, and Tris Speaker, who was also finishing out his career in Philadelphia, hit a line drive through the pitcher's box. I dove for the ball, got my glove on it and slowed it down enough so that it stopped in short centerfield just off the dirt. While I was scrambling after it I happened to get in Cobb's way—accidentally, of course—forcing him to pull up just enough so that I was able to throw him out at third to end the inning."

As Durocher was passing Cobb on the way to the visitors' dugout, Cobb said: "You get in my way again, you fresh busher, and I'll step on your face." Leo then recalled:

> I hadn't said a word to Cobb, and I still didn't. Hell, this is Ty Cobb. But Ruth, who was coming in from left field, wanted to know what Cobb had said. "Well, kid," Ruth said—he called everybody kid—"the next time he comes to bat call him a penny pincher." I'd never heard that word before, but just from the way everybody on the bench started to laugh I had a pretty good idea what it meant. What I didn't know was that Cobb had a reputation for being a very tight man with a dollar and had been ready to fight at the drop of a "penny pincher" for years.
>
> Well, naturally, I can't wait for him to get up again so I can go to work on him and holy cow, he turns in the batter's box, pointing his finger, and the umpire has to restrain him. Now, the game is over and the umpires don't have a care anymore. Both clubs have to use the third-base dugout to get to the locker room, and Cobb races over to cut me off. He's out to kill me and I'm looking for a place to run because I am not about to tangle with Mr. Cobb. Finally, Babe came running in and put his arm around Cobb, and he's kind of grinning at him and settling him down. "Now what are you going to do? You don't want to hit the kid, do you?" And while Babe has his attention—boom—I'm up the stairs like a halfback and into the locker room.[12]

Whatever else was true or false about that first game, Durocher knew he was going to pay for riding Cobb and other opponents without mercy, and before he was out of uniform that day he proclaimed, "Watch tomorrow's first pitch. And watch me when it comes up there"—pointing to his head. There was no pitch on the next day because of a postponed game, but on the following day Durocher got up to bat and waited for that pitch. "The throw came from the left arm of Ossie Orwoll, and it carried enough power to have torn Leo's head off," reported Arthur Mann. "But Leo was scrabbling unharmed in the dirt and the count was one ball. Leo arose, brushed himself off, and turned to Orwoll with three fingers upraised. 'Three more of them, pal,' he called in a rasping voice, 'and I'll be on first base where I belong!'"

Leo dove out of the way of three more balls aimed at his head and took first base. The Yankees won the game 1–0 and Leo bragged about his ability as a bean-ball dodger. With rare confidence Durocher predicted that Orwoll (who did not finish the game) would soon be gone from the major leagues and he would not.[13]

As the season progressed Durocher antagonized Cobb as well as other major opponents. By the end of May, after the Yankees had played every team in the league, Frank Graham wrote of Durocher in the *New York Sun*: "His days on the bench are spent annoying the opposing players on their appearance, their work and, occasionally, their antecedents."[14]

Durocher relished his new role, bragging that he was having a lot of fun riding the big fellows, especially Cobb, who he tried to put in the role of aggressor: "Any time the great Ty pulls a crack, he's going to get one right back."[15]

"Why don't you give yourself up?" he called to Cobb one day. "What are you waiting for them to do—cut your uniform off and burn it?"

Cobb snarled threats at him, and he laughed.

"Go home, Grandpa," he said. "Get wise to yourself. If you keep on playing with us young fellows, you might get hurt."[16]

Leo's big league debut had begun well. In his first four games he had six hits and drove in five runs—all batting as a right hander. He hit safely in his first seven games for a while, subbing at second for the injured Tony Lazzeri. After Lazzeri had returned he replaced the underperforming Mark Koenig at shortstop and continued to hit for almost four weeks. At the end of thirty-seven games his average was .312, and a few of the hits had been important ones, such as the game-winning triple with the bases loaded on May 29 against the Washington Senators.[17]

In the field his early reviews were great. "That circus stuff he has been doing with the New York team is every-day baseball with him," said Hank Gowdy, former player and now managing in the International League. "I've see some fielders in my time, but that kid's a wonder."

DURING THESE EARLY weeks in pinstripes, the Yankee rookie created a name for himself off the field as well. "Leo Durocher, Yankee infielder, is the only big leaguer with nerve enough to wear spats and carry a cane" was one report that became national news, thanks to the Associated Press.[18]

In early June during batting practice at Comiskey Park, as Durocher stepped into the batting cage, White Sox commentary could be heard from the dugout:

Buck Crouse: "Did you see that piece in the paper about this guy wearing spats and carrying a cane around New York?"

Moe Berg: "No."

Crouse: "On the level."

Bill Hunnefield: "I've seen him wearing spats."

Crouse (shouts): "Hey, spats, where's your cane?"

Hunnefield (shouts): "Take your cane up to the plate, maybe you can hit with that."[19]

Durocher had landed in Manhattan in the midst of Prohibition. He lived at the Piccadilly Hotel at 227 West Forty-Fifth Street, in the heart of the theater district just off Broadway, which was awash in illegal booze and the speak-easies, clip joints, and blind pigs where it was served. They called the district the "white light district," and it stretched from Fourteenth to Fifty-Ninth Streets along Broadway and two to three avenues on either side.

Texas Guinan, Manhattan's most famous speakeasy hostess, managed more than half a dozen joints herself in or near the district, including the 300 Club, the Texas Guinan Club, the Century Club, Salon Royale, Club Intime, El Fay, and the Club Argonaut. One of Guinan's entertainers was a dancer and would-be actor named George Raft, who hailed from the west-of-Broadway rough-and-tumble neighborhood known then and now as Hell's Kitchen. Raft made his gangster acquaintances in the clubs, of which he said, "If you were an entertainer on Broadway during those days you would have to be blind and lame not to associate with gangsters. Look, they owned the clubs." Raft and Durocher first met in a poolroom on Forty-Eighth Street and liked each other instantly. A former batboy and mascot for the

New York Highlanders before they became known as the Yankees, Raft was naturally drawn to the young ballplayer, who seemed every bit as brash as he was.[20]

Durocher hit the nightclubs with regularity, often beginning the night with a show at the Winter Garden Theatre in Midtown and then racing up to Harlem to catch the late show at the Cotton Club to see Bill Robinson or Cab Calloway.[21] This was the New York of Damon Runyon, and Durocher played it like a character from the second act of *Guys and Dolls*. "Three people could stand out in the rain under his hat brim when he first hit the big town," wrote columnist Jim Murray. "The pin stripes could be seen in the dark, the shoes came in two or more colors and the shoulders were wide enough for condors to light on."[22]

"It required no time at all for Durocher to attract a coterie of limelight followers in New York," wrote Arthur Mann. Traveling with the Yankees during the late 1920s, Mann became fascinated with Durocher and "made a close study of him," getting as close to him as any journalist ever would. "The Yankee uniform was a pass to everywhere," Mann observed. "Even his cacophony of words took on importance to listeners. He was a pushover for flattery and a flashy wardrobe, though his rookie salary was scarcely enough to clothe him in overalls. Wear now and forget the cost. You're a champion— dress like one. Always travel first class. Meet big people. And it was in prohibition days when you never asked your friend how he made his money for fear he would tell you."[23]

Durocher spent heavily. When one of his brothers became ill in early May, the Yankees gave him a day off and he motored to West Springfield and back in a brand-new car. Before he left Springfield he dropped in on a smoker at the Merrick Athletic Club, where he auctioned off a bat and glove he had autographed.[24]

His early success moved his newfound "friends" to organize "Leo Durocher Day" on June 23, 1928, at Yankee Stadium. A four-page brochure was printed to introduce their pride and joy as "the Regular Yankee Rookie":

> You all know "LEO" by now for he has taken New York baseball fans by storm, with his fiery personality and regular fellow spirit.
>
> Proclaimed by Critics to be the freshest and gamest Rookie ever to make a big league debut.
>
> A future Big League Star and a credit to Baseball.

The brochure was printed and first distributed on a day when Durocher had played only ten games in Yankee Stadium. The sponsors for the big day included names that lifted eyebrows even during the lawless days of Prohibition. Tommy Holmes of the *Brooklyn Eagle* later recalled: "The list was studded with the nightlight characters of Broadway and the roadhouse circuit, many of whom sooner or later were tangled up in the law."[25] The most recognizable name on the list was Conrad (Connie) Immerman, bootlegger and legendary operator of Connie's Inn, a nightclub at 131st Street and Seventh Avenue in Harlem, which had first featured the likes of Louis Armstrong, Fats Waller, and Fletcher Henderson.

As the big day approached, both the team and Durocher went into a slump in the West, which is what the midwestern teams were referred to before expansion to the West Coast. The Yankees lost six out of seven and Durocher was benched a week before his special day.

On the morning of Leo Durocher Day more than four hundred people from western Massachusetts boarded a special train for the event along with the drum and bugle corps from Our Lady of Hope Church. Durocher's parents traveled to the Bronx by car. Another contingent came by train from Hartford.

After the first game of that day's doubleheader, which the Yankees lost, Durocher was honored in an infield ceremony during which he was presented with two traveling bags and $1,500—a check for $500 and a traveling bag from the Springfield Chamber of Commerce and a traveling bag and a crisp $1,000 bill from his "friends." Because of the amount of cash involved, the bill was presented by Detective Dennis "Dinny" Mahoney, who headed the Detective Association of the New York Police Department and had also been one of the Day's sponsors.

The Yankees went on to lose the second game to the Red Sox before only fifteen thousand fans. As Harrison of the *Times* put it, "The only drawback to Durocher Day is that Durocher didn't play in either game." The awkwardness of Leo sitting out the games was compounded when the local contingent, sitting behind the Yankee dugout in a special VIP section, realized that they would not see Leo in action and began cheering for the Red Sox. If Durocher had been humbled by sitting out his day on the bench or embarrassed by the behavior of hometown friends, he didn't show it.[26]

There is no record of what the other Yankees thought of a substitute player having a special day, but it could not have been favorable. Waite Hoyt, who lost the first of those two Durocher Day games and got to watch his eight-game winning streak come to an end, did not get his day until 1965 and that was at Crosley Field in Cincinnati when he retired as a Reds broadcaster. Gehrig's came in 1939 when he delivered his "luckiest man alive" oration, and Babe Ruth finally got his day at Yankee Stadium in 1947 when he was riddled with cancer and near death.

After the doubleheader Durocher and his Broadway friends headed for Pelham in Westchester County to hear Vincent Lopez's orchestra play dance tunes at Joe Pani's Woodmansten Inn. The nightclub was a favorite for revelers from New York City carrying their own silver flasks of bootleg whisky, and members of the underworld. Lopez was another one of Durocher's sponsors.

Leo was now in the limelight. The next morning's *Springfield Republican* carried a photo of its favorite son holding up the $1,000 bill with an ear-to-ear grin on his face. The press played with the story of Durocher Day. "What Leo will do with two traveling bags is a question," wrote James Harrison in *The New York Times*. "Unless his friends think that the Yanks are going to send him on a long journey."[27]

Durocher saw little further action on the playing field until July 11 in Detroit. In the first game of the doubleheader Lazzeri was thrown out after arguing a call that had him out at third. He got the thumb as well for the second game and was suspended for the following day. Durocher replaced him and in the second game made a spectacular play to prevent the potential tying run and end the game.[28]

After Lazzeri's suspension was over, Durocher played occasionally, filling in when Lazzeri was ill or performing poorly. Lazzeri was benched on July 31 for poor fielding and Durocher doubled in that game, bringing in two runs. His work in the field was not only perfect but spirited. "Loquacious Leo has more pepper than a cage full of monkeys, and nowadays the Yanks don't need pepper any more than an automobile needs four wheels," Harrison of the *Times* wrote of that game.[29]

Durocher had a growing facility for quick one-liners, which netted him the nickname "Lippy," bestowed on him by Will Wedge of the *New York Sun*. He dealt deftly with the press. When his last name was mispronounced he was quick to insist that it rhymed with *kosher*, an apt rhyme for a team playing in the Bronx. His jibes from the bench filled newspaper columns. His most audacious bit of jockeying came in Detroit while he was playing second base during the second game of a September Sunday doubleheader.[30]

The Yankees led by two runs as Bob Fothergill, a pinch hitter who was five foot ten and weighed in the neighborhood of 240 pounds, came to bat with two outs in the ninth inning. Durocher called time and then yelled to the home plate umpire:

"I claim he is out for batting out of turn!"

The umpire scanned his lineup card and declared Durocher was wrong and that Fothergill was the rightful batter.

"Fothergill?" Durocher said, squinting. "Ohhhh, that's different. From where I was standing, it looked like there were two men up there."

Blind with rage, Fothergill took three straight strikes to end the game, dropped his bat, and came running after Durocher. Ruth grabbed Fothergill and put his arms around him, as he had once done with Ty Cobb, while Durocher scooted into the clubhouse, which was in an uproar. Huggins praised Durocher for his action, which to Durocher was praise from heaven. "No doubt about it," Durocher would later claim, "it was my greatest day as a Yankee."[31]

As an after-dinner speaker Durocher would tell this story for decades, positioning himself as a comic actor rather than a baseball player. From this point forward baseball was more than a game to Durocher—it was theater.

Meanwhile every small bit of news about Durocher was reported in the *Springfield Republican,* often alluding to him in terms of his Gallic heritage. The June 3, 1928, issue reported that the paper had received news that Durocher's picture now hung in the largest pool hall in Montreal along with other great "French athletes." Durocher was regarded both at home and abroad as French-Canadian, and his name was often pronounced *doo-row-shay.**[32]

Prior to the start of the 1928 World Series, the Yankees were practicing at Yankee Stadium, when Durocher spoke up within earshot of a group of reporters, claiming the Yankees would win the Series in a breeze. "I hate to be kept waiting on my base hits. If I can't get into the World Series myself I'm going to tell the other boys how to hit home runs."

He then beckoned to Ruth. "Babe, come over here and let me give you a lesson."

Ruth responded by heaving his mitt at the rookie. "Can you beat that,

---

* The first time Durocher is mentioned in a feature story in *The Sporting News,* it is in a feature on the impact of French-Canadian players on baseball.

kid?" said Ruth. "'The All-American Out.'" It was a nickname that stuck but not as strongly as the sobriquet "Lippy."*[33]

On October 4, the eve of the World Series, John Keller of Washington's *Evening Star* newspaper told his readers to keep an eye on Durocher as one of the reserves likely to make a difference in the days ahead. "This Durocher is in fact an unusually cocky chap ready to challenge the whole world when either his gameness or playing ability is challenged."[34]

The Yankees beat the St. Louis Cardinals in four straight games for the World Championship. Durocher played second base in the late innings of all four games, spelling Lazzeri and playing errorless ball. He had two at-bats and no base hits. Missing from the box score, however, was his role as bench jockey riding the Cardinals with special attention to their manager, Bill McKechnie, and Leo's boyhood hero, Rabbit Maranville. Leo and Maranville were promptly calling each other everything in the book. Maranville thought he had an advantage, because, according to Arthur Mann, someone on the Yankee team had presented the Cardinals with a cluster of carefully contrived expletives that seemed most likely to upset Leo. "But it didn't work," Mann later reported. "He returned every barb redoubled in vitriol."[35]

At the end of his rookie year Durocher's rogue reputation was established. The "chestiest youngster to hit New York in many years," wrote one reporter, and Grantland Rice later remarked, "No fresher busher ever came into the major leagues."[36]

THE WORLD SERIES share paid to Durocher and the other regulars that year was $5,813, the largest up to that time. Durocher had piled up considerable debts during the season, and yet he decided to buy a new Packard automobile instead of paying overdue bills.†

One of the largest debts was to the Piccadilly Hotel, but a significant

---

* Ruth explained that the "All-American Out" nickname was not his creation but what slugger Harry Heilmann had been calling Durocher in Detroit.
† The Packard was the great luxury car of that era whose owners included Tsar Nicholas II of Russia, the Japanese royal family, the Shah of Iran, and Babe Ruth, who ran through a number of them. After becoming a big league player, Ruth gave Brother Matthias, his mentor at Saint Mary's School in Baltimore, a new Packard. In two weeks, the car was demolished at a railroad crossing. Ruth bought him another.

debt was also owed to pool hall operators and restaurants where he had run up a tab.*

Durocher's trick to living beyond his means was post-dating checks and then not having funds on hand to pay them when they came due. He got away with this because he was a Yankee. One merchant located in the shadow of Yankee Stadium posted checks that Durocher had bounced in his store window, gaining Leo an extra share of bad publicity.

Durocher's return to Massachusetts in early October was supposed to mark the end of his football career, as Huggins had ordered him to steer clear of the gridiron to avoid injury. Leo obeyed at first and—save for appearing as a referee in the first game of the season—stayed off local football fields. This proved to be a great disappointment for the Merrick Athletic Association, for whom he had played football as well as baseball. "Leo was a demon kicker—from placement, from the drop or from the punt—speedy as a deer and in general a good offensive threat for a 140-pounder," one of his teammates recalled at a 1953 team reunion.

However, when Merrick played the Greenfield Athletic Association, a team they had lost to for the last three years, and the game was still scoreless in the fourth quarter, Durocher ran down from the grandstand, donned a Merrick uniform, and pleaded for a chance to kick a field goal. The Merrick coach, Fred Pezzini, agreed, and Durocher racked up three points with a perfect drop kick. Greenfield AA then scored a quick touchdown making the score 7–3, where it remained until the final seconds, when Greenfield fumbled and a Merrick back raced sixty-five yards for a touchdown. Durocher added the extra point with a drop kick; Durocher had supplied the margin of victory in the 10–7 win.†37

Whether Huggins ever learned of this is not known, but if he did it probably would have made little difference. Huggins saw Durocher as a high-spirited force who worked for the good of the team even if he angered others and broke the rules. "That boy Durocher is just chock full of courage" was one of his favorite descriptions of Leo. Huggins pestered writers, asking them for more—and better—coverage of Durocher. For his part, Durocher

---

* The hotel was razed in 1982. The site is now occupied by the Marriott Marquis Hotel.
† A drop kick involves a player dropping the ball and then kicking it when it bounces off the ground. Drop kicks are still legal in football for both field goals, punts, and points after but seldom employed. They were very important before 1934 when the blunt end of a regulation football was given more of a point to facilitate the passing game.

admired Huggins to the point of adoration. He wanted to be more like Huggins and sat next to him on the bench, where he kept a small black notebook in which he took notes on how Huggins managed the Yankees.

When the final batting statistics for the American League were announced on December 17, Durocher's season batting average was listed as .270 with eighty hits. He had appeared in 102 games and had had 296 at-bats. Statistically he was in the middle of the pack but below average for the Yankees, who led the league with a .296 average. The day those numbers were published, Ed Barrow, the chief executive of the Yankees, reaffirmed Durocher's role with the team: "Durocher is one of the greatest fielding shortstops in baseball and we can sacrifice hitting strength for defensive strength."[38]

Durocher's "lip" was news even in the off-season. Ed Barrow announced at the end of 1928 there was nothing to the rumor that Durocher's 1929 contract put limits on his "lingual output." Barrow added, "Huggins likes Leo's line of talk ... in fact it's the big reason for Leo's being with the Yankees." With a clear eye on Cobb, Barrow was asked:

"What if some big boy hurts him?"
"Well that apparently is Leo's lookout—and he can handle himself."[39]

Perhaps most important in all of this was that Jacob Ruppert, the owner of the Yankees, was delighted with Durocher's wisecracks and verbal attacks on opposing teams and their managers. Ruppert sat next to the dugout during the World Series and could be seen smiling and laughing at Leo's barbed banter. Ruppert, it was rumored, wanted to keep Durocher in place for his own amusement.

But in addition to making enemies of the big boys in the rest of the league, Durocher also lost favor with the New York newspaper writers who traveled with the team—or so claimed Albert Keane, sports editor of the *Hartford Courant*, who had closely followed Durocher's career since his days playing in that city. To the corps of reporters covering the Yankees he was seen as brassy, loud, and, in the slang of the era, "a pop-off."[40]

THE YEAR 1929 did not start out well for Durocher. He had been ill for a good part of the early winter and was hospitalized in New York City in late December at St. Luke's hospital for five days. He then returned to Springfield, where on January 8, while reading the newspaper at his new home, he passed out. After several days in a hospital there he was reported to be somewhat improved and released after a week. The *Springfield Republican* reported he was rapidly regaining strength. The reports on his ailment were confusing: a bruise, a strain, and, finally, an internal disorder that was never fully diagnosed.[41]

Finally recovered, Leo was getting ready for Spring Training on February 20 when his older brother Armand was arrested for passing bad checks in Hartford. The event made the newspapers not because Armand already had a police record but because he had signed Leo's name to the checks. He was on probation for a similar charge in Springfield and sentenced in Hartford to thirty days in jail.[42]

Durocher left with the first squad for Spring Training, stopping in Savannah, where Rud Rennie of the *New York Tribune* reported that Leo had already changed his suit seven times on the trip and had admitted he had been ill all winter but now had a fine bill of health and predicted he would make the team. Rennie was fascinated with Durocher's dress and grooming. "He gave two suits to the porter last night to have them pressed and then shaved before he went to bed," he wrote. "He must be getting ready for something but no one knows why." Rennie seemed to be saying that Durocher was already the odd man out.[43]

His jockeying was no longer confined to the ballpark but took on a new level of predetermination. Before the 1929 season started he had written a postcard to Ed Morris, the ace pitcher of the Boston Red Sox, and signed it *cousin*. In the parlance of the time, *cousin* meant a pitcher who was easy to hit for the player who called him by that name, suggesting that Durocher had the pitcher's number. Leo also made sure that word on the postcard got in the newspapers.[44]

On the eve of the 1929 season it had also become clear that Durocher was almost as irritating to the Yankees as he was to their opposition. He arrived at Spring Training with a new and even louder wardrobe and a stratospheric level of confidence untempered by the winter layoff and his own illness. He made no bones about the fact that he deserved to be a starter and help lead the team to another World Championship. He was going to win somebody's job, and he did not care whose it was.

According to Arthur Mann, who had traveled with the Yankees to Florida, a few of the starting players began to spread word to reporters that

Durocher was a phony who hung out with gamblers and had been seen in the company of Meyer Boston, a big baseball bettor. Such rumors were easier to spread when coupled with the fact that Leo's brother was serving a jail sentence.

One night in late March after an exhibition game, Huggins caught Durocher leaving the hotel in a tuxedo. Huggins asked him if he wore the tuxedo often, and Leo said only for special occasions and only in the evening. Huggins then told him that he had better forget that suit and concentrate on his baseball, which should be treated as a special occasion every day.

"I took off the tuxedo and went to my room," Durocher recalled later. "But before I went upstairs, he warned me about mixing too much away from the club, and that when things got tough, to keep away from people." Huggins had heard the whispered rumors of criminality and wanted Leo to lay low.[45]

On March 30, 1929, when the Yankees broke camp for their trip north, Huggins announced that Durocher would be his starting shortstop rather than Koenig or Lyn Lary, with whom Durocher had been competing. Lary was benched after an inept showing in the field and a .180 batting average. It was a big story, as the Yankees had paid $100,000 to purchase Lary's contract from the Pacific Coast League.

All during Spring Training Durocher had ridden every one of his teammates save for Lary. Unnamed sources claimed that behind the scenes Leo had gone on the offensive against the rookie, belittling his abilities and warning him that as he failed, Leo would be polishing up a place on the bench for him. Durocher allegedly insisted again and again that the only reason Lary had a chance was his hitting, and his hitting was what came under verbal fire from Durocher and as a result fell off. Columnist Ed Danforth of the *Atlanta Constitution* was quick to admit that the story lacked proof but had the flavor of authenticity, and he added, "and, goodness, sounds exactly like that irrepressible Leo."[46]

In making the announcement of Durocher's landing the starting position, Huggins said, "In Durocher we will have the fielding sensation of all the big league shortstops." Huggins believed that Durocher was a better infielder than he had been the year before. "Durocher is the most expert juggler of a baseball this year," wrote John Foster of the *Consolidated Press* after watching him play with a baseball. "He can toss one up, catch it coming down, bat it to one side with one hand and catch it with the other hand in time to throw it to first base; [he can] stand on one foot and get a ball; almost stand on his head and get another, then recover himself so gracefully and nimbly that he gets the runner at first base."[47]

Durocher's rise, Huggins's admiration, and Leo's lack of respect for the established Yankee order was big news. *Time* magazine's report from Spring Training was typical: "To fill in at shortstop, Huggins bought the services of one Lynford Lary from the Oakland, Calif., club . . . Florida sunshine, however, revealed serious faults in Lary's fielding. What to do? A young man on the substitute bench, Leo Durocher, had the answer . . . Huggins liked him because he was alive. When the old-timers 'rode' Durocher he talked back. He even wrote them fresh letters in his off hours."[48]

Opening Day against Boston was rained out, and Durocher was stuck in a hotel room where he gave an interview to Donald B. Bagg of the *Springfield Republican* in which he stated that he had learned the secret of steady batting and predicted that he would hit .285 or better. During Spring Training, Huggins had Durocher work on his hitting to the extent that he seldom worked out with the team. "Huggins has had me hitting all spring. For a long time down South I didn't even have a chance to work out on the regular field. It was hit and hit some more for me. Lyn Lary was out there at shortstop and it began to look to me as though I wouldn't get in there at all."[49]

The next day when the 1929 Yankees took the field for the opener they surprised their fans and those in the press box with new uniforms featuring large numerals on the backs of their jerseys. The Yankees were the first big league team to adopt this practice, which was seen as a great help to those keeping score. The numbers were assigned based on the players' everyday spots in the batting order, and Durocher debuted the number 7. Back in Springfield it was noted with pride that both Opening Day shortstops for the Yankees and the St. Louis Cardinals were local lads—albeit separated in age by fifteen years. The other difference was that Rabbit Maranville was probably one of the most popular men on the Cardinals roster both in terms of fans and fellow players. Leo on the Yankees was not.[50]

The teammates who disliked Durocher as a noisy disrupter of the status quo were given another reason to dislike him because Huggins was quite open about where he saw Leo in the club's future. In a late-April interview, when the team made its first trip to Boston, he said, "With men of the type of Durocher ready to take places in our lineup, it is for the best interests of the team that the veterans be let go." He also talked about the "careful weeding out of players" as a means to another pennant. This interview ran under a large photograph of Durocher swinging a bat.[51]

At about the same time that that interview appeared, Durocher's nose became swollen and red from an infection, giving opposition bench jockeys a special opportunity to razz him with a rude diagnosis—the mildest of which was that he got it from sticking his nose in other people's business. "It's a heartless world," observed columnist James Collins of *The Washington Post*.[52]

Meanwhile, the gossip about Durocher's gambling increased as the season got into full swing and it all seemed to be coming from his team-mates, who spread it to the writers and other teams in the league. "The sports writers ducked the stories," Mann observed. "They were too raw for print." Suddenly, if Durocher met friends at the clubhouse gate, the rumor-mongers saw it as a meeting with gamblers. Durocher soon realized that even if he stopped to sign an autograph on the street, someone would report that he had been seen taking part in some nefarious transaction. Durocher went silent and retreated from hotel lobbies. On the road he stayed in his room and dined alone.

Ruth continued to harass Durocher and, among other things, early in the 1929 season accused him of stealing his wristwatch. According to the most common version of the story Durocher was in a hotel elevator on the road with a few of his teammates late one night.

"Oh, am I drunk," said the Babe. "Somebody's got to undress me and put me to bed. You guys have to help me."

The other players backed away, but Leo agreed to help him. The next morning Ruth claimed he was missing his watch and pointed a finger at Durocher. Ruth biographer Robert Creamer disregarded the accusation: "Although he was drunk on the town the night before and had been in the Lord knows what places, he blamed Durocher. As Leo said, in a half-angry, half-mocking tone, 'Jesus Christ, if I was going to steal anything from him I'd steal his god-damned Packard.'"[53]

Creamer explained that, whatever the truth, the legend grew and was kept alive by Ruth, who took advantage of the incident and continually exploited it at Leo's expense. Creamer concluded that Ruth hated Leo Durocher and did all that he could to knock him and portray him as a sneak thief.

One night on the team train, as Ruth was getting undressed standing next to his Pullman berth, he called to Durocher.

"Hey, Leo, you want to see something?" He held up a glittering bit of jewelry. "See that, Leo? Isn't that beautiful? That cost me seventy-five hundred bucks, Leo. I'm going to give it to Claire when we get to New York. Tonight I'm putting it under my pillow. And, Leo, I want it to be there when I wake up in the morning."[54]

Making things worse, Huggins benched Durocher in mid-May, saying that he wasn't hitting well enough to hold his job. Lyn Lary replaced him. But even out of the lineup Durocher found that his antics provided good copy for the writers who followed the team. While in Boston for a weekend series against the Red Sox, a reporter from the *New York Sun* described Leo's venture into the world of literature.

Just after the team arrived in Boston, Durocher spotted Lyn Lary with a lot of books. "Where did you get all those books, Lyn?"

"That's a fine question in a town like Boston," Lary replied. "You can't walk a block here without stumbling into a bookstore."

The next morning Leo set out to buy a book and made his way into the dark, crowded, dusty aisles of a Pemberton Square secondhand bookstore.

"I'm with the Yankees ball club and I want something to read," he said.

Eyeing Leo over the top of his spectacles, the gray-haired proprietor said, "You will find much here to interest you; we have over seven thousand volumes in the front room alone. Take that step ladder and you will find some good sports literature on the upper shelf in the little alcove; some splendid things on hunting big game in Africa and trout fishing in Scotland."

Leo climbed up, guided by the words of the bookseller, though he was not interested in hunting or fishing. Unaccustomed to the darkness of used-book shops and their rickety stepladders, he slipped and tumbled down into a box of magazines and stubbed his toe.

"I couldn't find nothing I wanted there," he said in embarrassment, "but I'll take one of those old magazines on Western stories."

"Certainly; take it for nothing, for I'm sorry you hurt yourself," said the book dealer.

"Oh! I just banged my toe, but I won't take the magazine for nothing," said Leo. "I'll tell you what I'll do. I'll leave two tickets at the gate for you on Sunday at Fenway Park."

Because of blue laws, which governed stadiums' proximity to churches, the Sox were prohibited from playing Sunday home games at Fenway and had to play at the nearby home grounds of the Boston Braves.

But it was a get-even trick by Durocher. He told the *Sun* reporter, "That guy will go to the Red Sox park Sunday and we'll be playing at Braves Field. That will learn him. This reading racket is the bunk. I'm going to pull a Hornsby and save my batting eye in case I ever get back into the lineup."*[55]

He did get back in the lineup after fifteen games, but his isolation from his own team was becoming obvious. He did little to help himself and much to make it worse. During the same May trip to Boston when he stubbed his toe in the bookstore, Durocher and several other teammates took several rides in an airplane on a lark. They agreed to keep it a secret from Huggins, who regarded going aloft as an unnecessary risk. According to a story in *The Boston Globe* in late June, Durocher himself put Huggins wise to what they had done, and Huggins hit the roof, threatening a $1,000 fine to the next Yankee to fly on a plane without his permission.[56]

When Durocher did play he often put his own dexterity on display—which appealed to fans and provided good newspaper copy but showed up his teammates and opponents. In a June game against the Cleveland Indians, for example, Leo caught a Lew Fonseca pop-up in short left, lost it, caught it again, tossed it into the air, and finally grabbed it for keeps the third time it came down. One writer wrote of the play that Leo should have been credited with two assists and a putout.[57]

A July profile of Durocher in the *Brooklyn Eagle* said he had been "a despised and sometimes rejected batsman on the slugging Yanks." The article also noted that no pitcher struck him out without a tough battle of wits. "Somehow he keeps getting on base—through errors and puny little stabbing hits."[58]

About the same time as the article appeared in the *Eagle*, Arthur Mann began observing that Durocher was less able to make the back end of double plays and was more prone to error. He still handled batted balls well, but the throws that came to him from the infield, outfield, home plate, and even the pitcher's mound were wide, low, high, or came in on a hop. Mann concluded that "some of the Yankees were curving and even bouncing the

---

* The law in question was changed in 1932.

double-play balls at a shortstop to make him look bad and get him out of the lineup!"

Mann confronted Durocher at his hotel with this seemingly fantastic observation and Durocher said it was baloney. Mann pressed on and asked why he had suddenly become a lone wolf. Why did he suddenly become quiet and seem to be bitter?

"Orders, I take 'em from my only boss, Miller Huggins. He told me the best way to stay out of trouble was to stay away from the people who cause it. I'm not sure who causes it, so I don't mix with anybody if I can avoid it. I stay home a lot . . . eat alone . . . go to the movies alone, and sit with nobody near me." He then told Mann about the lecture Huggins had given him during Spring Training, which he had taken to heart.

As Mann was leaving the room to find Huggins, Leo called to him: "I came into this league to play ball for the Yankees. I may not stick around long, but those guys will never get me out by bouncing balls at me or whispering gossip. They'll have to take me up and heave me out feet first."

Next, Mann bearded Huggins with questions about those on the team trying to hurt Leo with bad throws. At first, Huggins evaded the issue, but then Mann asked, "What about a situation where the presence of a single player is jeopardizing the success of the whole team?"

"Well, they won't get him out!" Huggins said of Durocher. "He'll stay in there when every one of them is wasting away on the bench. Out of this whole team, I'll rebuild the Yankees with Combs, Gehrig, and Pipgras, Dickey and Durocher. I'll keep Durocher, because he is the greatest infielder that ever smothered a half-hop. I take six players, and I'll start over . . ."[59]

As the season began to slip away from the Yankees, Huggins's support of Durocher intensified and his praise became more lavish. In late August he proclaimed Leo to be the greatest fielding shortstop of his generation. He felt Leo was not getting enough good publicity and asked writers to give him a good write-up in the off-season: "He's worth it."[60]

But Huggins himself did not last until the end of the season. A painful carbuncle appeared on his cheek that kept him from managing on September 15, and he was admitted to St. Vincent's Hospital the next day. As coach Art Fletcher took over the Yankees for him, doctors diagnosed Huggins with erysipelas, a bacterial skin infection. The disease attacked the fifty-one-year-old Huggins, and despite multiple blood transfusions he was in critical condition when the Yankees hopped a train to Boston for a pair of games with the Red Sox. Somehow playing while their old manager stood on death's doorstep, the Yankees beat Boston 5–3 on September 24 and jumped out to a 5–2 lead by the third inning on the afternoon of the twenty-fifth. At 3:16 P.M. that day Huggins died.[61]

All American League games were canceled the following day as thousands flocked to Yankee Stadium to pay their respects while another two thousand passed by his open coffin at the Church of the Transfiguration, also known as the Little Church Around the Corner, on Twenty-Ninth Street. More than ten thousand waited outside as a funeral service was held inside the church.

"Well that's the finish of little Leo. Hug was the best friend I ever had," Durocher sighed to Arthur Mann as the mourning period began. "He was the only one who thought I might make good someday."[62]

On October 5 the Yankees played a doubleheader at Yankee Stadium. It was the first time the team had played at home since Huggins's death nineteen days earlier. Durocher got three of the Yankees' eight hits that day, which was also the last day of the season. The 1929 Yankees finished in second place but eighteen games out of first and were trending downward as a team. One pessimistic reporter wrote that the team was "in the throes of disintegration and rehabilitation."[63]

CHAPTER 4

The Red Menace

A T THE END OF THE 1929 SEASON, Leo Durocher was mailed a
contract from Yankee chief executive Ed Barrow that offered him
$5,000 with an additional $1,000 at the end of the 1930 season as a
bonus to be paid only with the approval of the manager. He was to defer
signing it until closer to Spring Training.

Meanwhile, Durocher's debts were piling up. Among other things, he
had moved his parents to the Bronx and installed them in a comfortable,
newly furnished rental home near Yankee Stadium. He was faced with
a mass of unpaid bills, IOUs, and overdrawn bank accounts amounting
to at least four times the amount he was being offered for the 1930
season. Merchants were now demanding cash in their dealings with him.[1]

In late October, the new Yankee manager, Bob Shawkey, returned from
the Canadian wilderness where he had been hunting to sign his 1930
contract and talk of reorganizing the team. Durocher's position on the team
was unsettled. Ben Chapman had been brought up from St. Paul, Jimmie
Reese had been brought in from the Pacific Coast League, and Lyn Lary
and Leo were both in contention for shortstop in the 1930 infield.[2]

Durocher chose to stay in New York over the winter months where he
would, among other things, pursue his second career as a pocket billiard
player, able to make the sports pages for beating some of the great professionals of the game in short fifty-point games. He bested Marcel Camp,
who was ranked ninth in the world, and he came within six points of
beating seventh-ranked Arthur Woods in a 125-point game. Durocher was
good enough for Camp to say of him, "He knows the game, has the

confidence and if he decided to take billiards seriously we in the pocket game would have something new to think about."[3]

In late January the *New York Sun* said that Durocher had signed with the Yankees, but on February 1 the *Springfield Republican* reported that Durocher had returned an unsigned contract, demanding more money. The same day that report appeared, Shawkey listed Durocher as one of the twenty-three players ordered to report to Spring Training on February 23.[4]

On February 4 Durocher walked into Chief Executive Ed Barrow's office on Forty-Second Street to demand $7,000 rather than the $5,000 plus the $1,000 bonus he had been offered. The timing could not have been worse, as the stock market had crashed in October 1929 and money was in short supply. One newspaper reported that Leo entered Barrow's office "extremely wroth" and saying he needed the extra thousand in advance to pay his overdue hotel bill at the Piccadilly. Barrow listened and then told Durocher to take it or leave it.

"Don't hold your breath," Durocher fumed, "because it is never going to happen."

Barrow then swiveled around in his chair, turning his back on Durocher and looking out the window.

Infuriated, Durocher headed for the door and called back and told Barrow to go fuck himself. Durocher claimed he uttered the line in a tone of voice so modulated that Barrow could hear him but was still soft enough that he could pretend he had not.

Barrow opted for the latter.

"What did you say?"

"Didn't you hear me?" Durocher yelled back.

"Yes, I did."

Durocher then swung around and looked him in the eye and said, "And it still goes."

Barrow then leaped from his chair pointed a finger at Durocher and said, "And so do you."

This was Durocher's account of the event. In Barrow's memoir, published in 1951, he gave a much more cordial and less confrontational—though not entirely contradictory—version of the meeting in which Durocher's parting words were "Good-bye, Mr. Barrow." Barrow's recollection did include a description of Leo's dress for the meeting: a derby hat, spats, and a velvet-collared coat.[5]

The mild-mannered Bob Shawkey, who did not like Durocher and later called him the "biggest mouth in the game," made the final decision to let him go. "I got rid of him because he did not help the team," Shawkey explained. "He caused more fights than anybody on the team. He was a good fielder but couldn't hit much." Shawkey was also good friends with many of the men whom Durocher targeted for verbal abuse.[6]

The Yankees put Durocher on waivers that very afternoon, but no American League team—not even the forsaken St. Louis Browns—wanted him. Under the waiver system then in place he was first offered to the last-place team in the National League. The Boston Braves turned him down after a short period of deliberation, a disappointment to fans in New England who would have enjoyed seeing Durocher and Maranville play on the same team. *Boston Herald* columnist Bob Dunbar wrote that it would be "quite a treat to hear the verbal fireworks and the incessant flow of chatter between Leo and Rabbit."[7]

After every team in the National League passed, the man who stepped up to acquire Durocher was Sidney Weil of Cincinnati, who had purchased the Reds in September 1928 for an amount probably double the team's actual value. He immediately increased all salaries for members of the staff and hired affable manager Dan Howley away from the St. Louis Browns to run the team. Before his first partial season as owner ended he was already making improvements to the ballpark starting with the installation of the first loudspeaker system in a major league ballpark. An avid Reds fan, Weil had become wealthy as the owner of a Ford dealership and the operator of the first multilevel parking garage in Cincinnati, and he looked at the team as a hobby more than a business.[8]

On October 29, 1929, Black Tuesday had hit Wall Street and Weil's financial situation had changed radically, as most of his money was tied up in stocks. He still had to field a baseball team, but now was looking for bargains.

The morning after Durocher walked out of Barrow's office, Weil got word that the Yankees wanted to get rid of him. He made a quick appointment with Barrow at his midtown office. Durocher was for sale, but Barrow's asking price was $25,000 plus one minor league player. "I was willing to part with the player, but not the money," Weil recalled. "After further talk, he gave me an opening to make an offer. I mentioned $7,500 and the player he wanted. He just swiveled around and looked out the window. I looked at his back so long I began to feel uncomfortable and then I said, 'Well, I've been thrown out of better offices than this,' as

I started to get up and get out. With that he turned around to face me, and in a few minutes I had bought Durocher for $10,000 and the player."*

When the transfer was announced, the press reacted with puzzlement. Why had so many teams rejected the finest fielding shortstop to come up to the majors in the last ten years? Was it because, as one writer put it, "he could not hit the floor with his cigarette" or that he had ridden every important player in the league "until their knees were sprained"? Perhaps, but Davis Walsh, sports editor of the International News Service, pointed out that baseball had a gentleman's agreement by which if an optioned player is refused by one team, the next club must also pass until the player is effectively banished from the league. Walsh quickly added, "However, if I was a major league club owner and needed a shortstop as the Indians, Red Sox and Braves do, I'd forget I was a gentleman."[9]

One rumored reason that all the teams in the American League passed on Durocher was that Babe Ruth let it be known he wanted Durocher out of the league.[10] Ruth continued to let everybody and anybody know about Durocher stealing his watch, and for years to come, opposition players stood in their dugouts and taunted Leo by holding a swinging watch. Ruth himself would take the belief that Durocher stole his watch to his grave. In 1948, as he lay dying in a New York hospital, he told the story one last time to then commissioner A. B. "Happy" Chandler, who had come to pay his respects.†[11]

The dapper, debt-ridden Durocher now headed to the National League. At this time, when the two leagues were separate empires with powerful presidents, the American League rejection meant that Durocher was

---

* The player named later was Clarke (Pinky) Pittenger, a journeyman shortstop who never reported to New York and was sent directly to the minors, where his baseball career ended.
† The most colorful rendition of the story appeared in Tiger pitcher Elden Auker's 2001 memoir, *Sleeper Cars and Flannel Uniforms* (Chicago: Triumph Books, 2001): "Because of Ruth's penchant for belching and passing gas," Auker wrote, "no regulars wanted to room with him on the road. So the team always had a young player room with him. Durocher was Ruth's roommate. He seemed to be dealing well with Ruth's personal habits, but Ruth and some teammates started to notice that money and valuables were missing. Suspicious, Ruth marked five $100 bills. He later found them, plus his pocket watch, in Durocher's bag. He woke Durocher and began beating him until hotel security arrived. Nothing ever appeared in the newspapers."

perhaps forever to be considered the property of what was then known as the senior circuit.*[12]

SHORTLY AFTER DUROCHER was acquired by the Reds on February 2, an anonymous assertion was made and circulated in baseball circles that Leo had been banned from the American League rather than simply rejected by the seven teams to which he had been offered. If true, it meant that Durocher was, according to the conventions of the time, tainted, and the Reds could and would not actually sign him and that he would be sent directly to a minor league team—effectively interrupting or ending his major league career. The public knew nothing of this until Arthur Mann revealed this assertion in the *New York World* in a bylined piece under the headline REDS MAY SHUNT DUROCHER OUT OF THE MAJOR LEAGUES.[13]

Weil quickly determined that the men who ran the American League had rejected Durocher because they did not like him and saw him as a source of clubhouse dissension, but that there was no outright ban. Weil then signed Durocher to a contract.

The Reds' new manager, Dan Howley, had expressed great admiration for Durocher as a nervy bench jockey when Howley managed the St. Louis Browns from 1927 through 1929. Howley made it clear that Durocher would be given every opportunity to exercise his vocal cords in the National League. *The Sporting News* looked at the purchase and noted, "Howley is so well supplied with infielders that just where he will fit Durocher in the Reds' lineup is rather difficult to figure, but Leo the Linguist talks a good game and may be used for that purpose."[14]

Clara Durocher once said that her son Leo could fall into the Connecticut River and not get wet. This certainly was the case when he came ashore in Cincinnati and was welcomed at river's edge by Sidney Weil, who treated him like a long-lost, albeit prodigal, son. Nonetheless, no sooner had Weil arrived back in Cincinnati from New York in early February 1930 than he began to get letters from Durocher's creditors, mostly hotels, demanding payment. He answered them all politely, telling each that Durocher had

---

* As Bob Ryan wrote in *The Boston Globe* on July 11, 2007, "Do fans today have any idea that there was no such thing as interleague trading until the early 1960s? It was a mighty big deal to cross from one league to the other. You only did it when you were young or old."

nothing yet coming from the Cincinnati club, but that when Durocher started to earn some money, Weil would do everything he could to get them paid.

Durocher, now twenty-four, reported to Spring Training in Tampa with high expectations. Dan Howley had already told Jack Ryder of the *Cincinnati Enquirer* that Leo looked to him like a .300 hitter in the games in which he had seen him play and Howley looked forward to Durocher's blossoming at the plate. That said, it was still clear that Durocher had to make his way into the starting lineup.

Before exhibition games began, Weil called Durocher to his hotel room and showed him the overdue bills, which amounted to more than a year's salary—more than $10,000, Durocher would later admit. (Others claimed it was actually closer to $20,000.) Durocher agreed that he owed all that was claimed and said he would pay it all eventually. "We made an agreement that I would withhold all of his salary except just what he had to have to live," Weil later recalled, "and apply the balance against his indebtedness."

Durocher was in hot water of another sort a few weeks after his meeting with Weil. On April 4, he missed the team train from Atlanta to Birmingham, Alabama, where an exhibition game was scheduled for later in the day. Durocher eventually located a friend from his playing days in Georgia who was a pilot at a local airport and convinced him to fly him to Alabama. When Durocher's plane finally swooped down over the ballpark, the Reds were already on the field taking batting practice. The plane landed nearby, and Durocher jumped into a taxi, raced to the hotel where the team was staying, changed into his uniform, and headed to the ballpark.

"Did you see that plane over you a few minutes ago?" Durocher asked his teammates. "Well I was in that 'bus,' and it only took me two hours to get here."

Howley was furious. He fumed, "Next time you have to take a plane to join the team, you better keep going to the Coast," alluding to the Pacific Coast League, where the Yankees had intended to send him before the Reds bought his waiver.[15]

As punishment, Durocher was benched for the remainder of the preseason exhibition games, on Opening Day, and beyond. But Howley's public benching of Durocher coincided with a call Sidney Weil got from Commissioner Kenesaw Mountain Landis on April 15, 1930, the morning of Opening Day.

"Weil," said Landis, "Durocher owes a lot of money in New York; do not permit him to play until he pays."

"Judge," Weil replied, "I know he owes the bills, but he has no money, and if he can't play, he'll never have any." Weil told him of the agreement that Durocher had made with him and that the bills would be paid eventually. Landis thought it over and reversed himself and said that under those circumstances Durocher could play.[16]

Weil genuinely liked Durocher, considered him a friend, and did the best he could to keep him out of trouble. His old debts were cataloged and prorated, and Durocher was put on an allowance, which he almost immediately exceeded. "Leo Durocher was a very natty dresser—the Beau Brummell type—and while we had agreed that he had enough clothes to do him for a long time, it wasn't a week later that I received a haberdasher's bill for $350," Weil later recalled. "I called him at once and asked him which of the purchases he had already worn. He said only the sweater he had on. I gave him enough to pay for it and told him to return all the other stuff, and he did. With all his faults, one couldn't help liking him."

Manager Howley liked Durocher but during the limbo period warned him: "Don't try any monkey business with me, young fellow. If you start popping off around here and getting yourself into jams, I'll first hit you over the head with a bat and then I will put 'Peoria' across the front of your shirt and make it stick. You've got a chance to become a great ballplayer—or to wind up in the minors in a hurry. Take your choice."[17]

On the field Durocher worked his way into the lineup on April 18 as a defensive replacement at second base at the end of the game. He finally got his first at-bat on April 28—seven games into the regular season. A few weeks later, the Reds traded infielder Hughie Critz to the Giants, allowing Durocher to start as the team's regular shortstop, with Hod Ford moving to second base, creating a combination that would soon lead the league in double plays and ultimately set a record.

The Reds were—with the exception of Durocher—a lackluster group made up of over-the-hill stars like Bob Meusel and Harry Heilmann and journeymen position players. The best that could be said about the team was that as a preseason Associated Press report put it, half the roster was made up of men who could hit and the other half, men who could play the field, but unlike Durocher, few could do both.[18]

The problem was that Weil, after the stock market crash, had become, in the words of baseball historian Robert Smith, "a hand-to-mouth type" who knew what it was like to get up early in the morning and rush to cover a check written two days earlier. "My scouts recommended enough players—whom I had to pass up for lack of funds—who eventually made their way to the Majors and made good with a capital 'G,' that I know that all that was missing in my operation was money. To name a few, there were Joe DiMaggio, Billy Herman, Big Bill Lee, and many others who could have made my team a lot better club than it was."[19]

The swiftness with which he had been shunted out of the American League had been a lesson to Durocher, and he chose to befriend rather than bedevil his teammates. On the other hand, he retained his credentials as a bench jockey, and his ability as a shortstop seemed to rise. The 1930 Reds ended up in seventh place, winning only fifteen of their last fifty-eight games, ending thirty-three games out of first place. Durocher batted .243 for the year with three home runs but he became the team's clear fan favorite.

DUROCHER, NOW TWENTY-FIVE, quickly found his way in Cincinnati, where he spent much of his time after dark playing pool and making new friends in the speakeasies and gambling joints located across the Ohio River from Cincinnati. Women were attracted to Leo, who was as dapper as ever and could afford to play the field. This made it all the more stunning when, out of the blue, he took a bride. Durocher married Ruby Hartley, twenty-three, on November 5, 1930, at St. Andrew Roman Catholic Church in Avondale, a Cincinnati neighborhood. Weil was not only surprised by the marriage but appalled by Durocher's choice. "One fall day I came home and Mrs. Weil told me Leo was married. She asked me to 'guess who?' Of course, I couldn't. When she told me it was Ruby who had sued the son of my partners in the automobile business for breach of promise in the amount of $50,000, I exclaimed, 'Can't that woman stay out of my family tree?'" The lawsuit had been for a broken engagement.[20]

Mrs. Leo Durocher was pregnant, and the couple's only child, Barbara, was born three months later. The marriage would quickly prove to be a bad match.

From the start Leo leaned on Weil for extra cash. "He would come and ask me for $100, and then we'd finally settle for $25," said Weil. He soon got the name of "C-note Leo." As the old debt was retired, he ran up new obligations. In Cincinnati, he could indulge his gambling appetite even more easily than in New York. Cincinnati was across the river—"over the Rhine," in local slang in the heavily German city—from the gambling casinos, brothels, and speakeasies of northern Kentucky where he spent much of his time. There were bookies, gamblers, and racketeers now in Durocher's orbit, whom he considered his friends and whom he would keep up with and tell stories about for decades to come. These men sported names befitting their professions—"Cigar" Charlie and "the Dancer."*

One was Louis Levinson, who was known as "Sleepout Louie," a notorious gambler who along with his brother Ed had the backing of Meyer Lansky, the gangster who headed Murder Incorporated, the enforcement arm of the American Mafia in the 1920s through the 1940s. Sleepout earned early fame as a second-story man, a gifted burglar, and, later, a well-connected gambler and owner of the Flamingo, a casino in Newport, Kentucky, which is where Durocher met him.

What Durocher never seemed to recall later as he told stories about his life in Cincinnati was that he had brought his mother, but not his father, to the city after the marriage and helped to get her a job as a chambermaid in a local hotel. A. B. "Happy" Chandler, then a state senator and later governor of Kentucky, met Durocher during this time in Cincinnati. As Chandler later recalled, "Leo would get all spiffed up, dressed to kill, spending all his money, while his mother was working at the Netherlands Plaza Hotel scrubbing floors." Using one of the bucolic metaphors he was famous for, Chandler said that Durocher would "hold the lamp while his mother chopped wood." Chandler regarded Durocher as a "bad boy."[21]

For the second time in his life, Durocher was in the Opening Day starting lineup of a Major League Baseball team. After losing seventeen of their first nineteen games, the 1931 Reds never got out of last place in the eight-team National League. For Durocher, a minor triumph was achieved on August 13 in Boston against the Braves when he hit his first home run of the season—an event that netted him a headline in the *Springfield Republican*. But the team's situation was so bad that by the middle of September *The Sporting News* declared that the team had sewn up its claim to last place so securely that no other team could hope to dispute their right to nestle in the cellar for the rest of the year. The team set a record that

---

* Later, when Durocher was with the Brooklyn Dodgers, he took team secretary Hal Parrott to a favorite dive and introduced him to these very men.

still stands for the most losses at home for any Reds team in their long history with fifty-one.[22]

The only bright spot was that Durocher was deemed the best fielding shortstop in all the major leagues by the United Press. This assertion was made during a streak from May 15 to August 5 in which Durocher handled 252 chances without making an error. Tom Swope of the *Cincinnati Post* wrote about Durocher during this 1931 streak: "Durocher now ranks pretty close to number 1 among the shortstops in his league, not because he is going so long without an error, but because of the plays he makes. He tackles everything and makes many a difficult play seem easy because of his speed and strong arm." For the year, Durocher batted .227.[23]

Writing at the beginning of the 1932 season, Henry McLemore of the United Press summed up Leo's greatest strength and greatest weakness when he wrote: "They shoot a cannon in Cincinnati when Leo misses a grounder—and they shoot two cannons when he gets a hit."[24]

Other than Weil, Leo's greatest allies were the Cincinnati fans who learned to love him on the field and off. "Inside those chalk lines nobody worked harder than Leo Durocher," Weil said some years later. "After a while, I started taking him around with me as a speaker. He was fast on his feet behind a platform too. He'd tell a lot of stories about his days with the Yankees, and they'd go over big."[25]

Not all the players liked Leo. Larry Benton, a Reds pitcher during all of Durocher's time in Cincinnati, had little use for him as a person but understood his value to the team. "I still want him behind me," Benton later said. "He saves me two runs a game. He goes after double play balls no one else would even try for."[26]

Manager Howley echoed Benton's assessment. One very hot night sitting on the lawn of the Forest Park Hotel in St. Louis with a young *St. Louis Journal* reporter named Red Smith, Durocher pulled up in a car driven by an attractive young woman. Leo stepped out of the car in white trousers, black-and-white shoes, a navy-blue jacket, and a straw boater cocked at a steep slant. As Smith reported: "Howley shook with laughter. 'Look at the bleep!' he said. 'Worth a million dollars on the ballfield, and not a bleeping cent off it.'"[27]

Leo managed to stay out of trouble and out of the headlines in the nation's newspaper sports sections, which thrived on discord and controversy, until May 12, 1932, when Commissioner Landis fined Durocher $30 and suspended him for three days for slugging shortstop Dick Bartell of the

Phillies in the jaw in a game played the day before in Cincinnati. It was Durocher's first major league fine and suspension.

In the eighth inning of the game in question, Durocher tried to steal second and missed; but as he slid in, his spikes scraped Bartell's wrist. Bartell told Durocher if he ever tried to knock the ball out of his hand again with his spikes he would punch him in the nose.

"I don't believe you're man enough to do it" was Leo's retort. Bartell, who shared Durocher's reputation for aggressiveness, stepped toward Durocher as if to make good on his threat; but Leo took the first shot and hit him on the chin, knocking him backward and onto the ground. Bartell got up and started toward Durocher when umpire Beans Reardon pushed him back so that his teammates could bring him under control. Durocher was ejected from the game, but Bartell was allowed to stay. In his notes on the game in the next day's *Enquirer*, Jack Ryder insisted that the umpire had not heard Bartell's challenge; if he had, Bartell would also have been ejected.[28]

The 1932 Reds were uncharacteristically 15–12 at the time of the ejection and ended the month in third place, but a ten-game losing streak in late June had the team sliding into the second division.

As Durocher continued to bait and berate opposition players, inevitably fans of the opposition came to verbally abuse Durocher. During an August 6 game in Boston, two men in the stands roasted Durocher throughout the game. After the game was over, they came out onto the field to shake hands. "But," in Weil's words, "Durocher happened to step on their feet with his spikes." Or, as the *Boston Herald* put it, Durocher planted his spikes with "considerable vehemence" on the feet of his tormentors. The men got a warrant for his arrest, but Weil shipped him to New York, where the team was to play next, before it could be served.*

In early September, the Reds played the Braves in Boston before the end of the season, and Durocher did not make the trip lest he be arrested. By the time of the Boston trip, the team had begun its final swoon, losing eleven of its last fourteen games and ending up 60–94 at the end of the season in eighth place. Howley was fired as manager with a 177–285 record for his three years in Cincinnati.[29]

---

* At this time in baseball history and for some years to come, fans were commonly allowed on the field the moment the last out was made.

Durocher's value as a player increased in Cincinnati, and despite his reputation as a poor hitter—and anemic 1932 batting average of .217—there were days when Leo excelled at the plate. In an August 14, 1932, doubleheader played in Cincinnati against the Boston Braves, Leo hit two doubles, two triples, and a single to drive in five runs in the two games. Even one of his outs was special—a line drive to left hit so hard that it sent outfielder Earl Clark sprawling backward. The fielding star that day was Durocher's boyhood idol Rabbit Maranville, who handled twenty fielding chances at second for the Braves without a misstep, some deemed brilliant in the next day's newspaper.[30]

Defensively, Durocher drew much attention by his ability to successfully play out of position. When Brooklyn slugger Hack Wilson came to bat, Leo parked himself in short left-center, fully fifteen feet from the edge of the infield dirt. And when catcher Frank "Shanty" Hogan of the Boston Braves came to the plate, he moved himself behind third base almost onto the outfield grass. Explaining why he played Hogan this way, Durocher said, "Frank's almost a sure dead left field hitter. He's slow enough so that I can throw him out from the back of the grass." Harold Burr of the *Brooklyn Eagle* thought that Durocher got the idea of playing out of position from his time with the Yankees when he watched American League infields swing way over to right when Babe Ruth came to bat and the second baseman played on the grass behind first base and the shortstop behind second base.* [31]

ON NOVEMBER 16, 1932, the St. Louis Cardinals' twenty-six-year-old shortstop, Charlie Gelbert, was out hunting rabbits in the mountains of Pennsylvania when he accidentally shot himself in the ankle with a 12-gauge shotgun after tripping over a vine. At the very minimum, he would be out for the 1933 season. Within hours of the mishap, the Cardinals began a drive to obtain Durocher as a replacement. A series of offers were made over the winter and into the spring by Branch Rickey, the former player, Cardinals manager, and now their business manager, the name then given to the general manager.

---

* Shifts of the kind made by Durocher were much less common during this period than they became in the late twentieth century. In the 1930s the practice was simply known as playing out of position.

Rickey had an uncanny ability to judge players and was building a Cardinal dynasty. Born into a pious Methodist household, Rickey eschewed the vices of drink and gambling common to many baseball men of his time. The closest he came to swearing was to bellow "Judas Priest," and his piety would not allow him to go the ballpark on the Sabbath. His one vice was smoking, and he was seldom seen in public without a large cigar clenched in his teeth.

Weil was not prepared to give up Durocher, who started the 1933 season as the Reds shortstop with the Boston lawsuit still pending. Early in the season, Weil called Emil Fuchs, the owner of the Boston club, and asked him to get an attorney for Leo because he knew that the first time the team appeared in Boston, the warrants would be served. They were, and he went on trial on May 4. The plaintiff, a traveling salesman named Walter James, denied having said anything provocative to Durocher. Weil, who was in the courtroom with Leo, observed: "A woman, who was a stranger to us, who knew all the Boston players, was Leo's chief witness (furnished by his attorney). She testified that she had been sitting behind the two who had done the heckling, and that they had called Leo atrocious names. The Judge asked her what they had said, and she responded that a lady just couldn't use such language." The result was a not-guilty verdict.[32]

At first Weil told Rickey he would talk about anyone but Durocher, but he insisted Rickey offer him pitcher Paul Derringer. Weil was desperate for a starting pitcher and was especially high on Derringer. He realized that Rickey needed Leo so badly that he was willing to part with players worth an estimated $150,000 for a $30,000 man. Weil tossed in two unimportant players—pitchers John Ogden and Frank "Dutch" Henry—and the Reds also got pitcher Allyn Stout and infielder Earl "Sparky" Adams. No cash was involved. Three days later, early on the morning of May 7, 1933, the deal was done.*[33]

The day of the trade, the Reds were in New York for a series against the Giants, when Weil called Durocher to his room at the Governor Clinton Hotel across the street from Penn Station and broke the news of the trade to him. Durocher had the deepest respect for Weil, who had by now helped him pay off all of his old New York debt, and begged to be kept. "I won't go!" he

---

* Derringer helped pitch the Reds to pennants in 1939 and 1940 and won fifteen to help the Cubs win the 1945 pennant.

asserted. "I like it here. I like you. You're the best friend I ever had. Trade someone else. I'll play for less money."

Weil explained that the deal was set and that it had to be made and that going without a fuss would be a favor and a way of reciprocating for the help he had given Durocher in Cincinnati. He asked Leo to step quietly into a Cardinal uniform.

"Then I'll hold up Rickey!" Durocher exclaimed. "He'll have to pay me a thousand more. Cash, now."

Weil guaranteed Durocher the extra thousand and promised that he would extract it from the Cardinals. Durocher and Weil then headed uptown to the Almac Hotel at Seventy-First Street and Broadway, where the Cards were staying while in the midst of a series with the Brooklyn Dodgers.

Rickey was in bed nursing a cold and smoking a cigar when Durocher burst into his room demanding an extra thousand dollars. Rickey stared up at Durocher, whom he was meeting for the first time. This, he thought, was the defiant maverick that the American League had rejected and whose baggage now included new debt and the burden of a marriage rumored to be on the rocks. Durocher demanded and got the extra thousand dollars but found out later to his shock and disappointment that Weil, not Rickey, had paid it. It was Weil's farewell gift to Leo, whom he still treated like a son.

Rickey now had the shortstop he needed to create a championship team for St. Louis, and Durocher had found another boss who, like Huggins and Weil, would always be in his corner—as he would put it later, his third baseball father.[34]

The original plan had been to announce the trade after the two teams had played that afternoon, but Rickey persuaded Weil to give him Durocher on the spot so he could play immediately. Durocher was still struggling with the impact of the trade and told Rickey he did not want to play that day.[35]

Rickey reminded Durocher that the deal was final and added:

"We've got a doubleheader in Brooklyn this afternoon. You may not play for us today. But how are you going to feel if our shortstop bobbles, and we lose both games? And how are you going to feel at the end of the season, if we lose the pennant by the two games that you could have won by being in there at shortstop? Answer that, son."

Durocher's resistance dissipated, and he agreed to play in both games, in each of which he singled and drove in a run. Abruptly, Leo stopped complaining about being sold to the Cardinals.

Before the day was over, Durocher had told Jack Ryder of the *Cincinnati Enquirer*, "I hate to leave Redland and the boys." It was a point well taken, because he had proven himself with the fans, his teammates, and the local press. Ryder himself wrote, "Leo has fire and pepper on the field and is one of the most colorful athletes in the business. He will be missed by both fans and players with all of whom his is a popular number."[36]

He also came away with a true friend and ally in Sidney Weil, whom for decades to come Durocher would call the best friend he had ever had. For his part, Weil treated Durocher like a son in the literal sense of a father playing catch with his son. During Spring Training in 1933, reporters witnessed an unusual sight: Durocher banging out hot grounders to the owner of the team.[37]

When Weil died in 1966 at age seventy-five in a car accident, his friend and fellow baseball owner Bill Veeck devoted one of his syndicated newspaper columns to his memory. "I'll make a wager, even give odds," Veeck wrote, "that Sidney Weil had more friends than anyone in the country, in the strangest places. And wealthy or broke, if you asked them 'Why?' their replies would sound like a broken record. 'D'ya know what Sid did for me?'"[38]

To his credit, Durocher never tired of extolling Weil and his indebtedness to him. In a 1955 interview with Robert Shaplen of *Sports Illustrated*, he said: "Sidney was a real wonderful man. He took good care of me. I was constantly in some kind of trouble and he did everything for me, always."[39]

One could easily make the case that Sidney Weil saved Leo Durocher's baseball career.

CHAPTER 5

Gashouse Tough

O N MAY 12, 1933, Durocher was back in Boston to play but also to participate in a baseball school sponsored by the *Boston Herald*. He and a handful of players from the Cardinals and Boston, including Rabbit Maranville of the Braves, gave a free morning clinic on fielding to forty-five hundred children and their parents. According to the *Herald*, Leo put on one of his slickest performances ever on the field; the *Herald* also noted that Durocher had taken extra time to give special instructions to a youngster named Bill Moran of Somerville. For all of his flaws and faults, Durocher reinforced at this event that a constant in his life was always going out of his way to be nice to children.[1]

The Cardinals won the game that day 2–1, and Leo was credited with several "fielding gems" that made the difference. In his first games as the new shortstop, the team went 19–7, and Durocher seemed to be a good fit with the Cardinals, where his swagger and arrogance were more of an asset than a liability. For the first time, Leo found himself on a team that immediately appreciated him for who he was. He found, among other things, that he and his teammates spoke the same profanity-laced language.

Leo was assigned uniform number 2, which seemed appropriate because he immediately assumed a leadership role on a team that often seemed to lack it. He would wear the number then and for the rest of his baseball career.

Despite the fine pitching of Dizzy Dean, who won twenty and lost eighteen, and the stellar play of Durocher at shortstop, the 1933 Cardinals were a disappointment. They played 153 games, winning eighty-two games, losing seventy-one, and finishing in fifth place. Durocher batted a respectable .258. The manager on the Cardinals was Frankie Frisch, also the team's second baseman. Frisch, whose hobbies were gardening and classical music, was not only Durocher's opposite but also a cultural world apart from his team. The only thing they all had in common was a fierce determination to win.

Meanwhile the 1933 Cincinnati Reds ended the year in shambles. With a 58–94 record, the eighth-place team was also last in the league in batting average, runs scored, and home runs. It had also gone through three managers. Then, on November 6, 1933, Sidney Weil, one of the best-liked men in baseball, resigned as president of the Reds, and the ownership of the team was taken over by the Central Trust Bank of Cincinnati. Weil had never fully recovered from the stock market crash and had to turn ownership over to the bank in order to prevent having to declare bankruptcy. The bank, which had no interest in running the team, appointed an energetic redhead named Leland Stanford "Larry" MacPhail as its new president. He had been named after Leland Stanford, a family friend and the great benefactor of Stanford University, which he had named for his son Leland Jr. During the First World War, MacPhail had been an artillery captain who, along with a few fellow officers, concocted a failed attempt to kidnap Kaiser Wilhelm II. While in the Kaiser's castle, MacPhail snatched a monogrammed ashtray, which he displayed on his desk in Cincinnati.

MacPhail's first job was to find a buyer for the team while improving its bottom line. One of MacPhail's first actions was to try to bring Babe Ruth to Cincinnati as the Reds' player-manager. Yankee owner Jacob Ruppert refused to release Ruth from his contract. Then, early in 1934, MacPhail convinced Powel Crosley to purchase the Reds as the head of a syndicate. The oldest Major League Baseball team had been saved.[2]

The 1934 Cardinals played a hard-nosed brand of baseball that fit Leo like one of his tailored silk suits. "We fought among ourselves," Leo Durocher once informed sportswriter Jimmy Cannon, "but we stuck together if anyone picked on us. There was a fight every day . . . with each other or the other ball club." The team was known for playing tough and dirty, and their weapon of choice was the beanball. Not only did they play rough, they also looked rough. As a team, they usually showed up at game time unshaven and dressed in uniforms still grimy from the previous game.

Frisch, despite his gardening skills and love of classical music, and Durocher were one of the great umpire-baiting duos of all time. With both men converging from either side of second base, the insults they hurled were terse, profane, and clever.

On April 12, 1934, three days before the Cards opened against the Pirates in St. Louis, the Durochers appeared in divorce court in Cincinnati. Ruby Hartley alleged that Leo had "punched her in the jaw and tied her in a bedsheet on one occasion when she had come home at 2 a.m., and Leo and his mother, who lived with them, had initially locked her out." Under cross-examination, she denied that she was drunk that night or that she had been "friendly" with other men. She then alleged that Leo had received telegrams at the house from women named Marie, Sis, and Virginia, one of which contained the line "I miss you, baby." It was disclosed that Durocher had already been paying $25 a week in temporary alimony. The divorce was granted.[3]

Frisch's Cardinals started out cold—they dropped seven of their first eleven games. They turned things around in May when they won twenty-one games and lost only six to climb back into contention.

When the team was winning, the players started to clown and carry on with a new intensity. The clubhouse featured hillbilly singing led by Pepper Martin, and the practical jokes grew ever bolder. For once, Leo let his teammates play the bad boys while he sat in the corner pretending to wear a halo—but it was a crooked one. Branch Rickey revealed in a 1955 interview with *Sports Illustrated* that the brains behind the most ingenious pranks came from Leo, whom he described as "the prime mover—the instigator." He added: "He was also the damnedest double-crosser that ever lived."

Late in May 1934, for example, when the Cardinals stayed at the Bellevue-Stratford Hotel in Philadelphia, Dizzy Dean, Pepper Martin, and utility infielder Henry "Heine" Schuble were inspired to don coveralls and workmen's caps and parade through the lobby, dining room, and kitchen carrying a ladder and all the while chattering about needed repairs to light fixtures, boilers, and other objects; they then invaded a convention of the United Boys Clubs of America and staged a mock fight. While all this was going on, Leo reported the incident to the house detective and there would be, in Rickey's words, "real hell to pay" for all involved save for Durocher.[4]

Between the play and the pranks, the Cardinals blossomed into one of the most colorful teams in the history of modern baseball. They featured Dizzy and Paul Dean, Ernie "Showboat" Orsatti, Ducky Medwick, Pepper Martin, Rip Collins, Bill "Kayo" DeLancy, and, of course, Durocher, who had been named captain of the team at the start of the 1934 season.

Durocher put his stamp on the team with his aggressiveness and drive and is usually credited with labeling the team the "Gashouse Gang." According to the most popular and widely accepted version of the story, the bestowing of the nickname occurred in May 1934, when Frank Graham of the *New York Sun* asked Durocher what he thought of the Cardinals winning the pennant. Before he could answer, Dizzy Dean drawled, "We could win the pennant in any league. The National or the American."

Durocher interrupted: "They wouldn't let us play in the American League. They say we're just a lot of gashouse players."

From then on, Graham called the team the Gashouse Gang. The term *gashouse* referred to factories in towns and cities that used to turn coal into gas for electricity and cooking in the days before the widespread distribution of natural gas. The plants were dirty and polluting, belching black smoke and giving off a foul smell. They were usually situated in the "bad end" of town, and those who worked in them were dirty with coal dust.*[5]

ON SEPTEMBER 27, only a few months after divorcing Ruby Hartley, Durocher married Grace Dozier, a prominent St. Louis businesswoman and fashion designer who had herself obtained a divorce only two days earlier. The two had been introduced by Branch Rickey and his wife, who were friends with Dozier and saw the pairing as one which would help Leo lead a more structured life.

Grace wore a black tailored gown with a white ermine cape. Durocher's

---

* There are several other versions of how the nickname was applied to the Cardinals. One has the St. Louis team coming into New York from Boston, where they had just played in the rain. Their uniforms were particularly dirty because they were a "sliding" team, and the equipment man did not have time to have them cleaned. When they appeared on the field at the Polo Grounds, one shocked reporter commented that they looked like "the gang from around the gas house." This version was given by Frisch (the *Saturday Evening Post*, July 18, 1959) and in a radio interview (May 11, 1963) in which he acknowledged that his was not the only version of the story. Frisch added that he thought the reporter was Frank Lamb of the *New York Evening Journal*. But in his biography of Dizzy Dean (*Ol' Diz*, New York: HarperCollins, 1992), Vince Staten questioned this version, because May 20 and July 23 were the only two days during the 1934 season that the Cardinals played in New York a day after a game in Boston—and both of those games in Boston were played under clear skies with no hint of rain.

best man was Cardinal outfielder Ernie "Showboat" Orsatti, who entertained the assembled by juggling the small box that contained the wedding ring.[6]

The new Mrs. Durocher immediately took over Leo's finances. All checks went directly to her as she worked to pay off some of Leo's substantial new debts. Dozier was widely admired, as was her line of clothing, which was marketed under her trade name, "Carol King," and was very popular. Durocher would later describe his bride as one of the most astute and successful women in the country.[7]

Getting married so late in the season would normally be considered a distraction, but matchmaker Rickey, not Durocher, had pushed for it. Rickey believed that the wedding would be good for Durocher as a player. The next day Durocher—now carrying the new nickname of "the Bridegroom Shortstop"—hit a double and a single and batted in two runs in a win over the Reds, which cut the Giants' lead to half a game. The day after that, the Cardinals tied the Giants, thanks in part to Durocher, who drove in two runs in another win over the Reds. Then, on September 30, the Cardinals clinched the pennant as the Giants lost and the Cards beat the Reds 9–0. The pennant-winning game was Dizzy Dean's thirtieth victory of the year. Durocher had two hits and drove in a run.

The final drive of the Cardinals was seen as one of the greatest uphill climbs in the history of the game. The team seemed on its way to losing the pennant on Labor Day after dropping a doubleheader to the Pirates, but came back to rob the Giants of the pennant by winning twenty of their last twenty-five games. The Giants squandered their lead by losing six of their last seven.

The chemistry of this team transcended Dizzy and Paul Dean, pitchers who could not have won without the team's power hitting and defensive skill. "The loss of a Durocher or a Collins would have been fatal to our pennant chances," Frisch pointed out later, "but the boys all realized also they could not have won without the Deans."[8]

Earlier in the season the Deans had been responsible for an explosion that almost blew the club apart when they staged what was essentially the first players' strike in baseball history. On August 12, after a home doubleheader against the Cubs during which both Deans lost their games, the team hurried to catch a train to play an exhibition game the next day against the Detroit Tigers. Neither Dean made the trip. Later, each admitted that he had missed the exhibition on purpose. Manager Frisch fined the Deans, and Dizzy raged, tore up uniforms, threatened to wreck the clubhouse, and was suspended for ten days by Frisch. The Deans then quit the team, demanding back pay so they could go to Florida and fish. Paul first, and then Dizzy, decided that they wanted to come back. Commissioner Landis held a hearing, and the suspension was cut to seven days and the fines rescinded.

With the revolt of the Deans over, the team seemed to come together with remarkable speed. Rebellion gave way to a fierce desire to win the pennant. Not known at the time but revealed after the Cardinals had won the pennant was that Durocher had called a clubhouse meeting and said something on the order of: "Listen, you dumb clucks. Do you realize that while we are doing all this, we are allowing a club to walk off with the pennant that it has no more right to win than a flock of schoolboys in Peoria, not to mention blowing about five thousand smacks apiece?" According to John Drebinger, who broke the story in *The New York Times*: "Those words apparently had a magical effect. Overnight the Cards became a happy family. Frisch's word became absolute law. And today they are heading into the World Series."[9]

On the eve of the 1934 World Series featuring the Cardinals and the Detroit Tigers, J. G. Taylor Spink of *The Sporting News* called Durocher "one of the most remarkable fielding shortstops the game has ever seen," adding, "He likes to smile and laugh, but how he loves to heckle the opposition and play ball." But now Durocher could heckle in print. Under the byline "Lippy Durocher," he wrote his own take on the Series for the syndicated Universal Service. On the eve of the first game he wrote: "I'm beginning to laugh already trying to imagine the swing-from-the-knees players like Goslin and Greenberg trying to hit Dizzy Dean." Even more to the point was the statement Durocher made to Walter Graham of the *Springfield Republican*, who was in Detroit to cover the Series. "I don't see how the Tigers can beat us."[10]

The crowd who took their seats for the first game of this Series at Navin Field in Detroit included humorist Will Rogers, surrounded by a cluster of celebrities including child movie star Shirley Temple, Henry Ford, the comedian Joe E. Brown, and George Raft, who played bad guys on the screen and who was Durocher's gambling pal from their days in New York and had kept in contact over the years as both men's fortunes rose. The writers who came to Detroit to cover the Series included Damon Runyon, "Bugs" Baer, and Henry McLemore.[11]

The Cardinals won the first game 8–3 and, if anything, seemed to become zanier than during the regular season. When Durocher came in from the field after that first game, he found that his brand-new white buckskin shoes had been autographed with green ink by Dizzy Dean. Nor had the Cardinals become any more respectful of their opponents. That night Durocher used his syndicated column to irk the Tigers: "Not meaning to rub it in or anything but, honestly, if that's the best the Detroit Tigers have, this is going to be the softest series ever."[12]

The Tigers won game two in the thirteenth inning on a Leon "Goose" Goslin single, but the Cardinals came back to win game three. John Kieran noted that Durocher had been hitless in three games, and he suggested that Leo was "striving valiantly to make this a no-hit series for himself." The next day the Tigers evened the Series at 2–2 with a 10–4 drubbing during which the Cardinals employed five pitchers. Durocher finally got his first World Series hit in that game.[13]

The Tigers won the fifth game and the Cardinals went back to Detroit for the sixth game, hoping that Paul Dean could even the Series and keep the Cardinals alive. The St. Louis team arrived in Detroit the night before the sixth game at about midnight and was greeted at the Cadillac Hotel by a howling mob of Tiger rooters. All night long, the shouting fans circled the hotel, jeering at the Cardinals and shouting epithets. They kept up the racket until dawn, apparently intending to keep the trapped Cardinals awake all night. In some cases they probably succeeded, but Durocher claimed that he slept like a hibernating bear.

The next morning, on the bus taking the players to the Tigers ballpark, Leo looked as chipper as ever as he paced up and down the aisle, rallying his teammates. "Let's go, gang, let's go! We can beat these Tigers easy . . . Let's go!"

Paul Dean and Detroit's Schoolboy Rowe were pitching with all their craft, and the score was 1–1 when Leo came to bat in the fifth inning. He hit a slow grounder toward second. Charlie Gehringer, the great Tigers second baseman, handled the ball cleanly, but Leo scooted like a scared rabbit and beat it out for a hit. Durocher came around to score the tie-breaking run, and before the inning was over, the Cardinals led 3–1. The Tigers fought back to a 3–3 tie. In the seventh, Leo came through again, driving an outside pitch off Rowe for a double and romping home with the winning run a moment later when pitcher Paul Dean singled. Not only did Leo score the deciding run, but he threw Detroit's Pete King out at the plate in the seventh. Walter Graham of the *Springfield Republican* reported that the "star act" that won the game for the Cards was Durocher and Paul Dean. "We've got them" was the lead to Durocher's column filed that night for the morning's newspapers. "I don't care who pitches for our club or theirs; the St. Louis Cardinals will be champions of the world tomorrow night, for the title really was won in today's sixth game when we beat the Tigers 4–3."[14]

Leo's most vital role in the Series may have been in the locker room before the seventh game. Manager Frisch was mad at Dizzy Dean for popping off at him and didn't want to let him pitch—especially with only two days' rest. Leo convinced Dizzy to apologize to his manager. Dean ambled across the clubhouse, slapped Frisch on the back, and said, "Stick with me, Dutchman, and I'll make you the best manager in the league." Frisch relented. Leo later claimed that the reason he intervened was the money. "I needed that winners' share. I wanted $6,000, not $4,000, because I owed eight."[15]

Dizzy Dean won game seven with an 11–0 shutout, which featured a defensive display by Leo. "Durocher made two of the greatest plays I ever saw today, especially the one where he had to come in behind the box to trap a high bouncing ball and make his throw off balance," opined Detroit slugger Leon "Goose" Goslin.[16]

For the Series, Durocher had seven hits, including a double and a triple, and a batting average of .259. He handled thirty chances in the field without an error, and his performance included bare-handed stops, over-the-shoulder catches, and acrobatics seldom seen before. Damon Runyon said the Series proved that Durocher was in a class by himself, calling him one of the greatest fielding shortstops of all time. Arthur Mann wrote, "No shortstop before or since looked quite as daring or as good as Leo did playing errorless ball through those 67 innings of thrills and nightmares."[17] Perhaps the greatest accolade came from retiring National League president John Heydler, who told *The Sporting News* that Durocher's hitting and fielding represented the margin of victory for the Cardinals.[18]

Leo's winning share was $5,389.57, which brought him closer to solvency than he had been in a long time, but he was still living on the debit side of the ledger. In addition, he was immediately beset with offers, including one from an entertainment syndicate and booking agency offering a dazzling big-money proposal that would involve a syndication of his life story, a radio show, personal appearances, and ultimately a motion picture story of his life.[19]

"Get it on the line!" Durocher responded to the agent for the syndicate.

The operator tried to convince Leo that what he was offering was a long-range program. "You'll make a barrel of money," he promised. "It'll come in from all directions."

But Leo said he didn't want a barrel of money; he wanted money now and from one direction.

"Put something on the line, or you get nothing."

The agent left in silence.

Despite this missed opportunity, Durocher was learning that his name and face had value in the marketplace. The World Champion Cardinals were early beneficiaries of paid testimonials. 21 OUT OF 23 ST. LOUIS CARDINALS SMOKE CAMELS was the headline to an ad in which Frankie Frisch proclaimed that the cigarette was the source of the team's "abounding energy." For Durocher, this would be the first of many advertising endorsements he would make. The ad appeared in all the nation's leading newspapers as well as *The Sporting News*. In the wake of the championship season, the Goldsmith Company introduced a Leo Durocher fielder's glove, an all-horsehide model with Durocher's autograph embossed in the leather, which retailed for a then-hefty price of $7.50.

IN 1935, AT the beginning of Spring Training in Bradenton, Florida, Charlie Gelbert, the man Durocher had replaced, was back with his wound healed and confident he could win his job back. After watching him work for a few days, Branch Rickey predicted that Gelbert would give Durocher a battle for the position.

In April, Durocher was the cause of a dispute that erupted with St. Louis–area trade unions, which voted to boycott Cardinals games because Durocher had taken actions that were alleged to be anti-union. In February, Durocher had been driving his wife to work at the Forest City manufacturing company where the workers were on strike. Grace's garments were manufactured at the plant and she had an office and design studio at the plant. As they pulled up in front of the factory, one of the women picketing the plant attempted to board Leo's car. The woman was arrested for disturbing the peace and, based on Leo's testimony, was fined $240 in a judgment rendered later in April.

The International Ladies Garment Workers Union did not dispute the incident or challenge the fine, but rather focused on what they claimed were anti-union statements made by Durocher. Leo maintained he had said nothing negative about the union, did nothing to intimidate them, and had nothing against them, but had been within his rights to issue a complaint against the woman who attempted to board his car. A complaint had been sent to Judge Landis claiming that Durocher had tried to intimidate members of the union and that an apology from Durocher was in order. Landis declared, "I never monkey around with that sort of thing. I don't know anything about it—and I wouldn't do anything if I did." Lacking an apology, the larger Central Trades and Labor Union, of which the ILGWU was part, voted on April 28 to call for a boycott of all Cardinals games by the seventy thousand members of the union.

For once, Durocher was in the crosshairs for something he apparently had not done. Nobody was able to point to a single anti-union statement he had made. The boycott was also tied up with the Cardinals' refusal to unionize the ballpark's ticket takers, ushers, and bartenders, who were represented by separate unions, all of which had pickets marching in front of the stadium. The boycott fizzled quickly and had disappeared by May 19 when the Boston Bees (the nickname taken by the Boston Braves from 1936 through 1940) came to town with Babe Ruth on their roster. Ruth was old and out of shape and had been let go by the Yankees, and many in Boston believed this might be their last chance to see the Bambino in uniform. The disturbance of the peace fine was appealed by the union in May and was thrown out after Durocher failed to appear in court.[20]

On June 11, manager Frisch sat Leo down for a doubleheader against the Cubs and gave Gelbert his first start since he had injured himself. Durocher was hitting an anemic .215 at the time. Yet, despite this slump, Durocher had a fine season. As the *Springfield Republican* declared, Leo had now reached a point where his hitting ability was no longer regarded as being as weak as a politician's promises. He played in 143 games, batted .265, and brought in seventy-eight runs—ranking fifteenth in the league in RBIs ahead of such stars as Bill Terry of the Giants and Chuck Klein of the Cubs.[21]

The Cardinals went 96–58 during the 1935 season and finished second in the National League behind the Cubs, but that was not good enough for Rickey, who let it be known that he was deeply disappointed in the performance and was willing to trade away the bulk of the Gashouse Gang to begin rebuilding the team. Only eight of the thirty-eight men on the team were listed as definite for the 1936 season—Durocher was one of the players who would not be traded.[22]

On the eve of the 1936 season, the two league presidents put out the word that fraternization on the baseball field by players would be regarded, in the

words of one writer, as "one of the seven deadly sins." The stronger of the
two manifestos was issued by Ford Frick of the National League, who told
his players and managers, "We want more of the gashouse stuff—good,
hard-playing and no lily pads around." In other words, baserunners were to
be regarded as enemy hostages rather than, to extend Frick's metaphor, frogs
at rest on the foliage atop the surface of a pond. With incivility the order of
the day, Casey Stengel, the manager of the Brooklyn Dodgers, took the lead
and refused to shake hands with Bill Terry of the Giants on Opening Day.

Durocher was soon in the mix. On May 12, 1936, the Cardinals played
the Dodgers in Brooklyn and lost 5–2 after Dizzy Dean gave up thirteen
hits. All afternoon, Durocher and Stengel had bickered and insulted one
another across the diamond. Stengel then demanded that the two men
settle their differences physically.

"I will see you later, punk, under the stands."

"You and what football team," Durocher responded.[23]

The initial reports said the fight was over quickly when Frisch intervened, and neither man suffered any major damage. Durocher claimed
that Stengel hit him in the right knee with a bat, but Casey said that Leo
had mistaken his fist for a bat. Frisch chose not to comment.

A day later, the AP's James "Scotty" Reston Jr. put the battle in the context
of the National League, where the boys loved nothing more than a well-
timed punch in the nose. According to Reston, Flatbush was celebrating
because their "warrior-manager" had cut Leo's lip and rolled on top of him.*

John Lardner, the popular son of Ring Lardner and the star sports
reporter for the North American News Alliance (NANA), then weighed in
with differing accounts of the brawl, including one in which fifteen
Brooklyn guys descended on Durocher with bats and another in which
twenty-five murderous Cardinals leaped on Stengel. Certainly tongue-in-
cheek, Lardner was out to mock Frick's call for a rough-and-tumble season.
"This is going to be a great baseball year, all right," Lardner concluded, "but
the cost to human life will be terrific unless something is done to harness
Mr. Stengel's murderous left jab to the knee."[24]

There was more to come. In St. Louis on August 11, 1936, Durocher was
ejected after a bitter eight-minute dispute following a call against the

---

* Reston would later go on to a distinguished career with *The New York Times*, where he
served as a columnist and executive editor. His 1986 *Times* obituary called him "perhaps the
most influential journalist of his generation."

Cardinals that led to a 6–4 loss to the Cubs in ten innings. After Leo was ejected, the players in the Cardinals' dugout responded by throwing bats, balls, and other equipment onto the field in the direction of umpire Bill Stewart. Three more Cardinals were ejected. Then at the end of the game, fans streamed onto the field with the expressed intention of attacking umpire Stewart, who punched one fan in the jaw before players from both teams formed a flying wedge and escorted him to safety.[25]

The 1936 Cardinals ended the season at 87–67 tied for second place with the Chicago Cubs, five games behind the New York Giants. Durocher batted an impressive .286 for the year, with twenty-two doubles. He also appeared in his first All-Star Game, gathering a single in three at-bats.

The 1937 Spring Training season opened on a new note. The Cardinals seemed to have lost their edge—both mentally and physically. Grantland Rice cautioned his readers that he feared that the Gashouse Gang was on its way to eating themselves out of the league. Rice had learned that a number of the Cardinals had reported overweight to Daytona Beach for Spring Training and noted that a Cards bathing-suit photograph of Durocher in Florida looked more like the immense Shanty Hogan than the trim Durocher of previous seasons. Rice lamented that the Gashouse Gang could—despite Frick's call for a reduced level of civility on the diamond— be the last link between the diminishing rough-and-tumble era and the "more effete" modern era.[26]

During Spring Training, Rickey called Leo into his office and asked if he and Frisch had been fighting much lately. Leo grinned and glibly replied: "No more than usual. I've been needling him again about getting a wheel chair, but we get along."

"Well, he's asked me to trade you," Rickey said. Leo's jaw dropped. "Trade me! That ungrateful rat! I've been holding him up for years and now he's out for my neck, eh? Well, what are you doing about it?"

"Nothing. Not now, at least," Rickey said.

Durocher and Frisch were barely on speaking terms by 1937. In early May, Frisch benched Durocher for light hitting and then suspended him on May 8 for a fierce argument on the bench. The team was in New York at the time and Leo was sent back to St. Louis for further discipline. He had decided he could manage the Cardinals better than Frisch, and he said it loud and often enough that Frisch, who was as abrasive and strong-willed as Durocher, told Branch Rickey there wasn't room on the team for both of them.

Despite this, the Cardinals started the season strongly, winning seven of their first eight games, and they were in second place as late as June 27, just half a game out of first place with a record of 35–24. However, they never rose higher, spending the rest of the year in either third or fourth place. They ended the season by losing six of eight and with their largest deficit of the year at fifteen games out of first place.

When the season was over, Frisch demanded that Rickey get rid of Durocher. Rickey countered that it meant breaking up a great infield. Frisch said it was either Durocher or himself who had to go. "Both of us can't stay on this club." Rickey sighed. "All right, if you're putting this on a personal basis, I'll have to do it."

Frustrated over Durocher's continued irresponsibility, Rickey traded Durocher to his friend Larry MacPhail, who had left Cincinnati and was now in Brooklyn. To get Durocher, the Dodgers gave up four players: infielders Jimmy Bucher and "Jersey Joe" Stripp, outfielder Johnny Cooney, and left-handed pitcher Roy Henshaw. The quick read on the trade was that the lackluster Dodgers had gotten the better of the deal. Grantland Rice wrote that the addition of Durocher gave the Brooklyn infield more "dash and color than it has had in many a campaign," adding that Leo still had pogo sticks for legs and was able to range widely between second and third base.[27]

Leo learned of the trade from the afternoon newspapers and demanded an explanation from Rickey. "If I just wanted to get rid of you," Rickey explained patiently, "don't you think I could have made a better deal than the one with Brooklyn?" Rickey told Durocher he thought he would have a great future in Brooklyn and that before long he could be the Dodgers player-manager, an argument that stopped Leo cold. Durocher was thirty-one, and it was possible that he had already seen his best years as a player. Despite his consistent ability as a defensive infielder, Durocher's 1937 batting average was an anemic .203.[28]

In the National League, the last seven pennants had gone to teams with player-managers. The nation was still mired in the Great Depression, and many team owners understood that a player-manager, like Frisch or Bill Terry of the Giants, could save them a salary and perhaps net them a first division finish or even a pennant. Rickey had now shoved this dream in front of Durocher, and Rickey noticed the effect of his words on Durocher: "You play the kind of ball you're capable of, behave, and you'll go right to the top of the game."

Outside of the two teams involved, the trade between St. Louis and

Brooklyn attracted little attention in the press. It was October, and the sportswriters were preoccupied with the World Series. The trade would later become a point of pride to Durocher. "Just imagine a .247 hitting shortstop being traded for four players," he later commented. "That is almost half a team and a pretty good one at that considering the good careers of Bucher, Cooney, Henshaw and Stripp."*[29]

ALTHOUGH NOBODY COULD have predicted it, Durocher and Rickey would soon take center stage in a narrative that would change the history of the game and the nation. MacPhail would provide the counternarrative.

One legacy they brought with them was that they were based in Sportsman's Park in St. Louis, the worst venue in either league when it came to accommodating African-Americans. Black fans were herded into a separate and inferior Jim Crow section of the park far removed from the boxes and better seats. The practice existed all through the Depression years. Tuesdays during the regular seasons of the early 1930s when either the Cardinals or Browns were in town was Ladies' Day, and women were allowed into the park without having to pay—white women, that is. Black women were forced to pay $.75 for an inferior seat. This practice was deemed an insult of the rankest sort by the *St. Louis Argus*, an African-American newspaper, which could not see how any person of color could under any circumstances find pleasure in going to or milling around Sportsman's Park.[30]

Doubtlessly aware of this situation, Durocher was getting another view of baseball on the other side of the color line. Unlike the Yankees and most other ball clubs, the Cincinnati Reds fielded their own All-Star teams to play against Negro league opponents in the off-season at home. Durocher, as a Reds alumnus, played for these Reds teams from 1935 through 1937. After the 1937 season, the Reds All-Stars played eight games against the Negro All-Stars, during which Josh Gibson hit three home runs. Durocher would later brag: "I played against Josh Gibson in Cincinnati, and I found out everything they said about him was true, and then some. He hit one of the longest balls I've ever seen. He caught hold of one of Weaver's fast ones, and I'll bet you it's still sailing."[31]

---

* Henshaw pitched for the Tigers through the 1944 season; Stripp was gone from the game at the end of the 1938 season; Bucher finished with the Red Sox in 1945; and Cooney finished with the Yankees in 1944.

CHAPTER 6

The Artful Dodger

ALTHOUGH HE WAS WIDELY known as Lippy, not until Durocher landed in Brooklyn did he become "Leo the Lip," or more commonly "the Lip." John Lardner may not have created the nickname, but he appears to have been the first to use it in print in his syndicated column of March 26, 1938. It was embedded in a quote on Leo's trade to the Dodgers:

"'Here's what it comes down to' says Leo the Lip. 'I've been traded from a first division club in a second division city to a second division club in a first division city. I like it.'"

Indeed, the Dodgers were a second division club to be sure. They had finished sixth of the eight-team National League in 1937, having lost sixteen of their last seventeen games, and attendance was about half that of each of the other New York teams. Durocher regarded the bulk of his new Dodger teammates as "has-been and never-was" ballplayers. In addition, the team was deeply in debt, and its stadium, Ebbets Field, had become a truly nasty venue, featuring broken seats, peeling paint, mold-infested dugouts and clubhouses, and a crew of thugs posing as ushers who would gladly beat a fan if a foul ball hit into the stands was not promptly returned.[1]

As the "fourth largest city in America"—which it was then and still is when separated from New York City—Brooklyn at this time had a distinct role in American life as the birthplace of many comedians and as a place whose natives were stereotypically feisty, contrarian, and voiced a dialect, "Brooklynese," all their own. The mere mention of the borough on radio got a laugh from the live studio audience. Short on sophistication, Brooklyn seemed to thrive on spirit and spunk. When Durocher arrived, Brooklyn had a heavily blue-collar population with more than ten thousand workers employed by the United States Navy Yard alone. Per capita, more declared members of the American Communist Party lived in Brooklyn than in any other American city.

As of January 1938, the Dodgers hired Larry MacPhail as the team's president and general manager. MacPhail was the red-faced, sandy-haired, heavy-drinking protégé of Branch Rickey who had revived the ailing Reds and turned them into a moneymaking contender. His innovations in Cincinnati included regular radio broadcasts employing another redhead, a young Floridian named Red Barber, and night baseball.

MacPhail had been hired to bring new life to the moribund Dodgers— he referred to them as a "collection of clowns"—and having Durocher on the payroll was part of his plan to give the club a new and more aggressive face. Durocher did not play in the first few exhibition games in Florida, as he was holding out for a $12,500 contract with an additional signing bonus of $2,500. MacPhail not only met Durocher's terms but threw in a set of top-of-the-line Bobby Jones golf clubs.[2]

After the Dodgers lost their last seven games in Florida, Durocher feared the worst for the season ahead. His despair was compounded by the outlook of Brooklyn manager Burleigh Grimes, a former major league pitcher known for his spitball, who sheepishly admitted to a reporter that he could not see the team finishing better than seventh place.

As the 1938 regular season got under way, it was clear that the Dodgers were still faring poorly both on the field and at the box office. On May 25, Grimes—with the approval of MacPhail—appointed Durocher as field captain in an effort to set a fire under the rest of the team. For Durocher, it was his second taste of appointed leadership and a possible signal that he was being groomed for a higher position.

By early June, after the Dodgers had posted a 9–19 record in May, attendance was plummeting, and MacPhail was pulling out all the stops to reverse the trend. He began by replacing broken seats and painting the grandstands. Before the season began, he had gotten permission from the league to install steel towers to support arc lights in order to stage a limited number of night games. He began hiring new ushers—men who, in the words of baseball historian Robert Smith, "did not have to be chained to their beds at night."[3]

On Wednesday, June 15, mired in seventh place, the Dodgers hosted their first night game at Ebbets Field, and the fans overwhelmed the turnstiles. Frank Graham of the *New York Sun* witnessed what was going on in the grandstands: "Latecomers, holding reserved seats, were shocked to find that in many cases their seats already were occupied. Furthermore, they were occupied by rugged and determined young men who had no intention of yielding them. Fights broke out all over the stands, and some were not halted even by the progress of the ball game."[*][4] More than forty thousand had already packed the stadium an hour before game time when the fire department came in and cleared the aisles of much of the overflow and then shut the gates with another ten thousand wanting to get in. The final paid attendance was 38,748, the largest on record for the Dodgers. The International News Service reported on "an amazingly large number of women present." Earlier in the day, the Giants, who were in first place, were able to draw only five thousand.[5]

What drew the crowds that night was not only the novelty of a game under the lights, but also the chance to watch 1936 Olympic hero Jesse Owens run an exhibition race against outfielders Lee Gamble of the Reds and Ernie Koy of the Dodgers, who was then regarded as the fastest man in baseball. Owens, who had won four medals at the Summer Olympic Games in 1936 in Berlin, was, as far as anyone could recall, the first black man to compete against white athletes at Ebbets Field.[†] The fans also came to see twenty-three-year-old Cincinnati left-handed pitcher Johnny Vander Meer, who had just pitched a daytime no-hitter at home at Crosley Field against the Boston Bees.[‡]

The pregame show also included two fife-and-drum corps, a full marching band, and the presentation of a gold watch by fans from Vander Meer's hometown of Midland Park, New Jersey. Vander Meer later admitted that he feared that all of this personal attention—especially having his

---

[*] "I will never forget one fellow," Tom Meany of *PM* later recalled of that night. "He had grabbed a front row seat in an upper tier box, and at the end of the game he still had a firm grip on the rail and sat there with his head bowed while the rightful owner of the seat kept belting him on the base of the skull. I don't know how much of the game he saw, but at least he scored a moral victory."

[†] The man who won the silver medal in the men's 200 meters at the 1936 Olympics, finishing just 0.4 seconds behind Owens, was Matthew "Mack" Robinson, Jackie Robinson's older brother.

[‡] Vander Meer had been signed by Brooklyn years earlier but had been lost to Cincinnati when Ducky Holmes, who managed one of the Dodger farm clubs, released him without permission from the parent club.

mother at the game—would jinx his pitching. After the watch presentation, special guest Babe Ruth was introduced and given a standing ovation. Ruth was becoming known in the press as the "man who baseball forgot," but not tonight.

The lights came on in time for the hundred-yard dash. The two baseball players started with a ten-yard advantage, and Koy was the winner, but later admitted that he had not been called back for gaining an early start before the starter's gun went off.

Because of the time the fire department needed to clear the aisles, the game was delayed, and Vander Meer had to warm up three times before he took the mound. When he eventually did, he made it through eight no-hit innings with a 6–0 lead, having walked six Dodgers. The local fans were now cheering for the young pitcher, as were reporters in the press box, where cheering was normally forbidden by unwritten rule.

In the bottom of the ninth with one out, Vander Meer walked three more, loading the bases. Koy then hit a grounder up the third-base line, and the lead runner was thrown out at the plate. Leo Durocher then came to the plate. "I never tried harder," he would later write. "Vandy was wild and with three on, I had him in a hole. Then I got the ball I wanted to hit—but I belted a long foul into the left-field stands. Finally, I did hit the ball hard. It was a drive which hung just long enough for Harry Craft to get under it in center field."[6]

Vander Meer had thrown the only back-to-back no hitters in baseball history. The Brooklyn fans broke onto the field and mobbed the young pitcher, who had to be led off the field by a flying wedge made up of his teammates. After the game, he admitted, "I was rattled in the ninth with the bases full and only Durocher between me and that shutout."[7]

Because of a five-year agreement between the three New York teams that forbade radio coverage, there was no broadcast of the game, so the fans in Cincinnati and elsewhere did not hear about Vander Meer's feat until the next morning when they opened their newspapers. The lead to the Associated Press story called it "the greatest pitching feat in the hundred year history of baseball," and John Kieran of *The New York Times* used an exclamation point when he declared, "Nothing like it ever before!"[8]

Two days later, on June 17, after the loss of a daylight doubleheader to the Reds with two-thirds of the seats empty, MacPhail approached Durocher on his walk back to the clubhouse and asked how he thought Babe Ruth would do with the Dodgers. Durocher knew Ruth was done as a ballplayer, and as he put it later: "I couldn't have been more surprised if he had asked me about exhuming the body of Abner Doubleday." MacPhail was quick to explain that he meant to hire Ruth as a coach who would bring in fans by belting balls out of the park in batting practice. The only at-bats he would get would be in exhibition games, which at that time were still played during the regular season for added team revenue.[9] Durocher admitted that Ruth would bring in fans even if he were carried in by rickshaw.

That night, MacPhail, Grimes, and Durocher met with Ruth and his business agent, Christy Walsh, in MacPhail's apartment in Brooklyn's Columbia Heights, which overlooked the East River. Ruth was offered $15,000 to coach the Dodgers for the last half of the 1938 season. He demanded $25,000, which was denied, and he and Walsh eventually and reluctantly agreed to the $15,000.

Before the evening was out, Ruth pulled Durocher aside and told him: "I'll be the boss around here before too long." Durocher saw red, and he and Ruth were off to another rocky start. Leo informed Ruth that Grimes was his man, but that the line for the next manager formed to Durocher's right and behind him.[10]

In terms of fan response, hiring Ruth worked beautifully. On his debut on July 19 for a doubleheader against the Cubs, the gate was 28,013, which would be the season's largest daytime draw. The Dodgers split the double-header, after which a sweating Ruth spoke for the club: "Well at least we scared hell out of 'em and we are going to do a lot better."[11]

From that day forward, fans came to see Ruth take batting practice, and the kids mobbed him for his autograph as he entered and exited the ball-park. Within two weeks, it was estimated that he had brought an extra twenty thousand paying customers to Brooklyn games. The demand for his autograph had become so intense that he had to have cards printed with a facsimile of his autograph to hand out so that he could be on time for work as batting practice slugger. For the moment, the man who baseball had forgotten was back in the game.

On only three occasions during his first fifteen home games in Brooklyn did Ruth fail to hit one or more batting practice home runs over the right-field fence onto Bedford Avenue. As early as July 2, George Kirksey of the United Press speculated that at the end of the season, Ruth would be made the next manager of the team, with Durocher likely to be made his assistant.[12]

Durocher's play was still good enough for him to be named to the

National League All-Star team for the game played in Cincinnati on July 6. In that game, Durocher was part of one of the rarer plays that can take place on a baseball field: circling the bases on a bunt. Frank McCormick of the Reds had opened the seventh inning with a single, and Durocher, the next batter, was ordered to sacrifice. He dropped a bunt down the third-base line as third baseman Jimmie Foxx charged in and fielded the ball. He threw it to second base, but the ball sailed over Charlie Gehringer's head into right field. Joe DiMaggio, a center fielder playing in right field in deference to Earl Averill, raced in, picked up the ball, and fired it home. The throw was too high and sailed over catcher Bill Dickey's head, allowing McCormick to score. Meanwhile, Durocher never stopped running until he reached home. Durocher also made several sparkling defensive plays. He received rave reviews for his All-Star Game playing. Francis J. Powers, reporting on the game for the *Washington Evening Star*, wrote: "In paying full credit to the Nationals, you cannot overlook Lippy Leo Durocher, the Brooklyn shortstop, who for money or marbles will be the next Dodger manager."[13]

On July 24, the Dodgers split a doubleheader with the Cardinals in St. Louis. The games lasted for more than five hours because of a long-distance hitting contest before each game. In the first contest, Ruth won by hitting a ball 430 feet—out of Sportsman's Park and onto the streetcar tracks on Grand Avenue. Roscoe McGowen declared in his account of the contest for *The New York Times* that Ruth was still the "Sultan of Swat."[14]

However, Ruth's efforts as a first-base coach, which began in mid-July, were primarily a sideshow. Bob Considine, the King Features reporter who would later write *The Babe Ruth Story*, watched Ruth on the job and described the Bambino's coaching style this way: "He slaps his fat hands together a lot, and his full fat lips holler encouragement in a resonant bass. He paces up and down on his impossible legs. Once he nearly fell down on a particularly close play at first base."

If anything, Ruth's instructions did more harm than good. Considine again reporting on Ruth's first day in the coach's box and an attempted steal: "The first man he sent down to second—Kiki Cuyler in the fourth—was thrown out by three yards. In the fifth inning with the bases clogged, an infielder's throw went through Collins at first and rolled over toward the Dodger dugout. Babe excitedly waved all the runners on, but they disobeyed him, and it was just as well, for the ball bounded off the wall of a side-line box and Collins could have thrown out any man by 40 feet."

Ruth's most cherished dream after his playing days ended was to manage a team, but the dream was crushed because he could not relay, let alone master, signals in his role as first-base coach. Durocher complained that Ruth forgot his signals walking from the dugout to the coach's box: "No wonder we're getting piled up on the bases," he said, underscoring Ruth's career-long problem with signs.[15]

Coach Ruth and Captain Durocher maintained a civil but chilly relationship until it all came to a head on July 27 during a night game against the Cubs in Brooklyn. With two outs and the Cubs leading 2–0 in the bottom of the ninth, Brooklyn had runners on second and third when Harry "Cookie" Lavagetto hit a line drive off the leg of shortstop Billy Jarvis, bringing in the two baserunners. Durocher was now at bat.

Durocher and Lavagetto had a private hit-and-run sign that Durocher flashed to Lavagetto as he led off first. Pitcher Clay Bryant of the Cubs suspected something was up and pitched out to Durocher. As Lavagetto broke for second Durocher threw his bat at the ball and hit a squibbler that fell just inside the line in shallow right field. Durocher was safe, Lavagetto scored, and the game was over.

After the game, one of the reporters asked Durocher if Ruth had flashed the hit-and-run sign. Durocher said no, he hadn't, and nothing more. The writer who asked the question filed a story claiming Ruth was a failure as a first-base coach and had not even been the one who, according to Durocher, gave the sign for the play that won the game. He called Ruth a "wooden Indian."

The next day, the Dodgers were at the Polo Grounds, and as manager Burleigh Grimes began his customary pregame clubhouse meeting, Ruth demanded the floor. Grimes declared that he was running the team, and Ruth had to wait until he was done.

When Grimes finished, Ruth stood up and said, "Durocher, I've wanted to slap you down for a long time—"

"What's eating you?" Durocher responded.

Ruth said the story in the paper belittled him by saying that he had not given the sign.

"Well, did you?" asked Durocher.

Ruth repeated that he had wanted to slap Durocher down for a long time and that it might as well be now.

Durocher rose from his seat, and the two men lurched toward one another. Durocher gave Ruth a violent shove, backing him into a locker, where he began slapping his face. It was quickly broken up by Grimes and the other players, but Ruth emerged—according to Durocher—with a mark under his right eye.[16]

Hal Parrott, former *Brooklyn Eagle* columnist and now the Dodgers public relations man, was a witness and said he saw Ruth lying against the locker in a crumpled heap. "It was as unthinkable as pulling a crutch out from under your grandfather."[17]

Whatever remained of Ruth's power at the plate seemed to ebb during the dog days of August as the exhibition games and the summer heat wore him down. He had three at-bats in an August 11 exhibition game in North Adams, Massachusetts, where the Dodgers played the local Sons of Italy team. He walked, grounded out, and flied out. After his third trip to the plate, the forty-five-year-old Ruth left the field and said loudly and to nobody in particular, "Sorry I can't go on playing, but I'm an old man now."[18]

The Dodgers finished in seventh place in 1938 and had never been in the race, but the team had drawn more than 750,000 at home, an increase of about three hundred thousand over 1937. Suddenly, as Tommy Holmes put it in the *Eagle*, "the pot was boiling" and everybody was talking about the Dodgers. "Now," said MacPhail "we're ready to roll."[19]

MacPhail moved quickly. On October 10, he announced that Grimes had been released and that six men were under consideration to replace him, including Durocher but not Ruth. When asked if Ruth would stay on as a coach, MacPhail responded, "That will be a matter for the manager to decide."[20]

On October 12, 1938, Durocher was named player-manager for the 1939 season and immediately named his coaches, with Ruth not being included. The Durocher-Ruth clubhouse tiff had not become a public issue until the World Series, when it was reported—and probably leaked—as a "fistfight" in the clubhouse that had eliminated Ruth from consideration as manager. The Associated Press report claimed that the Babe lost out when MacPhail sided with Durocher.

"The axe fell, as expected," Ruth's widow, Claire, recalled in her own memoir. "Babe found out about it in the newspapers . . . Babe was crushed. He had done everything they asked of him, and it hadn't been enough. He sat in the kitchen, head in hands, crying . . ." She added that her husband never heard a word from MacPhail despite the fact that, by any measure, his using Ruth to attract paying customers had been a roaring success. For the seven exhibition games in which Ruth started—most of which were added after Ruth signed on—sixty thousand tickets were sold. Ruth was now done with coaching and done with baseball unless he was offered a full-time position as manager in the major leagues.*[21]

Durocher's joy at being named manager was dampened by the fact he had to travel to Massachusetts the next day for the funeral of his father, George J. Durocher, who had died on October 10 without knowing of his son's latest achievement. Durocher had actually learned of the appointment during the opening games of the World Series in Chicago but thought it would be nice to surprise his father on the day it became official, but that turned out to be too late. "Dad died suddenly," he explained. "He was taken sick Monday afternoon and passed away just before midnight."

If Leo missed his father at this moment, he also missed former Yankee manager Miller Huggins, his surrogate father. "It's a shame though that Hug isn't alive to know about it. That guy sure went through a lot for me."[22]

The decision to appoint Durocher manager raised more than a few eyebrows. Tommy Holmes of the *Brooklyn Eagle* asked MacPhail why his final choice was Durocher.

> "It was this way," Larry said. "It seemed to me that Leo could better supply the thing that our club lacked, mostly during the past season."
>
> "Meaning?"
>
> "Well, call it morale, if you like. Call it anything you want. Whatever you call it, our club didn't have it. I think it's important. You can laugh at me, if you will, for trying to put the old college spirit into a team of professional ballplayers—but show me a big league team that ever got by without it. I think that's the spirit that Durocher can promote better than anybody else I know."[23]

As SOON AS the 1938 season was over, MacPhail's sights were on 1939, because Ebbets Field was close to Flushing Meadows, where the 1939 World's Fair—themed "The World of Tomorrow"—was to be held, almost certainly bringing a big boost in attendance.

During the winter months, MacPhail made big changes. On February 5,

---

* In 2012 a full Babe Ruth 1938 Brooklyn Dodgers road uniform was sold for $310,500 at auction at the Louisville Slugger Museum.

he announced that the Dodgers would be the first team to break the New York area radio ban, and all of the team's games would be broadcast on WOR—a fifty-thousand-watt powerhouse of a station. Sponsors had been lined up, and broadcaster Red Barber was hired to be the voice of the team. Barber went to Spring Training to get the lowdown on the players. New Yorkers had heard him before—and apparently liked his homespun Southern delivery—as the announcer for the 1938 World Series and the radio voice of the Army–Notre Dame football game staged at Yankee Stadium a few months earlier. Made for radio, his voice was soothing, and his approach to calling a game was colorful and rich in rural metaphor—Ebbets Field would soon become "the Flatbush pea patch." Barber was a man of "you alls" and "yes, ma'ams" headed for a place mocked for "dems" and "dose."[24]

Spring Training was set to begin in Hot Springs, Florida, early that year on February 2. After his first day on the job as a working manager, Durocher went out for dinner with his coaches to the Belvedere Country Club. After the dishes were cleared, the club's bingo night got under way. Durocher bought five $2 cards and proceeded to win the grand jackpot of $662 at the end of the evening. "This is going to be my lucky season," he told the United Press's George Kirksey.[25]

MacPhail brought in a leading trainer and dietician to get the team into physical shape. Two intense sessions of calisthenics were separated by a six-mile hike in the hills each morning. Baseball practice was initially limited to tossing the ball around and bunting the ball on the hotel lawn, as diet and exercise were the order of the day. "This may not seem important at first glance," Durocher said of this novel regime, "but if it works, we will have the best conditioned team in the Major Leagues when the season begins."[26]

Under Durocher, other things changed immediately. He encouraged players to bring their wives and children to Spring Training, a rare practice at that time, and he banned beer drinking until after the first exhibition game had been played on March 11. Any player who insisted on drinking would be fined $50 for each glass consumed.

On February 22, Durocher slugged a caddy during an altercation on a local golf course. The account of the event, covered on the United Press wire, said that Durocher was nursing a bruised right hand from a punch that "split the side of the caddy's face." The argument, it said, was over a lost golf club and turned violent when the caddy threatened Durocher with a stick.

A few days after the initial report, the story was given new life by John Lardner in his syndicated "From the Press Box" column. Lardner interviewed Casey Stengel, now managing the Boston Bees, on the matter. Stengel put it in the context of his 1937 fight with Durocher when Durocher was still a Cardinal. "It was my famous fishhook punch to the knee," recalled Casey. "Two feet closer and there might not of been no more Durocher. Leo's boyish laugh would have been stilled. The tinkle of his little fist on caddies' chins would have been stilled. I hate to think of it. A Stengel don't know his own stren'th."[27]

MacPhail then fired Durocher for gambling and fighting, but recanted the next day. This set the tone for the tumultuous years to come when Durocher would be "fired" more than a dozen times by MacPhail.

Opening Day of the 1939 season was broadcast live on the radio, and the Giants posted a 7–3 victory over the Dodgers. The intense rivalry between the two teams was about to become even fiercer under Durocher and Giants manager Bill Terry, who, before the 1934 season, was asked about Brooklyn's chances in the pennant race. He answered, "Brooklyn? I haven't heard anything from them lately. Are they still in the league?" This sparked a war of words and a wager of two new suits with then Dodger manager Max Carey. That year Brooklyn spoiled the Giants' pennant hopes on the final day of the season, winning 8–5 in ten innings.

As the first half of the season drew to a close, the Dodgers appeared to be heading to another second-division finish. Durocher had been on his best behavior and had gotten along so well with umpires that National League president Ford Frick was inclined to believe he had reformed and actually complimented him on his attitude.

But this all changed in a flash on July 1 as the team prepared for a three-game series with the Giants at the Polo Grounds. Frank Graham of the *New York Sun* watched the transformation during a meeting with reporters: "Goaded by the lackluster status of his team, nagged by MacPhail, and, for the first time, sensitive about some of the cracks the baseball writers were taking at him, he began to rip and tear in the old Durocher manner at umpires, rival players, anybody who stood in his way." When pressed by the writers, Durocher made no bones about the fact that his fiercest arguments with umpires often came when he believed that the call had actually been right but close and that his arguments were often nothing more than a smoke screen. "Maybe the ump will call the next close one my way."[28]

In the second game of a doubleheader at the Polo Grounds on July 2—the Dodgers had won the first game but were losing the second—after Leo had hurled insults at the entire Giants team, including the bench warmers, the situation turned physical. Hal Schumacher, pitching for the Giants, threw a fastball at Durocher's head, and Leo, hitting the dirt unharmed, came up screaming.

"So that's the way you want to play, is it?" he screamed at Schumacher. "All right, you son of a bitch!"

He dug himself in again, grounded the next pitch sharply to shortstop, and raced to first base. He was an easy out, but as he flashed across the bag, he spiked big Zeke Bonura. Enraged, the Giant first baseman threw the ball at him, trying to hit him in the head, then rushed after him and caught him in right-center field. Durocher whirled to meet him, and they swapped a number of blows until they were pried apart. In the melee, Leo punched Bonura in the nose.[29]

More than fifty thousand were in the stands that day. Many were Dodger fans who had come to Manhattan for the game, and the Brooklyn rooters were violently upset when Leo was ejected from the game along with Bonura by umpire Tom Dunn, who was new to the league and making his first appearance at the Polo Grounds. The fans yelled encouragement to Durocher, who had shaken off the players separating him from Bonura, and raged at Dunn, attacking the umpire with a shower of bottles and rotten produce, delaying the game. When it finally resumed, Durocher, peering out of a clubhouse window and, signaling instructions to Coach Charlie Dressen, saw his team beaten 6–4.

"From the press box it was difficult to tell exactly who was to blame and who got the better of the skirmish, except that it was a good fight while it lasted," wrote Louis Effrat in *The New York Times*.[30]

Upon receiving Dunn's report the next morning, Frick promptly changed his mind about Leo's reformation and slapped him with a $25 fine. A group of ardent Dodger fans, still incensed at the ejection of their manager, collected twenty-five hundred pennies, put them in a bag, and sent them to Leo with the message "Pay your fine with these."

Recalling a tale he had heard of a trick a minor league player once had pulled on an umpire who was the cause of his being fined, Leo said to MacPhail: "Do you know what I'd like to do? I'd like to stall on paying this fine until we catch up with Dunn again and then take this bag of pennies to the plate with me and dump it on the ground and say: 'There's your fine.

Pick it up.'" That appealed to MacPhail's sense of humor. "Swell!" he roared. "Do that."

One or the other must have told somebody about the plan. The next day, the telephone in the Dodger clubhouse rang. Ford Frick was on the line, calling Durocher. "I wouldn't advise you to do that," he said to Leo. "Do what?" replied Leo. "You know what," Frick said, and hung up. The pennies went to the bank, and a check went to the league headquarters.[31]

The Dodgers returned to Brooklyn for games against the Giants on Friday, Saturday, and Sunday. In six head-to-head meetings in early July, the two stadiums drew 142,357 paying customers.

Less than two weeks after his fine and ejection at the Polo Grounds, Leo was in hot water again. During a night game with the Reds at Ebbets Field, Dodger pitcher Whitlow Wyatt and Leo squawked in tandem so long and loud over a ball called on a Cincinnati hitter that both were ejected. Frick fined Durocher $50 and Wyatt $25.

In the season's second half, Leo's aggressive play on the field and ability to take risks as a manager gradually turned his second-division team into a contender. "He knew the game all right and he was a gambler," pitcher Freddie Fitzsimmons later recalled after Durocher took over the Dodgers in 1939. "He'd squeeze, he'd hit and run and he'd double steal." Under Durocher, the team learned to do a lot of things, including how to steal signs, which became an art under Leo's tutelage. Durocher loved cheating and loved to brag to his players about how he would use the sharp edge of his belt buckle to doctor the ball for Dizzy Dean and other pitchers when he was with the St. Louis Cardinals.[32]

On July 24, 1939, MacPhail, needing help in the outfield and willing to gamble on a man who could hit, picked up Dixie Walker from the Detroit Tigers on waivers. There was something about the big, open-faced, affable man that caught the fancy of the mob at Ebbets Field almost as soon as he went to the plate for the first time. Attesting to his popularity was the nickname bestowed upon him in Brooklyn, "the People's Choice," which the newspapers translated into Brooklynese as *people's cherce*.

As the team swept into August, it picked up steam, aided in part by Walker's bat. They were at their best when Durocher played and fell off a little when Johnny Hudson, a second baseman by trade, was used at shortstop. But Leo now and then felt the strain of his role as player-manager and occasionally had to take a day or two off.

As the season progressed, it was clear that the team and its noisy manager had a special identity in Red Barber's eyes. He created a unique vocabulary to describe events on the field with terms such as "sittin' in the catbird seat," "tearin' up the pea patch," "slicker than oiled okra," "one foot in the pickle vat," and "Oooohhh Doctor!"—a term he reserved for an unexpected occurrence. Durocher's arguments with umpires were known as "rhubarbs."

Brooklyn loved Red Barber and Red Barber loved Brooklyn. He saw the city as essentially a small town despite its three million residents. It had been the butt of one too many jokes and, as he wrote at one point, it had suffered under the shadows of the Manhattan skyline for too long. He learned early that the borough still resented having been dragged into New York City by the New York State legislature in 1898. To Barber, the Dodgers were Brooklyn's weapon for getting even, and he was the sweet voice of revenge.

Though Barber and Durocher had little in common, they paired well on the air and made history together. On August 26, 1939, the Dodgers hosted the Cincinnati Reds in a doubleheader at Ebbets Field. Some thirty-three thousand fans came to watch the match-up in person, but for the first time, roughly three thousand others saw the action and heard the roar of the crowd from television sets. Television was one of the stars of the 1939 World's Fair, featured in an exhibit by the Radio Corporation of America. Red Barber announced the game, and his live interviews included one with Leo, who took to the new medium like a fish to water. It was the first professional sporting event ever telecast, and it was produced by the National Broadcasting Company, the broadcasting arm of RCA, to display the compatibility of sports and the new medium.*

The Dodgers' record in August was 16–11, and it got even better in September at 23–13. The team ended the season in third place with a 97–57 record and had drawn more than a million customers. Durocher was named Manager of the Year by *The Sporting News*, and MacPhail was hailed as a genius for hiring him. As a player, Durocher came in eighth in the MVP voting and was second among shortstops. His batting average was .277.

As Durocher's stock rose, he was seen in more nightclubs—often with movie and Broadway stars, seldom with baseball people. During the 1939 season Durocher's earlier acquaintance with movie actor George Raft turned into a full-fledged friendship. They were spotted at boxing matches,

---

* When it was over, Barber, who had not been paid a cent for the event, asked NBC for a memento in the form of an engraved silver cigarette case. The case arrived a few weeks later along with an invoice for $38, which Barber paid.

and Raft was an occasional visitor to Ebbets Field, where he sat with Durocher's wife, Grace, and his personal bodyguard, a bruiser known as Killer Gray but whose real name was Max Greenberg.*

Raft was best known for his gangster roles in films such as the original 1932 *Scarface*, in which he played the coin-flipping henchman Rinaldo. He displayed a bravado typified by a comment he made many years later: "I must have gone through ten million dollars during my career. Part of the loot went for gambling, part for horses and part for women. The rest I spent foolishly." After his boyhood stint as a batboy for the New York Highlanders, the young Raft tried out for semipro baseball, boxed at the Polo Athletic Club, and hustled pool. Raft had a history of associating with racketeers, including Meyer Lansky and Bugsy Siegel, the leaders of Murder Incorporated. By the winter of 1939–40, the friendship was such that Durocher began parting his hair, dressing, and talking like Raft. Durocher visited with Raft when he was in California, and Raft stayed with Leo in New York. Durocher had a duplicate uniform—complete with his number 2—made for Raft.

THE MATTER OF African-Americans being systematically excluded from baseball had resurfaced in 1938 thanks to an incident of baseball infamy known as the Jake Powell affair. During a pregame dugout interview at Comiskey Park on July 29, 1938, WGN Radio announcer Bob Elson asked Yankees outfielder Jake Powell what he did during the off-season to keep in shape. Powell replied that he was a policeman in Dayton, Ohio, where he kept in shape by "beating up niggers and then throwing them in jail."

Outraged listeners besieged the station with angry phone calls. Others called the Chicago office of baseball commissioner Kenesaw Mountain Landis. Local residents and community organizations representing the heavily black neighborhoods of the South Side besieged the station, demanding Powell be permanently banned from baseball. Landis ultimately suspended Powell for ten games, marking the first instance in the history of American sports that a player was suspended for a racially intolerant remark. Landis then stirred up the situation again by stating that the matter was more due to carelessness than intent. The Yankees asked for

---

* The nickname actually came from the Yiddish term *killah*, for hernia, which Gray suffered from.

police protection, and rumor had it that Powell—who had been sent to a secret location—would not ever appear in a Yankee uniform again because of the proximity of Yankee Stadium to Harlem.[33]

One moment put baseball's unwritten but rigidly followed policy of Jim Crow back in the forefront. Amidst the commentary before the incident blew over, perhaps the most remarkable came from Westbrook Pegler, a nationally syndicated columnist of the right, who surprisingly suggested that Powell may have gotten his cue from the racial attitudes of the very owners whose hired disciplinarian had just benched him. Pegler then made another suggestion: "The Yankees or one of the Chicago teams easily could try the experiment of using a star Negro player from one of the semi-pro clubs. Customers would suffer no shock, and the Southern white boys would find after a few games that it didn't hurt them much at all." Powell was soon back in pinstripes, and the Yankees were free to move about the country, but more and more writers—and especially those whose bylines appeared in the New York newspapers—joined the fight for integration.*[34]

At the end of September, Al Monroe of the *Chicago Defender* (an African-American newspaper) tried to assess the progress being made on integration. Most managers and owners ducked the question, but one of the rare direct answers came from Brooklyn manager Burleigh Grimes, who said: "I would rather lose the pennant than to have Negro players on my ball club."[35]

Durocher, on the other hand, seemed eager to sign anyone who would help him win. In 1939, Lester Rodney, a sports reporter for the Communist *Daily Worker*, asked Durocher if he would sign Negro players if he had the chance. "Hell, yes!" Durocher shot back, "I'd sign them in a minute if I got permission from the big shots." He then added: "I've seen plenty of colored boys who could make the grade in the majors. I have played against some colored boys out on the coast who could play in any big league that ever existed. [Satchel] Paige, [Cy] Perkins, [George "Mule"] Suttles and [Josh] Gibson are good enough to be in the majors right now. All four of them are great players. Listen, there are plenty of colored players around the country

---

* Powell was actually not a police officer but simply a resident of Dayton who claimed to be one. Ironically, he died in a police station in 1948: while he was being questioned for passing bad checks, Powell shot himself to death. Westbook Pegler drifted further and further to the right until he eventually was banned from writing for the magazine of the John Birch Society because his views became too extreme.

who should be in the big leagues. I certainly would use a Negro ball player if the bosses said it was all right."[36] A leader in the struggle to integrate baseball, Rodney believed that Durocher, unlike Grimes, could see baseball integration coming.[37]

The interview appeared in the July 30 issue of the *Daily Worker* and was reprinted in several African-American papers, including the New York paper the *Amsterdam News* and, most importantly, the *Pittsburgh Courier*, where reporter Wendell Smith was working with Rodney to effect change. It attracted little attention, perhaps because the public and those who ran baseball paid little notice to the sports pages of the *Daily Worker* and the efforts of the Communist Party to integrate the game. In the late 1930s, as American Communists overcame some of the sectarianism that had isolated their party and tried to build broader popular support, they decided to focus on sports in general and on baseball in particular. In 1936, the Communist Party USA's Negro Commission had officially targeted Major League Baseball's Jim Crow policies. Rodney had been hired that same year as the *Worker*'s first sports editor.

Rodney was soon in the thick of the struggle. Yankee slugger Joe DiMaggio, in his second season in pinstripes, told Rodney in 1937 that "Satchel Paige is the greatest pitcher I ever batted against." For his part, Paige issued a challenge to white baseball via Rodney, offering to field a team of Negro leaguers to play against the 1937 World Series champions. "If we don't beat them before a packed house," Paige concluded, "they don't have to pay us!"[38] Durocher, who typically did not like reporters, was fond of Rodney as a writer and had extended conversations with him. One day, they were talking strategy after an important game. "Suddenly," Rodney recalled, "Leo leans over to me, grabs my arm, and says, 'You know, Rodney, for a fucking Communist, you sure know your baseball.'"[39]

Durocher's comment about not being able to sign African-American players would remain dormant for the moment, but he showed both tolerance and respect for African-Americans in a profile entitled "The Pop-Off Kid," which appeared in *Collier's* magazine on August 5, 1939. Quentin Reynolds, the magazine's star writer, wrote: "Funny thing about Leo: he wouldn't be playing ball today if it hadn't been for a big kindly Negro factory worker up in West Springfield, Massachusetts." The story of David Redd, who had convinced Durocher to leave his job and play in Hartford in 1925, was then told in detail. "Listen, boy," Durocher quoted Redd as saying, "you go to Hartford . . . I'm telling you, boy, you're as good as any of them."[40]

Before Huggins, Weil, and Rickey, Redd was one of Leo's benefactors. As a group, these four were always portrayed by him as his best friends and most dedicated protectors. For all of his flaws, racial and religious bigotry were not among them. Weil was an observant Jew, and Rickey was a Calvinist and a Christian who was so true to his faith that he wouldn't attend ball games on Sundays. What all these very different men had in common was a genuine liking for Durocher, which allowed them to tolerate his outlandish antics.

DUROCHER AND MACPHAIL worked hard to get the Dodgers ready for the 1940 season, including bringing two outstanding rookies north with them from Spring Training—outfielder Pete Reiser and shortstop Pee Wee Reese, Durocher's eventual replacement in the field. The team enjoyed an auspicious start. "With a motley crew of castoffs, misfits, fat men, erratic youths and one or two ballplayers," wrote Bob Considine, "Durocher led his team through its first nine games without a defeat, including a dazzling 3–0 no-hit game by James 'Tex' Carleton against the defending champions of the league, the Cincinnati Reds."[41]

Durocher made the National League All-Star team again, this time as a reserve, but his participation was still widely noted as a good-luck charm—especially since the 1938 miracle bunt. Durocher had been selected for the team three times, and the National League had won each time. Without him in 1939, the Nationals lost, but this time they won 4–0, the first shutout in the history of the All-Star Game.

The Dodgers ended the 1940 season in second place. It was their best finish in the final standings in sixteen years. Leo played in little more than half the games he had played the year before and came to bat only 175 times. Even though the Dodgers finished twelve games behind the Cincinnati Reds, it was clear that the Dodgers were now a strong team, with six of their members making the All-Star team. Reese showed he belonged on the team as Durocher's replacement. Injuries—including an inside pitch that hit him in the head and put him in the hospital for two and a half weeks—kept Pee Wee out of all but eighty-four games, in which he hit a respectable .272. More importantly Reese immediately distinguished himself as an adept infielder and first-class baserunner.

As spectators at the 1940 World Series, Leo and his wife shared their front-row box seats in Cincinnati with George Raft, along with the president of the Hollywood Stars ball club and the three Ritz Brothers, a popular comedy team. That winter, the Durochers were Raft's houseguests in Hollywood. Grace turned her ankle getting off the airplane, which allowed the boys to make the rounds while she recovered.[42]

The Dodgers went to Havana in 1941 on a Spring Training tour. Shortly after they arrived, they played a Cuban All-Star team. Leo got into an argument with a local umpire that became so heated that he was ejected from the game. True to form, Leo kept arguing and had to be escorted off the field at bayonet point by six military policemen. A longtime Cuban friend of Durocher's named Monchy de Arcos, who was with him during the incident as his translator, reported that Leo never ceased protesting and never missed a step as he was marched away. That night, word came to MacPhail in his hotel from the presidential palace of Cuban dictator General Fulgencio Batista: "Tell Durocher to keep it up. It helps draw the crowds." Leo told de Arcos that he wanted to reply to Batista: "I'll promise you an even bigger crowd if you will promise me a military funeral"—but the Cuban native convinced Leo that bandying jests with Batista was not a good idea.[43]

The Dodgers opened the 1941 season on a sour note, losing their first three games to the New York Giants, but then went on an incredible 22–3 run, slowing in July. The team picked up steam again in August with a 22–10 record.

Durocher's proclivity for fighting with umpires seemed to increase as the season continued, and with it he brought out the worst in the Brooklyn fans. On September 7, while playing the second game of a doubleheader with the Giants at Ebbets Field, Dodger Dolph Camilli was deemed by umpire Tom Dunn to have swung at a ball for a third strike. Camilli claimed he had checked his swing. Durocher came raging out of the dugout, coming face to face with Dunn and kicking dirt on him in the process. Durocher was ejected but refused to leave the dugout for several minutes while Dunn was subjected to a shower of glass bottles from the Brooklyn fans. Unarmed and alone, Dunn stood with his back to home plate and did not move even when one bottle grazed the peak of his cap. "No ball player under fire ever handled himself with more fortitude," wrote Bob Cooke of the *New York Herald Tribune* in an article praising Dunn and decrying the "mad fandom" behind the attack.[44]

On September 18, in the final game in Pittsburgh and with only nine games to go in the regular season, Durocher targeted Vince DiMaggio for a dose of verbal abuse. Pirates catcher Al Lopez, who was in the middle of the action that day, recalled later: "Leo yelled something over from the Dodgers' dugout, and it got Vince angry. Vince had a short fuse anyway. Next time up, he popped out, and that made him angrier. They spent the rest of the game yelling back and forth at each other."

The Dodgers were being shut out 4–0 until the eighth inning when they came up with five runs. In the bottom of the inning, DiMaggio singled and moved to second on a bobbled ball. Durocher then brought in reliever Hugh Casey. DiMaggio moved to third on a sacrifice fly, and the next batter grounded out. "That made two out and I'm the hitter," said Lopez.

Now, Casey had a way of going down to the ground in his windup and then coming up. Just as he goes down for his windup, DiMaggio makes a tear for the plate, as if he's going to steal home. He came so far down the line I actually thought for a moment he was coming all the way, but then he stopped. He must have distracted Casey, because Hugh hesitated for just a fraction in his motion—I thought he did anyway, so I jumped out of the batter's box and yelled "Balk!" Then the umpire, big George Magerkurth, ripped off his mask and yelled "Balk!" He saw it the same way I did. So DiMaggio is waved in and scores the tying run.

This threw Durocher into a tantrum. He whirled out of the dugout, all guns blazing, and was joined by a half dozen of his players, who held the game up for more than five minutes until Magerkurth threw most of them out. "I'm still up at the plate," said Lopez, recounting the event,

and Casey is out there boiling. The first pitch is right at my head. Second pitch, same thing. I'm ducking, and so is Magerkurth. Finally Mage says to me, "Hey, Lopez. Is he throwing at you or is he throwing at me?"

"I don't know," I said, "and let's not try and find out—he's mad enough as it is."

"The hell with this," Mage says. "I want to know." And out he goes to talk to Casey. Well, when that happens, here comes Leo again—he must've been hiding in the runway behind the dugout—along with Charlie Dressen, Fred Fitzsimmons, and some others. They go at it again. Magerkurth finally clears them off, throwing Leo out again.

So I step in again and look at Casey. He's got murder in his eyes. He throws two more at me. The fourth ball almost took my head off. I go down to first base. The next hitter is a fellow named Alf Anderson. Alf isn't too much with the stick, but don't you think he hits the first pitch just fair down the right-field line? I start running as hard as I can, while Dixie Walker is chasing the ball down in right field. The ball hugs the line all the way, and I score from first base.

The Dodgers went down in order in the ninth and the game was over, but Durocher and the Dodgers were not done for the day. After breaking a number of chairs and smashing some lightbulbs, Durocher and several other Dodgers chased Magerkurth all the way to the umpires' dressing room, where they continued what Duke Moran of the Associated Press called "vile personal abuse."* 45

On their arrival in Philadelphia the next morning, Durocher was notified by Ford Frick that he had been fined $150 for abusing the umpire, while lesser fines were levied on five other players. Leo, steaming over what he deemed an injustice, walked out of the hotel to get some fresh air for a few minutes and encountered Ted Meier, an Associated Press reporter who wanted a statement from him on the events with Magerkurth. One word led to another, and manager and reporter adjourned to an alley alongside the hotel, where Leo, although outweighed by some thirty pounds, flattened Meier three times with punches on the chin. Just as Meier was getting to his feet after the last knockdown and onlookers were pulling Durocher away from him, a cop appeared on the scene.

"What's going on here?" he demanded.

---

* Lopez would later use this game to illustrate how his non-provoking managing style differed from Durocher's. He told Donald Honig for his book *The Man in the Dugout: Fifteen Big League Managers Speak Their Minds* that what hurt the Dodgers most was Leo getting on Vince DiMaggio. "He should have left Vince alone. Instead he got him so worked up that Vince provoked Casey into balking, which got Casey so provoked he couldn't pitch to me. It ended up costing them the ballgame. So when you hear somebody say 'Let sleeping dogs lie,' you'd better believe there's a lot of good sense to it." He told Honig: "I used to warn my players not to antagonize anybody unnecessarily, especially the cellar clubs. Don't wake them up. Be nice to them, joke with them, get them relaxed—and then go out and beat their brains out. In a nice way."

"Nothing, officer," said Jerry Mitchell of the *New York Post*. "It's only that the Dodgers are in town."

"Oh!" the cop said, and walked away.[46]

Durocher and Meier went back to their hotel rooms and, according to eyewitness Tommy Holmes of the *Brooklyn Eagle*, returned to the lobby about a half hour later and greeted one another and insisted there were no hard feelings.[47]

Durocher's behavior during the game in Pittsburgh and his fight with Meier generated an immense amount of press then and after. The image of Leo and the hulking six-foot-four-inch former semipro football player Magerkurth having at it in Pittsburgh appeared in newspapers across the country, suggesting nothing less than an incarnation of David and Goliath. From this point forward, Durocher had the perfect villain for his tirades against authority.

The following day, Durocher and Meier shook hands again prior to the game, a move that was loudly applauded by the Brooklyn fans who had come to Philadelphia for a Sunday game. Accounts of that game also noted that George Raft was on hand to support the Dodgers. Raft's date for the game was Betty Grable, the immensely popular film star whose *Moon over Miami* had been the big hit of the summer movie season.[48]

GAMBLING HAD BEEN a constant in Durocher's life, dating back to his pool hall days in Massachusetts, but it reached a new milestone when, toward the end of the season, it became an open secret that Leo and the Dodgers were gambling a lot and sometimes under less-than-savory circumstances. Because Durocher and the rest of the team were gambling heavily and because the team was regularly in Cincinnati, Leo had kept up his association with Sleepout Louie Levinson and his cohort operating out of Covington and Newport, Kentucky.

Toward the end of the season the Dodgers were playing in Cincinnati, and after Leo had been ejected from a game and was sitting in a box seat, a messenger approached him and said, "You'd better win this game because Sleepout stands to win $100,000."

As Leo recalled years later, he told the messenger to get lost.

"O.K., so he goes. But now I start thinking, you know, and I worry a little. So we win 2–1 and who do you think I got down in the bullpen warming up? Two of my starting pitchers, that I want to make sure we won."

A week or so later, Leo got a call from Sleepout Louie instructing him to lay down as much money as he could on a horse named Anzac, which was running a few days hence at a racetrack in Detroit. Leo asked how much. Louie said just bet and keep betting.

"So it's already 4 o'clock and the race is at 4:20 p.m. and we're in Pittsburgh. I call a friend in New York and he gets down $2,000. He takes half and I take half. Chuck Dressen and a lot of the players got bets down too. But we don't know anything about the race. It wasn't until later that we found out it was a boat race"—twentieth-century slang for a fixed sporting event.

Durocher explained that when Anzac came charging for home, the other five horses just backed away and made room. "Our horse paid something like 30–1 and I never won so much money on a race in my life. But that was Sleepout Louie for you, you know, a gambler."[49]

Hal Parrott recalled the story differently, but the result was the same: Leo had gotten a tip from Sleepout on a horse named Anzac, the race was fixed, and Parrott and others, including some reporters, won a ton of money on the bet. In Parrott's version Durocher and he visited with Louie in Covington, Kentucky, and when Leo asked Louie for a sure bet because he was "carrying light"—short on cash—Louie told him to be on the lookout for a race featuring a horse named Anzac.*[50]

Despite the distraction of gambling, under Leo's leadership, in 1941, Brooklyn won its first pennant since 1920 with a record of 100–54, finishing two and a half games ahead of the Cardinals. After the team clinched the flag in Boston, MacPhail planned to meet their return train at New York's

---

* Stephen J. Gertz, Sleepout's distant cousin, addressed the issue of Levinson's nickname in a blog in 2009 and in subsequent conversations with the author. Louie lived at home but his professional activities were nocturnal, and he'd often return at all hours of the early morning, if he got home at all. More often than not, he'd just lie down on a table in the local pool hall and cop z's, hence "Sleepout." Gertz then added this: "When he didn't show up at home, his mother, my grandfather's Aunt Mary, a big bear of a Russian Jewess . . . would go out looking for him, her first stop the pool hall where she'd find him sawing logs comfy on the green felt, grab him by the ear and march him out of the pool room, down the street, and home like he was a five-year-old juvenile delinquent. This scene would invariably inspire hysterics in bystanders innocent and otherwise." Louie later became a person of interest to a couple of congressional subcommittees including one looking into the illegal affairs of Bobby Baker, a political protégé of Lyndon B. Johnson. When the gambling joints were closed by a reform sheriff in 1960, Louie moved to Las Vegas, where he ran the Fremont Hotel.

125th Street Station so that he would be aboard when they triumphantly reached a throng of fans at Grand Central Terminal in Midtown Manhattan. The train ride back from Boston may have established a record of its own— more than $1,400 was spent on beer, scotch, and champagne. The team members became more boisterous as the train moved toward New York. Actor and singer Tony Martin, who was traveling with the team, attempted to rise and give a stirring speech but was hit in the face with a well-pitched steak and told to sit down.* [51]

Upon hearing that some players were going to disembark at 125th Street, Durocher decided to skip the stop to ensure the entire team would disembark at Grand Central. Eagerly awaiting the train, MacPhail was left standing as the train rushed by him in a whirl of dust. When he finally caught up with the team, MacPhail was enraged and once again fired Durocher. Early the next morning and well before dawn, MacPhail called Durocher to discuss how they would play the Yankees in the World Series and did not mention the firing. As Durocher said when retelling this story, "There is a thin line between genius and insanity, and in Larry's case it was sometimes so thin you could see him drifting back and forth."[52]

One of Durocher's first acts in planning for postseason was to announce he was surrendering his four World Series box seat tickets behind the Dodger dugout to George Raft. Durocher's friendship with Raft was being watched by Commissioner Landis, who did not like Raft's association with gambling and horse racing. Landis, after all, had prevented a group headed by crooner Bing Crosby from buying the Boston Braves because of his racing interests. One of the members of Crosby's group was Raft, who, like Crosby, owned racehorses.

Landis suggested that giving the World Series tickets to Raft would not be a good idea. Columnist Joe Williams of the *World Telegram* understood that the way the Judge emphasized his "suggestion" to Durocher was by pounding his fist on the table with such force that everything in the hotel rattled.[53] Landis cajoled and threatened, but Leo refused to back off.[54] Finally MacPhail took Durocher outside and convinced him to agree to swap his box for four equally good seats from MacPhail's allocation, which he could give to Raft.

---

* A fifth of Johnnie Walker Red scotch in 1941 cost $2.98, and a bottle of name-brand California champagne cost $1.19, according to an ad from a local liquor store in the *Yonkers Herald-Statesman* in September.

While all of this was going on, Raft called Landis on the telephone to ask him why he was trying to keep him out of Durocher's box. Landis replied, "You own race horses, don't you?" Raft answered that he did, as did Alfred Gwynne Vanderbilt, the wealthy sportsman. The conversation then ended abruptly.[55]

In the first game, the Yankees' Joe Gordon homered and knocked in two runs for a 3–2 victory that featured a Red Ruffing six-hitter. Dodgers ace Whitlow Wyatt won 3–2 in Game 2, and the Yankees got a break and reclaimed the Series lead in Game 3, played in Brooklyn. The Dodgers' forty-year-old Freddie Fitzsimmons was locked in a 0–0 pitching duel with Marius Russo. With two outs in the seventh, the Yankees pitcher hit a low line drive that caught Fitzsimmons square on the knee. The ball bounced high in the air and Pee Wee Reese camped under the deflected ball and caught it to end the inning, but Fitzsimmons had to be helped off the field and was done for the day. Hugh Casey came in to pitch but was nailed for four hits and two runs in the eighth. His teammates were able to get only four hits off Russo and eventually lost 2–1. Durocher saw the loss in terms of a bad break: "We would have won 1 to 0 if Fitz could have stayed in there."

Despite the loss, the Dodgers felt as if they were in the driver's seat, because the next two games were at Ebbets Field. Sportswriters visiting the clubhouse after Game 3 found the team celebrating as if they had already won the Series. Brooklyn's pitching rotation was holding the Yankees sluggers to less-than-stellar stats. The Yankees managed only a single home run off the Dodgers, and in their thirty-four innings of at-bats preceding the fateful ninth inning of Game 4 had scored only ten runs. Things seemed to be headed in the Dodgers' favor with a 4–3 lead and two out in the ninth and no Yankees on base, but an error of catastrophic proportions turned the momentum of the game and inevitably the Series. Tommy Henrich swung at a low curveball from Hugh Casey for the final strike, but it got by Dodger catcher Mickey Owen and rolled all the way to the edge of the dugout. Henrich was safe at first. While this was going on, a dozen policemen, believing the game was over, poured onto the field, getting in Owen's way and giving the impression that the runner had a police escort. Durocher made the immediate claim that the police had been responsible for Owen not getting to the ball in time by blocking his path and blamed them entirely.

The Ebbets Field crowd—who had been poised for victory—suddenly watched in disbelief as their team fell apart. Joe DiMaggio followed with a single, and Charlie Keller put the Yankees ahead with a two-run double. After a walk to Bill Dickey, Gordon further quieted the Dodgers faithful with another two-run double. The Yankees' Johnny Murphy then turned in his second consecutive inning of 1–2–3 relief, and New York handed Brooklyn a devastating 7–4 defeat, which for years to come would be known by the Yankee faithful as the greatest World Series thriller.

Durocher sat in the clubhouse speechless for twenty minutes after the loss and then pointed to a bottle on the table. "Know what that ball game was? It was like the Yankees catching lightning in that bottle. They did it and beat us out of a game!"[56]

Leo then again blasted the police for the loss. Owen then emerged from the shower unaware of his manager's claim and was asked separately about the matter by Arthur Patterson of the *New York Herald Tribune*. "The police?" he replied. "Yes, they were out there, but that didn't make any difference, when I got to the ball, mister, the runner was on first base and I couldn't do anything about it." The headline in the next morning's *Tribune* was the last thing Durocher wanted to see: OWEN ASSUMES ALL BLAME FOR 9TH INNING COLLAPSE, SHUNNING ALIBIS FOR MISSING 3RD STRIKE.[57]

That night, Durocher did something that took him off the sports pages: he attended a huge political rally at Madison Square Garden. Along with an array of Hollywood stars and other celebrities, Durocher spent the evening with MacPhail at a demonstration in support of U.S. military intervention against Adolf Hitler as the only way to preserve world peace. This was not a popular position to take in the early autumn of 1941. Gallup polls conducted during 1940–41 found only about one-tenth of Americans willing to go to war for any reason other than to fend off an actual invasion of the United States. The rally, attended by an audience of more than seventeen thousand, had a script written by two of Hollywood's top screenwriters, Ben Hecht and Charles MacArthur. It was produced by Oscar Hammerstein, Moss Hart, and George Kaufman, with music and lyrics by Irving Berlin and Kurt Weill, among others.

Durocher and MacPhail not only attended "Fun to Be Free" but took part in it as well. After actress and singer Ella Logan sang "Tipperary," MacPhail stepped forward to give her a big kiss, and Durocher then rose and, according to *The New York Times*, "made a little speech to this effect: 'We don't want Hitlerism, we want Americanism. And the Yankees are a great ball club. Even if we lose, we'll be losing in a free country.'"[58]

Before the fifth game, Durocher tore into his team, trying to motivate them by getting them mad at him and the Yankees at the same time. "We're through," he snarled. "Finished. It looks like luck's run out on us and we don't have a chance. That's because you're all gutless." All through the game, he harangued and badgered his players, but to no avail.[59]

Ernie "Tiny" Bonham put the Dodgers out of their misery, tossing a four-hitter. Henrich homered in the Yankees' Series finale, clinching a 3–1 triumph. Despite winning their ninth World Championship, the Bronx Bombers had failed to live up to their nickname at the plate, managing only two home runs and a .247 overall batting average, but their crosstown rivals got even less offensive production with one homer and a .182 average. Columnist Henry McLemore observed wryly: "When you give the Yankees a reprieve, they get up out of the chair and electrocute the warden."[60]

Durocher was more sanguine than angry, insisting that the Yankee edge had boiled down to two lucky breaks for the Yankees and none for the Dodgers. After the loss, the *Brooklyn Eagle* covered its front page with the screaming headline WAIT UNTIL NEXT YEAR!

CHAPTER 7

Mutiny in Flatbush

AT THE SAME TIME that Grace Dozier Durocher's fame was spreading, Leo's name was showing up more and more in the gossip columns for partying with other women. Some women were clearly attracted to Leo, others not.

Metro-Goldwyn-Mayer film actress Laraine Day first met Durocher late in the summer of 1941 at New York's Stork Club. Born in Roosevelt, Utah, the twenty-one-year-old beauty had already acted in several dozen movies, beginning with a small part in the 1937 film *Stella Dallas*. She was best known for her role as a nurse in the Dr. Kildare series of movies. Day was on an East Coast promotional tour and dining with actor Allan Jones when Leo walked into the restaurant and immediately attracted a crowd. She knew nothing about baseball, much less about Leo Durocher. Jones, along with an MGM publicist, took her back to the Durochers' Manhattan apartment for a nightcap. She was ill at ease and became angry when Durocher attempted to patronize her with small talk. He seemed noisy and arrogant, and she had no wish to ever see him again. The two seemed as opposite as two people could be. Day was a practicing Mormon who neither drank nor smoked, nor did she tolerate the obscenities and crude talk that came naturally to a man like Durocher.[1]

As meetings with other women went on, Leo's marriage to Grace Dozier was showing signs of strain. When a feature article on baseball wives was published, she was quoted as saying: "My life with Leo has been so successful, because he is always away so much on trips." At the end of the 1941 season, after one of the New York papers reported that the couple would divorce after the World Series, Grace vigorously denied it, calling it the most absurd thing she had ever heard. The truth of the matter was that she had discussed getting a divorce from Leo during the season, but MacPhail had effected a reconciliation, arguing that a lawsuit could have a destructive effect on the team and its drive for the pennant.[2]

Leo left New York for Hollywood as soon as he could clear out his locker and pack his bags. He moved in with Raft without Grace, who spent the winter in St. Louis working while her husband played. On November 8, Durocher appeared live on Jack Benny's radio show broadcast from Hollywood. He was settling in as a comic figure ready and willing to work with the biggest names in radio.

"Well, well, Leo, I heard you were in Hollywood. Why didn't you let me know and come and stay with us?" was Benny's greeting.

"I'm stopping with George Raft," replied Leo. "And he's not charging me for room and board."

"It's guys like him who are ruining the tourist business," broke in Mary Livingstone.

Benny then said that Leo had assured him personally during the first World Series game that "we'll moider the Yanks" and that he had taken the tip and lost a couple of bets. "That's pretty bad."

"That may be true," retorted Durocher. "But you have some bad shows too, once in a while."

"Yes, one maybe," cracked Benny, "but not four out of five."

At one point in the broadcast, Livingstone asked Durocher, "How can such a sweet fellow have so much trouble with umpires?"

"That's easy, sister," responded Leo—the line giving him his biggest laugh.[3]

Durocher's infatuation with Hollywood in general and George Raft in particular seemed to intensify after winning his first pennant. Durocher was now dressing exactly like Raft, copying all of his details, including Raft's black knit neckties. Raft's own tailor now made Leo's clothes as well. Durocher became part of the Hollywood landscape and, as one gossip columnist put it, was "gradually talking half of Hollywood to death."

At one point in November 1941, Durocher met with Samuel Goldwyn, head of MGM, and writer Paul Gallico about playing himself in the screen biography of Lou Gehrig, *Pride of the Yankees*. But when Leo went for a screen test dressed as a Dodger, he balked at donning the Yankee uniform that had been tailored for him. The deal was off—or at least that was Leo's explanation for not appearing in the film. Other reports circulated that it was MacPhail who forbade him.[4]

Grace was a celebrity in her own right. A feature article on her in *Collier's* magazine in the fall of 1941 reported that the casual "junior-miss" dresses that she designed were sold in more than two thousand stores throughout the country, and that one could walk down any Main Street in America and be likely to see a dress designed by Grace Durocher and her team of eight assistant designers.[5]

ON DECEMBER 7, 1941, the United States was attacked by Japanese forces at Pearl Harbor, and the country was at war. The next day at the winter baseball meetings in Chicago, all the talk was about the impact of the war on the game. Bob Feller, the ace pitcher for the Cleveland Indians, had already decided to enlist, suggesting he might be the first of many. Mel Ott, the newly appointed manager of the New York Giants, spoke for many when he declared: "You can't look ahead and plan even for the next season. Young men, and I mean young ballplayers, aren't going to wait for the drafting. They're really mad, and they're going to be enlisting for this thing before the season gets here."[6]

On February 1, 1942, as Durocher signed a contract to manage the Dodgers for another season, the team got word from third baseman Harry "Cookie" Lavagetto, a licensed pilot, that he had enlisted in the Army Air Corps. He followed Claude Corbitt, a Dodger shortstop who had played in Montreal in 1941 and had enlisted in the Navy. The war quickly deprived the team of talent, but it also brought new fans as the industrial borough went on a war footing. The workforce at the Brooklyn Navy Yard was soon seventy thousand strong and working three shifts.

DUROCHER'S BATTLE WITH umpires resumed before the regular season began when he was ejected and fined in an exhibition game in Baltimore against the Yankees. Commissioner Landis himself imposed the penalty. Baseball's top officials were tired of Leo's umpire baiting and doing their best to support their men in blue. The rules of the game changed over the winter, in large part because of Durocher's antics. Beginning in 1942 a manager could be expelled and fined for delaying the game by arguing a ball-and-strike decision. Leo's first ejection under the new rule against arguing balls and strikes came on May 4 and was followed by a $50 fine the following day.[7]

Durocher soon came up with a new technique to try to thwart this new rule and the league's continuing battle with him over the use of profanity when addressing umpires. He would call time and then rush onto the field and blister the ear of the nearest Dodger, calling him all the nasty names he wished to apply to the umpire. It apparently worked for a while, saving him several ejections.[8]

The Communist Party of the United States had made baseball integration a high-priority target, and the team at the center of the target was the Brooklyn Dodgers. Beginning in 1939, members of the Young Communist League had fanned out everywhere with petitions—major league ballparks, Negro league games, busy street corners. They would go up to people and ask, "Would you sign a petition to get Negro ballplayers a chance to play in the Big Leagues?" In rapid order the YCL claimed to have thousands of signatures—fifty thousand or thereabouts by the end of 1939.*[9]

The war gave this effort new momentum—especially as more and more African-Americans were now in uniform. On May 6, the eve of his being drafted into the Army, Lester Rodney, sports editor of the *Daily Worker*, wrote an open letter to Major League commissioner Landis demanding integration. It appeared on the front page of the *Worker* and said in part: "Negro soldiers and sailors are among those beloved heroes of the American people who have already died for the preservation of this country and everything this country stands for—yes, including the great game of baseball. You, the self-proclaimed 'Czar' of baseball, are the man responsible for keeping Jim Crow in our National Pastime. You are the one refusing to say the word which would do more to justify baseball's existence in this year of war than any other single thing."

The letter also quoted Durocher from his 1939 interview, adding that the Dodgers had already been shut out by an African-American pitcher in

---

* Before seizing on racial issues, the party and the *Daily Worker* had seen baseball purely in terms of class struggle and exploitation. Mike Gold wrote on Dizzy Dean in 1934: "Dizzy seems to be a simple-minded, Ring Lardner 'You Know Me Al' ball player, raised down in the Southwest on grits and cornbread, gifted with a powerful pitching arm and a keen pair of eyes. But the stockholders of the St. Louis Cardinals and the racketeers and speculators who infest organized baseball as they do every other national sport in the country today have a keener eye than Dizzy's pitching ones and a stronger arm when it comes to counting the season's profits."

Havana during Spring Training. There was no immediate public response from Landis. Loath to discuss the color line, Landis finally broke his silence in July 1942, but only after he was shown the original Durocher remark in the *Daily Worker*, which implied that the commissioner was the obstacle preventing him from using a black player. Landis's public reaction to the Durocher allegation—along with the petitions—helped set the stage for integration.

There was little doubt that Durocher had made the original statement. However, Landis was so furious with Durocher that when the Dodgers next came to Chicago, he met with him behind closed doors and came out of the meeting announcing that Durocher had denied making the statement. Durocher himself was uncharacteristically silent, and by this time, Rodney was in an overseas war zone and unavailable to verify Durocher's comment.

One reason that Durocher may have been so quick to withdraw the statement may have been the belief that Landis was not the culprit but rather the owners collectively. In 1983, Richard Dozer, formerly of the *Chicago Tribune*, published an article in *Baseball Digest* in which he described a meeting of Durocher and Landis in the commissioner's office. Durocher recalled mentioning he had played in an exhibition against Josh Gibson, the great Negro league catcher, and observed that even though Gibson had great talent, he apparently was not welcome in the major leagues. "Landis looked down at me with that glare of his and said, 'Bring me the man who says you can't have a colored player in the big leagues, and I'll take care of him real quick.' I believe to this day that Landis would have accepted the player if an owner had signed one," Durocher said.[10]

The next day, July 18, a reporter from the *New York Herald Tribune* asked Landis for amplification of his position on race. "Not now or at any time in the 21 years I have been high commissioner of baseball has there been any rule or understanding against the hiring of Negro players." Stressing the point, he added that there was no rule, "formal or informal, or any understanding, unwritten, subterranean or sub-anything" against Negro players. "I told Durocher that he could hire one Negro or 25 Negro ball players just the same as whites."[11]

On July 21, 1942, Hy Turkin of the *New York Daily News*, which then had the largest circulation of any newspaper in America, wrote a column about Durocher's three-year-old comment: "A casual remark made by Leo Durocher to Lester Rodney, now in the Army, may do more for his place in history than all his shortstopping and managing histrionics. He said that he would hire Black players and this is like the tail of the tornado that has overwhelmed Judge Landis with two million signatures and threatens the democratization of our national pastime." The petitions came from several sources, but most of the signers had been recruited by the Young Communists.*

Suddenly it seemed as if everyone was talking or writing about why African-Americans were not in Major League Baseball and who would be the first to break the invisible "color bar" that existed in the game. "There is trouble and worry and a few headaches for the pilot who pioneers with Negroes in the big leagues, but there is nothing that intelligence and guts won't overcome," wrote John Lardner in the *Evening Star*. "The first man to make the move will knock the prejudice over on its back."[12]

Durocher had already focused on a Cuban named Silvio Garcia, having declared he would be worth one million dollars if he had only been white—Durocher described Garcia as "coal black." Leo had spotted Garcia in Cuba in 1942 when Garcia was part of a Cuban All-Star team that played five games against the Dodgers. During that series he hit Dodger pitching for a .381 (8 for 21) batting average and was flawless in the field. At one point, Durocher told Tommy Holmes of the *Brooklyn Eagle* that Garcia was the greatest shortstop he had ever seen. "He could do everything that Marty Marion could and a little bit more . . ."[13]

On the field, the 1942 Dodgers got off to a fast start and stood at 32–13 at the end of May. Unexpectedly, an incident from Leo's past reared its head again. On May 23, before the Dodgers game against the Giants, somebody on the Giants placed a half dozen copies of the new *Saturday Evening Post* in the Dodger dugout, opened to a short story by Stanley Frank entitled "The Name of the Game." Durocher either did not notice the magazines, or if he did, he did not appreciate their significance. Once the game got underway, the Giant bench started asking if he had read the *Post*. Caught by surprise, Leo turned to his own players to ask, "What the hell post are they talking about?"

After losing the game to the Giants, Durocher read the fictional story in which a young pitcher named Messlin witnesses the unmasking of a locker room thief who later becomes his manager. Two characters in the story were thinly disguised but totally recognizable as Babe Ruth and Leo

---

* As if to contradict himself on the matter of race, in October 1942, Landis issued an edict forbidding interracial competition during the winter off-season.

Durocher. The Ruth character, who is simply known as the Big Guy, is preyed upon by the Durocher character, known as Gaban, who is portrayed as a bully, a braggart, and a sneak thief. The story opens with the line "Messlin was in the clubhouse the day they found the Big Guy's World Series watch in Gaban's spare glove." Many clues linked Gaban to Durocher, among them his being termed "a poolroom bum at heart" with a voice described as a "brassy bellow." It was, as reporter Tom Meany put it, "pretty raw stuff."[14]

Durocher was furious, threatened to knock Frank's head off, and refused to dignify the piece with a denial, even as other teams made sure copies of the article appeared in the Dodger dugout before games. Bench jockeys again attempted to get Leo's goat by swinging pocket watches when they caught his eye, and players on one team made giant cardboard watches and waved them at Leo while their teammates yelled, "What time is it, Leo? What time is it?" Tom Meany watched all of this and concluded that Durocher's reaction to this incident was a perfect display of his ability to feign imperturbability.*[15]

On June 28, with a nine-game lead over the second-place Cardinals, Leo was ejected by umpire Tom Dunn in the first inning of the first game of a doubleheader against the Reds when he protested a decision at first base. He refused to leave the dugout, took a gulp of water, and then defiantly spat it onto the playing field. Dunn halted the game and started toward the dugout. Durocher emerged, repeatedly kicked dirt on the umpire's shoes and trousers, and as a parting gesture socked Dunn in the face with a wet towel. Durocher's obscenity-laden tantrum delayed the game by a full ten minutes. The next day, Leo was hit with a $50 fine and a three-day suspension.

A number of writers and columnists expressed amazement that such an offense netted such a mild punishment—at a minimum, they thought he deserved a five-day suspension. His behavior was deemed atrocious and comments came from all quarters. "This wet towel sweatshirt-Caesar stuff is as out of date as the horse car and cannot endure," Dan Daniel wrote in

---

* The Frank short story was controversial, but it was also seen as a first-rate short story; it appears in several major anthologies of baseball writing, including Charles Einstein's *The Fireside Book of Baseball* (1956). Einstein noted in his introduction that Frank had brought his true-to-life touch to fiction to the point that one baseball man "doubted grimly that it was fiction at all."

the *New York Telegram*, while C. M. Gibbs called Leo "a spoiled brat" in the *Baltimore Sun*.

Leo responded by banning Daniel and all but three of the thirty or so other "beat" reporters from the Dodgers clubhouse. The three who still had entrée had not offended Leo in writing critically about the incident with Dunn. The consensus was that Leo could dish it out but he couldn't take it. "No manager of recent times has gone out of his way to be disagreeable on such a scale as Durocher," wrote Francis Stann of the *Evening Star*.[16] Even more galling to many was that Durocher served his suspension while the team played the Phillies in Shibe Park and managed from a seat next to the Dodgers' dugout, attired in a blue sports coat, gray flannel slacks, cream silk shirt, and black knit tie. As much as they hated him, Leo—and his sense of fashion—was still good copy.[17]

Durocher's bad relationship with the press got even worse in July when Dan Parker wrote eight columns of his *New York Daily Mirror* column castigating Durocher for his treatment of the men who covered the team. Parker, whom Damon Runyon called "the most consistently brilliant of all the sportswriters," was not a man to be easily dismissed. For openers, Parker noted that Durocher was now isolated from the writers, with half not on speaking terms with him, because they were sick of being insulted by him, and the other half barred from the clubhouse because Durocher felt they had slighted him in print. The line from the Parker column that got quoted most often that summer was: "Durocher is manager of a big league ball club. That is quite different from being a big league manager, which Leo positively isn't."

What most irked Parker was Leo's set of rules barring newspapermen from the clubhouse except at certain times. "It seems they interfered with his gin rummy games with clubhouse visitors with far less right to be in there than the sportswriters who went as representatives of the fans." He added that these visitors included racetrack characters—in other words, bookies and gamblers, men like Sleepout Louie.[18]

Leo occasionally talked about his gambling and how much he could lose on the horses. He admitted in a dugout interview in 1969 that there was a time when he "had a ring in his nose" and once lost $8,000 two days in a row at the track. He finally learned that he could not beat the horses—but in 1941 it was a lesson that was still off in the future.[19]

The fact that Durocher was gambling and that his clubhouse was turning into a betting parlor was no secret and discussed in print by writers whose opinions of Durocher were becoming more and more negative. A few days after the Parker piece appeared, Jack Troy of the *Atlanta Constitution* used his column to tell about a contest in which Durocher was pitching bottle caps at a crack in the floor for so much a pitch. The cap that came closest to the crack took the money. Suddenly, Durocher grabbed his opponent's bottle cap and found a quarter stuffed in it, which provided enough weight to give it balance. According to Troy's source, Durocher screamed to the high heavens and threatened to punch the man in the nose. Just then, the man grabbed Leo's bottle cap, and it too was loaded with a quarter.[20]

LEO'S ANTICS WERE now catching up with him. At some point later in the season, as the team was faltering, Grace Durocher, fed up with his philandering, informed Leo that she was finally planning to sue him for divorce. Leo begged her to reconsider, insisting that it would be an added reason for MacPhail to fire him. MacPhail and the players and their wives liked Grace, who had become a devoted fan of the club and friend to the team despite Leo.

On September 10, 1942, at age fifty-two, Dodgers general manager Larry MacPhail shocked the baseball world by announcing he had accepted an invitation from the Army to go back on active duty with the rank of lieutenant colonel. He was forgoing the $75,000 a year, five-year contract he had signed in May. He expected to be back in khaki in less than a week.

Two days later, Durocher announced that once the World Series was over, he would enlist in the U.S. Navy. He added in an interview, which appeared in the *Springfield Republican*, that he had applied for a commission in the Navy earlier but had never heard back. When asked for details, he refused to talk. The reporter commented that this was approximately the second time in Leo's life that he didn't feel like talking. "Historians say that once, some years ago, Leo kept quiet long enough to have a tooth pulled."[21]

Later that same day, Durocher and coach Chuck Dressen got into a particularly nasty seventh-inning confrontation with umpire Al Barlick over a call at first base. The two men were ejected, and the team lost 2–1 to the St. Louis Cardinals, who thereby tied the Dodgers for first place. The following day, the Dodgers lost a doubleheader to the Reds, taking them out of first place and putting the Cardinals one full game in the lead. Durocher also learned that he had been fined $100 for the Barlick incident and was told bluntly by league president Ford Frick that if the pennant race had not been so close, he would have been suspended for five days. Durocher's fine was for prolonged argument, delaying the game, and using violent, profane language. Dressen took his fine and five-day suspension for laying hands on and pushing the umpire.[22]

After the double loss, MacPhail was in the clubhouse with Grace Durocher, who was crying. As he patted her on the back, he said, "Take it easy, kid, take it easy. Dry up your tears. There's nothing to cry about. We ain't licked yet. Not by a long shot."[23]

But the Dodgers never retook the lead, and MacPhail was gone before the end of the season. The Dodgers finished the month with a record of 16–10, but the Cardinals were 21–4, part of a remarkable final third of the season in which they won forty-three of their last fifty-one games. The Dodgers, despite a 104–50 record that resulted in a four-game improvement over their pennant-winning performance the year before, finished two games behind the Cardinals.

In late October 1942, Branch Rickey, now sixty-one, who had been at odds with the owner of the St. Louis Cardinals, left his position there and became the new president of the Dodgers, essentially what would now be termed its general manager. Durocher's future as manager was immediately called into question. Rickey knew Durocher's strengths and weaknesses as well as anybody, and Durocher was well aware of this. Rickey quickly summoned Leo to his country estate in Missouri and grilled him for hours about the team, its prospects, and its problems—especially that of low team morale, despite the fact that they had just won 104 games, which Rickey felt was caused, at least in part, by gambling in the clubhouse. There was no discussion of a 1943 contract.

Rickey's first job was dealing with the odious situation that had been allowed to develop around Durocher and his coaches. The Dodger clubhouse was overrun with gamblers, bookies, ticket scalpers, and racing handicappers. These fast "friends" had, in the words of Arthur Mann, "long enjoyed access to Ebbets Field and scurried from dugout to locker room like happy, squealing vermin in the rat runs of an aging barn."[24]

"It seemed like we always had someone hanging around that was a gambler and a bookie," said Dodger shortstop Pee Wee Reese in a later interview, adding, "All the Dodgers, it seemed, knew a bookie named Memphis Engleberg."

To his horror, Rickey found one player who had spent hundreds of dollars on a single horse race between the innings of a ball game. According to

Arthur Mann, another pitcher was so upset over his racing loss that he blew a ballgame. Players won, but they also lost, and they borrowed to cover their losses. Savings disappeared in the face of salary advances on future earnings. Rickey believed that the gambling cost the team an easy 1942 pennant.

The biggest clubhouse problem centered on high-stakes poker games, in which Leo played a hand. The writers all knew about these games and sometimes wrote about them as a phenomenon peculiar to Brooklyn. "A lot of big-league managers will not permit poker playing, even for a dime limit," *Boston Herald* columnist Bob Dunbar wrote, "and we can hardly recall seeing a poker game on a Red Sox road trip this entire year."[25]

Landis, who had all the facts on the situation—including knowledge of the several claims against team members for horse-racing debts that had landed on his desk—summoned Rickey to Chicago and told Rickey to clean house immediately or he would do the job himself. Charlie Dressen had to be let go—not only for his shortcomings as a coach, but for his open friendship with Memphis Engleberg, to whom he owed a large amount of money.[26]

Besides Engleberg, the big-name gambler associated with the Dodger clubhouse was Connie Immerman, who had been an original sponsor of Leo Durocher Day in 1927. He was a true Broadway legend whose exploits were adoringly chronicled by Damon Runyon and the New York gossip columnists. "I like Connie particularly for one thing," columnist Dorothy Kilgallen wrote in her widely syndicated "Voice of Broadway" column, "his great confidence in himself even when things aren't hitting on all cylinders."[27]

On November 12, 1942, after being pressed by reporters, Durocher finally admitted that he had not tried to enter the Navy. "I haven't ever seen anyone about a commission, tried for a commission or thought about trying for one." Leo had lied to look patriotic and was now confessing to this deceit as the war intensified. For those who disliked Leo, this was another log thrown on the fire.[28]

For this reason and others, many speculated that Leo's time in Brooklyn might be over and that the 1943 Dodgers would have a new skipper. But on November 19, Durocher was offered a new contract. Rickey had obtained two major concessions from Durocher. The first related to gambling. High-stakes games would be banned from the clubhouse and on railcars carrying the team between cities; poker games could continue, but with a fifteen-cent limit on bets. Players would not be allowed to go to the racetrack during the season. Crucial for Rickey was eliminating the players' associations with gamblers and their access to the clubhouse.

Durocher's response at the contract-signing press conference was defensive. He first admitted that clubhouse gambling was a bad practice but then said, "It has been pointed out that gambling was the reason we didn't win the pennant in 1942. It probably was harmful, although it caused no ill feeling." He then listed seven players—Arky Vaughan, Dolph Camilli, Ducky Medwick, Pete Reiser, Dixie Walker, Whit Wyatt, and Pee Wee Reese—who had never turned a card all season, pointing out, "So gambling doesn't account for their slump." Only later would Durocher admit that gambling had a "stranglehold" on the Brooklyn club.[29]

The second condition of the new contract required Durocher to again be listed on the Dodgers roster as an infielder. With these conditions in place, Durocher eagerly accepted Rickey's offer of $25,000 to manage the team.

Unknown to the public at the time was that Grace Durocher was present at both of these meetings and was there when the contract was signed. Despite the pending divorce and growing estrangement, she was the one who vouched for Durocher and said he would keep the promises he made to Rickey, thereby saving his job. Rickey was in awe of Grace, whom he called "an exceptional, extraordinary woman" who could talk Leo's language when she had to. Grace's reason for saving Leo will probably never be known, but one possibility is that she did it out of respect for Rickey based on the belief that the man about to be her ex-husband was the best man to run Rickey's team.[30]

But Leo's immediate concern was the military draft, which was edging toward conscripting his age group and could have him in uniform and in basic training before Spring Training began. When Durocher's draft status was examined, it was discovered that there was no birth record for Leo in Springfield but one for George J. Durocher, which his mother maintained was actually for Leo and that a mistake had been made. Confusion arose when she registered him for school and gave 1906 as his year of birth. When Durocher entered the big leagues with the New York Yankees, he gave his birthday as July 27, 1906. But in March 1943, a 1905 date was affirmed, and at age thirty-seven he was still eligible for the draft. The St. Louis draft board where he was registered immediately confirmed his draft status as 1-A. Questioned in Florida, where he was vacationing, Leo told reporters, "I'm ready to serve anytime they want me."[31]

He was in great physical shape, a point attested to by a January physical he had undergone at the Mayo Clinic in Rochester, Minnesota. At that time, married men with dependents were deferred, but his present wife was anything but dependent.

By 5:45 A.M. on March 1, 1943, the day slated for his induction, Durocher had already received four predawn calls from New York Giants fans out to bedevil him.

"Get out of bed, you bum," one voice said. "It's time for you to report to your draft board."

"Mind your own business," Durocher roared. "Why don't you beat your wife and leave me alone?"

When he finally reported to local board number 133 in Brooklyn, he was made a temporary corporal and placed in charge of a group of 162 selectees for a subway ride to the Grand Central Palace induction center in Midtown Manhattan, located on Lexington Avenue between Forty-Sixth and Forty-Seventh Streets. After his physical had begun, he noted a group of uniformed men following him from one examining station to the next.

"What do you sailors want?" Leo asked.

"We ain't sailors," one of the men shot back. "We're Marines, and we've been instructed to grab you off just as soon as you pass this exam." The most aggressive man in sports had been marked by the most aggressive arm of the armed services as a potential poster boy and recruiting magnet.

The last doctor in the gauntlet was Major S. P. Guidotti, who looked over his examination papers and declared Durocher to be 4-F—ineligible for military service. He had passed every medical requirement except one: rule 5C of the War Department's Mobilization Regulations, which declared someone unacceptable if he had a perforation of the *membrane tympani*—a punctured eardrum.

"The major told me I was perfect except for that eardrum," he told Sergeant Dan Polier, who was reporting on the induction for *Yank* magazine. "I asked him how serious it was, and he said that it wouldn't bother me ordinarily, but would interfere in martial duty. For instance, a gas mask would do me no good, because the gas would seep to my eardrum and ruin the inside of my head. And if I went swimming, water might cause mastoid trouble or some other serious infection."[32]

Rickey's response was that he was "both sorry and happy"—"I'm sorry from a patriotic viewpoint, but I'm naturally happy for the club's future."[33]

Durocher's rejection was big news in New York and received with mixed emotions, when first heard over the radio that day on the noon news and in the afternoon newspapers. Some, mostly in Brooklyn, were pleased, others neutral; but as Durocher feared, the 4-F determination was turned on him as wags pounced on the obvious. "He must have punctured it listening to himself bawl out the umpires" was one oft-repeated line. Headline writers embraced the event with puns held high: DODGER FANS DON'T SHED TEAR WHEN "THE LIP" GOES OUT ON EAR was how the *New York Herald Tribune* played the story the following day.[34] Durocher told Frank Graham that it was the result of a head injury suffered when he was hit with a pitched ball in St. Louis in 1933.[35]

When Durocher first met with Rickey that afternoon to let him know that he was free to manage the Dodgers, Rickey said: "My boy, you and I face the toughest job of our lives." The Dodgers were the oldest team in the National League and losing younger players to military service—Reese and Reiser were already gone. Rickey was forced to pick up old men like forty-two-year-old outfielder Johnny Cooney.

Because of wartime restrictions on travel, Commissioner Landis had ordered all teams to hold Spring Training close to home and the Dodgers complied by training on the grounds of the United States Military Academy at West Point, where they would have access to the sheltered field house several hours a day. The team was fed and lodged at the Bear Mountain Inn.

With Pee Wee Reese serving in the Navy, the Dodgers were desperate for a shortstop. In early June, therefore, Leo returned to the Dodgers starting lineup. Three others had tried and failed for their inability to make double plays. The assignment lasted only six games, during which he batted .222 with four singles. By mid-June, it was apparent that the Dodgers were faltering on the field. After losing five in a row, Sid Feder of the Associated Press wrote on June 19 that the team was well on its way to falling apart at the seams. "The panic is on in Brooklyn, chums," he wrote. Confounding the dire predictions, the Dodgers went forward, winning eleven of their next thirteen games.[36]

Durocher continued to show up in the many gossip columns originating from either Manhattan or Hollywood. One mention connected him to the war across the Atlantic. In his syndicated column "The Lyons Den," Leonard Lyons reported on June 28, 1943, that Durocher's name had been painted on one of fourteen 250-pound bombs dropped on the German city of Bremen by an Australian pilot who had been entertained on Broadway while training in the States. Durocher had been one of his Broadway "hosts" with a bomb named in their honor, along with the likes of Gloria Swanson, Tallulah Bankhead, Joe E. Lewis, and Sophie Tucker.

On July 10, with a record of 46–33 and more than seventy games left to play in the regular season, Durocher single-handedly sparked a revolt among his players. Some called it a rebellion and others a mutiny, but whatever it was called, it was a negative benchmark and a turning point in Leo Durocher's career.

The day before the mutiny, star pitcher Bobo Newsom had, according to Durocher, thrown a spitball in the third inning, surprising catcher Bobby Bragan and causing a passed ball on which a run scored. The Dodgers won the game in the tenth inning, but afterward in the clubhouse with writer Tim Cohane of the *World-Telegram* standing a few feet away, Durocher cornered Newsom, accused him of trying to show up his catcher, and suspended him for three games. Cohane reported the story in the next day's newspaper, which was the moment the rest of the club learned of the suspension and the reason for it. Newsom was not only a popular teammate but the club's best pitcher with a 9–4 record.

The headquarters and prime residence for the Dodgers during the season was the Hotel New Yorker near Penn Station on Eighth Avenue in Manhattan. Second baseman Billy Herman was having breakfast at the hotel with outfielder Augie Galan and future Hall of Famer Arky Vaughan, the team's hard-hitting third baseman, when they read Cohane's article and learned that Newsom had been suspended for three days without pay. Vaughan became very quiet, and Herman could tell that something was bothering him.

That afternoon, Vaughan dressed for the game, took batting practice, and then, a few minutes before infield practice began, barged into Durocher's office and demanded to know if the article was true. When Durocher confirmed that it was, Vaughan went to his locker and changed back into his street clothes. He put his uniform in a neat pile, returned to Durocher's office, and threw the bundle in Durocher's face. According to newspaper accounts, he yelled, "Here's another uniform you can have." Durocher then suspended Vaughan, who shot back, "You cannot suspend me, I've quit." According to Herman, the actual language of the encounter was too crude for the newspapers, as Vaughan had, among other things, told Durocher where he could insert the uniform.[37]

Infield practice was canceled, and Durocher called for a meeting of the club. With forfeiture looming and minutes to go before game time,

Durocher faced a revolt. Many in the park seemed to sense something was wrong when there was no sign of the Dodgers on the field at a time when ordinarily they would have been taking infield practice, so a group of reporters went to the clubhouse to see Durocher.

Frank Graham of the *New York Sun* was one of those who witnessed Durocher "white with rage and shaken by the hostility of the players, who glared at him from every corner of the clubhouse." Leo then denounced Cohane to the reporters and told them that he had been misquoted—that Cohane was lying.

"Where is Cohane?" he demanded.

"He's home. This is his day off," somebody said.

He then called Cohane at his home in Yonkers. "We are having a lot of trouble over here on account of you," he said. "You have been spreading false stories about me and you've got my ball club in an uproar."[38]

Cohane said he wanted to meet with Durocher and defend himself, but this was not heard by those assembled in the clubhouse. Durocher hung up.

Dixie Walker was the first player to speak. He chose his words carefully: "If what was printed in the papers is true, here's another uniform you can have."

"That makes two men," Durocher barked, and pointed to Vaughan.

Walker continued: "I don't see why this boy should suffer, and if he is out, I guess I am out, too."

At this point, a clubhouse attendant came into the room and announced that he had been sent by the umpires who were on the field and that it was time for the game to start.

Durocher then declared, "Well, let's see if we've got nine men to put on the field. If we haven't, we'll just forfeit the game."

Then he started from the top of his lineup card, asking each player if he was in or out. Everybody answered in the affirmative except Vaughan, who was in street clothes. The players then took the field and drubbed the Pirates 23–6.

During the game, Rickey convinced Vaughan to come down from the right-field grandstands where he sat with Newsom and to don his Dodger uniform. He returned to the bench for a few minutes with Rickey's assurance that he was not under suspension.[39]

Not only was the mutiny and lopsided score big news that day, but so was kitchen fat. Included in the crowd who came to Ebbets Field that day were

4,512 women who each brought a half pound or more of fat in exchange for free admission. The total for the day was 5,003 pounds, which was turned over to munitions makers to be turned into explosives. Such "Win the War" ballpark drives were common at the time and more commonly solicited fat, scrap metal, or blood donations.* [40]

During the game, Cohane called Rickey, told him that Durocher had, in effect, called him a liar, and demanded a chance to prove to the other newspapermen that he had only told the truth in his story. "I want you to call a meeting in the clubhouse before tomorrow's game," he said. "I want all the ballplayers and all the newspapermen there, and I'll face your Mr. Durocher and everybody will have a chance to find out who is lying."

A strange scene took place in the clubhouse that Sunday afternoon as Cohane cross-examined Durocher in the presence of players and reporters. Frank Graham reported: "Durocher sat on a uniform trunk, and Cohane, standing before him or walking up and down slowly, drew from him, question by question, an admission that he had said everything that had appeared in the newspapers. There wasn't another sound in the room but the rise and fall of their voices. And after the last admission had been made, Cohane shrugged. 'The prosecution rests,' he said."[41]

The consensus among the reporters gathered for the showdown was that Durocher was through—or should be. The following day, it was widely reported that Durocher was on his way out. But Durocher did not go; Bobo did. Newsom had tried to buy his outright release from the Dodgers but had not heard back. Three days after the mutiny, the Dodgers got waivers on him and sent him to the St. Louis Browns, getting in return Fritz Ostermueller and Archie McKain, two pitchers on whom all the other American League clubs had already passed. Newsom promptly stated that he would quit baseball before he would report to the Browns. He finally reported to them and then was traded to the Washington Senators.

The mutiny had been quelled. No disciplinary measures were taken against either Vaughan or Walker. Whatever Rickey said to Durocher was in private. For publication, Rickey issued a statement: "No player or players, no president, no public, nobody, can run a club for a manager. Durocher will have my undivided loyalty and support."

---

* One pound of fat contained enough glycerin to make about a pound of explosives.

Durocher's attack on Cohane specifically and the press in general would now fester and, with an occasional cease-fire, continue for decades. A few days after the mutiny, the mild-mannered Arthur "Red" Patterson of the *New York Herald Tribune* noted in his column: "Leo's attack on the integrity of some of the writers had the press corps lads set against him." Durocher would later throw salt in the wound in his May 1948 memoir *The Dodgers and Me* in which he again attacked Cohane for fomenting the mutiny. This time Cohane threatened to sue Durocher.* [42]

The day following Patterson's column, the Dodgers were in Boston to play the Braves, and Rickey summoned the whole team to Durocher's hotel suite for a two-hour pregame meeting. Rickey expressed total support for Durocher. The Associated Press reported "complete harmony" at the end of the meeting.[43] But in the wake of the revolt, Rickey got rid of two more popular players, Dolph Camilli and Joe Medwick. Both men were traded to the New York Giants. Camilli, who had been the Dodgers field captain in 1942, chose not to report in favor of retirement. On August 10, 1943, the Dodgers had a day off. They had lost ten games in a row and had won only one of their last fourteen. Rickey sat down with Durocher and compared the losing streak to a disease which would have to run its course. Tossing three popular players overboard was seen by the writers to be a vote of confidence in Durocher but also saw it as part of Rickey's avowed plan to purge the team of older players.[44]

Because of the mutiny and the ensuing losing streak, press coverage of Durocher turned increasingly negative. "Hollywood is thinking about doing a picture about Leo Durocher," Jack Troy wrote in his sports column in the *Atlanta Constitution* in mid-August. "That ought to be good, if the principal scenes are shot in a cellar."[45]

ON AUGUST 30, Leo was sued by Grace for divorce in circuit court in St. Louis where the couple still legally resided. Asking for alimony, all court costs, and attorney fees, Grace Durocher's petition charged her husband of being "constantly of a nagging disposition" and said he "possessed a very uneven temperament." She maintained that he had become very cold and

---

* Both Cohane and Patterson were bound for journalism glory. Cohane became sports editor of *Look* magazine, and Red Patterson became the longtime, immensely popular public relations director for the New York Yankees. Neither man ever hid his disdain for Durocher.

indifferent to her in the last four years, adding, "He stays away from home weeks at a time, indulging in unbecoming conduct." She also charged him with causing her to suffer "great embarrassment and humiliation," as newspaper columnists publicized his unseemly behavior in nightclubs with persons other than herself. She further charged Durocher with squandering his earnings on costly long-distance automobile trips and coast-to-coast airline flights, claiming they were for business reasons. Finally, she asked the court to restore her former name, Grace L. Dozier. Unlike his first divorce, Durocher did not contest Grace's petition.

Rickey led a parade of those saddened by the divorce. Grace was a popular public figure whose face and fashions often showed up in women's magazines. She had become an avid Dodgers fan with her own box at Ebbets Field where she entertained the stars of Broadway and Hollywood who had become friends of the Durochers.

Grace had also won the respect of the sportswriters who covered Leo. One of Grace's greatest fans was Dan Parker of the *New York Daily Mirror*, who had already declared his enmity for Leo. Less than two weeks after the divorce, Parker bylined a feature article entitled "Lippy Leo Out at Home" for the *American Weekly* magazine which was distributed with Sunday newspapers and claimed a circulation of fifty million. The piece was a total skewering of Leo and an appreciation of his ex-wife, who Parker pointed out "earns more as a designer of dresses than Leo does as a maligner of umpires." Parker went on to advance the thesis that Grace had awakened Leo's ambition and set the course for Durocher's rise as a manager. "Whether this line of reasoning does Leo an injustice or not," he observed, "the fact remains that he didn't really start to go places in his profession until he married the talented, attractive and faultlessly groomed dress designer."[46]

Parker ended the article by suggesting that if the divorce was coupled with the possibility of Rickey not rehiring Durocher as manager, it would be the costliest double play in which Leo had ever figured. Lawton Carver of the International News Service believed that the odds against Durocher remaining as Dodger skipper for 1944 were about a hundred to one. The mutiny was still fresh in people's minds, and Durocher and Dixie Walker were barely speaking to one another. Durocher himself said that there was one unnamed player on the team he could not stand, and everyone guessed correctly that it was Walker.

As the Dodgers landed in St. Louis on September 21, Durocher was met by a process server with a suit for a claim of $893 for nonpayment of his 1939 taxes, which was added to a pending suit for $554 for his 1938 taxes.

On September 29, 1943, with four games left in the regular season, Rickey called a press conference at which he stunned reporters when he released Durocher as player-manager, but then added that he might later consider him for the position of manager. He said that by releasing him, they both would be able to talk about 1944 without any feeling of compulsion. "If he wants to make a connection elsewhere, either in baseball, or radio, or the movies, he will be free to do so." The last reference was to published reports that Durocher might become an actor or a Hollywood agent. Confusion ensued. Did Rickey want him for 1944, or was this really a means of easing him out? Harold Parrott declared Leo was still a Dodger, but one "without portfolio."⁴⁷

Despite all the turmoil, Brooklyn finished third in 1943 with a decent 81–72 record. Bobo Newsom told Burton Hawkins of the Washington *Evening Star* that his respect for Durocher had not dimmed because of their tiff. "If anyone should ask you," he said, "Durocher is a pretty good manager—a sound baseball man who really battles to win."⁴⁸ On October 8, columnist Leonard Lyons reported that the Dodgers had refunded to him all of the $600 for the six fines Durocher had been assessed during the season. The Dodgers regarded them as "inexpensive publicity," a comment MacPhail had made before he left for the Army.

But with Leo's future with the Dodgers now in limbo, the long knives came out. "Durocher probably is the least liked figure in the National League," former Dodger Alex Kampouris told Burton Hawkins of the *Evening Star.* "Everybody on the club hates him." Hawkins, in a column entitled "Unpopularity Fails to Hold Back Durocher," listed the names of umpires, journalists, and fellow managers who did not like Leo.⁴⁹

After considerable soul-searching and consultation with his friend and confidant Sid Weil, who was always squarely in Durocher's corner, Rickey decided he would bring Leo back and summoned Durocher to his office on October 25 to sign a contract for the 1944 season. Lawton Carver of the International News Service marked it down as Leo's greatest victory. At the signing, Leo was asked about the revolt, and he said that he had reconciled with all the players, save one whom he would not name but everyone knew was Dixie Walker.

In announcing the signing, Rickey said to the thirty reporters who had assembled to hear about the rehiring:

A year ago, my chief problem in deciding on my manager concerned the matter of associations with professional gamblers which I found to exist in the club. There is no secret about this. I wanted it stamped out, and I am happy to say it was stamped out. What is more, I want to say Durocher did his full share to bring this condition about. This time my problem dealt with other matters. I am hopeful that Leo can regain control of the players, and I think he is going to do another good job. I know at heart he is for the players, and I do not think the players' feelings toward him are hopeless.[50]

Durocher later admitted that he had not reconciled with Walker because Walker had sided with Newsom and Vaughan during the mutiny. At one point, Durocher wanted Walker off the team. Rickey intervened. He signed Walker early after he got the two men to shake hands.[51]

In November 1943, Durocher announced that he and the Brooklynite movie comic Danny Kaye were rehearsing a comedy routine that they would take overseas to entertain U.S. troops in war zones. One skit would cast Kaye as an umpire and Durocher as an umpire-baiter, and another would be a take on baseball in the time of Shakespeare. The routines were written by Kaye's wife, Sylvia Fine, who was also a professional screenwriter. Kaye would perform his recent musical comedy numbers, and Leo would answer questions about baseball. The trip was postponed several times until it was finally canceled early in 1944. Durocher spent much of the waiting time staying with George Raft in Hollywood. Then suddenly the show was on again. Durocher and Kaye would not go overseas but rather to Army camps in the southern United States. In three weeks in February 1944, they hit seventeen camps and never did fewer than two shows a day and some days as many as five.[52]

In addition to the stage shows, the duo visited military hospitals where men wounded in the war were being cared for, spending hours going from ward to ward. At first, Durocher balked at visiting the severely wounded, fearing he would have nothing to say. But he was assured that these men really wanted to talk to him—to ask him about the player revolt, to ask him what he thought about Bobo Newsom, and to ask what it had been like to play with Dizzy Dean. Durocher was a big hit with the troops and found that he was able to keep the troops engaged and keep them laughing.

When Durocher headed for Spring Training, George Raft was in New

York after returning from his own overseas tour and, as had been his custom for many years, was staying at Durocher's East Sixty-Fourth Street apartment—now a bachelor's lair—while Leo was at Spring Training. Leo's Manhattan headquarters was a plushy terrace apartment with a built-in bar whose stools were made of catchers' mitts mounted on baseball bat tripods. Raft's new film *Follow the Boys* opened at the Palace Theatre while Leo was at Bear Mountain. After the premiere, Raft took some friends to Durocher's appartment for a party. Raft was playing gin rummy with sportscaster Bill Stern when a businessman who had tagged along suggested a dice game. A pair of dice was found, and a fateful session of craps began that ended close to dawn with Raft ahead by $18,000.[53]

During Spring Training, Durocher seemed to be testing Rickey's patience, which ran out one blustery morning in early April at the Bear Mountain Inn. Rickey suddenly needed Durocher for decisions on trimming the Spring Training roster, and Leo was nowhere to be found. He discovered that Durocher had left camp and was in a Times Square radio studio rehearsing a guest appearance on Milton Berle's slapstick radio show *Let Yourself Go*. Leo still wasn't around that evening for a press conference at the inn, with Rickey presiding. "That young man," he boomed, "will have to make an election of professions!"

Rickey was bothered not only by the absence but by Leo's new career. On March 28, Leo had appeared on the radio sit-com *Duffy's Tavern*, and the week before on Jack Benny's show. Weeks before that, he had been on the Fred Allen show, where he visited with the fictional characters who inhabited Allen's Alley. Durocher was seen as a guest whose very name brought laughter from a live studio audience and he gladly played the fall guy to fictional characters. Miss Duffy of *Duffy's Tavern* called him "a very verbose guy who besides talks too much." For each of these guest shots, Leo was paid $1,500 to $2,000.

Rickey's statement about choosing professions was carried in the early editions of the next morning's tabloids, so Leo read all about it before he started back across the George Washington Bridge at midnight after Berle's show had aired. The next morning, Durocher entered the inn's dining room grinning from ear to ear as he approached Rickey's table and opened the conversation.

"You won the election, Mr. Rickey."

"What election?" asked Rickey.

"You were running against Milton Berle, and I voted for you, that's all."

Then a pause: "What I mean is, I like this job, and I won't leave camp any more without your permission."[54]

But Durocher kept testing Rickey. Early in May, the Dodgers were scheduled to play an exhibition contest in Kingston, New York, and Dodgers public relations man Hal Parrott and some of the beat writers showed up for the night game. According to Parrott, "The ballpark lights were so poor you could barely read the scorecard." The game was of no import, and Durocher chose not to attend, which might not have been a problem except that Rickey and his son Branch Jr., nicknamed Twig, had traveled to Kingston to have a look at a few new prospects the Dodgers dressed for the exhibition. When Rickey noticed Durocher's absence, he was furious and suspended Durocher on the spot, making Clyde Sukeforth the manager.

When Durocher arrived the next day, Rickey wasted no time demanding to know why Leo had gone AWOL.

With hesitation he said, "I went to the race track!"

"If you had told me anything but the truth, you'd have been finished for good." Then, clenching his teeth, Rickey added: "I knew you were at the track."[55]

In one version of this story, Branch Jr., who was then working for his father and had overheard the whole conversation, came into his office after Leo had left, and smiled:

"I knew all along you wouldn't fire Leo, Dad," he said.

"You did, eh?" Rickey replied. "How did you know?"

"Because Leo is your favorite reclamation project, and if you fired him you would have to admit defeat."

Rickey smiled. "You are right, son."

Before the season began, the Dodgers lost more men to military service, and it looked as if the only way to plug the middle infield was for Durocher to play second base. On April 8, in an exhibition game against the Boston Red Sox in Brooklyn, he attempted a bare-handed catch of a wild throw from an eighteen-year-old rookie shortstop named Gene Mauch, which fractured his right thumb in two places. Mauch, whom Durocher was training as a middle infielder, said later, "I think he was happy about it, because he didn't have to play anymore."[56]

On April 14, 1944, the Dodgers and Phillies played a preseason exhibition game at Ebbets Field to benefit the Red Cross War Fund. The featured pregame attraction was crooner Frank Sinatra, who sang "Take Me Out to the Ball Game" as well as some of his hits accompanied by a grand piano that had been rolled onto the field and placed atop home plate. When Sinatra finished, Durocher and Freddie Fitzsimmons stepped up to the microphone to sing "You're Driving Me Crazy," accompanied by the Dodgers comic off-key Washtub Symphony. Durocher would later date this as the moment when he and the man they then called "the Voice" first became friends.[57]

The Dodgers lacked not only Durocher as an infielder, but Gene Mauch, who had played in the first five games of the season before he was off to serve in the armed forces. From the outset, the best that could be said of the 1944 team is that it was a patchwork of young men who should have been still learning their trade in the minors and old men who would have been long retired had it not been for the war. Given the manpower situation, Durocher and his coaches worked more and more as instructors. Mickey Owen later reported that Leo had become "more patient" as the war progressed—patient, that is, with his players, not with the umpires.[58]

In May, the Dodgers took the field in St. Louis in new satin road uniforms intended to shimmer under the lights of night baseball. The uniform was the color still known as Dodger Blue, with white piping on the shoulders and a white stripe down the legs. The blue caps featured a white visor. Dizzy Dean, who announced the Cardinals games, was dumbstruck: "There ain't nothing I can say." Cardinal shortstop Marty Marion said the Dodgers looked like a girls' softball team. An unnamed commentator said Durocher was "dressed as if he were ready to ride Pensive in the sixth race."[59]

On June 4, 1944, umpire Jocko Conlan threw Durocher out of a game for arguing a call. Durocher screamed obscenities at Conlan and, as was his style, kicked dirt on the umpire's pants. The confrontation prompted yet another salvo of glass bottles—those aimed at Conlon from the Brooklyn fans. Durocher was fined $50.[60]

Between June 28 and July 16, 1944, the Dodgers lost sixteen games in a row, leaving them with a 33–46 record. When the Cubs came to Brooklyn on July 25, the Dodgers lost the first game in the series 14–6, marking their twenty-second loss in twenty-five starts. They were tied with the Braves for last place. A large part of the problem was the loss of Pee Wee Reese. "Few people realize," Durocher told Grantland Rice, "what a good shortstop means to a ball club. The difference between a good shortstop and only a fair shortstop can mean 10 or 12 games."[61]

Durocher's expulsions took an unprecedented turn on August 18 during the first game of a twi-night doubleheader in Cincinnati when he was ejected after arguing a called strike with umpire Dusty Boggess. He then made the round of the bases, pleading to no avail with umpires Babe Pinelli and Lee Ballanfant, with whom he exchanged harsh words before finally leaving the field. After the game, Durocher barged into the umpire's dressing room to have the last word.

"You don't belong in here," said Ballanfant. "Get out."

"Who's going to make me?" said Durocher as he struck a defiant pose with his arms folded across his heaving chest. With that, he left the dressing room.[62] He was fined and suspended the following day for five days, after which he took a seat within four steps of the Brooklyn dugout and managed the game from there in clear violation of the rules.[63]

As the Dodgers kept losing, Leo became more and more of an attraction, as wire service photos of him fighting with umpires became a staple of sports pages across the country. Nobody could deny that many fans went to Ebbets Field just to see Leo in action. On September 25, the Dodgers lost their eighty-eighth game of the season in front of 1,583 paying fans at Ebbets Field out of a total of 2,207 attending. The disparity between the two numbers was largely because anyone bringing in ten pounds or more of scrap metal was given free admission. For Durocher, it was a celebratory moment, because the paid attendance had gone over 600,000, yielding him an immediate $5,000 cash bonus. At least one baseball writer, C. M. Gibbs of the *Baltimore Sun*, put into print what others must have been thinking when he asked his readers if Leo's "endless umpire baiting exhibitions" might have been staged to boost his bonus.[64]

Two days later, Leo was signed by Rickey for his seventh season. When it was announced to the press, one reporter asked Rickey if the contract would restrict any of Leo's outside activities, such as his growing popularity as a radio personality. "Leo is as free as any man in this room," Rickey responded.[65]

The war-depleted 1944 Dodgers finished in seventh place with a 63–91 record. Other than Dixie Walker, who led the league with a batting average of .357, and a handful of relief appearances by a promising eighteen-year-old named Ralph Branca, it was as poor a roster as the Dodgers had fielded in years; later some actually nominated it as the worst Dodger team of the twentieth century.

In the face of this, Durocher was in high spirits and expressed great optimism about the future of the team. Just after the 1944 World Series, Durocher granted an extensive interview to Bob Considine of the

International News Service in which he predicted that three seasons later, in 1947, the Dodgers would come out on top and stay on top for years to come—specifically, after that first pennant, six out of the next ten years. He said that Considine would not recognize the names of as many as half of the ballplayers that the Dodgers would build this dynasty with. "Some of them are in short pants now, others in uniform." He then drifted into hyperbole when he boasted: "We've got more young ballplayers ticketed right now than any other ball club ever had, and that goes for the Cardinals. We got so many players that baseball will have to start a lot of new leagues after the war to take care of them. We know exactly where they are, what they can do and what they'll be able to do by the time we need them. There's never been a more comprehensive system of rounding up young talent."[66]

Meanwhile, as more and more African-Americans entered the armed forces, the pressure to come to grips with Jim Crow on and off the field increased. On May 4, 1944, the two St. Louis ball clubs announced that their old policy of restricting Negroes to the bleachers at Sportsman's Park was being abandoned, and they could now purchase tickets and sit in any part of the stadium.[67]

What Durocher chose not to acknowledge in public was that the Dodgers were actively scouting Negro ballplayers. At Durocher's instigation, Silvio Garcia had been scouted by the Dodgers in 1943 and was scouted again in 1944 in Mexico but not signed. Then in 1945 O'Malley went to Cuba with a check for $25,000 to sign Garcia. "When I arrived in Havana," he later told Doc Young, "I learned that Silvio had been conscripted into the Cuban military and was in a pup tent on the Prado. We're looking for players to fill the void caused by the draft of U.S. athletes. Silvio already was in the Cuban Army."*[68]

On November 14, 1944, Leo's reputation took a hit, albeit not of his own making. New York district attorney Frank S. Hogan announced that his office was investigating a crooked dice game held in Durocher's apartment

---

* Another version of the Rickey rejection has it that when Rickey asked Garcia how he would handle racial taunts or being abused by another player because of the color of his skin, Garcia's response was short and simple: "I kill him." This version appears in a 2014 report from the Center for Negro League Baseball Research (*Forgotten Heroes: Silvio Garcia, Dr. Layton Revel and Luis Munoz*) and several other online accounts of Garcia's flirtation with the Dodgers that unfortunately are unsourced in the absence of further evidence, the story must be spiked as apocryphal. Another source claimed Rickey rejected him as a drinker.

the previous March 24, while he was managing Spring Training at West Point. The allegation was that George Raft used loaded dice to take $18,500 from Martin Shurin Jr., president of the Hudson Aircraft Company, which manufactured small aircraft parts. Shurin had initially taken the loss in stride, but exploded when the wife of one of the other players in the game came to Shurin and reported that he had been cheated and that her husband had been Raft's confederate and received a cut from the game's profits. The wife was also suing her husband for divorce.

Raft was quick to respond angrily, arguing that the charge was "ridiculous," pointing out that the game was on the level and that Shurin himself had goaded Raft into playing for high stakes. He also insisted that he came away from the game with $10,000, not the higher amount claimed by Shurin. Raft added that he had had a hard time collecting the debt, but when he did get the money, which was paid in checks, he reported it on his income tax.

Raft regretted that the name of Leo Durocher, "one of my best friends and one of the finest fellows I've ever known," had been dragged into something with which he had no connection. Raft said he planned to sue Shurin for slander, vowing to turn over every cent of his winnings to charity. "No penny pinching big shot's gonna make a sucker outta Raft."[69]

Durocher seemed more amused than appalled—as if he were a willing cameo player in a George Raft film. No formal action was taken against Raft, and no slander lawsuit was initiated. Yet, despite his apparent innocence, Durocher's name was now linked to an allegedly crooked dice game.[70]

The Durocher-Raft relationship was now more newsworthy than before the Shurin incident. Irv Kupcinet of the *Chicago Sun Times* was one of the columnists who kept his eye on these two. "Their friends are eagerly awaiting the next meeting of George Raft and Leo Durocher. They were Damon-Pythias buddies until a few weeks ago when Raft was accused of using loaded dice in Durocher's apartment."[71]

On November 25, 1944, with the loaded-dice story still in the news, Judge Landis passed away after having just been elected to another seven year term as Commissioner. Two weeks after his death, he was voted into the National Baseball Hall of Fame by a special vote. For Durocher, the man who called himself "the high commissioner" had been more of a blessing than a curse. As both judge and jury in baseball matters, Landis had been quick to discipline Durocher, but also quick to give him another chance. One object that would be kept and turned over to the next commissioner was the file on Durocher, which contained information that was anything but flattering.

Durocher headed off to Europe in December 1944 to entertain the U.S. troops in the Mediterranean war zones. This tour—entitled *Here's the Pitch*—was all about baseball and did not include Danny Kaye or any other entertainers. The man in charge of the tour was Tom Meany, sports editor of the newspaper *PM*. Others in the touring group included Joe Medwick of the Giants and Nick Etten of the Yankees. The small troupe drew audiences as large as 9,500 and as little as zero in one locale where the mud was waist-deep and the troops couldn't get through. The general routine was to show films of the 1944 World Series and then discuss baseball and answer questions. One group in northern Italy was cheated out of seeing the film because the Germans had captured the movie projector and the power generator that afternoon. The show went on in a blacked-out tent, and questions were answered in the dark. As was the custom, autographed baseballs were given out. Etten commented: "I'm not sure but that last fellow I gave a ball to was Kesselring"—the Nazi field marshal in charge in Italy.[72]

"Neither Etten, Medwick, nor I hold any illusions about our talents," Meany wrote in *PM* on his return.

> We just got up and talked and did the best we could. And then we turned Leo loose. He never spoke less than a half-hour, usually about forty-five minutes. He confined himself to two stories, but Durocher's stories, like his disputes with umpires, have a way of running on and on. Durocher is an extrovert, pure and simple. Give him an audience, and he's off . . . All told, I must have heard the stories a hundred times before the trip was over, but I never failed to enjoy them. And, which was more important, neither did the men. When I looked out and saw the soldiers roaring with laughter as Leo strutted his stuff, I felt that it was going to be pretty hard to second-guess him next summer. Your GI is tough to fool. He's seen a lot and his senses have been sharpened. He can spot the phony a mile away. Sincerity becomes pretty important when you're away from home, and Durocher had to have something on the ball to get the reception he did.

Durocher's trick in setting up his audiences was to come onstage after Meany introduced him and push the microphone away with disdain, bellowing: "Who ever heard of a guy from Brooklyn needing a mike?" The response was intensified if there were a few Brooklynites in the crowd, and as Meany reported, "It seemed there invariably were."[73]

By the time the tour ended, they had covered twenty thousand miles and played to seventy thousand soldiers in a period of forty-two days. The one thing they had missed was an audience with Pope Pius XII. As they were leaving for the States, Meany had asked Durocher if he thought there was any chance of such an audience, and Durocher said, "I hope we do because I know the Pope."

"You what?" Meany reacted.

"I know the Pope" was Leo's calm reply. "I met him out in St. Louis in 1934 at Archbishop Glennon's house when he was over here as Cardinal Pacelli, the Papal delegate."

Meany confirmed the story and retold it later to show how Durocher could make good on his boasts, as the group did get its semiprivate audience with the pope when they were in Rome. Many years later, Durocher would claim that Medwick snuck two baseballs into the audience, one of which he got the pope to autograph. "Can you believe that? Getting the Pope to autograph a baseball. That Medwick was some crazy (bleep)."[74]

Pulling a few strings, Durocher was able to get back in time for the start of Spring Training at Bear Mountain. Once there, he looked over his club and said to himself, "Leo, what was your big hurry?"[75]

CHAPTER 8

Game Changer

SHORTLY BEFORE NOON ON APRIL 6, 1945, Joe Bostic, sports editor of the Harlem newspaper *The People's Voice*, arrived unannounced at the Dodgers' Spring Training camp at West Point accompanied by Jimmy Smith of the *Courier-Journal* and Nate Low of the *Daily Worker*. They were accompanied by two Negro league veterans, pitcher Terris McDuffie and first baseman Dave "Showboat" Thomas, hoping for a tryout.

Bostic told Harold Parrott, now the Dodgers traveling secretary, that he wanted to speak to team president Rickey about scheduling a tryout for these uninvited and unannounced ballplayers. Parrott said Rickey couldn't be disturbed, because he was watching a game at another practice field at the academy. Parrott then returned with Bob Finch, Rickey's top assistant, who said the team gave tryouts only to players who had invitations. Bostic asked why the team had never invited a black player. Finch had no answer. He told Bostic that Rickey would discuss the matter over lunch.

At about 2:30 P.M. Bostic and the ballplayers were escorted to a dining room where they were met with a tirade from Rickey, who said that he would grant the tryout but that he forbade other writers from attending. He also made it clear that showing up without notice was a bad idea. "I'm more for your cause than anybody else you know," he said, "but you are making a mistake using force."

Rickey asked that nobody in the room discuss the particulars of the meeting with the press, but both the Associated Press and United Press were on the story immediately. Rickey gave no details, but he said unequivocally "that I will look at any ball players of any age, color or creed, even Eskimos or members of the cabinet when I please." He added that he was ready to hire Negro talent, had the backing of the board and full ownership group, and was already thinking of bringing Negro teams into Brooklyn to play at Ebbets Field.[1]

Bostic was immediately on the phone to sports columnist Al Laney of the *New York Herald Tribune* with the full story. In his "Views of Sports" column the next morning, Laney took delight in writing how Bostic had surprised Rickey, leaving speechless the loquacious executive, whose long news conferences had been dubbed "the cave of winds" by sportswriters. "It would have been a real pleasure to be at Bear Mountain yesterday," Laney said. "To catch Brother Rickey thus with his guard down was an extraordinary achievement. The situation had elements of immortal comedy."[2]

Comedy it was not. Bostic's noon meeting with Rickey the next day was no more pleasant than the first meeting. "I was thoroughly raked over the coals for breaking the agreement not to tell anybody about the tryout so that it would be held in comparative privacy," Bostic said.

To Durocher came the unenviable task of trying out two journeymen who were old and seemed to lack the skill to make it in the major leagues. After the workout, Rickey issued a personal report, as he did for all prospects. McDuffie's control was "very good," wrote Rickey, trying to be kind. "His fast ball is good and his curve is good. I believe he can get a better change." The report also included Durocher's comment that he had a dozen kids with more stuff and was not interested in a thirty-two-year-old with no major league experience. Their take on Thomas was even more lukewarm. "He showed power. But on a change of speed was very weak. I would not be interested if he were 24 instead of 34."*

Then, and in the future when the story of baseball integration was retold, Durocher was cast in an unfavorable light because of the frankness he used in dismissing these two.

While Bostic was confronting Rickey at Bear Mountain, a Boston city councilman, Isadore Muchnick, told the Red Sox he would revoke their license to play games on Sundays if they did not consider at least one black player. *Pittsburgh Courier* sports editor Wendell Smith, who had been calling for the integration of baseball for nearly a decade, recruited three

---

* Neither Thomas nor McDuffie ever made the majors. Thomas had one last splendid season with the New York Cubans in 1946, hitting .393 and retiring. McDuffie had several more good years in the Negro leagues and finished his career in 1954 with one season in the minors, going 3–4 for Dallas of the Texas League.

high-quality ballplayers—Jackie Robinson, Sam Jethroe, and Marvin Williams—and the Red Sox agreed to look at them.[3]

Whereas Rickey treated McDuffie and Thomas like any other prospect, the Red Sox assigned high school pitchers to throw batting practice to Robinson, Jethroe, and Williams. Whereas Rickey scrutinized the abilities of McDuffie and Thomas, Red Sox officials said nothing to the players, dismissing them with instructions to put their home addresses on postcards that would be mailed to them if and when they were needed.

Smith called Rickey from Boston to tell them how Robinson had excelled in his tryout. He asked Rickey if he could detour to Brooklyn to discuss Robinson. "Jackie Robinson! I knew he was an All-American football player and an All-American basketball player," Rickey explained. "But I didn't know he played baseball." The two met, talked about Robinson and other Negro players, and promised to keep in touch. Rickey began to scout Robinson with the full awareness of Durocher.[4]

On April 18, 1945, during the second game of the season, Durocher took his last official at-bat as a major leaguer. It was his 1,637th game and 5,829th big league plate appearance, the first having come twenty-five years earlier. His lifetime batting average was .247.

In the American League, having returned from active duty, Larry MacPhail was settling into his new job as president of the New York Yankees. Prior to his military discharge, MacPhail had been part of a group that bought the team, and he was now a co-owner. In his new job, he took an active role in the search for a new baseball commissioner and quickly got behind the candidacy of Albert "Happy" Chandler, a sitting United States senator from Kentucky, to succeed the late Judge Landis.

The initial front-runner for the post had been National League president Ford Frick, whose candidacy encountered broad support but faced opposition from Philip Wrigley, owner of the Chicago Cubs, and Warren Giles, the owner of the Cincinnati Reds, for a reason or reasons never made public. Rickey was Frick's strongest supporter, while MacPhail led the fight for Chandler.*[5]

---

* In 1945, members of the United States Senate earned around $10,000; the baseball commissioner's post paid $50,000, which was a considerable enticement for Chandler, who was not the only politician to be considered for the job. A member of the Chandler family later confirmed that the salary boost made the decision to take the commissionership a "no-brainer."

When the team owners gathered in Chicago on April 24 to consider a replacement for Landis, Chandler's name was not even on the initial short list of candidates; but as others were ruled out, Chandler moved up the list. Deadlocked, the owners took an informal vote, and Chandler was among the top three candidates. After further balloting, he received enough votes from the owners to become the new commissioner. He was a Democrat and a graduate of Harvard Law School who had served as a private in the First World War. That he was of a different caste and cut than Landis was summed up in the fact that everybody called Chandler by his apt nickname, "Happy."

Within hours of his election, Durocher sent a telegram to Chandler: "Butch Nieman hit ninth-inning homer that beat me (Tuesday.) Hereby file first protest. What do you intend to do about it?" Chandler went along with the gag and announced he would give the game to the Boston Braves. Nieman had hit a homer with two men on in the ninth inning of the game in question, giving the Braves an 8–6 victory. Durocher seemed to be testing Chandler to see where his limits lay. Sending such a gag message to Landis would have probably invited a stern rebuke.

Chandler was not immediately popular in his new post. When he announced his plan to relocate the commissioner's office from Chicago to Cincinnati because it was much closer to his home in Versailles, Kentucky, both writers and team owners expressed disappointment. Chicago was central, with a team from each league. Cincinnati was not. One of his first spats was with his benefactor MacPhail, whom he told not to raise ticket prices for the 1946 season. MacPhail said that Chandler was "out of order," and he raised them anyhow.[6]

In May, Rickey announced the formation of a new franchise, the Brooklyn Brown Dodgers, and a new Negro league, the United States League. He then dispatched his best talent hunters to observe black ballplayers, ostensibly for the Brown Dodgers, but in reality for the Brooklyn National League club. The subterfuge was effective, as many of the men scouted and/or contacted by Rickey as potential Brooklyn Dodgers thought they were being looked at for the Brown Dodgers. One such candidate was Roy Campanella.

Although Chandler would not actually take office until November 1, when his resignation from the Senate became official, he soon had a matter to keep his eye on. It centered around Durocher, who was already on his watch list as a troublemaker from his days in Kentucky when Durocher was with

Cincinnati. Toward the end of a night game at Ebbets Field on June 9, a young war veteran named John Christian, who had been heckling Durocher and the Dodgers all night, left the park with a number of bruises and a broken jaw and headed to Kings County Hospital for treatment. The following day, Christian filed a criminal complaint against Leo and a special policeman named Joseph Moore, who were brought before him in his hospital bed where they were identified as the assailants. The two men were arrested and jailed and then released on a $1,000 bond set by Judge Samuel S. Leibowitz, who was known for having been the lawyer for the Scottsboro Boys, nine southern African-American youths who were falsely accused of rape and sentenced to death in Alabama in 1931. Durocher had missed the game that afternoon, and when bail had been posted, a call went out in the press box: "He's been sprung."

The story hit the newspapers the next morning. The *Brooklyn Eagle* noted that Christian, an employee of the U.S. Customs Service, had been razzing Durocher and the Dodgers from the mezzanine level of the grandstand from the beginning of the season. It was also noted that Christian had been honorably discharged from the Army with a knee injury. Branch Rickey said that he didn't think the charges would amount to anything.

But they did amount to something. On June 19, the case came to court, but it was postponed because Christian's jaw was still wired shut, and he could not speak distinctly. On July 9, the case was postponed again as Christian was back in the hospital and his jaw was still wired. Finally, on August 7, the case was heard, and the court decided that it would next go to a grand jury.[7]

But the Durocher case was lost in the news. The day before his court appearance, an American B-29 bomber dropped the world's first deployed atomic bomb over the Japanese city of Hiroshima. The explosion wiped out 90 percent of the city and immediately killed eighty thousand people. Tens of thousands more would later die of radiation exposure. Three days later, a second B-29 dropped another A-bomb on Nagasaki, killing an estimated forty thousand people.

On August 14, crowds across the nation celebrated Japan's surrender. More than a million people gathered in New York's Times Square. The impromptu block party stretched from Fortieth to Fifty-Second streets. A frenzy of hugging and dancing ensued that came to be symbolized by a *Life* magazine photograph of a young sailor's passionate kiss of a nurse in a crisp white uniform.

On September 7, Durocher was brought back to Brooklyn to be arraigned before a grand jury for the indictment charging him with assault in connection with the beating of John Christian on June 9. The *Brooklyn Eagle* sent a reporter to New York Municipal Airport to meet Durocher, who had returned from Pittsburgh for the arraignment. The reporter noted that Leo, after giving no comment to all queries, was "hustled away in the company of two blondes." The grand jury decided that the case would go to a full jury trial in criminal court with a date to be determined.[8]

The Dodgers ended up in third place with a solid 87–67 season. When the season was over, Eddie Dyer, manager of the St. Louis Cardinals, with an eye on players returning from military service and fresh talent in the pipeline, named the Dodgers as the team to beat in 1946, despite the fact that the team had finished in third place eleven games out of first.

AT THE END of the 1945 season, Durocher's overseas USO trip with Danny Kaye was suddenly on again. This was to be the first of many postwar star-studded shows sent to the war zones of Asia in the days immediately following V-J Day. Upon hearing this news, the Brooklyn district attorney's office again postponed his jury trial for criminal assault until Leo's return from Asia. Leo's overseas trip had been approved by none other than General Douglas MacArthur, who was in charge of the occupation of Japan.

Durocher left Philadelphia after the last game of the season and linked up with Kaye in Los Angeles. They then flew on to Manila with a third man, an accordionist, and arrived on October 4. They performed multiple shows in the Philippines, Guam, the Marshall Islands, and the Japanese island of Okinawa, then went to Tokyo to entertain the American occupation forces and gave their first show at the half-completed Meiji Shrine Stadium, which had been the planned site of the 1940 Olympics. In Tokyo, Leo met with Sotaro Suzuki, the newspaperman who had set up the 1934 baseball tour that brought Babe Ruth and Lou Gehrig to Japan. Leo got the sense that the Japanese were eager to start playing baseball again. While in Tokyo, Kaye and Durocher also had a chance to meet face to face with General MacArthur, who surprised them with his knowledge of both show business and baseball.[9]

At every venue, Durocher predicted that the Yankees and Cardinals would win the 1946 pennants but to look out for the Dodgers in 1947 when the team would be refreshed and rebuilt. While Durocher was still in Japan, on October 23, Jackie Robinson was signed by the Dodgers. The historic first signing of a Negro player, which took place in Montreal, called for Robinson to play with the Montreal Royals of the International League for the 1946 season. He was to be paid a $3,500 cash bonus and $600 per month in salary.[10]

Durocher was fully aware that the Dodgers were scouting Robinson and knew that Rickey wanted to bring him aboard, but he first heard about the actual signing when he read about it in the Asian edition of *Stars and Stripes*, the daily newspaper of the American armed forces. From that point forward, the GIs wanted to know more about Robinson and to get Durocher's take on the signing.

"If he's good enough to play Major League Baseball, that's all I care about" was Durocher's standard response, often adding, "I have never seen him play baseball, but I saw him play football, and if he is as good at baseball as he was at that, I'm for him."

Durocher reported that the soldiers he met who asked about Robinson thought it was "really great" that the Dodgers had signed a Negro ballplayer. One Army major told Durocher he thought signing Robinson was the greatest thing that could happen to the game of baseball. The fact that Robinson had seen military service, that Durocher seemed keen on the idea, and that blacks had been in combat in the South Pacific and were scattered through these GI audiences, contributed to this high level of approval. Baseball—or more commonly fast-pitch softball—had already been racially integrated in the combat zones. Larry Doby, an African-American player who would immediately follow Robinson into the big leagues and integrate the American League, was still on duty in the South Pacific when Robinson signed. Doby played softball and basketball with Billy Goodman, who went on to a career with the Red Sox, and with Washington Senators veteran Mickey Vernon, with whom Doby established a lifelong friendship.*[11]

In America, Durocher's name was invoked in the Robinson debate—but sometimes in a less-than-heroic context. Rumors were afloat that Robinson

---

* The three men played together on Mog-Mog in the Ulithi Atoll in the Pacific, a tiny fog-shrouded speck of a place that one veteran later said reminded him of the "eerie island in the movie *King Kong*."

might not have been a good choice to represent his race and that he was a "trouble-maker." Will Connolly of the *San Francisco Chronicle* confronted the issue, insisting that Robinson's personality, whether agreeable or disagreeable, should not be the basis for judging him. "Baseball," he wrote, "embraces a whole sloth of disagreeable whites,* and the more obnoxious they are, the more publicized they become as 'characters' and the higher the salaries they command because of their orneriness, as witness Lippy Leo Durocher, who, with ironic appropriateness, may one day manage Robinson at Ebbets Field."[12]

Not all of the reaction to the Robinson signing was positive. The man who headed the minor leagues, William Bramham, called Rickey a "carpetbagger." Durocher's own right fielder, Dixie Walker, said of the Montreal signing, "As long as he's not with the Dodgers, I'm not worried."[13]

Before the tour was over, Kaye and Durocher had covered thirty-six thousand miles and given more than ninety-eight shows, including one close to Hiroshima, where they got to fly over the city at one hundred feet to see the unbelievable devastation. In all, they had entertained 275,000 troops.[14] On their return from Asia, the two men landed in Los Angeles, and Kaye placed a call to gossip columnist Hedda Hopper to report that Durocher had gotten bigger and better laughs with his baseball stories than he had with his scripted gags. By Kaye's account, the showstopper had been their song-and-dance routine and Leo's line "This is what killed vaudeville."[15]

Leo headed straight from the airport to George Raft's house, where he brought in a barber to shave his beard and chop off his long hair. Raft's bodyguard Killer Gray commented on his arrival, "He looks so tough he scared even me."[16]

For Leo, the trip and its attendant publicity set him up as bone fide celebrity both inside and outside the game of baseball. After the trip to Asia, he was a constant network radio guest and a major fund-raiser for war bonds, peaking at the Victory Bond Show at Madison Square Garden in Manhattan on December 3, which was staged to raise $8 million in war bond purchases. Leo was a headliner in a list that also included Bing Crosby, Frank Sinatra, Danny Kaye, Duke Ellington, and Joe E. Brown. The only other baseball names on the marquee were Joe DiMaggio and Hank

---

* Here Connolly is employing a seldom-used application of *sloth*, which is a collective noun for a pack of bears.

Greenberg, who, like Leo, were known to people who had never been to a baseball game.* [17]

On January 2, 1946, Durocher signed a new one-year contract with the Dodgers despite the criminal charges pending against him. Rickey asked him to stay in Brooklyn to overhaul the new team. Perhaps Rickey implied that Durocher would be an ideal manager once a Negro player joined the team. Rickey understood intuitively and correctly that Durocher would fight for one of his own guys on the field, regardless of color, creed, or anything else extraneous to the winning of ballgames.

Out of public view, opposition was building to racial integration, and Rickey and Durocher were well aware of it. Weeks before the signing, Larry MacPhail, in his role as president of the New York Yankees and co-owner of the team, sent a letter to a committee appointed by New York City mayor Fiorello La Guardia to study baseball's color line. A copy of the letter was sent to all teams in both leagues in official American League envelopes. The letter said, in short, that black athletes simply didn't have what it takes to play in the big leagues. "There are few, if any, negro players who could qualify for play in the major leagues at this time. A major league player must have something besides natural ability."†

MacPhail's letter showed that the Yankee executive had little use for what he called "political and social minded drum-beaters." He claimed they did not know anything about baseball and didn't care about the national

---

* Durocher was so popular, he was built into jokes, such as this one told by Jack Troy in his *Atlanta Constitution* column, which he said was a favorite of returning servicemen:

"A horse showed up one day in Brooklyn: asked Durocher for permission to work out with the Bums. Leo, surprised by a talking horse, agreed. The horse was a sensation at all infield positions, fielding and throwing expertly. Came batting practice and line drives whistled over the fence. The horse could really hit. Durocher now knew he had something the fans of Brooklyn would love: a baseball-playing horse.

And so the horse was in the lineup one day. All went well. The Dodgers put men on base and then the horse came up and drove the pitch between center and right. As the runners raced around the sacks the horse stood there and watched.

'Run, run, you fool!' Durocher yelled from the coaching lines.

'Run? Listen Leo, if I could run,' the horse replied, 'I'd be over at Belmont Park.'" (*Atlanta Constitution*, June 17, 1945, p. 8-C)

† MacPhail chose not to capitalize the word *Negro*, which was standard style at the time. To capitalize the word was seen as one of the few ways in which respect was shown to Americans of color.

pastime. "They have singled out Organized Baseball for attack because it offers a good publicity medium for propaganda," the report said. Integration, MacPhail argued, would also cost major league teams substantial revenue: "Negro league clubs rent their parks in most cities from clubs in Organized Baseball," the report said. "The Yankee Organization, alone, nets nearly $100,000 per year from rentals and concessions in connection with Negro league games at Yankee Stadium in New York, and at their minor league stadiums in Kansas City, Newark and Norfolk."

MacPhail then added: "In conclusion: I have no hesitancy in saying that the Yankees have no intention of signing negro players under contract or reservation to negro clubs."*

At the same time as Durocher signed, an announcement was made that he had settled the civil suit filed by John Christian. Leo was first reported to have paid damages of $5,000, later revealed to be $6,750. One published rumor claimed that Danny Kaye had helped. Another suggested that Sidney Weil had also added to the fund. As was to be become public later, settling the civil suit was a major condition for Durocher getting a new contract.

On January 16, Judge Louis Goldstein declared that the many postponements of Durocher's criminal trial had been kicked around for so long that it was bordering on a "public scandal" and set a date for March 6. Durocher and Joseph Moore showed up on the sixth, but the lawyers representing the two men in a common defense got the trial postponed until April 22 because a number of the defense's key witnesses—including Dressen, Coach John "Red" Corriden, Augie Galan, and pitcher Curt Davis—were in Florida with the Dodgers in Spring Training. Given that this was a criminal case, it was clear that Durocher was now being given unusual latitude as to when the case would actually be tried.

Earlier that month, Commissioner Chandler was in Tampa delivering his first speech to major league teams. His message was loud and clear: Keep away from gamblers. He explained: "Baseball will lead the way in the big post-war sports boom in our country and it is up to you young men to make sure the game is kept on the highest moral plane." Later that day, word reached Chandler that two leading sluggers—Ted Williams of the Red Sox and Dick Wakefield of the Detroit Tigers—had bet each other $1,000

---

* An original copy of this letter was sold in 2015 at auction for $9,235.19 to the Negro Leagues Museum in Kansas City.

on who would have the most hits during the regular season. Chandler repeated his no-gambling edict, and the two players insisted that they were "only kidding."[18]

On the same day that Chandler began his anti-gambling tour of the training camps, Jackie Robinson arrived with Rachel, his wife of three weeks, in Daytona Beach after a thirty-six-hour journey from his home in Los Angeles. During the trip, they were denied entry to white-only restaurants and hotels and were twice bumped from planes and replaced with white passengers. At one point, Robinson was ordered to the back of a Greyhound bus by the driver who called him "boy." By the time Robinson reached Daytona Beach, he wanted to quit what was called "baseball's great experiment," but two journalists, Wendell Smith and Billy Rowe, working for the black newspaper, the *Pittsburgh Courier*, convinced him that he had to endure certain indignities so other blacks could have opportunities that were now closed to them.

On March 17, Robinson was penciled into the Montreal starting lineup for an afternoon game against the Dodgers in downtown Daytona Beach. It was to be Robinson's second exhibition game against a major league team. He told reporters that he had played in an earlier exhibition game with players from the Chicago White Sox when a junior college student in Pasadena.*

As was the custom, black journalists were denied press credentials and were forced into a special section down the right-field line more than one hundred feet from home plate. Photographer Rowe was therefore at a disadvantage in trying to document this special day. Durocher spotted him and, so that all could hear, invited him down to the dugout to get a proper picture of Robinson. As Rowe began to walk across the field, someone in the white section of the segregated bleachers yelled, "Get that nigger out of there!"

Rowe froze, but Durocher motioned for him to keep walking. Rowe got his pictures, and Durocher went to the ballpark officials and demanded the removal of the spectator. Moments later, a man was escorted from the ballpark. "I don't know if it was the right guy or not, but they made somebody leave," Rowe remembered with a smile some years later.[19]

Robinson failed at the plate that first day, but Durocher was the first to

---

* In 1942 Robinson requested a tryout at a White Sox training camp in Pasadena, California. Robinson impressed White Sox manager Jimmy Dykes but nothing came of the event.

come to his defense. "Although Robinson didn't get a hit today, he looked like a real ballplayer out there," he told Wendell Smith of the *Courier*. "Don't forget he was under terrific pressure. He was cast in the middle of a situation that neither he nor the fans had ever experienced before. But he came through it like a champion. He's a ballplayer." Through Spring Training, it was Durocher—not Rickey or O'Malley—who made it clear that Robinson would get a trial with Brooklyn in 1947 "if not sooner" in Durocher's words.[20]

At the end of Spring Training, the issue of returning to Daytona Beach the following spring was broached. In a clear allusion to his inability to house and feed black and white players under the same hotel roof, Durocher told the *Daytona Beach Evening News* that he was opposed to a return to the city because he did not like having his players spread all over the place. "I like to keep my eye on my players at night," he said. "They're down here to train and it's my business to see that they behave themselves and stay in shape."[21]

The 1946 home opener was everything Durocher and Rickey could have hoped for, as evidenced by Roscoe McGowen's lead in his coverage of the game for *The New York Times*: "Leo Durocher's Gashouse kids ran wild in Ebbets Field yesterday as the new Dodgers blew off the home opening lid with a decisive trouncing of Mel Ott's Giants."

The following day, April 19, the postponements for the assault trial were over, and Leo was ordered to appear in court the next Monday. After a half dozen delays, the wheels of justice suddenly moved quickly. A jury of twelve men—eleven of whom identified themselves as Dodger fans—was picked to judge the two men on the charge of second-degree assault. The Associated Press reported that the man selected to be the jury foreman was an accounting clerk who was "a great admirer" of Leo Durocher but, after making the statement, was challenged and replaced by another prospective juror who said "a Brooklyn Dodger can do no wrong."

If found guilty, the maximum penalty would have been five years in prison and a fine of $1,000. Durocher and Moore faced the very real possibility of having to go—as the newspapers then liked to put it—"up the river to Sing Sing," the state prison on the Hudson River in Ossining, New York. As if there were any question, the *Brooklyn Eagle* reminded its readers that if Durocher were not acquitted, he faced lifetime banishment from baseball by Happy Chandler, who was keeping an eagle eye on the trial.[22]

Durocher appeared in court in a light-gray suit and listened attentively as

John Christian testified that Moore had hit him with a black object—presumably a blackjack—and that Durocher had punched him in the jaw. He said that he ran out of the room where he had been taken but Durocher again began to beat him with his fists, and that the attack was now unrestrained and that Moore cried out, "What are you doing, Leo? What are you doing? Let him go."[23]

Christian testified that, after the attack, Moore escorted him to a first aid station for immediate treatment and then escorted him through the gates, warning him never to return. Christian then went to the hospital where his jaw was wired and remained for seven days.

Under cross-examination, Christian admitted that he might have called Durocher a thief but never accused him of throwing a game. Durocher's lawyer also got Christian to admit that he had made a $5 bet at odds of two to one against the Dodgers, who that night handed the Phillies a one-sided beating.

"Wasn't that bet the cause of your yelling and calling Durocher a bum and a crook?" Leo's attorney, Hyman Barshay, asked him.

"Not exactly," Christian responded. "I yelled at the other players too."

Christian was asked by the defense if he had accepted Durocher's civil settlement as "easy cabbage," and he denied the accusation.

Jacob Garfinkel, a former Army sergeant who was sitting with Christian during the game in question, then testified that he had seen Durocher "raining blows" on Christian after he left the room behind the dugout. He added that he did not report it to police at the time, because he was then stationed at West Point, where the Dodgers trained, and feared that "Durocher might go to the general and make a report on me." Under cross-examination by the defense, Garfinkel admitted that the two-hundred-pound-plus Christian had actually fended off Durocher's blows. When the prosecution rested, the jury was excused while Durocher's lawyer argued to have the case dismissed, but the motion was denied.[24]

As all of this was going on, Ed Hand pitched a no-hit game for the Dodgers, winning 5–0 over the Boston Braves. The team, now 6–1, was managed by Chuck Dressen while Durocher was in the courtroom.[25]

The next day, Leo, who was under oath and speaking in a clear, firm voice, portrayed Christian as a loudmouthed and abusive pest who had bedeviled his players before the night in question. Leo focused on Christian's prior attacks on his rookie third baseman Bill Hart. On one occasion, while Leo was coaching at third, Christian yelled that Leo should take Hart out of the game and send him back to New Orleans where he came from. "Send his wife back too," he added. "She's running around with other men." Durocher said Hart turned white as paper. "He was so jittery, I had to take him out of the game." On the night of the alleged assault, Durocher said that Christian had started in again on Hart as well as pitcher Curt Davis, whom he accused of throwing the game in the fifth inning. Durocher also accused Christian of hurling insults at an umpire who had made a disputed call on a hit-and-run play, which was also upsetting to Davis.

Leo, unsurprisingly, remembered what happened next differently from what Christian had testified. Christian was escorted by Moore to a small room behind the dugout where Durocher asked: "Have you a mother? Well, how would you like it if . . . I went to your house and called her the names you have been shouting out tonight?"

Durocher then claimed Christian came back with an obscenity. Leo said at that point: "I ran at him. I saw him fall against a wall. He fell into a water trough. I did not pursue him." He then added dolefully, "I don't know what might have happened if I had gotten my hands on him."

When asked about his willingness to settle the civil suit, Durocher said that he had paid the $6,750 to Christian to settle because the team warned him through his attorney that he would not be re-signed unless the issue was resolved. His attorney argued that having settled the civil suit had nothing to do with Leo's guilt or innocence.

At the close of testimony on the evening before the case was handed to the jury, Bob Considine wrote: "Brooklyn crime authorities, who haven't been as aroused over a court case since the trials of Murder, Inc. hoodlums, were almost unanimous in predicting that Leo would be cleared."[26]

The jury was out thirty-eight minutes, and after just one vote for each man, Durocher and Moore were found not guilty. When the jury foreman handed the verdict to Judge Louis Goldstein, he termed it "fair and just" and then launched into a lecture on the sanctity of the game. "I am glad for the sake of the Brooklyn baseball team that their manager has been vindicated and that no discredit has been placed upon the great American game of baseball."

With that, Durocher was mobbed by supporters, some 150 of whom were in the courtroom, another three hundred in the hallway, and thousands in the streets outside. They shook his hand and pounded him on the back. Neither Durocher's attorneys nor the prosecution had any comment on the verdict, but Leo insisted that he knew all along he would be cleared and added with a grin, "I had better luck here than I do with the jury on the ballfield, didn't I?"[27]

A few days later, Branch Rickey praised Durocher at a Brooklyn meeting of Rotary International, declaring, "We are a team of ferocious gentlemen," and vowed to stand as a unit against indecent and vulgar remarks from the stands. Remarkably, one of the most respected writers in the business seemed to use the verdict as an excuse to give an opinion on those, like Christian, who heap verbal abuse on athletes. Stanley Woodward, sports editor of the *New York Herald Tribune*, wrote of fans who insulted players and umpires: "Being law-abiding we hesitate to reveal the secret conviction that all of them should have their jaws broken in three places." Woodward also pointed out that one of Durocher's key arguments—that pitcher Curt Davis was visibly shaken by Christian's taunts—was invalid because Davis did not pitch that day. Woodward quoted the Associated Press box score for the game and ended the column with the line "No, Mr. District Attorney, Davis didn't play." Not only had Davis not played, but he did not testify, even though the need to have him as a witness was one of the reasons that Durocher got the postponement from March to April.[28]

On July 5, 1946, the Brooklyn Dodgers were in first place in the National League. Their archrivals, the New York Giants, were in seventh place—next to last. As his team was about to play the Giants at the Polo Grounds, Durocher held court for a group of sportswriters. Although the Giants had beaten his team the day before, Durocher ridiculed their pathetic record and dinky home runs. Red Barber asked Durocher why he didn't admit that the Giants' home runs were as good as anyone's. "Why don't you be a nice guy for a change?" he asked.

Durocher leaped to his feet. "A nice guy?" he shouted. "A nice guy! I've been around in baseball for a long time and I've known a lot of nice guys. But I never saw a nice guy who was any good when you needed him. Go up to one of those nice guys some time when you need a hundred to get you out of a jam and he'll always give you that, 'Sorry, pal. I'd like to help you but things are not going so good at the ranch.' That's what they'll give you, those nice guys. I'll take the guys who ain't nice. The guys who would put you in a cement mixer if they felt like it. But you get in a jam and you don't have to go to them. They'll come looking for you and say, 'How much do you need?'"

Winking to his colleagues, a reporter asked Durocher if he was a nice guy. "No," said the Dodgers manager. "Nobody ever called me that."

Durocher pointed at the Giants' dugout, saying: "Nice guys! Look over there. Do you know a nicer guy than Mel Ott? Or any of the other Giants? Why they're the nicest guys in the world! And where are they? In seventh place! The nice guys over there are in seventh place. Well let them come and get me." He waved contemptuously toward the other dugout. "The nice guys are all over there. In seventh place." The exchange was reported by Frank Graham of the *New York Journal-American*, who devoted his entire Graham's "Corner" column of July 6 to it. Quickly, the quote morphed into "Nice guys finish last."*[29]

THE 1946 NATIONAL League season went down to the wire, and the Dodgers and Cardinals tied at the end of the season with identical 96–58 records. The tie was seen as a triumph for Durocher, as the Cardinals were considered a stronger team. Jesse Linthicum, sports editor of the *Baltimore Sun*, observed that Leo Durocher had made a big difference in the play of his team. "The Dodger manager turned in baseball's outstanding job . . . Somehow," Linthicum added, "Durocher was able to keep his players battling into the ninth inning, even when the fans were exiting the ballpark."

Because of the tie, a best-of-three-games playoff was ordered: the first tie-breaker series in major league history. In the opening game, played at Sportsman's Park in St. Louis, Durocher used Ralph Branca, who in his last outing against the Cardinals had pitched a three-hit shutout. Enos Slaughter and twenty-year-old rookie Joe Garagiola each drove in a run with a single in a two-run third inning that gave the Cardinals a 4–2 win.[30]

Then the playoff moved to Brooklyn, where St. Louis won the pennant 8–4 in the 156th game of the season. Durocher was defiant in defeat, telling his players that they had done a better job than the Cards. "Where'd you think we'd finish up in the spring?" he asked a group of reporters after the loss. "We had a bunch of kids and old men. They did a helluva job and I'm proud as hell of all of them."†[31]

---

* Although he originally claimed he had been misquoted, Durocher was soon proud of the misquotation, and he said years later that the line "has got me into *Bartlett's Quotations*— page 1059, between John Betjeman and Wystan Hugh Auden—and will be remembered long after I have been forgotten. Just who the hell were Betjeman and Auden anyway?"

† The tie-breaker games—the 155th and 156th of the regular season for both teams—counted in the regular-season statistics.

The Cardinals faced the Boston Red Sox in the World Series and took the championship in seven games.

Adding to the frustration of losing, Rickey once again had to deal with Durocher's all-consuming friendship with George Raft. Immediately after the loss to the Cardinals, Rickey tried to enter the Dodger clubhouse but was momentarily barred from entering by Killer Gray, who told him, "Just a minute, Pop. Stand back!" Gray informed Rickey that Raft and Durocher did not want to be disturbed. Rickey was furious.

There was no mistaking the fact that MacPhail's arguments against integration based on economic self-interest had gained ground. On August 27, 1946, a report was delivered to Happy Chandler from a major league committee that included MacPhail, Phil Wrigley of the Chicago Cubs, and Thomas A. Yawkey of the Red Sox, which included all the main points and in many cases used the exact words that MacPhail had used in his eight-month-old letter, especially when it came to the economic impact of integration on major league rentals and concessions.[32]

AFTER THE 1946 World Series, a number of events brought new melodrama to Leo's already melodramatic life. On his way to one of his many postseason speaking engagements and while still living with George Raft, Durocher found himself booked on the same plane departing from the Los Angeles Airport as the movie star Laraine Day, now considerably more famous than she was when he had first met her in 1941. Day still had no interest in Leo. "I turned to this lady I was with and said, 'Let's hope we don't sit anyplace near him,'" Day later recalled.[33]

When they got on board, Durocher had theatrically saved them two seats. By the time the plane landed, Day had been won over by what she described as a funny, charming, and warm man. Beyond that, she summed him up in one word: vitality. Within two weeks they were planning to get married, despite the fact that Day was already married.

Late in 1946, journalist Arthur Mann suggested that somebody or some group of people badly wanted Durocher out of Brooklyn: "No other explanation can be offered for a leak of confidential data from the offices of Brooklyn district attorney Miles F. MacDonald to syndicated columnist Westbrook Pegler." Pegler had begun as a sports reporter covering, among other things, Durocher during his Yankee years, and had since become a muckraking conservative columnist who was virulently anti-Roosevelt and anti–organized labor. He was also a dogged researcher who in 1941 received a Pulitzer Prize for a series of articles exposing labor racketeers. Pegler's column ran in more than two hundred newspapers in the Hearst chain. He was much read and much feared.

Frightening information was relayed to Rickey by Pegler. Having tapped Leo's phone, the district attorney had proof that he had talked to racketeer Joe Adonis, and Leo's signature had appeared on checks in an $800,000 check-cashing scam—known as "the Mergenthaler swindle."[34]

Rickey leaped into action and found that both accusations were true, but neither had merit. Leo had indeed talked to one of Adonis's henchmen, not Adonis himself, and it had been about Durocher's promise to send autographed bats and balls to a New Jersey church for a fund-raiser. The check signature was indeed Leo's, but proved nothing other than the fact that he had written it and it had ended up in the hands of a swindler who had stolen thousands of checks. As Mann put it: "The mountain of drafts might have contained anyone's signature."[35]

Rickey got back to Pegler, who told Rickey that he wanted Durocher out of baseball and that he was going to make Leo a key figure in a forthcoming series of columns on the sad and corrupt state of sports in America. On October 27, Pegler published his first of three columns linking Durocher to Raft and Killer Gray—and, by extension, to major figures in organized crime. Pegler retold the story of Martin Shurin Jr. being taken for $18,500 in Durocher's apartment two years earlier—and suggested in his melodramatic retelling that Durocher's involvement had been less than innocent, implying a classic case of guilt by association. This was Pegler's warm-up pitch, because in his next column, he invoked the specter of the 1919 Black Sox scandal. In the final column, he went for the jugular: "The moral 'climate' of Durocher's circle and Raft's is ominously similar to that in which the corruption of 1919 occurred," which he labeled "a coup of underworld gamblers by the friends of George Raft, the friend of Leo Durocher." This conclusion was coaxed from old news, but fresh in Pegler's hands in that it alleged a link between Durocher and the notorious gangster Bugsy Siegel. Pegler alleged that Siegel had dined with Durocher at Raft's house in Coldwater Canyon. Pegler then detailed the twenty-year friendship between the actor and the mobster, who was linked to the Luciano crime family, and connected Raft to a killer named Owney Madden and other gangsters.[36]

After that third column appeared, Pegler called Rickey to demand that he fire Durocher as a "moral delinquent" who would eventually bring down the team. Pegler reminded Rickey that despite what had been said in the columns, Leo was still living with Raft as they spoke. Rickey stood his ground and defended Durocher, but he was also perplexed and concerned to the point where he secretly sent Arthur Mann to Cincinnati to talk to Chandler and ask the commissioner to convince Durocher to cut his ties with his unsavory friends and force him to move out of George Raft's Hollywood home. Rickey had become fed up with all the adverse publicity coming from Durocher's relationship with Raft and, by extension, men like Bugsy Siegel who were friends with Raft. Mann also asked Chandler not to let anyone know that Rickey had made the request.[37]

Chandler was receptive to Rickey's request, and with Mann standing by, the commissioner called Raft's home and asked for Durocher. He was told that he was at a rehearsal for *The Jack Benny Show* that night. He called the NBC studio and, when he got through to Leo, told him to meet him on the following Friday at the Claremont Country Club in Berkeley. Leo said he had business in Texas that day, but Chandler told him to cancel the Texas trip and meet him in Northern California.

Durocher at this point was not only living with Raft but making news from the West Coast as he talked up the Dodgers and their great Negro prospect. At a charity breakfast in Los Angeles on November 16, he said about Robinson: "He is a great bunter. I'd say he's better than Shoeless Joe Jackson. Robinson also is a magnificent pivot man on double plays. Actually, he can't be beaten playing third base. There is no finer gentleman on the Montréal ball club." Here and in other speeches, Durocher had Robinson playing third base for the 1947 Dodgers.

In Brooklyn, Rickey was also growing more and more impatient with Durocher for not having come to terms with the club for a 1947 contract. On November 19, Rickey made a public statement to the effect that if Durocher was not ready to renew his contract with the Dodgers by the following Monday, he was prepared to name another man.

On November 22, Chandler and Durocher met on the golf course privately with a cold rain falling. The meeting began with Chandler asking Durocher to name all of his friends and acquaintances outside of baseball whose reputation might be questionable. As he mentioned the names— George Raft, Memphis Engleberg, Connie Immerman, Joe Adonis, and others—Chandler told Leo he had to break off the friendships and avoid all contact with all of them. He was asked if he knew a man named Bugsy

Siegel. Durocher replied that he had a "nodding acquaintance" with him. Chandler said, "Don't nod at him anymore." In addition, he was ordered to move out of Raft's house immediately.[38]

Leo then stunned Chandler with a confession. He was in love with a movie star named Laraine Day and planned to marry her. Earlier in the fall, he explained, he and the star had flown together on an airplane, and he had fallen madly in love with her. The only thing in their way was that she needed to get a divorce.

Then, according to Chandler, Leo told him that he had just been in Day's bedroom arguing with her husband as to which of them would get to take her.

Chandler said: "I remember giving him a look and I'll never forget what I said to him. 'You come down to my country,' I said, 'and do that—well, I'll make a set up for you and I won't have to be bothered with you any more, Durocher.'"

"Why?" asked the puzzled Leo.

"They'll kill you," Chandler answered. "If you go into some fellow's bedroom and argue with him about who's going to take his wife, they'll kill you. I won't have to be bothered with you anymore, Durocher."[39]

The meeting ended, according to Durocher, on a cordial note, with Leo promising to follow Chandler's instructions, and the commissioner putting his arm around him and saying: "Leo, I like you. I'm for you."[40]

Rickey and Chandler got Durocher to promise never to let Raft use his apartment again. Raft, in turn, got a call from Joe Adonis commenting on the Shurin business now back in the headlines: "This is bad business, George. You should know better than to get wrapped up in a third-rate crap game with strangers. The papers will cut you and Leo to pieces."

For nine years in a row, Durocher had stayed with Raft for the eight weeks following the end of the baseball season. After meeting with Chandler, Leo met with Raft at his Coldwater Canyon home to pick up his belongings.

"Go ahead and say it," said Raft.

"Well," he said, "you know how it is. I'm in the great American game—and Chandler says . . ."

"I know what he says," Raft interrupted. "You'll hurt your career chances hanging around with me. I don't want that to happen, you better move out."

Leo looked away and said, "Yeah, I better."

He packed his bags that night and moved out the next morning. The two men were never seen alone together again.[41]

Four days later on November 26, Durocher was back in Brooklyn to sign his 1947 contract to manage the Dodgers. Despite Durocher getting himself into deeper and deeper trouble on many fronts, Rickey continued to believe that Leo's determination and temper could be used as a tool to ease Robinson into place. As Red Barber noted in his book *1947: When All Hell Broke Loose in Baseball*, "Rickey knew Durocher would fight for Robinson." He added: "The rest of the league would be against the black man. Leo relished such a fight."

The one-year contract was rumored to be in excess of $60,000. At the end of the news conference, Rickey announced that each of the players and their coaches had donated $250 to the new ballplayer Pension Fund, and that the team had matched that amount with a donation of $8,500, making Durocher a charter member of the fund. This fund had been Chandler's idea and a step forward in his campaign to become "the players' commissioner"—a term he appropriated for himself. The pension fund for players was largely established from the sale of World Series broadcasting and advertising rights through 1956 for over $10 million with Mutual Broadcasting and the Gillette Safety Razor Company. All of the money was paid directly into the pension fund.[42]

Immediately following the Durocher news conference in Brooklyn, Larry MacPhail fueled a growing feud with Rickey by announcing that he withheld news that he had hired Bucky Harris to manage the Yankees for twelve days as a "personal favor to Leo Durocher," implying that he was helping Leo to squeeze extra money out of Rickey. Jack Hand of the Associated Press labeled the MacPhail-Rickey feud "synthetic" by pointing out that this feud over Durocher was going on as the two teams were scheduling six exhibition games against each other for the following spring—three in Havana and three in Brooklyn.[43]

Two weeks after his meeting with Durocher, Chandler was blindsided by charges that widespread gambling and game fixing were taking hold in some of the minor leagues. The issue was made public in early December at baseball's winter meetings in Los Angeles when retiring minor league commissioner William Bramham used the meetings to make the situation public. Bramham claimed he had strong evidence that players in one of the southern minor leagues were throwing games, betting against their own clubs, and working in collusion with gamblers. For the first time since the Black Sox scandal of 1919, he claimed, there was evidence of "general decadence" in professional baseball, and the situation had gotten worse as the season progressed, such that gamblers blocked the aisles in minor league stadiums, crying out betting odds like auctioneers.

The story was big news carried by all the major wire services. The United Press story led by calling it the biggest crisis since the 1919 scandal and called gambling the "evil now plaguing the game." Local stories followed, confirming the allegation. The *Advocate* of Baton Rouge, Louisiana, pointed out that the local Evangeline League was the one mentioned in the speech, and despite the efforts of owners to purge gambling from their teams, the situation in the league was "rotten."[44]

Chandler was in Los Angeles at the winter meetings, and when told of the speech and the allegations made, he told reporters that nobody had mentioned anything about this situation to him and that he had no idea what it was all about. Then he said that the gambling situation in the minors was "no affair of mine unless the minors appeal to me for help," bragging that the major leagues in 1946 were free of gambling—that confidence in big league baseball had never been higher.

Chandler had just proven to anyone reading the sports section of any newspaper in the country that he bore no resemblance whatsoever to Judge Landis, to whom such an accusation would have been red meat. Associated Press sports columnist Whitney Martin reported that Chandler had "blurted out" a rather peculiar remark about not knowing what was going on in the minors. This, Martin argued, would be like a cop covering one beat while having no idea of what was going on in the beat next to his. Martin gave Chandler the benefit of the doubt when he wrote that he thought that the commissioner had probably spoken first and thought later.[45]

The next day, a new minor league commissioner was appointed; he pledged to wage a ruthless war on baseball gambling and asked Chandler to help him wage that war. Regaining his lost footing, Chandler said he would help.

On December 12, Pegler went into full attack mode. He wrote that he had just learned from reading in a Hollywood gossip column that Durocher was back bunking with George Raft, despite a promise from Rickey that Raft would no longer be seen with Durocher. Pegler was reacting to faulty gossip, as the two had actually gone their separate ways at this point. However, the real focus of the attack was not Durocher, Raft, or Rickey but Chandler, whom he accused of fostering a "new spirit of comradeship between elements which formerly were as distant as virtue and sin." His windup was: "There has been a change of atmosphere in baseball since Judge Landis died. Your nose knows."[46]

The next day, which was two days before the National Football League playoff between the New York Giants and the Chicago Bears, it was revealed that Merle Hapes and Frank Filchock, the Giants fullback and quarterback, had each been offered $2,500 in bribes to lose the game by more than the ten-point spread. Both declined the offer but were obligated to report it. Hapes admitted being offered the cash before the game, and commissioner Bert Bell banned him from the championship game. Filchock didn't come clean until after the game but probably wished he, too, had been banned, as he threw six interceptions in the Giants' loss.

Chandler had been caught flat-footed on the issue of corruption in baseball's minor leagues. Not only was he now under attack from Pegler, but a shadow had been cast over baseball's next-door neighbor, pro football. To those who covered and read about professional sports, it looked like the gamblers were gaining the upper hand.

The pressure to clean up baseball continued to build. In a major speech at the Baseball Writers' Association of America dinner in New York later in the month, former postmaster general and leading Democratic politician James Farley deplored players' associations with gamblers and urged baseball leaders to "take every precaution by both rule and example to protect the player against himself and the public."

Shortly before Christmas, in the wake of the Pegler columns, Nixson Denton, sports editor of the *Cincinnati Times-Star*, wrote his own column criticizing Chandler for failing to take action on Durocher in the crap game case. On Christmas Eve, Chandler wrote back to Denton and said that he could not be held accountable for disciplining Durocher for an event that took place while Landis was commissioner. He also told Denton that he had met with Durocher to curtail his association with unsavory individuals such as George Raft.[47]

At year's end, Chandler's relationship with the sportswriters, especially those in New York, was at low ebb, and one had to look long and hard to find any journalist in his camp. As *Time* magazine summed it up: "Chandler, onetime pork-barreling U.S. Senator from Kentucky, had indeed done little as baseball's chief of police except to treat baseball-club presidents to ice-cream sodas to demonstrate what plain, folksy and moral people they all were."[48]

Happy had earlier summed up his job to a newspaper reporter: "As baseball commissioner I'm compelled to spend the winters in Florida and attend baseball games during the summer. If there is a better job than that, I don't know about it." The line was oft-repeated as he came under tighter and tighter scrutiny.

ONE OLD FRIEND who was squarely rooting for Chandler was the former governor of Michigan and then Supreme Court justice Frank Murphy, who wrote to Chandler during this period: "Don't let the critics bother you. Each day you are growing stronger in public esteem and that is because you are a man of character and good judgment. Only the game fish swims upstream and you're that sort."

When Chandler booked into the Sherry-Netherland Hotel just after the first of the year, George Raft came to see him to argue that Durocher be allowed to remain his friend. Chandler cut him off before he could state his case.

"George, do you have a contract in baseball?"

"No" was Raft's response.

"Then we haven't anything to talk about. What you do is not my business. If Durocher plays cards and gambles, I have to be concerned with him. But not you. So, please, just go away."

"But," Raft blurted, "I got a bum rap!"

"I didn't give it to you" was Chandler's last word.[49]

CHAPTER 9

Exiled

As the new year began, Durocher was clearly conforming to Chandler's orders, and at the same time making headlines off the sports pages with his relationship with Laraine Day. The coverage began on December 4, when Day's husband, a man named Ray Hendricks, who managed an airport owned by radio star and ventriloquist Edgar Bergen, reacted to her divorce petition, which had actually been filed before she began seeing Durocher. He accused Leo of posing as a friend of the family while "clandestinely wooing my wife in my home and under my eyes." The tabloids feasted on the story. LARAINE DAY HAS WORD FOR LIPPY: "SNAKE IN THE GRASS," blared the New York Daily News.

Day's divorce petition was granted in California on January 20, 1947, with the stipulation that she not marry until the decree became final in one year. The next day, she and Durocher flew to Juarez, Mexico, where she obtained a "quickie" Mexican divorce. They came back over the border, and later that day, they were married by a justice of the peace in El Paso, Texas.

Judge George A. Dockweiler, who had granted the California divorce, was greatly displeased with Day's actions. He spoke of setting aside her decree and voiding her divorce, and ordered her to show cause why he shouldn't rule against her. At this, Durocher called the judge a couple of times to make sure it was all right for Day to reenter California. The judge said that she could return to California if she did not reside with Durocher there—at this point Day lived with her mother in Santa Monica—and warned that if they lived together in California, Day could be arrested and tried for bigamy.

Durocher returned fire, stating that the couple was legally married and intended to remain so for the rest of their lives. He then called the judge "a most unethical and publicity conscious servant of the people." The judge then lamented that Durocher was "a very facile talker, but this is one umpire he will have a hard time convincing."[1]

In early February, Day began shooting a big-budget Technicolor film called *Tycoon*. Her costar and love interest was John Wayne, who later said that Durocher was the most openly jealous husband he had ever met. "The Lip" hovered on the set each day, making rude comments or glaring at Wayne whenever he and Day were filming romantic scenes. Wayne complained that Durocher watched him as if he were a baserunner preparing to steal home. Ultimately, Wayne got so fed up that in order to keep Durocher off the set, he ordered it closed—the only time in his career he ever did so. Wayne later complained that Leo's presence was, as much as anything else, responsible for the decided lack of passion in the love scenes.[2]

Although Durocher's earlier marriage to and divorce from Grace Dozier, a divorcée herself, had brought little if any public moral outrage from Durocher's fellow Roman Catholics, this situation proved to be much more explosive. Rickey was a target of the rising tide of protests. Letters from troubled spiritual leaders reached him. When he was petitioned in person by Reverend Vincent J. Powell, Brooklyn diocesan director of the Catholic Youth Organization (CYO), whose fifty thousand members were part of the thriving Knothole Club, Rickey confidently turned the matter over to Dodgers legal counsel and minority owner Walter O'Malley. Being of the same faith, O'Malley met Father Powell at least twice in Rickey's office in hopes of avoiding an all-out ban on attending Durocher-led Dodger games that the CYO had ordered for Brooklyn's young Roman Catholics.

Rickey then received a written plea to release Durocher. It came from Bishop Bermingham of the Washington, D.C., archdiocese, who was Father Powell's predecessor as CYO director in Brooklyn. In reply, Rickey explained that Durocher had not violated his contract with the team and there was no cause for his dismissal. Regardless, sweeping dirt under a rug did not make the house clean. He closed the letter by expressing surprise that "a man of your cloth or any cloth" would admit that one human soul was beyond redemption.

Why the church was so upset now when it had made no such protests during Durocher's earlier divorces would later puzzle Damon Rice, who wrote in *Seasons Past*, his historically accurate novel about this period of baseball history, "Miss Day, cool and beautiful, was desired by a million red-blooded American boys." Leo was living out a million adolescent fantasies, seducing a movie star—and not just any movie star, but a devout Mormon who neither drank nor smoked nor used crude language.[3]

Westbrook Pegler had let up on Durocher momentarily, but not on Chandler. A column in mid-January accused baseball of selecting Chandler because of, not in spite of, his many defects, one of which was his ability to "see a silver lining in a sewer." Under Chandler, baseball was headed in a "dirty way," and Pegler predicted it was just a matter of time until the underworld secretly owned a major league team through loans to an inept and stupid owner. Pegler went on to attack Chandler's past, claiming that he was, among other things, "a machine politician from a political environment in Louisville that includes professional underworld types . . ."[4]

Durocher and twenty-five players left Penn Station in New York on February 18 for Miami and flew to Havana the next day for preseason exhibition games. Leo had just been informed he had been picked as one of the ten best-dressed men in America by the Custom Tailors Guild, just behind Supreme Court justice Robert H. Jackson and ahead of movie stars Douglas Fairbanks Jr. and Clifton Webb. The *Brooklyn Eagle* ran the best-dressed story on page one. A few weeks later, Hollywood gossip columnist Jack Lait Jr. wrote: "Filmtown wags are saying the Dodgers are a sure bet to win the pennant this year— that's the only way Durocher can get back on the sports pages."[5]

On his first night in Havana, Durocher ate dinner in the Hotel Nacional's dining room, only to be visited by a "well-known New York gambler" and some of the gambler's friends. "I had to be very tough with those birds," Durocher told Dan Daniel, "and ask them to leave." In order to avoid gamblers in Havana, Durocher took to eating dinner in his room and refused to answer his telephone. "I have been forced to become a hermit in Havana," Durocher said, "because of the presence of gamblers who want to say 'Hello.'"[6]

One of the first actions taken by Durocher in Havana was to ban all poker games from the Brooklyn clubhouse for the duration of the season— this was, he insisted, his own rule, and Rickey had had nothing to do with it. When he was not on the practice field or working with the team, he was by himself, and his public comments were few and far between. The Lip had been buttoned by Chandler. "Nobody was ever more faithful to a promise than Leo was to Chandler," said broadcaster Red Barber, who watched him avoid any suggestion of wrongdoing.[7]

On February 28, while Rickey and O'Malley were in Havana with the club, Reverend Powell announced he had withdrawn the entire CYO from the Knothole Club in protest against Durocher, claiming he was "undermining the moral training" of Brooklyn's Roman Catholic youth. The club had about 125,000 members, of whom it was estimated about half were Catholic.

On March 3, Durocher gave an impromptu press conference in his hotel room. He was dressed in a maroon bathrobe and delivered a series of declarations to a group of reporters to the effect that he was staying away from "everybody." He declared that the Dodger dugout and clubhouse were now totally off-limits to anyone who did not have press credentials or was not involved in maintaining equipment for the players, with no exceptions. He then attacked the practice of releasing the names of the pitchers for the next game, claiming it was a "spur" to the gambler and gambling. Gamblers needed odds to post, and without the names of the pitchers, odds-making became much more difficult.

Also on March 3 in a "Durocher Says" column, which was, as always, ghosted for him by Dodgers public relations man Harold Parrott, Durocher issued "a declaration of war" against the Yankees. He charged that Larry MacPhail "had resolved to knock me and make life as hard as possible for me," and that in the following games with the Yankees, the Dodgers would be out for blood. "These nine games—three in Venezuela, three in Cuba and three in Brooklyn—may give me a little line on the type of ball clubs MacPhail and Rickey are going to steer through 1947. Personally, I think the Yankees are going to have plenty of trouble and I hope it starts right here tomorrow."[8]

Early in the morning of March 4, Leo and his coaches and twenty-five players flew to Venezuela for three exhibition games against the Yankees. The trip began with a bang. On his way from the airport to his mountaintop hotel, Durocher had a close call when the car he was sharing with Parrott and two players collided with another on a narrow road and was saved from plunging down a two-thousand-foot cliff by a three-foot stone barrier that fortunately held.[9]

In Caracas, MacPhail and Durocher were on a war footing in the wake of Leo's column, which acted as kerosene thrown on a fire. "Messengers in the afternoons scurried from the Dodger hotel on a side street to the Yankee hostelry on a hill, bearing challenges, defies, and ultimatums and always brought back threats, sneers, and promises of vengeance," Harold Burr said, describing the battle that raged between the men in Venezuela, where they left the natives trying to comprehend the mad Americans.[10]

In the first game a crowd of ten thousand watched the Yankees beat the Dodgers 17–6 as Yankee rookie Yogi Berra clubbed three doubles. The next night, the Dodgers thrilled eight thousand fans with a five-run ninth-inning rally to win 8–7. The teams concluded their Venezuelan series on March 6. Charlie Keller and Phil Rizzuto each doubled as the Yankees scored four runs in the sixth inning en route to a 4–0 victory in front of nine thousand fans. The teams awoke at dawn the next morning to begin their twenty-mile descent from the mountain to the airport for their flights back to Havana for exhibition games at El Gran Stadium. Rickey brought the Durocher situation to a climax on March 8 when he saw two familiar figures in Larry MacPhail's official box during the first of the games. Both qualified as "undesirable" under the standards emphasized by worried baseball leaders throughout the winter. One was handicapper Memphis Engelberg, the other Connie Immerman, manager of the Havana gambling casino, of which expatriate Lucky Luciano was part owner. Rickey denounced MacPhail and the presence of the characters to two New York sportswriters. He raised the question of one standard for managers and one for club presidents. The outburst was reported to the Associated Press.

Leo went to the ballpark early that day and to his great surprise spotted Immerman and Engelberg sunning themselves in MacPhail's box. "Righteous wrath, which was housed in an inadequate minimum security cage in Leo's breast, came bursting forth," recalled Heywood Hale Broun, a witness to Leo's rage as a reporter in Havana for *PM*. "First there was a fine flow of what are now coyly known as 'F words' and 'S words.' Among them were enough 'O words' (for 'ordinary') to make the two witnesses present, myself and Dick Young of the *New York Daily News*, understand that he was not mad at Memphis and Connie, who were good friends and kept cleaner books than a number of banks recently in the news. Neither was Leo mad at MacPhail, with whom he had a love-hate relationship of many years' standing. At the end of all this came the fatal words—to me logical words— 'If those guys were sitting in my box, I'd get banned from baseball.' He added the 'if' is important here but was subsequently ignored."*[11]

---

* Broun's eyewitness account appeared a few days after Durocher's death in 1991, but he had spiked it at the time: "Young, either a better reporter than I, or a more ruthless person, or both, printed the whole thing. I, aware that the baseball Establishment was laying snares for Leo, printed none of it, though I later wrote to the commissioner offering to testify. There is a use for such letters, they are now called 'recycled toilet tissue.'"

Durocher went on: "Are there two sets of rules, one applying to managers and the other to club owners?" Recalling the commissioner's admonition on the golf course that had made Engelberg a "former friend" of his, Leo added indignantly, "Where does MacPhail come off, flaunting his company with gamblers right in the players' faces? If I ever said 'hello' to one of those guys, I'd be called up before Commissioner Chandler and probably be barred."

Within a week, MacPhail twice demanded that the commissioner punish Leo. He said, "I feel it my duty to myself and my colleagues to request Commissioner Chandler to investigate my charge that Durocher is guilty of conduct detrimental to baseball." There were three elements to the complaint: the "Durocher Says" columns in the Brooklyn Eagle ghosted by Harold Parrott, remarks by Rickey about MacPhail's guests in the Havana ballpark, and various quotations attributed to Durocher about MacPhail.

On March 12, he demanded the commissioner call a hearing to determine the responsibility for and the truth of the statements, even those regarding the men sitting in the box, which had been witnessed by many at the game. Chandler first asked MacPhail to "cool off" before making the charges formally in writing, but MacPhail insisted that the verbal charges were sufficient and refused to cool off.

Jackie Robinson had been scheduled to travel with the Dodgers and the Montreal team to Spring Training. The more lenient racial attitude in Cuba, as opposed to Florida, had been one of the reasons the Dodgers returned to Havana for Spring Training in late February 1947. They had trained at Havana's La Tropical Stadium in 1941 and 1942, abandoning Cuba only because of wartime travel restrictions. Because of those earlier visits, Durocher already had his own Cuban nickname, which would be used in the Spanish language programs for the 1947 trip: "El Famoso LIPIDIA."

Upon reaching Cuba in late February, Robinson found the white Dodgers were lodged at the superb Hotel Nacional, which did not share the racial tolerance that was the Cuban norm. The soon-to-be Dodgers of black descent stayed at the Hotel Boston in old Havana, while their minor league Montreal teammates stayed in the dormitories of the Havana Military Academy, a prep school. Since major hotels in Havana did not accommodate blacks, the Boston was the place where Negro leaguers had been staying for decades when they played in the Cuban winter league. It was, as Herbert Goren of the New York Sun called it, "a musty third-rate hotel . . . that looked like a movie version of a water-front hostelry in Singapore."

Harold Burr of the *Eagle* called it a "ramshackle old Spanish hotel." Both reporters knew the hotel firsthand, as they had gone there to interview Robinson.[12]

To Robinson, Roy Campanella (who had played in Cuba), and Don Newcombe, this was aggravation as well as insult. Robinson was irate when he discovered that the segregation was due not just to Cuban customs but to arrangements made by the Dodgers. Rickey wanted no chance of a racial incident in the Dodger or Royal camp. However, the Boston did provide a haven from an atmosphere at the Hotel Nacional that would have been tense if not hostile. Its environs were friendly, familiar, and had over the years built a kind of support system for these players.

All but invisible at this point, Robinson got into his first game in a Montreal uniform against the Brooklyn "B" squad on March 13 in Cuba, and then it was off to Panama for a series of exhibitions with locals and then with the Dodgers. Initially, the plan had been to take Robinson to Panama, where he would play for the Panama national team against the Dodgers, but this plan was abandoned. Then it was decided to keep the Montreal team in Havana while the Dodgers with Robinson in tow were in Panama. The reason the Dodgers went to Panama was to play a series of fourteen exhibition games against Army teams, local teams, and their Montreal farm club, which would come over to Panama a few days later—and get a chance to see Robinson in action.

Durocher and the rest of the Dodgers "A" squad arrived first. Durocher was a paragon of virtue in Panama, even to the point of eschewing contact with a pool table in the lobby of the officers' quarters at the U.S. Army barracks at Fort Gillick where he bunked. Instead of playing cards, his evenings were devoted to a study of Chinese pottery from a book given to him by Laraine. Tommy Holmes, who dubbed this man "the New Durocher," commented: "He aims to learn as much about the Ming Dynasty as he did about Hoyle."[13]

Even before the Royals arrived, the team knew that Panama would become a stage for Robinson's tryout and potential elevation to a starting position on Opening Day, bringing the issue of race into play for the first time as a team matter. Branch Rickey at first believed that the integration of Robinson into the Dodger squad would occur with little or no opposition. He believed that the Dodgers would embrace Robinson for the simple reason that he would help the team to win more games.

Shortly after arriving in Panama, Harold Parrott told Durocher he had learned from pitcher Kirby Higbe that a group of his players were drawing up a petition to stop Robinson from taking the field in a Dodgers uniform. Durocher had also heard from one of his coaches that something was in the works aimed at ending Robinson's major league career before it started.

At first, Durocher thought the story might not be true: "What did the damn fools think they were going to do—strike?" To check it out, the next day he spent time around some of his players, praising Robinson's talent. The response was discouraging. That night he lay awake and decided to take action before anyone signed a petition. He saw this as an open revolt, woke all of players and coaches, and staged an early-morning meeting to break it up. After telling the players that they "could wipe their ass with the petition," he informed the team: "I do not care if the guy is yellow or black, or if he has stripes like a fuckin' zebra. I'm the manager of this team and I say he plays." Durocher continued: "From everything I hear, he's only the first. Only the first, boys! There's many more coming right behind him and they have the talent and they're gonna come play. These fellows are hungry. They're good athletes and there's nowhere else they can make this kind of money. They're going to come, boys, and they're going to come scratching and diving. Unless you fellows look out and wake up, they're going to run you right out of the ball park."*[14]

The next morning Rickey arrived and took up where Durocher had left off. He used his time in Panama to confer individually with players, including Bobby Bragan and Dixie Walker, about accepting a player of a different race.

On the morning of March 17, less than forty-eight hours after the early morning meeting, Durocher flew to Los Angeles from the Panama Canal Zone to pick up his bride and bring her back to Havana for a "honeymoon" in Cuba, where Day's Mexican divorce was recognized. She had just finished ten weeks of shooting *Tycoon* with John Wayne, and Durocher felt it was proper to be there to help her through customs. As he left, he was asked by a reporter about Robinson and had no comment, adding that he had not yet seen him play that season.

Robinson was still the odd man out when he arrived in Panama with the rest of the Royals later on the day of Durocher's departure. All of the

---

* This meeting was depicted accurately in the recent film 42, with actor Christopher Meloni playing Leo. In real life, Leo wore a yellow bathrobe, while he is shown in a blue one in the film.

Dodgers and all of the Royals were housed inside the Canal Zone, which was then still part of the United States, and as such, was administered under an ad hoc Jim Crow umbrella. Robinson and Roy Campanella had to sleep outside the zone in Panama City, where there was no segregation to speak of. After Robinson arrived in Panama, all of the games were played in the Canal Zone. As Tommy Holmes of the *Eagle* put it, Robinson had gotten a far better break in Florida than he was getting in a territory under control of the U.S. government. In Florida, he at least knew the rules and got to bed and board with local families. Here he was exiled—literally forced to leave the United States—to find a place to sleep. This put added pressure on him and fueled the anger he had already expressed over his living conditions in Havana.

In another complication for Robinson, the Dodgers wanted to see what he could do playing first base for the Royals, so he was also learning to play a position he had never played before. Instructed to move Robinson to first, Royals manager Mel Jones bought a secondhand first base mitt from the Dodgers clubhouse custodian, Dan Comerford, for $15. When Jones asked Robinson how it fit, Robinson said that he did not know, because he had never worn one before.[15]

Hours after Durocher's plane departed, Robinson made his debut as a Royal against the Dodgers. It was, as Harold Burr wrote in the *Eagle*, "the day this town has been waiting for all winter." In the debut game, Robinson played flawlessly at first base and got two hits, one of which resulted in Montreal's only run. He also made a dazzling catch of a wide throw to first base. The game was called on account of darkness and declared a 1–1 tie. Two days later, Robinson got three hits against the parent club but also made a throwing error that yielded three unearned runs. In Panama, Robinson hit safely five times in eight at-bats against the Dodgers.

The fact that the majority of the large press contingent stayed in Cuba while the Dodgers went to Panama helped keep the racial issue under wraps. The *Brooklyn Eagle* had its two main baseball writers—Burr and Holmes—in Panama, and a few members of the Negro press there who were following Robinson, including Sam Lacy, but that was it. Burr alone was aware of dissension about Robinson, which he reported on March 22 after the Dodgers returned from Panama. He termed the excursion a disaster on several levels. The heat was like a furnace, and the team was actually shuttling some of its regulars back twelve hundred miles to Cuba to cool off. The local teams they played against were not very good, and as few as five hundred people had showed up for some of the games. Burr added: "Mentally the players are sore about the bringing in of Jackie Robinson and morale is at a low ebb," and he added that Rickey seemed to have his head in the sand regarding Robinson's effect on the team, stating that a poll of the team would run heavily against allowing Robinson to don a Dodger uniform. Voting against Robinson in a straw poll was not the same as refusing to play with him, but a problem still existed, and both Rickey and Durocher were aware that work still had to be done.[16]

Durocher returned to the Dodgers training camp in Cuba on Friday, March 21. Rickey said: "Leo was very much in favor of bringing Robinson up. As a matter of fact, he asked me to do just that when the club returned to Havana from Panama, but I didn't because I didn't think that it was the proper time." The next day, the Dodgers beat a Cuban all-star squad 5–2. Laraine Day watched the proceedings from a box seat behind the Dodgers' dugout and was part of a scheme adopted by the Dodgers management to pave the way for Robinson. During the next group of exhibition games, Leo would leave the ballpark for the hotel in the seventh inning after his starting players had come out of the game. Day would leave with Durocher, leading the reporters to think he was going back for an extra shift behind closed doors with his new movie star wife. It became the stuff of headlines: LOVE-SICK LEO DESERTS TEAM FOR LARAINE.

What Leo was actually doing, Day later revealed, was meeting privately with individual Dodgers, including veterans such as Pee Wee Reese, to convince them to accept Jackie Robinson as a teammate. "Robinson was up against the world in his efforts to integrate baseball. Durocher quietly tried to make it easier," she recalled. When Day finally told the story in 1952, she asserted that this was probably the hardest work Leo had ever done in baseball. "Talking is his favorite pastime, but this was talk with a vital purpose, talk meant to overcome deep-seated feelings of centuries." She added: "There were nights when he returned from one of those meetings worn out from the strain. We could laugh privately at the lovesick-Leo legend, but I was inwardly boiling at the injustice of it all."[17]

IN THE MEANTIME, Rickey learned that Chandler had called a hearing for Monday, March 24, at Sarasota, Florida. He was not worried. The defense consisted merely of identifying the guests in the Yankee box as known gamblers, submitting proof that they used Yankee tickets, and making a deposition as to who got them for free distribution. Ford Frick arrived on Saturday to invoke the National League's interest in a discussion with Rickey the next day.

Late Saturday night Rickey's wife learned that her oldest brother Frank had died in Ohio. Rickey wired Chandler requesting a postponement of the hearing and belatedly registered with the commissioner a protest against the gamblers having been in the Havana ballpark. He departed early the next morning by plane in characteristic haste and confusion, leaving word that if there was no postponement, the Dodger interests would be represented by O'Malley, who at that moment was having breakfast with Frick in the hotel dining room in Florida.

Later in the day at Sarasota, the commissioner announced that the request for a postponement had been denied, that there might be two hearings, and that newspapermen would be barred. Upon reaching Sarasota, President Frick announced that he had declined Chandler's invitation to the hearing with no reason given.

MacPhail's rambling set of charges against his old club and against the things that Durocher had said about him had, in the words of Francis Stann of the *Washington Evening Star*, touched off "a roaring bonfire." The issue had become what Leo had said and written about MacPhail—or so it seemed at the time—which was enough to bring reporters from all over the country to Sarasota. More than thirty newsmen and photographers were at the airport to greet Durocher, who somehow gave them the slip. He was simply not available for comment either before or after the meeting.[18]

Arthur Mann, who was in the room, later wrote about the meeting in his 1957 biography of Branch Rickey: "The next day's hearing was essentially a travesty on democratic procedure. It resulted in a black day for baseball. A permanent stain will remain if the stenographic transcript of the testimony is ever uncovered. Not a single word was spoken in defense of Durocher by the Brooklyn Dodgers or even by himself. Under questioning, Leo tried to say that his protest in Havana echoed the warning he had been given on the Berkeley golf course against unsavory associations, but Commissioner Chandler hushed him quickly. The subject of gamblers in the ballpark, so important during the winter, was carefully avoided. At the last minute, entry into the record was made of proof that (1) the two occupants of the Yankee box were undesirable to baseball, and (2) they received gratuitous tickets from the New York Yankee supply."

After the session was over, Durocher headed back to his hotel. "It went off easy as pie," he reported to Day. "They hardly asked me anything at all. I can't figure it out." Day recalled that he looked somewhat baffled.[19]

On March 28, Durocher finally got to see Robinson in action. Back in the lineup despite his ongoing stomach problems, he went one for three, but "he was far off his usual brilliant form, being guilty of two errors," wrote Roscoe McGowen in *The New York Times*. "Robinson booted two plays at first base, leading to four of the Dodgers' runs as Brooklyn beat the Royals 5–2."

The rest of the day did not favor Durocher. Pegler had penned another column tying Leo to Bugsy Siegel (who, according to the columnist, was now involved in a secret plan to take over the state of Nevada). Later in the day, the second hearing addressing MacPhail's charges against Durocher and Rickey shifted to the Pennsylvania Hotel in St. Petersburg, Florida. Instead of testimony from multiple witnesses, this meeting with Chandler included only Rickey, who had returned; MacPhail, and Arthur Mann, who had just left reporting to become a special assistant to Rickey. The Associated Press's story before the meeting declared, "No one now expects the commissioner to do anything drastic to any of the leading figures in the quarrel, including manager Leo Durocher of the Dodgers. It can be said that he does not feel any evidence has been introduced which calls for drastic action on his part."

Rickey opened the long session with a detailed explanation of his outburst in the lobby of the Havana Hotel. He had not seen the sports-writers' quotes, but he would not deny them, since both writers were responsible reporters. What he had done, and wanted in the record, was to protest against the presence of Engelberg and Immerman as guests in the Yankee official box. Regardless of what may have been said on his behalf at the first hearing—a protective "general denial" had been entered—this was the reason for his outburst. And, if his manager, Leo Durocher, had protested similarly after the second game, he had done so with good cause, as the commissioner well knew.

Chandler then sent for Arthur Patterson, traveling secretary of the Yankees, and questioned him about courtesy tickets to the Yankees-Dodgers games of March 8 and 9 to see if he could deny that the gamblers had been guests of the Yankees. Patterson admitted handling the club's free tickets. He admitted knowing both Immerman and Engelberg and admitted giving some of the tickets to MacPhail, who was in the hearing room but not ques-tioned on this point. Asked if he had given free tickets to Immerman and

Leo at the end of the 1925 season, photographed by Charles M. Conlon, whose portrait of Durocher as a Yankee suggested a quiet, shy young man seated at the end of the bench.
NATIONAL BASEBALL HALL OF FAME LIBRARY

These three St. Paul Saints, (left to right) Norman McMillan, Oscar Roettger, and Leo Durocher, created a formidable double-play combination.
GETTY IMAGES

Leo Durocher and Babe Ruth, presumably before Babe accused Leo of stealing his watch. GETTY IMAGES

Leo Durocher, shortstop for the Cincinnati Reds, as he appeared in 1931. Because of the protective influence of owner Sidney Weil, Leo began to thrive in the National League. Weil genuinely liked Durocher, regarded him as a friend, and did the best he could to keep him out of trouble. GETTY IMAGES

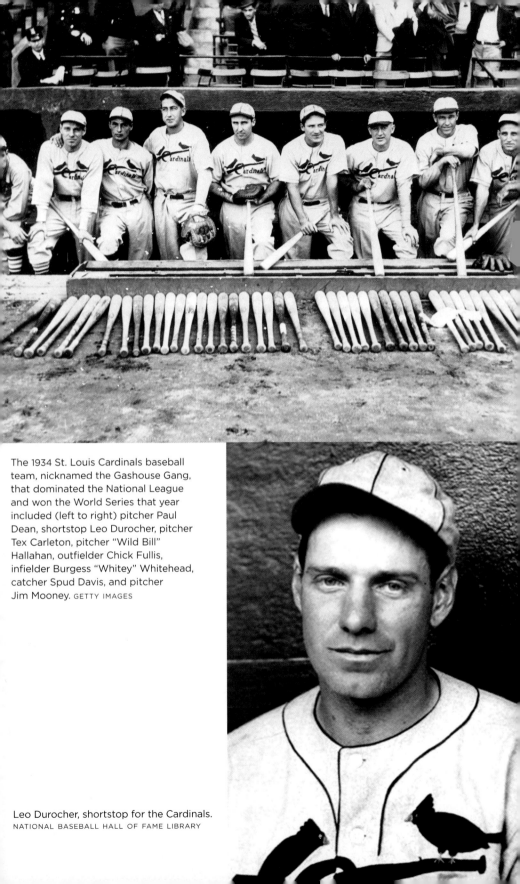

The 1934 St. Louis Cardinals baseball team, nicknamed the Gashouse Gang, that dominated the National League and won the World Series that year included (left to right) pitcher Paul Dean, shortstop Leo Durocher, pitcher Tex Carleton, pitcher "Wild Bill" Hallahan, outfielder Chick Fullis, infielder Burgess "Whitey" Whitehead, catcher Spud Davis, and pitcher Jim Mooney. GETTY IMAGES

Leo Durocher, shortstop for the Cardinals.
NATIONAL BASEBALL HALL OF FAME LIBRARY

Gashouse Gang Leo "talking it over" with an umpire, as depicted on this novelty postcard.

Dodgers executive vice president Lee MacPhail and Durocher, moments after it was announced that Leo would manage the team for the 1939 season, replacing Burleigh Grimes.

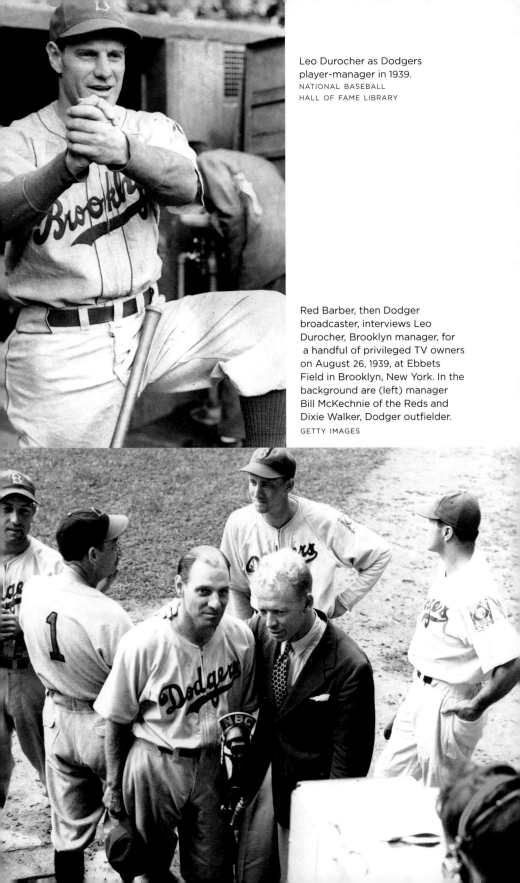

Leo Durocher as Dodgers player-manager in 1939.
NATIONAL BASEBALL HALL OF FAME LIBRARY

Red Barber, then Dodger broadcaster, interviews Leo Durocher, Brooklyn manager, for a handful of privileged TV owners on August 26, 1939, at Ebbets Field in Brooklyn, New York. In the background are (left) manager Bill McKechnie of the Reds and Dixie Walker, Dodger outfielder.
GETTY IMAGES

Leo as Brooklyn skipper always had the ear of sportswriters, as he was always good copy.
NATIONAL BASEBALL HALL OF FAME LIBRARY

Leo and umpire Al Barlick argue. It was one of several arguments that broke out in St. Louis on September 11, 1941. NATIONAL BASEBALL HALL OF FAME LIBRARY

Leo and his second wife, Grace Dozier, attend the Joe Louis vs. Lou Nova prizefight in September 1941. Durocher is dressed in his traditional black knit tie, a fashion habit he picked up from George Raft. AUTHOR'S COLLECTION

Leo reports to his local Brooklyn draft board on March 1, 1943. He moved on to his induction exam, where he was found to be ineligible for service due to a punctured eardrum. AUTHOR'S COLLECTION

Danny Kaye, Leo, and Brooklyn native J. Arbeeny on October 13, 1945, at Atsugi airstrip during a tour of Japan. The Flatbush sign was sent to Arbeeny by New York mayor Fiorello La Guardia. The photo is a Signal Corps Radio photo. AUTHOR'S COLLECTION

Leo Durocher and Danny Kaye ham it up, posing on an airplane fuselage at Kadena, Okinawa, in 1945. The two performed on the island shortly following a typhoon. PRINTS & PHOTOGRAPHS DIVISION, LIBRARY OF CONGRESS

After Leo's Brooklyn Dodgers were eliminated by St. Louis in the 1946 playoffs for the National League pennant, Leo took in a game of the World Series in Boston with (left to right) actor George Raft, restaurateur Toots Shor, and New York Yankee great Joe DiMaggio.
GETTY IMAGES

Leo with radio comedian Jack Benny on one of his guest appearances on Benny's show in the 1940s. In one famous episode, Leo tried to explain baseball to British actor Ronald Colman. AUTHOR'S COLLECTION

Leo Durocher with Branch Rickey, who was Leo's mentor and savior in St. Louis and Brooklyn.
NATIONAL BASEBALL HALL OF FAME LIBRARY

Leo with Jackie Robinson before the Dodgers played their Montreal farm team at Spring Training in Havana on March 29, 1947. Robinson would make his major league debut as a Dodger on April 15, the first day of Durocher's suspension from baseball.
NEW YORK DAILY NEWS PHOTO FROM GETTY IMAGES

Leo listens to the "not guilty" verdict from the jury foreman at his 1946 assault trial. Standing to Leo's left are his attorney and Joe Moore, special policeman and co-defendant.
AUTHOR'S COLLECTION

Newlyweds Leo Durocher and Laraine Day on the set of the movie *Tycoon* two days after their 1947 marriage and three days after her divorce.
AUTHOR'S COLLECTION

Leo and commissioner Happy Chandler strike a jolly pose in the days before Durocher's suspension by Chandler for the 1947 season. Chandler later stated, "Leo Durocher made me more trouble during my time as Commissioner than all the other Baseball players in both the Major Leagues." NATIONAL BASEBALL HALL OF FAME LIBRARY

Leo Durocher, at the end of his suspended season, with wife Laraine Day and actor Danny Kaye at the opening game of the 1947 World Series on October 1. AUTHOR'S COLLECTION

The New York Giants new skipper Leo Durocher with team owner Horace Stoneham.
AUTHOR'S COLLECTION

Leo Durocher, Willie Mays, Hank Thompson, and Monte Irvin.
BETTMANN COLLECTION, GETTY IMAGES

Owner Horace Stoneham (left) and New York Giants manager Leo Durocher (right) hug Bobby Thomson in the clubhouse after the Giants' third baseman's three-run homer in the ninth inning gave them a 5–4 victory over the Brooklyn Dodgers in the final game of a playoff series for the 1951 National League pennant. The victory gave the Giants their first pennant since 1937. BETTMANN COLLECTION, GETTY IMAGES

Durocher and NBC broadcast partner Lindsey Nelson in 1958. Durocher was an immediate hit as a sportscaster because he played himself and did not fear saying things that were controversial. Nelson got along with Durocher and said of him in his autobiography, *Hello Everybody, I'm Lindsey Nelson*, that Durocher would be the manager he would choose if he had to win only one game. "He might steal it, or whatever, but somehow, he would figure out how to win it." AUTHOR'S COLLECTION

Leo with comedian Alan Young and
Mister Ed, the talking horse, on the
third season opener of *Mister Ed* on
the CBS television network, Sunday,
September 29, 1969.
AUTHOR'S COLLECTION

Leo, at fifty-nine, on his return to
managing as skipper of the
Chicago Cubs in 1966. This image
was created by James Hansen of
Look magazine for a feature
entitled "Return of the Lip" in which
the author commented: "He still
struts, but after standing around a
ball park for three hours, he's tired."
PRINTS & PHOTOGRAPHS DIVISION,
LIBRARY OF CONGRESS

Houston Astros manager
Leo Durocher with César Cedeño.
When Durocher joined the Astros,
he compared Cedeño to a young
Willie Mays. NATIONAL BASEBALL HALL
OF FAME LIBRARY

Durocher's third wife, Laraine Day,
now seventy-three, accepts for him
on his posthumous induction into the
National Baseball Hall of Fame in 1994.
NATIONAL BASEBALL HALL
OF FAME LIBRARY

Engelberg, Patterson replied, "I can't recall." When asked if, conceivably, he could have given them the tickets, he said, "Yes, conceivably I could have."

Chandler then excused Patterson and asked all to leave the room, including the stenographer, except O'Malley, Rickey, and Mann. When the door closed, Chandler rose, went over to the Dodger table, and said, "How much would it hurt you folks to have your fellow out of baseball?"

"Branch Rickey emitted a gasp of amazement," Mann reported. "His mouth flew open like a man hit in the solar plexus or lower. His gnarled fists went up into the air and came down against the table with an angry whack. Tears rolled down his suntanned cheeks. He exclaimed in a half-sobbing voice, 'Happy, what on earth is the matter with you? Why, that boy has more character than the fellow you just sent out of the room!'"

Ignoring the pointed reference to MacPhail, the commissioner insisted he was trying to do his best—that he was under great pressure from "outside of baseball," that he "had to do something," and that he just wanted to know "how you all felt about it." Chandler would not specify who or what those forces were outside the game, but when asked, he pulled a hand-written letter out of his pocket "from a prominent Washington official" who was demanding Durocher's expulsion. As he waved the letter, Chandler explained that people like the "big man" who had written it could not be disregarded.[20]

What Chandler would not reveal in 1947 and for some years to come was the identity of the man who had written the letter. The most common guess at the time was FBI director J. Edgar Hoover. This made some sense, as one of the rumors among the press corps in Havana was that Chandler had borrowed FBI agents to look into Durocher's connections. At least one writer, Chauncey Darden of the *Richmond Times-Dispatch*, wrote in a March column about FBI men supposedly borrowed by the commissioner.*[21] Finally in 1955, in an interview for a profile of Durocher in *Sports Illustrated*, Chandler revealed that the letter had come from Supreme Court justice Frank Murphy, an influential Catholic layman and a friend of the commissioner.[22]

The men at the Dodger table were shocked and angry that Durocher could be expelled on the suggestion of an unnamed but important public

---

* When Mann published his account of the events of 1947 in his 1951 book *Baseball Confidential: A Secret History of the War Among Chandler, Durocher, MacPhail, and Rickey*, he still could not get Chandler to tell him who the mystery man had been.

figure. Chandler, now on the defensive, assured the Dodgers that everything, to paraphrase Mann again, would be taken care of all right, and
he had asked about expelling Durocher to find out how the Dodgers
would react.

As the three men left the room, MacPhail pushed O'Malley out of the
way and demanded to talk with Rickey in private. After edging Rickey into
a nearby restroom and closing the door, he asked if he was interested in left-
handed first baseman Nick Etten. Rickey bolted from the room in anger
and frustration. Mann concluded that what he called "incongruity" had
now reached either a new high or low.*

The sandbag landed with a thud two weeks later on April 9, 1947, while
Rickey was working the blackboard with his staff in his office and a few
hours before the Royals would play the Dodgers in Brooklyn in an exhibition match. The decision whether to bring Robinson to the Dodgers still
had not been made. The commissioner's assistant, Walter Mulbry, tele-
phoned to relay Chandler's decision on the hearings, one highlight of which
was the fining of both the Dodgers and the Yankees $2,000 for "engaging
in a controversy." Harold Parrott, the Dodgers traveling secretary, who had
ghosted Durocher's column, was fined $500. The final pronouncement was
that Leo Durocher had been suspended from baseball for a year "as a result
of the accumulation of unpleasant incidents in which he has been involved
and which the commissioner construes as detrimental to baseball."†

A startled Durocher exploded: "For what?"

The full written version of the decision, which Rickey obtained later in
the day from a United Press reporter, showed what Mann termed "a palpable
perversion of the stenographic record of the hearings in at least one of the
commissioner's findings." Chandler claimed that "evidence produced at the
hearings shows that the alleged gamblers were not guests of MacPhail and
did not sit in his box at Havana." Mann had transcribed who attended
both of the secret hearings, had entered the documented evidence, and

---

* Etten, who had gone on tour with Durocher, was finally traded to the Phillies, for whom he
played in seventeen games before retiring. Whether or not MacPhail offered his first
baseman with an eye to checkmating Robinson will probably never be known, but he did tell
reporters that Etten would be a good fit for the Dodgers.

† Durocher later asserted that Chandler himself made the telephone call and that Rickey
had told him, "You can't do that." (*Nice Guys Finish Last*, p. 257) Mann and others in the
room insisted from the start that Mulbry made the call and not the commissioner, who in
his own memoir says he ordered Mulbry to do it.

insisted that the exact opposite was true. He added that photographs of the gamblers in the Yankee box and the testimony of Patterson added to the proof. The lengthy decision closed with a firm admonition: All parties to this controversy were silenced from the time the order was issued.

In the pandemonium that followed, Rickey reflected on the bitter fact that, having lost two coaches, Chuck Dressen and Red Corriden, he had now been deprived of his manager. The wholly unexpected blow caught him on the threshold of a decision on Robinson. Five steps of the six-stage program had been cleared. Robinson was undeniably the right man on and off the field. By April, Rickey was certain of a good reaction from the press and public, because both had challenged him to promote Robinson to the Dodgers or explain the delay. Robinson had qualified fully in Spring Training by batting .625 in exhibition games and making excellent use of the first baseman's mitt handed to him in Panama.

While Durocher and Rickey worked behind the scenes to smooth the way for Robinson among a few recalcitrant Dodgers—namely, Dixie Walker and catcher Bobby Bragan—Robinson had made it clear that he was not going to push himself on the team and that if he was not wanted, he would just as soon return to Montreal, where he got along fine with everybody. He told Herbert Goren of the *New York Sun* in late March that the last thing he wanted to do was disrupt the morale of the parent club and spoil its chances for the pennant, that his attitude was "devil may care," and that he would not feel badly if he did not make it, adding that the main reason he hoped to make the Dodgers was purely economic. "They've got a minimum salary in the majors which is more than I am making now."*[23]

"Jackie was extremely level-headed," recalled sportscaster Bob Wolff, who interviewed Robinson in 1947. "When he was asked about race rela-tions, he would tell the story of how he went to UCLA, and USC was their biggest rival. 'They would taunt me and yell at me,' Jackie said. 'But after we played for some time against each other and got to know each other, we went from bitter rivals to friends. The more we got to know each other, the more we found we had a lot in common.' It was a great way to build unity and harmony about people."[24]

On April 10, Jackie Robinson signed a contract with the Brooklyn Dodgers and later that day Durocher stopped by the Dodger clubhouse to

---

* He was making $4,000 with the Royals, but he would get a minimum of $5,000 with the Dodgers.

tell the players to put their faith in Rickey, who would bring them through. "You've got a great chance to win the pennant," he said. "I'll be with you every day of the season. Good-bye and good luck."[25]

On Opening Day of the 1947 season on April 15 against the Boston Braves, the main topic in New York newspapers was Durocher's departure after eight years as the Dodgers manager. The next biggest item was Pete Reiser's triumphant return to center field after breaking his ankle the previous year. Somewhere in the last few paragraphs, most stories got around to discussing Brooklyn's many new players, among them the "Negro lad" who was twenty-eight at the time. To the New York press, Robinson was not such a big deal—especially after he grounded out, flied out, and hit into a double play. Dick Young mentioned Robinson in the last paragraph of his *Daily News* story, describing Robinson merely as "the majors' most-discussed rookie." Arch Murray of the *Post* first referred to Robinson in his third paragraph, noting: "Jackie Robinson, the first colored boy ever to don major-league flannels, started at first base and batted second for the Dodgers."* In light of Durocher's ban and the commotion surrounding it, Red Smith later called Robinson's major league debut "a whisper in a whirlwind." *The Boston Globe* was one of the few newspapers saying that a new era had begun. On its editorial page, it wished Robinson good luck.[26]

As HE WAS preparing to fly to the West Coast, Walter O'Malley, the Dodgers vice president, pledged to bring Durocher back to Brooklyn as soon as possible. "We're going to have a great team this year, and to Leo and Laraine, we're not saying 'good-bye' but 'we'll be seeing you soon.'" Dixie Walker was the most outspoken of the players. Referring to the Chandler decision, he declared, "I can't see anything fair about it in any sense of the word."

Overlooked that historic day was that the Dodgers still lacked a manager. Clyde Sukeforth, who had turned down the job, managed for the first two games of the season. Rickey needed a new manager in a hurry, so he called his old friend Burt Shotton, now sixty-two years old, who was scouting for the Dodgers in Florida. Shotton was close to Rickey and had been for many

---

* "I wondered how I could have been so blind to the meaning of it all," Young would later write. "And then I remembered Robinson had not been a factor in the ballgame, and in those days we wrote what happened on the field. Period."

years. Back in 1925, when Rickey managed the Cardinals and Shotton was a coach, Shotton took over on Sundays when Rickey observed the Sabbath by staying away from the ballpark.[27]

He had not managed full-time since 1933. He told Shotton, "Be in Brooklyn in the morning. Call nobody, see no one." According to Shotton, he didn't know the job was his until ninety minutes before he arrived at the Polo Grounds to manage the third game of the season. Shotton was a quiet, considerate man, one of whose conditions for taking the job was that he did not have to put on a uniform. It would have been hard to find two men in all of baseball as different as Leo Durocher and Burt Shotton. There was no question that Durocher was Rickey's man in the matter of bringing up Robinson. Red Barber, who watched it all up close, said there was no question that Rickey had "carefully schooled" Durocher on handling Robinson's debut.[28]

When Leo's plane landed in Los Angeles on April 14, he refused to make any comment on the suspension or anything else. He brushed by reporters, answering the multitude of questions with a staccato burst of "No comments." A short Associated Press piece in the *Herald-American* carried the headline LIPPY'S NEW NICKNAME "THE CLAM."

For many, the most distasteful part of the whole affair was the gag order that was ordered by Chandler, which denied all of those disciplined a chance at a rebuttal. Columnist Henry McLemore wrote, "In short, he rammed gags down their throats—gags of the same size and texture that have been standard equipment in totalitarian nations for many years. I don't know where the baseball commissioner got his gags, but it could be that an Army friend found them while snooping in the medicine chest of Adolf Hitler's Berlin bunker retreat."

Regarding the severity of the punishment, McLemore wrote that Chandler was not content with throwing just the book at Leo Durocher, but let the Brooklyn manager have the entire library, including the librarian and the scrubwoman. Arthur Daley of *The New York Times* compared Leo's punishment to the chap hauled into traffic court for running a red light and being given the electric chair, using the term *bum rap* to describe Durocher's harsh punishment.[29]

BILL MARDO IN the *Daily Worker* likewise expressed strong editorial support, underscoring the point that Durocher's strongest and most immediate support came from the far left. "As a Brooklynite and a Dodger fan," said New York Communist councilman Peter V. Cacchione in a public statement deploring Chandler's act, "I am strongly opposed to the arbitrary suspension of Leo Durocher." Cacchione suggested that Chandler spend his time making sure that the rest of the other fifteen teams in baseball signed Negro players. The Kings County Committee of the American Labor Party—a proudly Red organization—declared that the people of Brooklyn were entitled to know the facts upon which so drastic a penalty was imposed, and based on what had already been published, called on Commissioner Chandler to reconsider the suspension and to reinstate Leo Durocher as the manager of the Brooklyn baseball club for 1947.[30]

Chandler reacted badly to the press criticism and told Dan Parker that an unholy alliance existed between Parker, Tom Meany of *PM*, Dave Egan of the *Boston Daily Record*, the whole of the *New York Herald Tribune* sports department, and others who did not see eye to eye with the commissioner. "And I wouldn't be surprised," Chandler told Parker, "if there's a lot of money behind it." Red Smith of the *Tribune* gleefully pulled Chandler overboard. "I wish to state using the first person, that if I can get paid for thinking Happy Chandler has performed like a clown and a mountebank, I want all of that kind of money that I can get. Ordinarily, I have to work for mine," said Smith's boss, *Tribune* sports editor Stanley Woodward. "Knowing he was under fire for timidity, Chandler took refuge in overreaction . . . the most colossal piece of injustice and bravado yet perpetrated."[31]

But criticism also came from those Chandler chose—or dared—not to attack because of their influence. When Grantland Rice, still regarded as the dean of sportswriters, called Durocher's punishment "much too severe," Chandler was just as silent as when he had been attacked by Pegler.

Others, especially those at the center of the event, would never comprehend what Chandler had done to Durocher. "I can't understand to this day why he did what he did," Red Barber said in an interview more than thirty years after the fact.[32]

Some even believed that Durocher's banishment had to do with an assault on Rickey and the breaking of the color bar. Dr. Dan Dodson, the sociologist who chaired the group looking into baseball integration, Mayor Fiorello La Guardia's Committee on the Unity of New York City, later wrote: "Many of us will always believe that it was Chandler's way of getting at Rickey, who he could not touch personally but whose manager was vulnerable." In his memoir, *The Lords of Baseball*, Hal Parrott stated his belief that by suspending Durocher the lords of baseball made Robinson's ordeal more difficult.[33]

A few cheered Chandler's decision. John Christian claimed the last laugh was on Durocher, who now had his jaw wired shut. Many of the Hearst newspapers, including the *Chicago Herald-American*, took a bow in print for carrying the Pegler columns, which they insisted had been the reason Durocher was now in exile. A handful of sportswriters agreed with Leo's banishment. "Commissioner Chandler's suspension of Leo Durocher will outrage the hoodlum element," wrote Arch Ward in the *Chicago Tribune*, "but fans who have the long range interest of baseball at heart will applaud."[34]

If Durocher had become a pariah to some, he was a maverick hero to others. A Brooklyn Congregational Church group petitioned Chandler to reinstate Leo. In Cambridge, Massachusetts, a call went out from the students of the Harvard Athletic Association in a letter published in the *Harvard Crimson* the day after his suspension to sign Leo as assistant baseball coach. A few even found humor in the whole thing. Shirley Povich of *The Washington Post* said that Durocher had been sentenced to "a year and a Day." But *Time* magazine may have had the last word when it said that Chandler had done the seemingly impossible, which was to turn Durocher into a sympathetic character.

Despite his role in the melodrama, MacPhail most unexpectedly leapt to Leo's defense, claiming Chandler did not have the grounds for a five-minute suspension of Durocher, let alone a year. MacPhail also argued against those who said that Chandler had been lenient on him because he had engineered Chandler's election to commissioner. Not so, he told Harry Nash of the *Newark Evening News*—he had not voted for him until the sixth ballot.[35]

On April 15, MacPhail sent a letter to American League president Will Harridge asking for his intervention in the suspensions of Durocher and Dressen. Then, on the twenty-first, Rickey, National League president Ford Frick, O'Malley, Arthur Mann, and Henry L. Ughetta (a part owner of the Dodgers franchise) flew to Cincinnati to plead for Durocher, but to no avail. As the Brooklyn delegation was en route home, Chandler turned down their requests, stating that the case against Durocher was closed.

But the case against Chandler was not. On the eve of the Dodgers delegation's departure for Cincinnati, Leonard Lyons noted in his Broadway column that J. Edgar Hoover, who had been unavailable at the time of

Chandler's election because World War II was still being waged, was now free to take the job of commissioner—an indication that some people wanted to see the short reign of Happy Chandler come to a quick end.

A growing cadre of sportswriters simply did not like the thin-skinned Chandler. As columnist Edwin Rumill wrote in the *Christian Science Monitor*: "Mr. Chandler suspends Leo Durocher for actions 'detrimental to baseball' yet he himself publicly blasts the nation's writers for criticizing his management. Wouldn't you say that was poor publicity for the national pastime?"[36]

Chandler was silent for the moment on the matter of Durocher, but one answer he gave almost immediately and for decades to come had to do with the harshness of his treatment of Durocher: "People asked me if it wasn't hard suspending him for a year. But, hell, I signed 36 death warrants when I was governor, including two men they hung in the courthouse yard for rape. If you ask me, I was lenient on Durocher."*[37]

In early May, Durocher returned to Brooklyn and watched the Dodgers beat the Cardinals 7–6. The club was off to a 10–3 start. Durocher talked to a few members of the press after the game willing to talk about everything but his exile. About his golf course meeting with Chandler the previous October he observed: "Ever since that meeting, I defy the commissioner or anyone else to look me in the eye and say that I haven't been on the straight and narrow."

Durocher expressed no bitterness about his situation and stunned Bob Cooke and the other writers by declaring, "Although it's the first time in twenty-three years that I've been out of baseball, I want to say that I've never been happier in my life than during the last few weeks. I've had a lot of offers, on the radio and in the movies." Durocher made no bones about the fact that he was in Brooklyn to talk to Rickey about returning to the Dodgers for the 1948 season. Durocher behaved as if the suspension was already in his rearview mirror.[38]

On May 9, Day's divorce in California was upheld in Superior Court.

---

* Some five years after the suspension, Chandler began answering the question of whether or not he would have done the same thing again by insisting that he would. He said the underlying reason he took Durocher out of the game was to "keep Leo from killing somebody." In 1955, while running for governor of Kentucky, he denied ever having said such a thing when interviewed by Robert Shaplen of *Sports Illustrated*, but Chandler later reverted to his belief that Leo was homicidal and in fact expressed the thought in his own memoir.

The California court, however, still did not recognize the Texas marriage, and based on legal advice, Leo and Laraine continued to live at separate addresses in California.

Westbrook Pegler continued to stir up trouble. The day after Day's divorce was upheld, he used his column to take on sportswriters who he claimed were allowing gangsters to overrun professional sports. "The sports run and the police beat now overlap, but sportswriters are notoriously aloof to problems outside their comfort zone." The proof of this, he declared, was the inability of newspaper writers to dig deeper into the Durocher-Raft-Siegel matter. Pegler claimed to have obtained wiretaps showing that Raft had once used Durocher's New York phone to call Longie Zwillman, a notorious New Jersey racketeer, and other underworld contacts. As had been true of the earlier attacks, Durocher chose not to respond.

On June 20, gangster Benjamin "Bugsy" Siegel was shot dead in his girl-friend Virginia Hill's Beverly Hills home just south of Sunset Boulevard. The murder set up new speculation about the relationship of baseball to this deceased member of the Luciano crime family.

Tommy Holmes of the *Brooklyn Eagle* unveiled a series of revelations in his column the day after the killing that put others into Siegel's orbit. Del Webb, one-third owner of the Yankees, was reported to have had a one-third interest in Siegel's Flamingo Hotel in Las Vegas. The columnist then called Webb's partner, Larry MacPhail, to verify Webb's involvement: "Of course, Del was interested in the Flamingo," said MacPhail. "I say 'was' not 'is,' because it's my understanding that he got his money out. And when I say 'he,' I don't mean Del personally, but as president of the Del E. Webb Construction Company." MacPhail ended the conversation by saying that he didn't know how Siegel was connected with the corporation or even that he was, and that he did not know if Webb knew anything about such a connection.

Holmes reported that while Durocher was getting himself into a jam in Cuba, the New York Giants were training in Phoenix, Arizona, and owner Horace Stoneham decided he wanted to throw a party in Las Vegas for the baseball writers following the team. He phoned Webb for a suggestion, and Webb not only suggested the Flamingo but joined the party himself with Siegel. One reporter told Holmes that he had won a chunk of money playing roulette, but that another member of the press corps got into an argument with Siegel. Apparently, the writer insisted on calling him Bugsy, while Siegel insisted on being addressed as Ben.[39]

Holmes ended his column, entitled "That Link Between Baseball and Bugsy," by puckishly suggesting that the commissioner should take stern action when it was shown that Durocher, Webb, Stoneham, or a baseball writer had pointed the gun that fired the slugs found in Siegel's body.* [40]

Over the course of the season, Rickey and Chandler had gone back and forth on the matter of Durocher. What was not known then but revealed later was that Rickey had actually threatened to quit the game of baseball if Durocher were not allowed to return for the 1948 season with all rights and privileges restored.

LEO LIVED A much different life in California. He became Laraine's yardman and gardener. Working with her twin brother, Lamar, they cleared four acres of brush, cut down two hundred trees, and installed a sprinkler system for a new, lush, rolling lawn. The Durochers' best friends during the suspension were Corny Jackson, a West Coast advertising and public relations executive, and his wife, Gail Patrick, the former movie star. Leo and Laraine became godparents to the Jackson children. The Jacksons were active in show business and together would package the popular *Perry Mason* television series, which began in 1957. Corny became Leo's greatest advocate, and their friendship would extend for years to come. In 1955, when *Sports Illustrated* ran a three-part profile of Leo, Corny gave him an extraordinary testimonial: "Leo's love of people, his gratitude for friendship, is both his greatest asset and weakness. He'll act and talk toughest with people he likes most. But no matter where you are, you can stock a room with 20 people with better minds and better looks, and he'll somehow take charge." [41]

At one point during the suspension, Leo learned that people who had written to Chandler protesting the suspension got the response that they would view the matter differently if they knew the full case against Durocher. At this, Leo blew up and tried to get Chandler on the phone. He

---

* Years later, when Chandler was elected to the National Baseball Hall of Fame, he penned an article for *The New York Times* in which he claimed that one of the reasons he was voted out of the commissionership was because he had started an investigation of Del Webb for his associations with gamblers. He wrote: "After I left, nothing came of the investigation. Ford Frick, who replaced me, stopped it. Webb was very much in Frick's corner." Chandler also claimed that Webb boasted that the greatest contribution he had made to baseball was getting rid of Chandler." (*The New York Times*, March 21, 1982)

had to settle for Walter Mulbry, Chandler's assistant, who told him he could not talk to the commissioner. "My advice to you," said Mulbry, "is to keep your mouth shut."[42]

This was a major source of frustration for Durocher, as well as the fact that he was not being paid by the Dodgers and had no cash coming in. He was receiving numerous business offers, but he knew that if he went down that road, he would have to leave baseball. Durocher finally sought legal advice and was prepared to sue for his wages in civil court. According to Day, in her memoir of her years with Leo: "His case was so strong—since no formal charges had been made against him—that his Brooklyn salary was finally paid in full."[43]

In early September, MacPhail again defied the gag order by making a series of odd and disjointed remarks about Leo and Rickey. He asserted that Rickey could have prevented the suspension but chose not to, effectively orchestrating Leo's year away from the game. He argued for Leo's innocence. "I'm still offering a suit of clothes to anybody who can show me what evidence Durocher was suspended on." He also predicted that Durocher would not return as Brooklyn manager.

Upon reading MacPhail's remarks, Rickey exploded with rage. "I've taken all I can stand. I'm suing MacPhail for a million dollars," he said. Rickey never followed through on this threat, but the feud between the two had now escalated.

The next day MacPhail claimed that he had never held a news conference, and that all of the quotations ostensibly from it were bogus. As Lawton Carver of the International News Service pointed out, the quotations attributed to him in various newspapers under the names of different reporters were virtually identical, and to repudiate them was an "incredibly bold gesture." A growing belief developed among those who covered the Yankees that MacPhail was experiencing a mental breakdown.[44]

On the baseball field, the Dodgers and the Yankees were both faring well. Under Burt Shotton, Brooklyn moved into first place in July thanks to a thirteen-game win streak, and they spent the rest of the summer vying for the pennant with the Cardinals. By midsummer—with Brooklyn on a torrid pace at the head of the National League—very little was being written about Leo, and what did appear in print depicted him as baseball's forgotten man. "No front-page figure in the history of baseball ever disappeared so completely from view in such a short period of time," wrote Ed Rumill in his column on August 1, 1947.[45]

On September 22, the idle Dodgers clinched the National League pennant when the second-place Cardinals lost to the Chicago Cubs. "It's been a long pull, but a pleasant one," Shotton observed. "I'll congratulate the boys when they report at Ebbets Field tomorrow for the game with the Giants." They ended up with a five-game lead over the Cardinals. At sixty-two years and eleven months, Shotton was about to become the oldest manager ever to make his World Series debut. The Yankees finished with a 97–57 record, a dozen games ahead of the Detroit Tigers.

Under Shotton, certain players flourished who could have wilted under Durocher. Early in the season, during the Dodgers' first western trip, rookie pitcher Harry Taylor had a rough outing against the Reds. Back in Brooklyn, the Dodgers front office wanted to send the hurler back to the minors, but Shotton was convinced that Taylor had it in him to be a successful big leaguer. He said this to the front office and repeated it to Taylor. The youngster responded with a number of solid outings before pulling a tendon in his arm in August. He finished the season with a 10–5 record and a 3.11 ERA.[46]

Eddie Stanky, who had come to the Chicago Cubs in 1944, was another Dodger who made a difference in 1947 when he was elected to his first All-Star squad. He got 141 hits, scored 97 times, and made just 12 errors at second base in helping to lead Brooklyn to the pennant. There were others, but Shotton had the right mix of new and veteran players he needed to win.

Chandler, who was already unpopular with the writers, became more so when he refused to approve Bill Corum as a broadcaster for the 1947 World Series because Corum—despite his past history with Durocher—had been highly critical of the commissioner's punishment of Leo. "If you want to be critical of me," Chandler told Corum, "you do it on your own time. This is my time. You're not gonna do it with my time."[47]

The World Series was a classic with five of the seven games settled by two runs or less. In the fourth game Yankee pitcher Bill Bevens carried a no-hitter into the ninth inning only to lose when Cookie Lavagetto doubled with two outs and two on. In the sixth game, Dodger outfielder Al Gionfriddo robbed Joe DiMaggio of a game-tying extra-base hit with one of the most memorable catches in baseball history. The Dodgers' Red Barber's radio call of the play became one of his most famous: "Swung on, belted . . . it's a long one . . . back goes Gionfriddo, back, back, back, back, back, back . . . heeee makes a one-handed catch against the bullpen! Oh, Doctor!" Tied at three games apiece, this set up the seventh game in which Brooklyn jumped to a 2–0 lead, but the Yankees, behind ace reliever Joe Page's five shutout innings, won 5–2, claiming their eleventh championship.*[48]

As Rickey left the field, MacPhail caught up with him, put his arm around his shoulder, offered his hand, and started to congratulate him on the fine job he had done with the Dodgers. "I am taking your hand only because people are watching us," Rickey said. Rickey then launched into reasons for his disappointment in MacPhail as a man, and he severed their relationship once and for all: "Don't you ever speak to me again."

MacPhail's glee turned to deep anger as he entered the Yankees clubhouse. He turned the clubhouse celebration on its head when, in a drunken rage, he unleashed a barrage of insults, punched a writer, and announced his resignation. His behavior continued at the Biltmore Hotel, where MacPhail tearfully announced his retirement again and proceeded to harass members of the press and the Yankees organization. Co-owner Dan Topping dragged him into the kitchen to shake some sense into him. MacPhail was chastened briefly, then fired farm director George Weiss in an irrational burst of anger, leaving Weiss in tears. MacPhail had single-handedly turned a victory celebration into a horror show.

Del Webb and Dan Topping bought out the fifty-seven-year-old MacPhail the next day for $2 million. MacPhail had doubled his investment but was now gone from baseball for the rest of his life. As Yankee historian Neil J. Sullivan concluded: "His was one of the tragic lives that spot the game's history—brilliance lost in alcohol, drugs, or mental illness."†[49]

After the Series, when the Dodgers voted to give Durocher a full share of the team's World Series money, Chandler vetoed the move and warned the team not to give him even a gift. If the Dodgers decided to take up a collection to give Leo a gold watch, the commissioner warned that he would fine each player in the amount of his contribution. It was as if Chandler was determined to give Leo an extra measure of punishment. Even those who genuinely disliked Durocher were beginning to feel that he was being unfairly punished twice for the same crime.[50]

Jackie Robinson, who had gone on to bat .297, score 125 runs, and steal

---

* For the first time, a World Series produced total receipts over $2 million with a significant amount going to the ballplayer Pension Fund. Chandler also upped the number of umpires on the field for a World Series from four to six.
† He was elected to the Hall of Fame in 1978, three years after his death.

29 bases, was named the first Rookie of the Year in the postseason. Over the course of the season Robinson had come to respect the even-tempered Burt Shotton. The two men were suited to one another in the sense that a general was suited to a soldier under his command—more on the order of Dwight D. Eisenhower than George Patton or Douglas MacArthur. Shotton was simply his boss, and there was nothing paternalistic or stressful about their relationship. Robinson, like Branch Rickey, regarded Shotton as a friend.

On November 12, Walter Mulbry got a call from *Brooklyn Eagle* sports editor Louis Niss asking where the commissioner stood on the reinstatement of Durocher. He was told that Chandler had no objections. Then, in early December, the Brooklyn Chapter of the Knights of Columbus came out opposing Leo's reinstatement. The group gave no particulars, leading Red Smith of the *New York Herald Tribune* and others to conclude that the opposition by the Catholic fraternal group was because of his marriage to Laraine Day and the legal circumstances surrounding the divorce. Smith spoke for many in the press when he concluded: "This is an uneasy business especially if the K of C's attitude should be the deciding factor in costing the man his job. It is not so very far from such a position to a boycott against all divorced men in sports."[51]

Just when it looked like the edict of the Knights of Columbus might have had an effect, the Catholic Youth Organization announced it was withdrawing its objections to Durocher. On December 6, 1947, he was reinstated as manager of the Brooklyn Dodgers. Shotton, now sixty-three, was made supervisor of the managers of the club's twenty-six farm teams. "It is a nice old man's job," he said.

On December 8, Day announced her devotion to Leo by ripping up her contract with RKO, which still had six years to run and would have netted her approximately $1 million. She told the studio that she didn't want to make a movie during the time Leo was with the Dodgers, and that she preferred to do freelance work, but only when he was not working. She also told Hollywood columnist Louella Parsons that the two would be remarried in California after the Los Angeles divorce became final.[52]

On December 17, Ford Frick announced that Durocher would manage the 1948 National League All-Star team, the honor accorded to the manager of the National League champions.

CHAPTER 10

Over the River

DURING HIS MONTHS IN EXILE, Durocher resisted any impulse to appear in public as a speaker or perform on the radio or write for a newspaper despite many requests to do so. However, he secretly began formulating the idea of producing a memoir about his Dodger years, with Hal Parrott as his ghostwriter. Leo did not want to do anything that would attract Chandler's attention—especially since the commissioner had told anyone who would listen that his punishment for Durocher had been too light.

But this all changed the minute the ban was lifted. Leo dusted off his black tie and hit the winter banquet circuit as a popular and well-paid after-dinner speaker. During the wartime tours with Danny Kaye and others, Durocher had polished his innate sense of timing, which he combined with an ability to spin good yarns, many of which involved making fun of himself. He was now able to wow large audiences for high speaking fees.

"Your Excellency"—turned to the governor to begin a dinner engagement at the Connecticut Sports Writers Association in Hartford—"I trust I am correct in calling you Your Excellency."

The governor nodded his approval. Durocher then turned to the mayor.

"Your Honor—I presume it is in good taste to refer to you as Your Honor."

There was a smile of assent.

"Thank you very much," said Durocher. "I just don't want to make any mistakes this year with Chandler listening."[1]

While Durocher was on the banquet trail, the writers who covered the

Dodgers and who genuinely liked Burt Shotton decided to throw a banquet of their own in Shotton's honor at Toots Shor's restaurant. More than a hundred sportswriters showed up, along with a number of baseball officials. It quickly turned into a lovefest for the man they called Old Barney. Shotton himself used the occasion to talk about the "family of writers" who had traveled with the Dodgers in 1947: "They were all my friends"—a line that Durocher would have gagged on.

Hugh Casey represented the players in praise. "Shotton was more than just the manager of the Dodgers," Casey said. "He was a father to the players. I could see some of 'em grow into men under his guidance. I saw that happen myself."

Durocher did not make it to the event but did call in to convey his best wishes by telephone. No doubt some of those in the room would have resented his sharing the spotlight with Shotton.

If there was an odd note to the event, it occurred when the amiable *Brooklyn Eagle* sports editor Harold Burr deviated from all the toasts wishing Shotton good-bye by rising to declare: "They tell me that this is supposed to be a farewell dinner, Burt. I don't think we're here to say good-bye. I predict you'll be back with the Dodgers by next July."[2]

Burr, Tommy Holmes, and most of the other Brooklyn beat writers felt that Shotton had done a good job leading the Dodgers to a pennant, and that Rickey and the rest of the Dodgers front office felt they had to bring Durocher back as part of their belief that he and they had been wronged by Chandler— not because Leo was necessarily the better man for the job. Holmes believed that Rickey had begun to lose interest in Durocher during the John Christian affair and would have let him go if he had not done so well in 1946.

Holmes and other writers believed Shotton had lowered the temperature in the Dodgers clubhouse and dugout and that the team had blossomed under the man whose idea of challenging an umpire was to shake his head in disbelief. Shotton managed from deep in the dugout and seldom if ever appeared on the steps leading to the playing field.

On the other coast, a year after her divorce, Laraine and Leo were married again on February 15, 1948, in a private Mormon ceremony at Day's residence in California. Everything the Durochers now did seemed to make news, including the purchase of an oversized bed in which they would sleep when they were cohabiting in California. According to an Associated Press feature, the new bed was fitted with an antique headboard shipped from New York.[3]

"I can't change Durocher," Leo said, referring to himself in the third person in an interview with magazine journalist Caswell Adams early in the year. "I'll be hustling and scraping to win every ball game I can. The way I know how. A year away from the game didn't take any of the fire away from me. And my voice is still good. Shotton did a swell job but I will have to hustle to do as well. Otherwise a lot of guys will be on my neck."[4]

Come spring, Rickey had negotiated a deal with dictator Rafael Trujillo for a short Spring Training tour to the Dominican Republic—a tightly controlled military state that was a far cry from the "anything goes" atmosphere of Cuba. The deal that Rickey had struck with the strongman guaranteed the Dodgers $50,000 for the tour. Trujillo was there for the opening exhibition and, in an elaborate ceremony before the game, presented Durocher, Rickey, and Walter O'Malley with baseballs he had personally autographed. Early the next morning, a colonel from Trujillo's staff came to the hotel and without explanation or apology took the balls back.[5]

The tour of the Dominican Republic was demoralizing on numerous levels. The weather was hot, the local competition was lousy (the Dodgers beat the All-Stars 23–5 in one contest), and the field they were given for practice was in terrible shape. Durocher and Jackie Robinson were at odds as soon as Robinson showed up in Ciudad Trujillo (the name for Santo Domingo from 1936 to 1961, after Dominican dictator Rafael Trujillo named the city for himself). Leo took one look at Robinson and claimed he had lingered too long at the banquet tables that had been set in his honor and had put on too much weight. Leo told him that he was fat and slow. Robinson had in fact gained more than twenty pounds and had lost a step moving between bases.[6]

While still in the Dominican Republic, second baseman Eddie Stanky, the man widely regarded as the sparkplug of the 1947 Dodgers, was suddenly dealt to the Boston Braves. Stanky blamed Durocher, who had said that Stanky was not worth the one-third raise in pay he had asked for. "Leo's statement was unjustified," Stanky told Jack Cuddy of the United Press. "I battled for him and never said anything about his $60,000 salary. And I played 145 games last year when he wasn't even here. So how does he know what I was worth? In short, he knifed me in the back, he really put the skids under me." Stanky finally settled for a 25 percent raise before being traded to the Braves.

Durocher's behavior in the Dominican Republic and later at the new Dodger training camp in Vero Beach was disturbing to Rickey—so disturbing in fact that he compiled a six-page memo on April 2, 1948, detailing Leo's transgressions. Written more than two weeks before Opening Day, it was marked CONFIDENTIAL and conveyed a deep sense of betrayal. It opened by pointing out that Durocher's 1948 contract forbade him from gambling. Rickey had spelled it out: "Under no circumstances was Durocher, at any time during his employment, to play games of chance, e.g., cards for stakes of any amount whatever, with any of his players. Nor was he to gamble in any direction whatever, anywhere or at any time, or with anybody." But Rickey asserted he did play for stakes in the Dominican Republic with various parties and included, on occasion, a player or players. "He even had the effrontery to tell Mrs. Rickey that at [Ciudad] Trujillo he won $300 in one night," Rickey noted, "but I have considerable information that he did not refrain from any games in which he had an opportunity to participate."

Durocher also seemed to be going out of his way to disobey Rickey's direct orders in other matters. He refused to show up for an exhibition game that Rickey had insisted he attend and manage. Leo's presence had been promised to the Dominican officials, and Rickey felt his absence may have caused the relationship between the Dodgers and the Dominicans to sour to the point where the team might not be invited back. In order to deter "hustlers and touts," Rickey had also ordered Durocher not to invite any friends not in uniform to sit on the bench during practice and exhibition games, but Leo chose to disobey this simple edict as well.

What especially irked Rickey was Durocher's attitude toward the new Dodger training facility in Vero Beach, Florida, nicknamed Dodgertown. It was a sprawling complex with three ballparks and roads with names like Branch Rickey Boulevard, Walter O'Malley Way, and Durocher Trail. This was Rickey's pride and joy and seen as a new chapter in a program to develop ballplayers. The new facility could accommodate more than four hundred players from all levels of the Dodgers system. Suites were built to accommodate Dodgers officials, including the board of directors. But when the team returned from the Dominican Republic, Durocher refused to stay in the apartment that had been prepared for him and Laraine, declaring it unfit and demanding a suite in a luxury hotel. Durocher made his point with "great bombast" and then went to the press ridiculing the Dodgers and their camp. Bill Roeder of the *World Telegram* was one of several who quoted Leo's negative take on Dodgertown. Rickey wrote in his memo: "Leo's attack on the camp was not only offensive to him personally but was extremely hurtful to the team's scouts and field workers. Copies of these articles in the hands of our competitive clubs and circulated freely among free agents seriously damage our chances to sign prospective players. It is the belief of our boys in camp that these articles would not have been written if Durocher had stayed in the camp."

Rickey was not through. Durocher had ridiculed Dodgers coaches and marginalized several of them to the point where they were rendered ineffective. He had mocked outfield coach and Rickey friend Ray Blades in front of the team. Durocher had also proposed that the team release players who would then be lost to the Dodgers organization to the tune of $250,000. One of the players Leo would have discarded if his plan had been adopted was Gene Mauch, who would have been sold on waivers.

Finally, Rickey recounted an incident in which Durocher had created a deliberate and unnecessary public confrontation with him. Prior to Spring Training, Rickey had asked the National League to assign him an umpire to use with his B squad, which would be on a separate barnstorming tour at the end of the stay at Dodgertown. The league offered him Jocko Conlan, and Rickey hired him with pleasure. But several days ahead of his arrival in Vero Beach, Conlan called Rickey and said that he was a major league umpire and did not want to officiate at the B level. Rickey explained that this was a special case and that Rickey needed a top umpire for the tour. The conversation ended cordially with Conlan prepared to travel with the B team.

The day before the B team was scheduled to travel to Mobile, as his memo revealed, Rickey learned that Conlan had met with Durocher, and the two men decided that Conlan was going with Durocher and the A team. Quoting from Rickey's memo on what happened that evening: "At the entrance of the dining room," Rickey related, "and in the presence of a number of people, including Mrs. Durocher and Mr. Conlan and a number of my friends and theirs, Mr. Durocher stopped the egress and ingress of everybody to and from the dining room while he told me, with great gestures and in loud voice, that Mr. Conlan was going with him to Ft. Worth and that he was going to carry both Larry [Goetz] and Conlan with him on his entire trip."

Conlan sided with Durocher, and Rickey told Conlan he should leave immediately for New York because the Dodgers no longer needed his services. Conlan came back to Rickey later in the evening and apologized profusely. He said he would be pleased to go with the B squad the next morning, which he did.

Rickey feared that this recent display of Durocher disloyalty would appear in the press, which it did not. But after many years of putting up with Leo's antics, Rickey was finally becoming fed up.[7]

In Florida, the relationship between Durocher and Robinson deteriorated. It seemed to have nothing to do with race but rather two strong personalities at odds. Robinson saw Durocher as a vain man who wore too much cologne and was obsessed with his clothing and grooming. Durocher called Robinson "fatso" and complained openly about his lack of discipline to the press. "He was skinny for Shotton but got fat for me."[8]

On the other hand, Durocher was immediately impressed with African-American catcher Roy Campanella, who later recalled: "Leo liked my style. He told me he'd open the season with me behind the plate. That's what he told Mr. Rickey too. 'I'm going to switch [Gil] Hodges to first base,' Durocher told Mr. Rickey. 'That's where he belongs.'"

Rickey then asked: "Who will catch for you if Hodges plays first base?"

"Campanella," Leo said unhesitatingly. "Campanella and Bruce Edwards."

Durocher felt that Campanella was the best catcher in camp and that Hodges was a natural at first. However, he could sense he was fighting a losing battle on behalf of playing Campanella and finally agreed to do without him. Leo was allowed to keep him around until the then mandatory cut-down time on May 15, but only to sit on the bench, not to go behind the plate except to finish out a game. Durocher did get Rickey to promise that if Campanella was needed for the pennant race around midseason, he would be recalled from St. Paul. "At the time," Campanella said, "I didn't know any of this, but what difference would it have made if I had?"[9]

Although a number of writers predicted that the Dodgers were odds-on favorites to win the pennant again in 1948, things did not go according to plan as the regular season got under way. From the start, it looked like a different team. Stanky was gone and the team lost four of its first seven games without a single Dodger pitcher going the distance, a rarity at a time when pitching a complete game was still the norm.

Impatient, Durocher wanted to toy with the entire lineup. Things got worse, and Durocher's temper followed suit. He bawled out outfielder Pete Reiser and continued his criticism of Robinson, accusing both of not being in shape. Campanella observed: "Jackie said his arm was sore, Leo wouldn't listen. He vowed he was going to get Jackie in shape or else. The next day he had coach Clyde Sukeforth hit grounders to Jackie until he nearly dropped. It started a feud between Durocher and Robinson that lasted a long time."

Campanella later commented: "It probably was not racist, it was based on the fact that Jackie and Leo were two of the fiercest competitors I ever saw."[10]

Durocher replaced Robinson at second base with Gene Mauch and things got worse—the Dodgers were immediately shut out by Boston 3–0 on a three-hitter. He then wanted to switch Billy Cox from third base to second and put Spider Jorgensen on third. Cox didn't want to play second, so he left the club and went home to Harrisburg, Pennsylvania.

Durocher was desperate, so after losing two games in a row, he put Campanella into the lineup for the second game of a doubleheader on April 27 against the Boston Braves, which the Dodgers lost 3–2. The next day, Campanella was benched because Rickey hit the roof, insisting that Durocher had played the catcher against his explicit orders. In the days that followed, Durocher pushed Rickey on the matter of Campanella, but Rickey became even more adamant that the catcher belonged on the bench, where he stayed for the next sixteen days. The issue was not as much about Campanella as it was a battle of wills between Rickey and Durocher.

When May 15 arrived and the Dodgers faced their cut-down date, Campanella was sent to the Dodgers farm club in St. Paul, the transfer occurring on May 17. Throwing salt on the wound, Durocher asked Campanella what Rickey was paying him, and Leo decided it was too little. Durocher then confronted Rickey with a salary demand for Campanella that Campanella had not asked for. At first, Rickey blamed Campanella.

On the day that Campanella headed west, the Dodgers began an eight-game losing streak that extended to May 23 when they blew a 5–0 lead to the Reds in a game that lasted three hours and seven minutes—an extraordinary duration at the time. That game put the team seven games below .500 and deep in the second division.

In the midst of this losing streak, Leo's book *The Dodgers and Me: The Inside Story* was published. It had originally been titled *Dem Bums*, which was vetoed at the last minute by Rickey, who had always loathed the nickname and deemed it offensive. The book had been ghostwritten by Harold Parrott and was reviewed widely and received poorly. "No feelings spared, as the author attacks people as though they were all umpires" was an early assessment from the Kirkus reviewing service. The greatest criticism was the degree to which details of Leo's story were either edited out or retold in a light flattering to Durocher. His friendship with George Raft was never mentioned and the John Christian affair earned just four lines, which Arthur Daley of *The New York Times* said was depicted as a most unusual accident in which a cement water trough leaped off the ground and conked Mr. Christian in the head. "You might say that Mr. Durocher was not so well tailored for biography as for fiction," wrote columnist Robert Ruark, who added, "He has the imagination and the skill, and all he needs now is a good subject."[11]

John Durant, a popular writer of illustrated baseball histories, reviewed the book for *The New York Times* and criticized Durocher for his reticence about the events leading up to his banishment and about the Christian episode. But Durant really called him to task for his "plain distortion" of facts regarding the 1943 mutiny. Among other things, Durocher claimed that *Telegram* reporter Tim Cohane was a "snooper" who had overheard Durocher from a half-opened door, rather than admitting he had given Cohane the information in a face-to-face interview. Twisting the knife, Durant pointed out that the ghostwriter for the book was Hal Parrott, who as a writer for the *Brooklyn Eagle* had taken Leo apart for his behavior during the revolt. Durant pointed out that the clubhouse mutiny was told so unfairly that Tim Cohane was threatening to sue Durocher for libel.[12]

What seemed most upsetting to both sportswriters and fans was that Durocher had been, in the words of one editor, "inexcusably blunt" in some of his comments about men who had played for him in Brooklyn or were still on the roster. Great exception was taken to what he wrote about infielder Luis Olmo, whom he termed a flop both defensively and offensively: "I rode him hard because he did not like to be pitched tight, and the pitchers discovering that, knocked him down again and again and sidearmed him to death. When his hitting fell off, he lost his hustle in the field, and I really went after him. Instead of trying harder, the Puerto Rican folded up." The comments were not only unfair but displayed Durocher at his most venal.

Leo was unimpressed by the critics of the book. "Hell. It wouldn't be much of a book if I didn't unload a few blasts. Let them knock my brains out. It'll sell more copies."[13]

As Durocher promoted the book, he once again proved that he had an uncanny ability to make news—not all of it good. In the midst of an autographing session in a Boston department store at the beginning of June, Durocher predicted that unless manager Mel Ott of the Giants began winning, he would be fired by the end of the season. The writers at the event pounced on Leo, who immediately denied ever having made the statement, which he had just made in front of them all. On the spot, Durocher decided that he was done promoting his book and would hold no more autographing sessions. Later that day, he performed a tasteless dugout pantomime that, according to the *Boston Herald*, had Braves president Lou Perini "purple with indignation." He ended the day by telling *Herald* columnist Will Cloney that the Cardinals—not the Dodgers—would win the pennant.[14]

Rickey had now lost confidence in Leo's ability to lift the club up and inspire his players: "I intended to give him the opportunity to resign if he felt he couldn't pick up the club." Rickey felt that he had gone all the way down the line with Leo, and in the words of Tommy Holmes, Rickey holding on to Durocher was getting to be a little bit like trying to hold a tiger by the ears.[15]

On July 4, Hal Parrott came to Durocher and told him that Rickey wanted him to resign. Durocher refused, saying the Dodgers would have to fire him if they wanted to get rid of him. Parrott was unable to locate Rickey but did get to Rickey Jr., who asked if Durocher had quit. Parrott said he had not. Rickey Jr. replied that he guessed that Leo was still managing the team.[16]

On the morning of July 15, according to Arthur Mann, who was in the middle of what was going on, National League president Ford Frick phoned Rickey and asked him to come to his office that afternoon. Horace Stoneham, owner of the Giants, had a matter to discuss with him. Rickey hurried over to the National League offices in Radio City and found the Giants owner waiting for him. Stoneham got right down to business.[17]

"Branch, Mel Ott has resigned as manager of the Giants," he said to Rickey. "I have his resignation here in my pocket. And I'd like to know whether Burt Shotton is available to manage the Giants."

Rickey pondered silently for a minute. "I'll tell you, Horace," he said finally, "I don't honestly think I'd like to let Burt go. It's no secret that we're having a little trouble in our organization, and I need Shotton more than ever where he is, keeping an eye on our minor league talent. No, I'm sorry, Horace." Rickey shook his head. "I'd like to help you out, but I wouldn't want to let Shotton go."[18]

"How about Durocher?" Stoneham shot right back.

"You'd be interested in Leo?" asked Rickey.

Stoneham nodded. "Very much so." Rickey puffed his cigar energetically. "Very well, you have my permission to talk to Durocher. I'll have him flown back to New York immediately."

The next day, a bewildered and apprehensive Durocher sat alone with Branch Rickey and Arthur Mann in the Dodgers Montague Street office.

"I had a rather interesting meeting with Horace Stoneham yesterday, Leo," Rickey said, easing into the discussion. Durocher waited silently for Rickey to go on.

Rickey dropped the bombshell quietly.

"He asked me if you were available to manage the Giants."

"What did you tell him?" Durocher inquired evenly.

"I told him he has my permission to discuss it with you."

"Does that mean that I'm fired?"

Rickey blinked. He took out a fresh cigar, lit it, and blew a cloud of smoke at the ceiling. "No it doesn't mean that at all. But it may well be, Leo, that there's a better future for you with the Giants. I know the agony you're going through here in Brooklyn. You're in an impossible position. With the Giants, you will have a new challenge, a fresh start. And perhaps a great deal more security."

"That's all I wanted to hear, Branch," Leo said, rising from his chair. He shook hands with Rickey. "I'll call you as soon as I get through talking to Horace Stoneham."

Horace Stoneham showed up at Leo Durocher's apartment on the evening of July 15, 1948, before Leo returned home from that evening's Dodgers game. Laraine Day greeted him politely, fixed him a drink, and asked the reason for his visit.[19]

"Leo has agreed to manage the Giants, and I expect the announcement will be made tomorrow," Stoneham replied.

Day walked over and clicked off a radio station carrying Red Barber's play-by-play of the Dodgers game. "Then what am I listening to this for?" she said.

Leo got home later that evening, and after the game, which the Dodgers won in the small hours of July 16, the telephone rang in the home of Bill Corum, the popular sports columnist for the *New York Journal-American*, who just a few months earlier had threatened to sue Durocher.

The caller did not identify himself, nor did he need to. In what Corum later described as "clear, piercing tones that I could recognize anywhere on Earth," the man said, "You are now talking to the new manager of the New York Giants."

Corum phoned his newspaper, then sat down at the typewriter. A few hours later, the early edition screamed the news with a huge, red headline: DUROCHER TO MANAGE GIANTS. Corum went on to call it "the second coming." It was the first and only sports story ever to be recorded on the tape produced by the Dow Jones ticker.

Rickey and Stoneham had agreed to release the story simultaneously the following day and Rickey was enraged by Durocher's giving Corum the scoop. Giants public relations man Garry Schumacher, who had known Durocher since meeting him on a train in 1925 on the way to Yankee Spring Training, was so sure that Durocher would leak the story in advance that he spent the night with Stoneham lest he take the blame.[20]

Almost before the ink was dry on the first headlines, the Dodgers announced that Shotton was returning to manage the Dodgers. The cliché that was broadly adopted was to call it the "greatest managerial shakeup in baseball history"—a judgment that still remains valid to the present day. "A flash opinion would be that Leo Durocher is the luckiest man in Baseball," wrote syndicated columnist Bill Cunningham. "With the wolves hard on his traces in Brooklyn he moves over the Bridge to inherit a club with so much power that it'll move if it ever gets some pitching."[21]

On the forty-sixth anniversary of the great John McGraw's hiring as the Giants manager, former team enemy number one Leo Durocher took the Giants' helm. The move shocked baseball fans across the country, but the reaction in the greater New York City area was unprecedented. The Dodgers and Giants were the bitterest rivals in sports history. When the teams met, as they did twenty-two times a season, fights frequently erupted in bars, on the street, and in the grandstands at Ebbets Field or the Polo Grounds during games. Umpires dreaded coming to New York.

"In the supercharged New York baseball atmosphere of 1948," columnist Dick Heller wrote later, "Durocher's move across the Harlem River was just as much a shocker as Harry Truman's presidential upset of Thomas Dewey 3½ months later." To Heywood Hale Broun, it was Robert E. Lee defending Gettysburg instead of attacking it. "Giant fans hated Durocher because he was a Dodger," wrote Ken Smith of the *New York Daily Mirror.* "To drop him suddenly in the Polo Grounds, where the feats of McGraw, Terry, Ott, Matty and the others are a sacred memory, was a shock too abrupt for acceptance."[22]

But for all of the shock some saw the move as brilliant from the Giants' standpoint. Arnold Hano, a twenty-six-year-old freelance sportswriter and book editor living in New York at the time, was thrilled. He loved Ott but thought he was a terrible manager and Durocher was a supremely good leader who could take the Giants to a pennant. "He was shrewd and cunning and had a great managing spirit."[23]

The day he moved to the Giants, Durocher sat alone for a time with Broun, who was then with the short-lived *New York Star*, waiting for the arrival of the Giants press. "His clarion voice was muted like a Cootie Williams trumpet and his face was wretched. 'What'll I do, Heywood?' he asked. 'These guys hate me.'"[24]

On July 26, Durocher returned to Brooklyn in a new uniform, still bearing the number 2. The event was nicknamed "D-Day" and "The Big One," and reserved seats sold out days in advance. A long line for general admission tickets had begun forming at dawn. A large police contingent was on hand, including five mounted and more than sixty foot patrolmen. Fearing problems from the many fans who had come to boo Durocher, National League president Ford Frick sent Bill Klem, his supervisor of umpires, to meet with Durocher before the game to warn him against any unnecessary bickering. In a soft voice, Leo responded, "I'll manage my club the same as always."[25]

The Giants won the game, but the headline writers won the day: D-DAY IN BROOKLYN SEES LIP GIVE BUMS BRONX CHEER, 13–4, read a typical example.[26]

The feud between Durocher and Jackie Robinson took on new life when Durocher moved to the Giants. Durocher coached and rode the opposition from the coaching box at third, and not only launched verbal tirades against Robinson but downplayed his talent whenever he talked about him to reporters. Robinson fought back and became a thorn in Leo's side. Monte Irvin witnessed it firsthand: "The feud between Jackie and Leo Durocher was especially nasty. Leo used to tell Jackie he was swell-headed, and Jackie would call Leo a 'traitor' for leaving the Dodgers. Sometimes it got very personal."[27]

As the season wound down, Brooklyn finished in third place and the Giants in fifth. The Boston Braves took the pennant and were beaten by Bill Veeck's Cleveland Indians in the World Series.

Soon after the season ended, Durocher signed two coaches—Frankie Frisch and Freddie Fitzsimmons, the latter still under contract to Boston. The Braves quickly pointed out that Durocher was welcome to the coach, as he was no longer needed in Boston, but Chandler saw it as "tampering," and Durocher was called to the carpet again. The two men met privately at the winter meetings in Chicago, where Leo's defense was that Fitzsimmons had come to him looking for a job, and all that he had done was to offer him one. Fitzsimmons was then signed by the Giants front office, not Durocher. Chandler said he would rule on the infraction sometime in the future—January at the earliest. Large numbers of reporters were in Chicago for the meetings, and their reaction did not favor the commissioner. Red Smith, who by this point was referring to Chandler as the "despot of the diamond," wrote of the Chandler-Durocher meeting, "It is perhaps the smallest tempest in the tiniest teapot to be set before the king before his accession to baseball's low throne."[28]

On January 12, 1949, Chandler fined Leo and Fitzsimmons $500 each and Fitzsimmons was suspended from the first of March until the first of April. The Giants were fined $2,000. The suspicion grew that Chandler was now using Durocher as his whipping boy, exercising his authority against Leo at convenient intervals, which Chandler denied.

The Giants' 1949 season got off to a slow start, opening with two shutout losses to the Dodgers in Brooklyn. On April 28, the Dodgers pummeled the Giants 15–2 at the Polo Grounds. All during the game, Fred Boysen, an Army veteran, kept ragging Durocher from the box seats. At the end of the game, Boysen ran onto the field and swooped past Durocher, grabbing his cap. Leo made a quick lunge to recover the cap, during which he came into brief contact with Boysen, which may have sent him sprawling.[29]

After riding to a hospital in a taxi accompanied by his lawyer, Boysen fell into an impressive but phony faint. Whether he had come with a lawyer to the game or picked him up on the field after the incident, Boysen was clearly preparing for litigation. Boysen immediately told reporters from his hospital bed that he was filing a suit for assault, charging that Durocher had hit him, thrown him to the ground, and then kicked him in the stomach. "I didn't even see Durocher behind me when he first hit me. But when I fell down after the first punch I saw that it was Durocher and he kicked me."

The first reaction of Commissioner Chandler was that Leo had done it again. Since the incident took place in a National League park and involved a National League manager, it seemed to lie within the jurisdiction of league president Ford Frick. But because Durocher was in the middle, Chandler told Frick he would handle it.[30]

Chandler ordered Durocher's immediate and indefinite suspension, and without a hearing. Years later, in his autobiography, Chandler stated the reason he had acted so quickly was that he had gotten a call from his friend Bill "Bojangles" Robinson, the famous tap dancer and actor who had cofounded the Negro league New York Black Yankees team in 1931. According to Chandler, Robinson told him that Durocher had hit "a little black boy behind second base at the Polo Grounds" and he felt he had to act immediately.[31]

At first blush, the story looked bad for Durocher. The next morning's headline in the *Chicago Sun-Times* was DUROCHER "SLUGS" BROOKLYN ROOTER and the *Boston Herald* bannered the story with LEO DUROCHER CHARGED WITH KICKING FAN. The Associated Press ran a wire photo of Dr. Charles Kessler holding a stethoscope to Boysen's chest. Initially identified in print as Puerto Rican, Boysen was also clearly black.

In the wake of Chandler's action, New York assemblyman Elijah Crump went a step further and demanded Leo's permanent expulsion from the game. He suggested that if he were not expelled, a boycott of Giants games by his Harlem community was in order. Crump framed the incident in terms of bigotry and racial intolerance, and since the Polo Grounds was located in Harlem, the threat of a Harlem boycott hit home. Crump was quickly backed by an ad hoc committee of twenty-five Brooklyn citizens who planned to travel to Cincinnati to petition Chandler for a lifetime ban.[32]

However, the picture quickly changed after an X-ray examination proved completely negative. Durocher said little but did ask, "Do you think I could knock him down in front of hundreds of spectators and no one would see it?" Dick Cueller, a player, called the whole thing "a *crucifiction*," and Giants infielder Sid Gordon called it "exaggerated nonsense." "Leo did nothing to that guy," he said. "He merely pushed him aside."

The mail over the next two days seemed to bear Gordon out. Scores of telegrams and letters poured into the Giants office and into Chandler's, protesting the new suspension and giving eyewitness testimony that Durocher had done nothing more than stand his ground. Then a railroad fireman named George Cronk delivered an affidavit stating that he was behind Boysen when he fell and that it was he, not Durocher, who had made contact. "I was so close behind him I couldn't help myself. I tripped over him. I suppose I kicked him in the leg or some other place in so doing and then stepped over him. I apologized. I said sorry and then walked out of the Park."[33]

The most incriminating evidence against Boysen came from a cabdriver named Maxwell Katz, who in his own sworn affidavit stated that he had picked up Boysen and several other passengers at the Polo Grounds to go to the hospital. He said that Boysen was "hale and hearty" and talked about the large sums of money which would soon come his way. Katz added that when they got to the hospital, two of the men with Boysen supported him while the other two took pictures. One of the passengers was Morris Golding, the lawyer representing Boysen. According to the International News Service dispatch on Katz's affidavit, Golding refused comment.[34]

The press had meanwhile backed Durocher. The baseball writers who had traveled with the Giants to Boston gave Leo a unanimous vote of confidence. The wife of the *New York Mirror's* baseball writer, Kenneth Smith, reported that she had been forced to move from her box seats because of the nature of Boysen's remarks.[35]

Red Smith used his *New York Herald Tribune* column to point to an insistent and growing public clamor for Chandler's removal. Smith explained that if Chandler had suspended Leo as a precautionary measure pending investigations of the charges against him, the whole matter might have met with less public anger. But by issuing an immediate disciplinary suspension of indefinite length without explanation, Chandler had lost all chance of public support. Smith's own take on Chandler was that he was an obstinate and self-important little king: "His official acts reflect such an abiding respect for the wisdom, the personal charm of A. B. Chandler that the failure of others to share his hero worship must be difficult for him to comprehend."[36]

On the eve of the hearing, the St. Louis Cardinals voted unanimously to ask the commissioner for leniency in dealing with Leo. The spokesman for the team was Coach Terry Moore, who admitted he did not know whether or not Leo had hit the man, but the team wanted the commissioner to know that the abuse players were taking from the stands was on the increase and becoming intolerable. Ragging now meant "low cracks" about a player's wife and family. "The worst thing now, though, is that people are rushing onto the playing field during and right after games, stealing gloves, grabbing caps off players' heads and even trying to get away with favorite bats." There was growing sentiment all over baseball and among both players and umpires that fans must be kept off the field at the end of a game.[37]

By the time Chandler got around to holding a hearing in his office, more than one writer covering the event felt that Chandler was on trial, not Durocher. The hearing in Chandler's Cincinnati office lasted for just under two hours, and he found that there was not sufficient evidence to indicate Durocher had deliberately assaulted Fred Boysen. "Under the circumstances, the suspension against Durocher is lifted immediately and Durocher will rejoin his team on Wednesday, May 4." But Chandler used the hearing to admonish Stoneham for his policing of the Polo Grounds and for allowing fans to run onto the field before the players and umpires had left.

Boysen's case had totally collapsed, but it still had to be addressed in court, where Durocher was required to appear. Boysen formally requested the court's permission to withdraw the summons. "I have no case. I'd like to take it like a good sport and forget the whole thing." The Giants attorney then stated that a great injustice had been done to Durocher and asked Boysen to apologize. For a moment, Boysen hesitated. Then he put out his hand and said, "Sorry Mr. Durocher. I hope you have luck." Durocher grasped Boysen's outstretched hand and, forcing a smile, thanked him.

While the resolution of the Boysen affair had nothing to do with the team, it had everything to do with reestablishing Durocher in the public eye. Even those who did not particularly like the man rallied to his defense. "The whole thing boomeranged in his favor," said Garry Schumacher of the Giants. "From that day, he felt the fans were back with him and not against him. It's made a big difference." Ed Fitzgerald of *Sport* magazine went even further: "All in all, the case was the greatest thing that could have happened to Leo. It put him in solid with the reluctant Giants fans."[38]

Chandler later insisted that the reason he had suspended Leo without a hearing was that he feared what would happen in the Harlem neighborhoods near the Polo Grounds when word got out that the man who was assaulted was black. "I didn't want a riot," he told Robert Ruark not long after exonerating Durocher. "I suspended Durocher until I could find out what's what. After all, the precedent is against Durocher." Then he added, "like that thing in Brooklyn, when Durocher was accused of hitting that John Christian with a blackjack, and the court found him not guilty. I made Durocher sit right here and tell me, Ford Frick and Horace Stoneham that he had hit that man in the jaw with a blackjack. No matter what the court found he told me and Frick and Stoneham that he was guilty and he paid off $6000 to Christian for it."

While discussing Leo with Ruark, the commissioner pointed to a four-foot-thick dossier that he claimed contained the activities of Durocher, including material going back to the administration of Judge Landis. Chandler told Ruark that most of the material in that file was uncomplimentary to Durocher.[39]

Ten days after returning to the team, Stoneham signed Durocher to a two-year contract extension to manage the club through the 1951 season. His salary was not mentioned but was believed to be about $60,000 a year.

On July 8, the Giants brought up Henry Thompson and Monte Irvin from the team's farm club in Newark, New Jersey. Both men were veterans of the Negro leagues, and both had served in combat zones during the war. Thompson had been in the Battle of the Bulge, and Irvin was part of the force that landed in Normandy in the days following D-Day. Thompson, who followed Robinson and Larry Doby of the American League, had originally come up with the St. Louis Browns in 1947 as the third Negro to enter the majors, and now had integrated two teams and became the first African-American to play in both the American and National Leagues.

In early August, Durocher granted an interview to Wendell Smith, now with the *Chicago Herald-American*. Smith claimed the Giants were still in the pennant race but would need better pitching to give the Dodgers and Cardinals a run for their money. "We have the hitting and fielding. We've fixed the gap at second base by adding Henry Thompson the Negro kid. He's doing a fine job for us. He can hit, run and throw." The interview signaled how far racial integration had moved in two years, because not only had the Giants integrated, but Smith was also now reporting as a member of the Baseball Writers' Association of America—the first African-American in the organization.[40]

Despite Durocher's midseason optimism, the Giants finished in fifth place, behind the Boston Braves. Their record was 73–81, and their poor attendance mirrored the record. Some Giants fans had pledged to boycott the team as long as Durocher was managing it, and others who stayed away, or were content to take the games on radio or television, simply couldn't see any difference in the team under Durocher. "To them it was just as futile as it had been under Ott and not nearly as exciting," Frank Graham would write. "With the Yankees and Dodgers winning again, the plight of the Giants was desperate."[41]

ON DECEMBER 14, Leo, who at this point was for all intents and purposes both manager and de facto general manager of the Giants, made a decisive move. It was one he had been contemplating for months as he had watched his ball club sag. He outraged most of the fans and strengthened the Giants by trading away a significant chunk of his team—shortstop Buddy Kerr, outfielders Willard Marshall and Sid Gordon, and a young pitcher named Sam Webb—to the Boston Braves for Eddie Stanky and Alvin Dark.

The move was controversial, but Leo was quick to justify it: "We haven't had a good second base combination for a year or more. Until we can get better pitching, that is what we need. Two fellows out there who can make double plays. The one player I didn't want to give up was Gordon. But unless I did, I couldn't have made the deal."

One more important addition was made to the club that winter. Sal Maglie, the hard-eyed, blue-jawed "Sal the Barber," who had been pardoned for jumping the Mexican border to play in the outlawed Mexican League, returned with no questions asked.

"We'll be the youngest team in either league and the fastest," Leo bragged during Spring Training in Phoenix in 1950. "Even with Eddie Stanky—he's 32—I'll have a club that averages only about 25 years." In the words of Frank Graham, "Leo was beginning to get his kind of ball club."[42]

The 1950 season started slowly for the Giants as the team gradually worked its way out of the second division. And it was not long before Leo was in trouble again, this time for a tirade against umpire Babe Pinelli that was picked up by a television microphone and broadcast over the air. Before the mike was cut off, he had called Pinelli a four-eyed bandit and a son of a bitch. The station got many complaints, and the incident generated many headlines employing the initialism S.O.B.[43]

It was not long before Maglie was winning, and the infield was clicking thanks to Stanky and Dark. Durocher had been disappointed with Monte Irvin's initial season—he had appeared in thirty-six games in 1949 and batted .224 with nary a home run. During 1950 Spring Training in Phoenix he had his eye on Irvin. "He saw that I wasn't swinging the bat well, so he sent me down for a couple weeks. When I came back I started hitting." Indeed two days after he came back from the Giants' Jersey City farm club—where he had batted .510—in mid-May he drove in five runs with a single and a grand-slam home run in a rain-shortened six-inning game against the Cubs. The next day he followed up with a three-run homer.[44]

There was a new kind of action off the field that year. On Opening Day of 1950, Laraine Day became the host of the Giants pregame show on WPIX television. The fifteen-minute program was called *Day with the Giants*, and it was broadcast at 1:15 P.M. before home games. It was a cozy, chatty show in which Day sat with the players on a small couch flanked by table lamps made from small statuettes of ballplayers. She looked enchanted by every word and smiled. But she knew how to put on a show. She coaxed Freddie Fitzsimmons into square dancing, and when she learned Pee Wee Reese's nickname came from his childhood prowess at marbles, she got him down on the floor to do some shooting.*

Day never hid the fact she was on the Giants' side, and two months into her first season, she made headlines by exhorting Giants fans to vote for Eddie Stanky as the National League's All-Star second baseman. The problem was that Stanky was up against Jackie Robinson, who had been the league's MVP the year before. This did not faze Day. "Robby won that reward for his value in 1949, not 1950," she said. "When it comes to sheer value, Stanky has been far more valuable to the Giants than Robinson to the Dodgers, because he has been hustling harder." Robinson won in a landslide, but the strain between Durocher and Robinson was now intensified. Day was criticized in the black press for her All-Star picks, who were all white; she also neglected to name a National League catcher, white or black, when everyone else was naming Roy Campanella.[45]

In June, as Irvin continued to succeed, the Giants signed another African-American ballplayer. Willie Mays did not get any headlines in the papers and few, save those who followed the Negro leagues, had ever heard of him. The Giants had sent two men to Birmingham to scout a first baseman. They passed on the first baseman but suggested signing the young outfielder, who was still enrolled in high school and could play only on weekends lest he jeopardize getting his diploma. His contract was bought from the Birmingham Black Barons on the day following his graduation from high school, and he was immediately sent to the Trenton Giants of the Class B Interstate League. Mays got a $5,000 bonus for signing with the Giants. For Trenton, he batted .353 in eighty-one games and was lauded for his work on defense in the outfield.†

---

* Pee-wee is the name for a marble of about a half inch in diameter.

† The late Jules Tygiel wrote that according to an unconfirmed report, the Boston Red Sox, the last major league team to have a black player, could have signed Willie Mays. They didn't because their white scout refused to be inconvenienced by staying over when bad weather forced postponement of the game at which he was scheduled to see Mays. "On another occasion," Tygiel wrote, "a Red Sox 'superscout,' who made the final evaluation on promising players, was advised of a Negro tournament in the Southwest. 'How long is this nigger tournament going to last?' he asked. 'I'm not hanging around here three days to watch a bunch of black kids.'" He did not spend even one afternoon at the tournament and reported to the Red Sox that he hadn't seen anyone worth signing. (Tygiel, *Baseball's Great Experiment*, pp. 290–91)

As the Giants integrated there were accusations that Leo was ordering his pitchers to knock down Jackie and, according to Sam Lacy of the *Afro-American*, countercharges that Jackie was trying to intimidate the Giants' all-white pitching staff with accusations based on race. In due course there were challenges to meet under the stands that, again according to Lacy, led to warnings by Happy Chandler to stop.[46]

In 1950, the winning started too late to get the club higher than third place. It appeared that Durocher's Giants could win games only after the pressure of any real shot at the championship was off. Leo, however, was confident, maintaining in a November press conference that the team was already a contender for 1951 because of the confidence it had gained in the last two months of the season when the team came to believe they could beat anybody. Irvin was one of the players who convinced Durocher that he had the nucleus of the team he needed. Irvin appeared in 140 games, batted .299 and drove in 66 runs.[47]

Then there was the pitching, which for the second half of 1950 was the equal of any other in baseball. Larry Jansen was the workhorse of the pitching staff, ending up with a 19–13 record for the year. Jim Hearn, who had been obtained from the Cardinals midseason for a modest price, blossomed with the Giants. Hearn was 11–3 with the Giants and wound up with a respectable 2.49 earned run average (1.94 with the Giants). Then came Sal Maglie, who worked his way into the rotation the second half of the season and was suddenly unbeatable, finishing the season with an incredible 18–4 record, completing twelve of his sixteen starts and a team-energizing, headline-grabbing eleven victories in a row.

If Durocher treated players like Irvin gently, veterans got to deal with a different Leo. A story that Durocher told and retold many times in years to come involved a game in 1950 when Leo did not like the way Maglie was throwing the ball and had gone out to the mound with nobody warming up in the bullpen. He yelled at Maglie, told him he was pitching like a girl, and called him a dago.

As retold by reporter Ron Rapoport, who heard the story from Durocher at a banquet, "Maglie had hated that, but he had started getting his back into his pitches and throwing harder and he had finished the inning without any runs scoring. He had come back to the dugout and gone to get a drink and then, on his way to his seat on the bench, he had spit a mouthful of water all over Durocher.

"After the game, Maglie had come up to Durocher to apologize but Leo had told him to forget it. They had won, hadn't they?"[48]

As if the point still had to be made, Durocher had an uncanny ongoing ability to charm celebrities, which he displayed once again in December 1950 when he spent eight hours sitting next to Swedish actress Greta Garbo on an airplane from Los Angeles to Newark. Durocher immediately noticed she was so nervous that her hand was shaking on the arm of the seat.

"What the hell is it with that shaking?" he asked. "What the hell are you doing with that rapping on the arm? You are making me nervous!"

As Leo later reported to columnist Earl Wilson, he then realized Garbo was in need of a bit of Durocheresque counseling.

"What are you nervous about? It goes up and comes down either safe or in a heap, so why worry."

This calmed her once aloft. The two ordered their meals—steak for Leo and a salad for Greta. Leo was taken aback by her order and said: "I never touch salads. I got an expression: 'Salads make your bones soft.'"

On arrival in Newark, they shared a cab to Manhattan, and Leo declared Garbo to be a wonderful woman. He told Earl Wilson that he wished she could play second base. Garbo, who is best remembered today for the accented line "I vant to be alone," was apparently willing to make an exception for Leo Durocher.[49]

CHAPTER 11

Miracle Man

N OW SETTLED IN WITH the Giants and happily married, Durocher seemed to be living a new life. During the season, he lived on Park Avenue, lunched at '21,' and commanded a place of honor at Toots Shor's restaurant. In the off-season, he and Laraine lived in Santa Monica, where as "Baseball's First Couple" they were the toast of Hollywood, picking up tens of thousands of dollars in fees for joint appearances on radio and television shows. Day had become "the first lady of baseball" and a fixture among the Giants wives in Section 19 at the Polo Grounds, and her hit pregame show was renewed quickly for the 1951 season.

The Durocher-Day marriage became a national fixation during Leo's early Giants years. Dozens of magazines put the two on their covers; several had them on twice. For many Americans, Durocher symbolized the guy from the wrong side of the tracks who got to marry the movie star. Durocher claimed Day had civilized him, and he was now eager to talk about antiques, Persian carpets, and modern art. Day was an avid square dancer and brought Durocher into that fold.

Durocher was, as one journalist put it, the first ballplayer to become a celebrity in his own right, able to play that role with skill. In one interview with Gilbert Millstein of *The New York Times*, he showed his fascination with antiques and fine décor by discussing two old silver buckets he had bought at auction and made into lamps to fit a pair of French Provincial tables. "And you know what else I did with them?" he said. "I planted philodendrons all around the lamp bases. They're simply gorgeous." He ended the interview on a lyrical note: "Ah, my life's been wonderful."

Lest there be any question, the old Durocher was on hand for the same interview, especially when it came to baseball. He uttered one of his most famous quotations: "Look, I'm playing third base," Durocher told Millstein. "My mother's on second. The ball's hit out to short center. As she goes by me on the way to third, I'll accidentally trip her. I'll help her up, brush her off, and tell her I'm sorry. But she does not get to third."[1]

His mother notwithstanding, Durocher's civility in dealing with writers and reporters was shocking to many of the old-timers who had fought with him for years. In early 1951, Ed Fitzgerald, the editor in chief of *Sport* magazine, was able to interview Durocher for a major article. Durocher presented himself as affable, witty, and successful. "He can be one of the friendliest, gentlest men you could hope to meet," wrote Fitzgerald. "He is a far cry from the fresh young rookie who spat back at Babe Ruth in the Yankee clubhouse." Fitzgerald's article was entitled "Leo Durocher: Man with Nine Lives," and this new Durocher was presented as one of those lives.

Leo was not only cooperative but also willing to talk about things he had not discussed before—at least not in front of someone with a pencil and a notebook in hand. He was finally willing to talk about his alleged gangster friends.

"Bugsy Siegel? All right, let me tell you about that. To begin with, sure I used to live with George Raft off-season. Why not? I figured him for a nice guy. I had no reason to think anything else. At least not until he borrowed my apartment and got me in all that trouble about a crap game when I wasn't anywhere near the place. But the thing is, Raft was always okay with me. People always say 'Durocher and Raft and Bugsy Siegel' like it was a business firm or something. You want to know how close I was to Siegel. I'm staying at Raft's place and this night, I've got a date. I'm going out. So I get dressed, put on my coat, start out. The door opens and this man comes in. He looks like a banker. Raft is behind him and he says, 'Leo, Bugsy Siegel.' I say 'Hiya' and I go out. The papers have me palling around with him all my life. They even got me vouching for his character in a court case. A lie. A dirty lie. But I go around denying it, and who believes me?

"Joe Adonis? Sure, I met him. How could I help it? He's at ballgames, he's at fights, he's everyplace. But if I see a fellow like that now, I don't even say hello to him. I keep right on going."

Durocher was unwilling to talk about Chandler other than to demand that he stop telling people he had things in his files that would show that his suspension had been lenient and that proof of darker deeds lurked in

Chandler's "private files." Durocher wanted Chandler to open the files for all to see or to stop telling people they existed.

Fitzgerald saw Durocher as a man who had made a specialty of bouncing off the floor and rising to greater heights. He noted that during those four short years after the suspension, the wheel had turned full circle: Chandler was desperately trying to hold on to his job, while Durocher was sailing into the 1951 season in the enviable position of a $65,000-a-year manager of "a red-hot pennant contender" in the biggest city on the circuit.[2]

Chandler's contract as baseball commissioner had not been due to expire until April 1952, but he had asked for the owners to extend it in December 1949. The owners voted against offering the extension at that time, but promised to reconsider the request in December 1950. The vote in 1950 was nine votes for Chandler and seven against, leaving him three votes short of the necessary three-fourths majority. Chandler asked that the extension be considered again at the owners meeting on March 12, 1951, but the vote was again 9–7. Upset that his contract was not extended, Chandler resigned, effective July 15, 1951. From that point until 1969, when Bowie Kuhn became commissioner, Chandler was virtually ostracized by the baseball establishment and was never invited to World Series games or Hall of Fame inductions.[3]

To replace Chandler, Ford Frick was given the job and signed a contract worth $65,000 a year for seven years. Just before his announcement, the major league team owners voted that the commissioner's office should be located in a city with two major league teams. Frick decided to relocate the office from Cincinnati to New York.

For Leo, redemption was in the air.

On Opening Day 1951, Al White wrote an article for the *Chicago Defender* predicting that this would be the best year yet for Negro major league players. In his discussion of the New York Giants, the only black rookie named was Artie Wilson, and Willie Mays was conspicuous by his absence.[4]

Mays was assigned to play for the Giants' top minor league club, the Minneapolis Millers of the American Association. The major league team trained in Lakeland, Florida, and their minor league camp was in nearby Sanford. A game was arranged between the team's two top farm clubs, Minneapolis and Ottawa, because Durocher wanted to see Mays play. In the match played at 9 A.M. with few spectators other than Durocher, Mays hit a double and a long home run. Durocher began lobbying for Mays to play for the big club immediately, but owner Horace Stoneham resisted. He said Mays was going into military service "any minute" and needed more experience in the minor leagues. Stoneham had his way, and Willie began the season with Minneapolis as planned.

After a truly wretched start in which the Giants won two of their first three games but then lost eleven in a row, Leo was deeply frustrated and determined to somehow move the Giants into the first division. Those eleven losses made Durocher a new man in the way he related to his players. As Shirley Povich said later about the 1951 season, "Mellowness had set in somehow." One common theory was that Durocher was turning into a nice guy because of the influence of Laraine Day; another was that he realized Willie Mays and some of his other young players could not flourish under the old Leo.[5]

Meanwhile, Mays had collected twelve hits in his first week with Minneapolis and played a spectacular center field. Durocher again began pleading with Stoneham to bring Mays up to the parent club, arguing that Mays was needed to add a long-ball hitter to the lineup as well as to allow Whitey Lockman to move to first base, leaving Monte Irvin and Mays to defend the outfield along with Don Mueller. Stoneham strongly opposed the move of Lockman and was even more strongly opposed to bringing Mays up with scant minor league experience.

Durocher countered that the team needed Mays if it wanted a serious chance at the pennant. On April 29, the Giants had been 2–12 but then went on a 15–7 run. By May 24, they were only two games below .500, but not good enough to win the pennant. At this point, Mays had played thirty-five games with Minneapolis and was hitting .477. Stoneham finally relented, and Mays was put on a plane to fly to Philadelphia, where he would start the next day in center field against the Phillies. Leo then announced to the New York press that he was betting the store on a very young rookie who was only 339 days out of high school. To make room for Mays, Artie Wilson was optioned to Ottawa.

The next day, when Mays officially became a Giant, the *Brooklyn Eagle* published an article that ran without a byline and opened with a prescient lead sentence: "The Giants today brought up a 20-year-old Negro with less than a year of experience in organized baseball and asked him to win the National League pennant—beginning tonight." Probably written by Tommy Holmes, the article went on to say that Durocher and the Giants front office were thumping the tub for Willie Mays to the point where they predicted he could make New York forget about Yankees rookie phenom Mickey Mantle.[6]

After ripping line drives into the upper decks during batting practice on Friday, Mays was hitless. He was hitless again on Saturday. Sam Lacy interviewed Mays on Sunday morning for the *Baltimore Afro-American*, and Mays admitted that he was more than merely nervous; he was "scared to death." Mays was hitless again that afternoon.

Despite his batting woes, when the team returned to the Polo Grounds, Willie's first home game saw him batting third against the Boston Braves and their star southpaw, Warren Spahn. In his first at-bat, he hit Spahn's offering atop the left-field roof for a home run, his first major league hit. After that homer, Mays went on an 0-for-13 slide, leaving him hitting .038 (1 for 26).

At this point, Willie sat in front of his locker in tears after taking the collar again. Seeing Mays in distress, coaches Freddie Fitzsimmons and Herman Franks sent for Durocher. Mays said he just couldn't hit big league pitching. Durocher replied, "As long as I'm the manager of the Giants, you are my center fielder . . . You are the best center fielder I've ever looked at." Then he told Mays to hitch up his pants to give himself a more favorable strike zone. Willie then went on a 14-for-33 tear.[7]

Meanwhile Durocher was moving his players around. Left fielder Whitey Lockman was sent to first, first baseman Monte Irvin was sent to the outfield with Mays, and finally, on July 20, center fielder Bobby Thomson was sent to third. Although not without precedent, the movement of players as if they were pieces on a chessboard was highly unusual in mid-twentieth-century baseball.

"He was exciting to watch as a manager, since he was the third base coach," recalled Neil Gillen, who watched it all as a young vendor at the Polo Grounds. "Whenever Willie Mays got on base, everyone in the Polo Grounds knew he was going to steal second, and possibly third. Durocher was more animated when Mays was on base, always swinging and waving his arms. We always thought that Mays would go from first to home on a single. He would round third in a bluff and the place would go wild. Durocher would spin around with a huge smile on his face. Willy would take big leads from third base and the place would go wild. Durocher would have his hands cupped around his mouth yelling at the pitcher." Gillen, who worked the Polo Grounds from 1951 to 1954, added: "Durocher and Mays brought an excitement to the Polo Grounds that has never been duplicated in any other ball park since. It was a special time."[8]

Arthur Mann had been working on a book that would address Durocher's 1947 suspension and put it into the context of all that was right and wrong with baseball. Mann wrote to Mrs. Durocher on May 23, 1951, asking for her and Leo to take a look at his manuscript. He wrote, "I want you and Leo to like it for what it is: an overall explanation of an 'American Dreyfus case'"— alluding to the scandal that rocked France in the late nineteenth and early twentieth centuries involving a Jewish artillery captain in the French Army, Alfred Dreyfus, who was falsely convicted of passing military secrets to the Germans. He added that there were ways that the manuscript could be converted into a motion picture script.[9]

Mann met with the Durochers on May 28, and many corrections and additions were made to the book before it was ready for syndication beginning on July 8 in the *New York Journal-American* and another dozen major newspapers. The book would follow on September 7 under the title of *Baseball Confidential*.

The Dodgers were especially tough on Leo. When Dick Williams came to the Dodgers in 1951, manager Chuck Dressen, who had replaced Burt Shotton, assigned him the task of ragging certain individuals, especially Durocher—he later called himself a "verbal hit man." Dressen disliked Durocher and believed he had, in fact, stolen Babe Ruth's watch, so almost every time the Dodgers played the Giants, Dressen ordered Williams to scream at Durocher about the watch. As Williams recalled many years later after he had become a Hall of Fame manager: "The dugouts were near each other at Ebbets Field, so I could shout from one end of our bench and Durocher could hear me loud and clear. 'What time is it, Leo?' I'd yell to him. 'How's Ruth's watch running? Still working? Bringing you good luck? Lee-ooo. Oh Leee-ooo!' Dressen would be laughing like hell, while a flustered Durocher wanted to kill me. I knew this because every time I batted against the Giants I got knocked on my butt presumably on Leo's orders."[10]

On July 18, 1951, the Giants lost for the sixth time in nine games, falling eight games behind the Dodgers in third place and clearly struggling. The next day Durocher called a team meeting while the rain washed out all major league games east of Cleveland, including a doubleheader scheduled at the Polo Grounds. Among other things, Durocher asked his players how many would benefit from a system by which the type of pitch could be determined in advance by stealing the catcher's signs. About half said yes and the other half declined based on the belief that such information could be wrong and do more harm than good. Monte Irvin was one of those who told him no. Durocher replied: "You mean to tell me, if a fat fastball is coming, you don't want to know."

The scheme that went into effect the next day began when Durocher sent coach Herman Franks, a former catcher, to the clubhouse at the Polo Grounds high up in center field. Monte Irvin confirmed that Franks, with the approval of Durocher, would look through a telescope and decipher the catcher's signals, then send the information via an electrical buzzer to the bullpen. From there, someone would relay the sign to the batter by a visual cue.

This move came at a time when using mechanical devices such as telescopes and binoculars were not forbidden and the Giants were far from the only team using such a device—the Cleveland Indians had used a telescope Bob Feller had brought back with him from his time in the U.S. Navy during World War II.

In early August the Giants dropped three games in a row to the Dodgers at home. Dick Williams recalled during one of those victories hearing Jackie Robinson through the wall that separated his shower from Durocher's in the other clubhouse, yelling above the steam and the spray, "Leo, eat your heart out! Leo, eat your heart out!"[11]

As late as August 11, the Giants were still thirteen and one-half games behind Brooklyn, rated by some experts as the best National League club since the 1934 St. Louis Cardinals. From that point the Giants drew with the help of television, radio, and the rivalry with the Dodgers— what *Newsweek* later said was probably baseball's greatest succession of "national gasps."

The first gasp came with a defensive play on August 15 at the Polo Grounds against the Dodgers when Mays ran down a long Carl Furillo drive in right-center, some 330 feet from home, wheeled, and threw out Billy Cox trying to score from third base. Because of its singularity, that play later came to be known as "the Throw." Mays was quickly proving he had defensive skills that set him apart.

In a key two-game series at the Polo Grounds on September 1 and 2, Don Mueller—who had eight home runs in his previous three seasons with the Giants—hit five, thus tying a record held by Adrian Anson, Ty Cobb, Tony Lazzeri, and Ralph Kiner. According to Bobby Thomson in his 1991 memoir, "Mueller's slugging feat became the focal point of a controversy that continued for the rest of the season that Mueller and other Giants were benefiting from signs stolen by the Giants from the center field clubhouse with the aid of binoculars, without which Mueller never could have hit five home runs."*[12]

The Giants roared down the home stretch, sustained by the pitching of Sal Maglie (23–6), Larry Jansen (23–11), and Jim Hearn (17–9); the hitting of Irvin (.312, with twenty-four homers and a league-leading 121 runs driven in); Mays (.274, with twenty homers and sixty-eight runs batted in); and the hustle of second baseman Eddie Stanky.

They moved into the final week three games behind the front-running Dodgers, at which point Durocher observed, almost despairingly, "We've got to win 'em all." The Dodgers began behaving like a ball club in panic. On September 27 the Dodgers dropped a doubleheader to the Boston Braves, and then after a third defeat in Boston, several Dodgers in fury kicked in the door of the umpires' dressing room. Three Dodgers were fined but not suspended, although Durocher suggested that one of the culprits, Jackie Robinson, be suspended. After beating up the rest of the league for most of the first 152 games, Brooklyn went into the last two scheduled contests tied with New York for first place.

The Giants won their last two in Boston, giving them a record of thirty-seven victories in their closing forty-four games. The Dodgers also won their last two games in Philadelphia, although the final one was a fourteen-inning, 9–8 cliffhanger that Robinson prolonged with a driving bases-loaded catch and then won with a homer.

With identical 96–48 records, the teams began a best-of-three playoff, the first game to be played on October 1—the first National League playoff since Durocher, managing the Dodgers in 1946, had lost to the Cardinals.

The Giants won game one at Ebbets Field 3–1 with home runs by Bobby Thomson and Monte Irvin while the Dodgers came back to win at the Polo Grounds in Game 2, 10–0. The third game at the Polo Grounds went the Dodgers way up to the last half of the ninth inning. Don Newcombe outpitched Sal Maglie and the score was 4 to 1 as Alvin Dark led off the ninth. He singled past Gil Hodges into right field. Don Mueller, known as Mandrake the Magician for his ability to slap a hit through an infield hole, did just that with a single to right, and Dark raced to third. After Irvin had fouled out to Hodges, Lockman doubled to left, scoring Dark and sending Mueller

---

* Mueller also became a father during the second game and when he hit the second homer in the eighth inning of that game got to shout to Durocher in the third-base coaching box. "It's a boy! It's a boy!"

scrambling to third. Mueller slid into the base at an awkward angle, twisting ligaments and tendons in his left ankle. He was carried off on a stretcher and Cliff Hartung ran for him.

Dodgers manager Chuck Dressen took Newcombe out and fatefully waved Ralph Branca in from the bullpen to replace Newcombe with Thomson coming to the plate. "The delay really helped me," Thomson later said.

> I walked out to talk to Leo and he said: "If you ever hit one, hit one now." I could see he was plenty excited, too, and I calmed down a bit.
>
> On my way back to the plate, I said to myself: "You're a pro. Act like one!"

The first pitch came right down Thomson's alley, and he took it for a strike. Durocher then recalled, "Bobby looked at me, his eyes lifted in disgust, and I hollered, 'Come on! He'll throw you another one.' I'm not thinking of a home run; a home run never occurred to me. This is the last inning, *we've got to get that tying run in*, that's about all I'm thinking about."

His second pitch was a fastball high and inside. Thomson connected. "Now," Leo recalled, "when the ball left Thomson's bat I knew it was going to hit the wall, but it didn't occur to me it was going over. There were very few home runs hit into the lower deck at the Polo Grounds because of the overhang from the upper deck. Only a line shot—a rising line drive—ever went there. This one was far too low to hit the overhang, and it was a *sinking* line drive. I can't remember any ball hit like that ever going in before . . ."

Then Durocher blanked out, with the last picture he recalled seeing being that of the fans reaching and jumping in the left-field bleachers "frozen and unmoving, like a still photo." Eddie Stanky had charged out of the dugout and landed on Durocher's back, pulling him down and causing him to lose sight of Thomson rounding third and crossing the plate.[13]

To his everlasting credit, New York Giants play-by-play man Russ Hodges's description matched the drama: "There's a long drive! It's gonna be, I believe! The Giants win the pennant! The Giants win the pennant! The Giants win the pennant! The Giants win the pennant!"

With that one swipe of his bat, Thomson had settled everything. The Giants had won the pennant for the first time in fourteen years. He was a hero and Durocher a genius. "It was the most famous home run ever made," Garry Schumacher said. "He hit it in 3,000,000 living rooms, to say nothing of the bars and grills." The next morning, Red Smith wrote what would become his most famous and hyperbolic lead: "Now it is done. Now the story ends. And there is no way to tell it. The art of fiction is dead. Reality has strangled invention. Only the utterly impossible, the inexpressibly fantastic, can ever be plausible again." The home run was given a pair of nicknames that still resonate decades later—"The Shot Heard 'Round the World" and "The Miracle of Coogan's Bluff."[14]

Before the Giants had time to catch their collective breath, they met the New York Yankees in the World Series. "Leo didn't hold a meeting when we got together," Monte Irvin reported on the eve of the first game of the Series. "All he told us was to keep on playing the way we had been, that we were doing just fine."

Because of Mueller's damaged ankle in the playoff game, Leo moved Hank Thompson into the outfield with Mays and Irvin for the Series, thus creating the first all-black outfield in the history of the big leagues. The racial aspect was not lost on the black press, which saw this as a victory for Harlem, home to the Polo Grounds. HARLEM GETS IT ALL—PLAY-OFF AND SERIES was the headline in the *Defender*, which was an accompanied by a photograph of Durocher posed with his color-bar–busting outfield, Willie and Leo with their arms around one another. The *Defender* and the other voices of black America did not hesitate to point out that the Yankees still lacked a black player.*[15]

With twelve championships in their last thirteen World Series, the Yankees were the favorites. Many people felt they could win by simply showing up. But Monte Irvin's four hits and his first-inning steal of home, along with lefty Dave Koslo's seven-hit pitching, gave the Giants a 5–1 winning jump. Eddie Lopat's shrewd five-hit performance stopped the Giants in the second game 3–1, but the Giants had a five-run fifth inning off Vic Raschi in the third game, leading to a 6–2 victory.

---

* Durocher was still sending David Redd World Series tickets at this point in his career. Redd himself made news in 1951—at least in Springfield—where he was lauded on the editorial pages of the *Springfield Republican* for giving all of his overtime pay for a number of weeks to help pay off the mortgage on his church. Besides the $750 he donated himself, he also raised an additional $1,250 from others. In 1955 Redd told Robert Shaplen of *Sports Illustrated* that Durocher had sent him free World Series passes until 1954.

"The Yankees," mourned columnist Jimmy Cannon in the *New York Post*, "don't make the other people fold up any more." But Joe DiMaggio, who was hitless during the first three games, came through with a two-run homer and another hit as the Yankees won the fourth game 6–2. The next day with the score tied at 1–1 in the third inning, Yankee rookie Gil McDougald became the third man ever to hit a World Series homer with the bases loaded. The Yankees went on to a 13–1 triumph that blew the Series open, and won it in the sixth game with a 4–3 victory on Hank Bauer's three-run triple. Bauer also made a ninth-inning sliding circus catch of Sal Yvar's sinking line drive to keep the Giants from tying the score.

The Yankees now had their third straight World Championship. As they headed for the Biltmore Hotel to celebrate the victory and honor Joe DiMaggio on the final game of his career, another story was developing. Laraine Day told Louis Effrat of *The New York Times* that just prior to the game, she had turned over a letter to baseball commissioner Ford Frick. The letter, postmarked October 6, offered Leo and the Giants $15,000 to lose the next three games. According to Day, the letter had been on Leo's desk for several days along with other unopened mail. She explained, "Leo opened some of his mail Tuesday night and found this one." The letter was typewritten and also contained a threat: "If you want to keep Laraine, better keep your mouth shut." The story broke the next morning in the *Times* and was picked up by the wire services. Frick refused comment, and the assumption was that he had turned the letter over to the police or the FBI or both. It added extra melodrama to what is still regarded as one of baseball's most dramatic seasons.[16]

Even with the Series loss, Durocher was cast in a new light. The 1951 season was Durocher's masterpiece. "Durocher was an inspired manager that year," said Monte Irvin. "He kept making the most astounding moves and seeing them pay off. Things like the right pinch hitter at the right time, the right pitching change at the right time, moving his fielders around. It seemed that over the last few months of the season he just couldn't make a wrong move."[17]

Mays was now the toast of New York City and was given the nickname "Say Hey Kid" by sportswriter Barney Kremenko of the *Journal-American*, who recalled later that Mays, in his rookie season, "would blurt 'Say who,' 'Say what,' 'Say where,' 'Say hey.' In my paper, I tabbed him the 'Say Hey Kid.' It stuck."

On October 19, 1951, the baseball fantasy movie *Angels in the Outfield* was released. The story focused on a volatile, obscene, and comically controversial manager named Guffy X. McGovern, played by Paul Douglas, managing the Pittsburgh Pirates. McGovern was clearly based on Durocher. Among other things, he fought with the press ("Dogs have fleas, managers have reporters," McGovern says) and waged battles with umpires that seemed choreographed by Leo. Even Durocher's mellowing after marrying Laraine Day is mirrored as the Douglas character is transformed from savage to nice guy after meeting the character played by Janet Leigh.

The plot was simple enough. Douglas's abusive behavior seemed to be responsible for the position of the Pirates, eighth in the National League. Then one day, an angel makes a deal with him whereby the Pirates would win a pennant if Douglas would calm down. He does, and they do. At the movie's conclusion, it is revealed that the title angels, the Heavenly Choir 9, included the ghosts of Babe Ruth, Lou Gehrig, Walter Johnson, John McGraw, Christy Mathewson, and Eddie Collins.

The film had special appeal, because the behavior of the Douglas character mirrored Durocher's 1951 behavior. "At first, Durocher was suspect last season when he adopted an almost saccharine sweetness toward his athletes who were losing their first 11 games in a row," wrote Shirley Povich in *The Washington Post*. "It appeared to be only a pose by the tyrant who once said that nice guys finish last, but as the season wore on, and Leo gave out with no bombast at all, then a smile for everyone, his reformation was undeniably complete."* [18]

The film was quite popular and attracted a few who were obsessed with it, including Dwight D. Eisenhower, who made it a White House favorite when he became president in 1953. He later told the film's director, Clarence Brown, that he ran through three celluloid prints of the film while in office. In *Going Home to Glory: A Memoir of Life with Dwight D. Eisenhower, 1961–1969*, grandson David Eisenhower reported that this was still Ike's favorite film and according to the projectionist at the Eisenhower farm in Gettysburg, Ike watched the film precisely thirty-eight times in retirement. "At the conclusion of every showing, Granddad would sit silently allowing his eyes to adjust to the light. 'Wonderful show,' he would say, almost inaudibly, rising from his chair and wandering off to bed." [19]

---

* The team had actually won two of their first three games and then lost eleven in a row.

On October 22, Willie Mays was named National League Rookie of the Year. Two days later, Durocher was named major league Manager of the Year, polling almost double the number of votes as Casey Stengel of the Yankees. Finally, the Dodgers' Roy Campanella was named MVP, beating out Stan Musial.

OVER THE WINTER, various baseball writers tried to get a handle on Durocher's come-from-behind success during the 1951 season. Some, such as Povich, saw it as his new ability to motivate his team with pats on the back rather than kicks in the pants. Others attributed it to Durocher's skill at switching players around—namely the Lockman-Irvin-Thomson triple switch. When Spring Training started in 1952, Jack Hand of the Associated Press reported that Leo might have created a trend with his lineup twists: "First basemen are buying fielder's gloves. Lifetime third basemen are studying books on 'How to play second.' Outfielders are turning into shortstops."[20]

As Spring Training got under way, Jackie Robinson let it be known that he was ready to stop feuding with Durocher if Durocher would also agree to stop. The feud had become even more nasty in 1951 when at one point in the regular season, after being hit by two Giants pitchers, Robinson sought to strike back by placing a bunt where pitcher Sal Maglie would have to field the ball in his path. Robinson barely missed running him down, and there was a momentary flare-up. Then, innings before the Thomson homer in the final playoff game, the two men were at it again. At one point, managing from his usual perch as third-base coach, Leo became so engrossed in his efforts to unnerve Dodger pitcher Don Newcombe that he walked a third of the way toward home plate so he could appear in the pitcher's field of vision. Robinson called time and demanded that the umpire order Leo back into his box. Umpire Larry Goetz gave him a warning. The headline over the Sam Lacy story of the playoff game in the Baltimore Afro-American read: JACKIE WINS BATTLE OF WORDS, DUROCHER THE PENNANT.[21]

At the 1952 All-Star Game, Robinson bobbled a couple of balls on a wet Shibe Field in Philadelphia, and the crowd booed. Durocher, who was managing the National League All-Stars, jumped to his defense. "They should boo Robinson?" Durocher said sarcastically. "On a field like that all muddy and slippery." When Robinson tried to take the blame, Leo broke in: "Jackie, you were great!" The headline in the next issue of Jet magazine, an African-American newsweekly, was JACKIE, LEO MOVE TO BURY HATCHET.

The magazine reported this as a distinct contrast to the years of tooth-and-nail fighting between the two.[22]

Early in the 1952 season, Mays was drafted into the Army after a much-criticized effort to gain a deferment due to his financial support of nine half-siblings. He was inducted on May 29 when the Giants were in first place with a 2.5-game lead over the Dodgers. A few days later, they dropped out of first place for the remainder of the season. Durocher claimed the loss of Mays hurt the team psychologically, as he was always able to make that game-saving catch, and that with his "contagious pep he gave the team a constant lift."[23]

While in the military, Mays's main duty was to play baseball, which he did exceedingly well. He was in the Army as an entertainer, playing a game a day and batting, by his own estimate, ".420 or something like that."[24]

Although the Giants finished second in 1952 with 92–62 record, 4.5 games behind the Dodgers, some people argued that Durocher might have even done a better job of managing that year given the talent available to him with Mays in the Army and Irvin out most of the season with a broken ankle. Despite losing the pennant to the Dodgers, the Giants had a 14–8 record against them during the regular season. With a .301 batting average and 73 RBIs, Alvin Dark was Durocher's standout player for the 1952 season.

Nineteen fifty-three was a different story. Durocher had become such an object of public fascination that *Pageant*, a general-interest magazine with about four hundred thousand subscribers, commissioned Dr. David Tracy, baseball's practicing psychologist, to put Leo "on the couch" and see what made him tick. Tracy had made headlines in 1950 when he used psychology—mostly relaxation techniques and hypnosis—to try to help the hapless St. Louis Browns out of a perpetual slump. The work made little difference, as lack of talent bedeviled the Browns, not an inability to meditate or relax.[25]

In his off-the-cuff analysis of Durocher in the March issue of *Pageant* and, by extension, in wire service stories that picked it up, Tracy predicted that the man he called "the Dandy Little Manager" would eventually be banned from the game for life. His entire professional life—indeed, his entire life—led the New York psychologist to that inevitable conclusion. Durocher's philosophy, said the doctor, has always been: "I don't care how I win, as long as I win." Tracy asserted that this personal policy was sure to prove Leo's undoing. He claimed that Durocher had an inferiority complex that caused him to start arguments. "His small stature and limited education have to be covered up by over-aggressiveness. Leo is not an outgoing personality—that is, he gives little of himself. He shows no sincere interest in other people, as a general rule."

While Tracy felt Leo could become less disturbed internally, "any thoughts of reversing his character are out of the question."[26]

As if to give credence to Tracy's analysis, Leo did not behave well when the 1953 Giants were flat and lacked both hitting and pitching. Leo's battles with umpires seemed to increase in direct proportion to the inability of the Giants on the field. In early June, after being ejected from two games in a row—in one, for kicking dirt at umpire Frank Dascoli—Leo insisted that five National League umpires, including Dascoli, carried a grudge against him and called on new league president Warren Giles to do something about it. Giles demanded that Durocher substantiate his charges or retract them or face indefinite suspension. Leo both retracted the statement and apologized to Giles.[27]

Nevertheless he decried a recent effort by the league to curb headhunting—i.e., throwing balls at opponents' heads. "Why when I broke in they used to pitch at my ear all day. It was part of the game. It made for better baseball," he opined on a quick visit to Springfield in late July. "But now the president of the league doesn't want it. He says it will cause riots. Did you ever hear of a riot at a major league game?"[28]

On September 6, Durocher almost got to see that riot. With the Giants thirty games behind, and after Dodgers manager Chuck Dressen had proclaimed "The Giants is dead," Durocher told pitcher Rubén Gómez to hit Carl Furillo of the Brooklyn Dodgers. As Furillo made his way to first base after being hit, Durocher wagged his finger at him. Furillo charged the Giants' dugout, got Durocher in a headlock, and began choking him. In the melee, Furillo's hand was broken, and he was shelved for the rest of the season. At the time, Furillo led the National League in batting. The Giants finished in fifth place in the National League in 1953 with a 70–84 record, thirty-five games behind the Brooklyn Dodgers. It was the first Giants team with a losing record in four years. The Dodgers lost again to the Yankees in the Series. Broadcaster Ernie Harwell later commented that the loss of Furillo may have cost the Dodgers the Series.[29]

As LATE AS the spring of 1954, reports of a campaign to get Durocher out of the game appeared. One of the reasons given by Peter Govern in the March issue of *Confidential* magazine was that certain owners were still furious with Durocher for his role in integrating the Dodgers and Giants and then conspicuously bringing up—and making stars of—other black players. For this reason, it was claimed the most bigoted owners wanted him out of the game as punishment. This can never be proven, but only half the major league teams had been integrated at the time Govern's article appeared.

When Willie Mays returned to the Giants in 1954 after his stint in the Army, he seemed bigger and stronger. He had gone from 170 to a muscular 190 pounds. On first seeing him in Spring Training in Arizona, Durocher turned to the rest of the team and said: "Here comes the pennant."[30]

His performance in Phoenix was extraordinary and began with the first exhibition game. Durocher said a few days later: "I sent him in as a pinch hitter and he tied into the first pitch that must have traveled nine hundred feet for a home run. At the end of the inning he went out to centerfield and would you believe it? He made one of the greatest plays I ever saw, climbing up on the wall for a one-handed catch and following it up by throwing a strike to first to double up a runner." Leo then added, "There's only one Willie."[31]

The team got off to a slow start but then posted a 24–4 record in June. During this streak, Durocher, on a whim, started to write checks for $100 and gave them to his players when they hit a home run. The practice was short-lived, as National League president Warren Giles forbade it after a game on June 21 and threatened to fine Leo $500 for each infraction. One of those who lost his C-note that day was pinch hitter Dusty Rhodes—a man who Durocher explained couldn't run, couldn't throw, and couldn't field, but was an extraordinary hitter, especially as a pinch hitter.

Durocher said that on days when he started Dusty to give one of his other outfielders a rest, he could almost count on Rhodes misplaying at least one fly ball into a hit, or maybe a single into a double, usually by the fifth inning. "You couldn't trust the guy in the field," Leo said. "But then he'd come into the dugout after an inning like that and he'd say: 'You better get me out of there, Skip, before I kill myself.' Now how could anybody get mad at a guy like that! I don't know why Rhodes hit so well, and I don't think he did, either. But I've been around a lot of ball clubs for a lot of years, and usually when you look down the bench for a pinch hitter, most of the guys are trying to hide behind each other. Oh, they'll pinch-hit if you ask them, but for most of them it's the worst kind of pressure."

After a six-game losing streak in late July, the Giants were able to dominate the National League, in part thanks to Durocher's new system of platooning in which he had six "regulars" for three positions. When the opposition started a right-handed pitcher, Leo used Whitey Lockman at first, Hank Thompson at third, and Rhodes in left field. Against left-handed pitchers, Bobby Hofman went to first, Billy Gardner to third, and Monte Irvin to left field. The platoon system did not last the entire season, but while it did, Durocher gained an amazing degree of flexibility in terms of the use of position players.[32]

Leo made no bones about the fact that he really liked this group of men, with a genuine and abiding devotion to Mays and Rhodes. The chemistry between them was also a factor. Rhodes was a free-spirited Alabaman who regarded the black players and was regarded by them as, to use Mays's term, a brother. Irvin said he was "color blind."

Durocher may have had the talent he wanted, but that year he also let one of the most talented pitchers get away. In 1954 Durocher's Giants had a peek at an unsigned eighteen-year-old left-handed pitcher from Brooklyn named Sandy Koufax. A scout named Gene Bonnibeau had approached Koufax's father, asking him if his son would like to stop by the Polo Grounds for a tryout. Young Koufax agreed and Bonnibeau escorted him down to the clubhouse to meet the Giants pitching coach Frank Shellenback who put him into a uniform and sent him out onto the field with a borrowed glove to toss a few to catcher Bobby Hofman.

Shellenback told Koufax to loosen up and he immediately wound up and threw the ball over Hofman's head, landing three rows deep in the grandstand. The rest of his performance did not get much better and by his own admission he had made a fool of himself, and to the relief of everyone involved was sent back to the clubhouse to shower and change back into his street clothes.

"The only thing I remember clearly was that there was a Coke machine in the clubhouse and that suddenly I was thirstier than I had ever been in my life," Koufax later recalled. "Having very little experience with clubhouse etiquette, I decided that the proper thing to do was to ask the manager, a kindly chap named Leo Durocher, whether it would be all right if I took a Coke. The kindly manager had a few other things on his mind, in the summer of 1954, like, for instance, winning the pennant. To borrow one of Leo's own pet expressions, he looked at me like I had nine heads. 'I don't give a *blankety-blank* what you do,' he snapped . . . I slunk off into a corner to sip my Coke, then slunk out of the clubhouse."*[33]

---

* On December 14, 1954, Koufax was signed by the Brooklyn Dodgers as an amateur free agent for a $6,000 bonus.

The Giants took the pennant with a 97–57 record, five games ahead of the Dodgers. Mays was sensational and won the National League batting championship (.345, 41 homers, 110 RBIs). On the eve of the World Series, Leo called Mays the greatest all-around player in the game.

Rhodes was also a key figure, batting .341 as a part-time player with fifty RBIs. Team pitching was excellent, led by Johnny Antonelli (21–7, 2.30 ERA), Rubén Gómez (17–9, 2.88 ERA), and Sal Maglie (23–6, 2.93 ERA). Leo's World Series opponent was Al Lopez and his Cleveland Indians, who had 111 wins and had overtaken the Yankees by eight games. The Giants were the clear underdogs, with the posted odds against them being 18–10 on the eve of the Series.

On September 29, with the first game at the Polo Grounds tied 2–2 with two on in the eighth inning, Indians slugger Vic Wertz belted a ball some 450 feet, only to have Mays, his back to the plate, race for the wall in distant center field, make an over-the-shoulder catch, spin as his cap whirled off his head, and fire a perfect throw to the cutoff man so that Al Rosen at first base could not tag up and advance to second. Even now, the Mays feat is still referred to as "the Catch" and remains the most famous defensive play in baseball history. In the bottom of the tenth inning, also with two on, Dusty Rhodes lifted a soft fly ball to right field that barely cleared the fence above the 257-foot sign, giving the Giants a 5–2 victory. Rhodes' hit was a glorified pop fly but it cleared an eleven-foot fence and landed among astonished fans in the right field seats.

The next day, Rhodes delivered a pinch single in the fifth and a home run in the seventh against future Hall of Famer Early Wynn to highlight a 3–1 Giants win. Then, in the third inning of Game 3, the Series having shifted from New York to Cleveland, Rhodes came in cold off the bench and delivered a two-run single in a game won by the Giants 6–4. The Giants took the fourth 7–4 without any help from Rhodes, but his exploits (.667 batting average, 2 homers, and 7 RBIs in just six at-bats) had already made him a household name. "It was just as well," the hard-drinking Rhodes recalled years later. "After the third game I was drinking to everybody's health so much that I about ruined mine."

Bob Considine called the stunning sweep "one of baseball's most appalling routs." Another unusual aspect of the Series was that there had not been a rhubarb or any controversial or disputed decisions in all four contests. Durocher was remarkably quiet before, during, and immediately after the Series. This may have had more to do with superstition than humility, as Leo had ordered Laraine not to talk about the Giants in the final weeks of the season because it could jinx the team. Al Lopez probably delivered the best line on the Series: "They say anything can happen in a short series. Well, I knew that. I just never thought it was going to be *that* short."[34]

Within minutes of the sweep, Durocher got a telegram from Branch Rickey: YOU DID A GREAT JOB. IN MY BOOK YOU RANK AMONG THE GREAT MANAGERS OF ALL TIME. Durocher was not only named Manager of the Year by a landslide vote in the annual Associated Press poll, but he also won a new award: the William Wrigley Jr. Award for the baseball comeback of the year, awarded by the Chicago Baseball Writers.

In 1985 when fully retired and out of the game, Durocher was asked by a reporter which of all the teams he managed was the most amazing. Without hesitation, he said the 1954 Giants. The reporter reminded him of the 1951 miracle team, and Durocher stuck to his guns. "Why?" asked Phil Elderkin, staff writer of the *Christian Science Monitor*. Durocher replied: "Going into that Series I didn't think we had a chance. We beat the Indians four straight, mostly because of a guy named Dusty Rhodes." Leo continued: "You know what Rhodes was? He was a buffoon, and I say that affectionately. I loved having him on my ball club because of his personality and the funny things he did that kept everybody loose. But I couldn't have stood two of him."[35]

WITH A WORLD championship under his belt, Leo was feted from coast to coast during the winter. The most noted—and notorious—event was a stag dinner in Leo's honor at the Hillcrest Country Club in Hollywood, where Leo's Hollywood friends—including George Burns, Dean Martin, Jack Benny, Bob Hope, Frank Sinatra, and Milton Berle—roasted Leo. The star of the event was Danny Kaye, who served up an imitation of a drunken Giants owner Horace Stoneham in an argument with Durocher in which Kaye played both parts. In the skit, Stoneham was depicted as the genius behind the championship team and Leo as his loudmouthed errand boy.

Yet it was not the skit that people remembered but rather the lead into it in which Kaye portrayed Stoneham at his most besotted. Kaye gathered empty bottles, dishes, and utensils around him. Then he stood up, mussed his hair, pulled up his shirt, pulled down his unzipped pants, staggered for a moment, and then went sprawling across a table, sending glasses, knives, and forks everywhere. He pulled himself up, teetered, screwed up his face, and asked in a slurred voice, "Where can a guy take a piss?" At this point, according to Durocher, Kaye withdrew his member from his trousers and placed it on a saucer. Kaye's lewd depiction of Stoneham was alluded to in the Hollywood gossip columns and described in some detail in *Variety*, the show business weekly. *The Sporting News* said, "They'll be talking about it from Toots Shor's to the Stork Club for weeks."[36]

Stoneham was furious. Durocher claimed the skit was Kaye's idea, but Durocher took the blame in Stoneham's eyes, especially as reports had it that he had laughed as loud as anyone in the room. Stoneham was still angry at Kaye and Durocher when the Giants reported for Spring Training in Arizona. The difference between 1954 and 1955 was evident from the beginning. Willie Mays arrived weary from his season of winter ball in Puerto Rico, pointing out that he had played in 230 games since the previous March, and admitting to Rud Rennie of the *New York Herald Tribune* that he was "a little bored with baseball."[37]

Durocher admitted that pitching was his greatest concern. "If we could have made a deal for a pitcher, we would have done so," he said on the eve of Opening Day. "But who wants to trade with a pennant winner? Know anybody? Send them around if you do."[38]

Although Leo and Laraine were still deemed the ideal couple in the popular press, the reality was somewhat different. Giants broadcaster Ernie Harwell recalled the time at Spring Training when Laraine took to calling Leo by the nickname "Horseshit" because of his intransigent attitudes and general stubbornness. One night at an Arizona dog track, she got into an argument with him over leaving: she wanted to go, he didn't. Finally, she walked away from him and then had him paged on the public address system. "Paging H. S. Durocher, Paging H. S. Durocher," the PA announcer intoned. Soon they were on their way home. Harwell believed that the real manager in that household was the actress, not the manager. "She had Leo pretty much where she wanted him."

The 1955 season started badly, with the Giants losing their first three games and committing infield errors in each. The team seemed unable to jell, and in June, there were published rumors that Durocher had either been fired or was on his way out. Stoneham denied the rumors, but they persisted. After an exhibition game on June 28, when the team had a record of 33–37, the Associated Press reported that Leo's players collectively seemed to have given up and conceded the 1955 flag to the Dodgers. In the same article, entitled "Giants Through? They Act Like It," Durocher was quoted in an atypical mood of despair: "The club is at its lowest ebb right now.

Everything is going wrong for us. Nothing we do turns out right. When the players don't foul up, I do."[39]

Leo's mother, Clarinda, died at age seventy-eight on July 24, with the funeral several days later. The ceremony was a simple, solemn one attended by about fifty mourners. But it was accompanied by two carloads of flowers—including floral displays from each of the sixteen major league clubs and from many individuals, including restaurateur raconteur Toots Shor and Pee Wee Reese of the Dodgers.

On September 23, with two games still to play in the regular season, the United Press reported that Durocher would leave the Giants at the end of the season and be replaced by Bill Rigney, then managing the Minnesota Millers. The report stated that the divorce was by "mutual consent." The Giants finished the year with a respectable 80–74 record, albeit 18.5 games behind Brooklyn, which had gotten off to a spectacular start. The next day, Durocher reported he was quitting and accepting an executive non-baseball job in California. But as Jimmy Cannon pointed out a few days later, Durocher had quit a job that he did not have. Stoneham had fired him by not offering him a contract for 1956. He clearly wanted Leo out. The two had fought during the season on several occasions. The worst of these battles was not about the team but was waged when Durocher demanded tickets for Giants-Dodgers games from Stoneham, which simply were not available. Cannon also reported what had really gotten under Stoneham's skin and had festered during the season was Danny Kaye's depiction of him the previous winter.[40] Durocher had managed the Giants for almost seven and a half seasons and finished with a .549 winning percentage.

Monte Irvin, who was close to both men, recalled Durocher's departure: "I think Leo wanted to have full control of the team and be its general manager and I think Stoneham had his eye on Bill Rigney." Interviewed decades later at age ninety-six, Irvin still had nothing but good words to say about Durocher. "He was the best manager I ever worked for. He was always ahead of the manager he was playing against. Leo always knew how to pick you up when you were down."[41]

During the last game of the season—the second game in a doubleheader with the Phillies in New York—Durocher called Mays over and pulled him into a tunnel behind the dugout. He placed both hands on his shoulders and said: "I want to tell you something. You know I love you, so I'm prejudiced. But you're the best ballplayer I ever saw. There are other great ones, sure, but to me you're the best ever. Having you on my team made everything worthwhile. I'm telling you this now because I won't be back next season."

"How can you leave?" Mays responded.

Durocher said the decision had already been made, and that Bill Rigney would be his new manager, adding that if there were ever anything Mays needed, he could call on him.

Mays had tears in his eyes. "But Mr. Leo, it's going to be different with you gone. You won't be here to help me."

Durocher then said, "Willie Mays doesn't need help from anyone," and leaned over and kissed him on the check.

Mays would later describe this as his saddest moment in baseball.[42]

Unknown to Mays, Stoneham, or any but a few select friends at the time, Leo had already had an exit strategy in mind a year before he left the Giants. Emmanuel "Manie" Sachs, a top official at the National Broadcasting Company, had been after Leo for a long time to get out of baseball and come work for the network.

"What do you want?" Manie said to Leo on several occasions. "What are you trying to prove, Leo? Come with me."

"I can't do it yet," he told Manie. "When I was a kid I wanted to be a baseball player. Then I wanted to be a major league player. Then I wanted to play on a pennant-winning team. After that I wanted to be a manager, and then I wanted to manage a pennant winner. Now I want to manage a world championship team."

Finally, after Durocher won in 1954, Manie called him again and said, "How about it, Leo? You coming with me now?"

As Leo told a reporter for *Sports Illustrated* in 1961, "I told him I couldn't. I had another year on my contract. Then at the end of the 1955 season I went with him."[43]

CHAPTER 12

Hollywood Dodger

O N SEPTEMBER 28, 1955, the National Broadcasting Company announced that Leo Durocher had taken a $50,000-a-year job where his primary responsibility would be in the area of "talent relations." He would also appear on NBC as a comedic presence and would serve as a sports commentator and a guest on variety shows. At a cocktail party at Toots Shor's restaurant later in the week, the appointment was celebrated, and Durocher was asked if he would ever return to baseball.

"Take a look at the NBC release," he responded.

In the formal press release, Durocher was quoted: "I am happy and elated to have this association with the National Broadcasting Company and look forward enthusiastically to a long period of pleasant and lucrative undertaking."

Leo was then asked what *elated* meant.

"It's the way I felt when Bobby Thomson hit the homer in 1951," he said.[1]

It was an odd response, especially given that his first major assignment with NBC was to become a comedian and to host *The NBC Comedy Hour*. The show was slotted against the very popular *Ed Sullivan Show* on CBS on Sunday night at 8 P.M. in the East. Sullivan owned Sunday night, and he had knocked an earlier version of *The NBC Comedy Hour* off the air two years earlier. NBC wanted Leo to agree to do fifteen shows, but he would agree to only three. His first show was to be on January 8, 1956, and NBC had him take acting lessons in preparation all during December. On the eve of the show, he did not hide the fact that he was ill at ease with the assignment. "I don't want to be an actor," he told one reporter who covered television. "I want to be Leo Durocher."[2]

Despite the fact that his guests included supposedly surefire funnymen Jonathan Winters and Henny Youngman, the show was a disaster, and Durocher was a flop. Leo was "unfunny," according to more than one critic, while others pointed out that he was wooden and paid much more attention to the teleprompter than to his live studio audience. John Crosby of the *New York Herald Tribune* took one look at the show and wrote, "Sunday's show was so bad that almost anything else—a Shakespearean reading, a barn dance, a 1912 movie—would have been an improvement." Jack Gould of *The New York Times* commented, "Leo Durocher's return to baseball should be arranged as soon as possible."

Durocher tried to get out of doing the second show, but NBC convinced him to give it one more try. In terms of ratings and critical reception, the second show was worse than the first. Durocher was colorless, cold, and widely derided for chewing gum in front of the camera. Leo walked out after the second show, battered by more bad reviews and an inability to generate laughs—despite having ten writers crafting comedic lines for him. Durocher had been humiliated, and he took at least one return shot aimed at NBC in which he said he was not a comedian and had only agreed to do the show to be cooperative. "If I get a pitcher," he told *The Sporting News*, "I don't send him to center field."[3]

The laughs finally came—but at Leo's expense. At the Baseball Writers' Association of America dinner at the Waldorf Astoria Hotel in February, comedian Phil Silvers summed up the Durocher situation: "I used to know Leo when he was in your business," he said to the 1,600 baseball folks in attendance. "Come to think of it, I used to know Leo when he was in my business." One of his writers later noted that Durocher made the deadpan Ed Sullivan look like Noel Coward.[4]

By March, columnist Bob Cooke acknowledged he had been told by an NBC executive that Leo's $50,000 was being written off as a short-term loss, and rumors were rife that Leo would be back in baseball by the time of the 1956 All-Star Game in July.[5] But in June, Leo's contract with NBC was renewed. In September, he was given the role of lining up talent for the new *Dinah Shore Show*. A very popular singer herself, Shore wanted Frank Sinatra to be the primary guest on her first show. At this time, Sinatra was turning down all television appearances, and Durocher did not relish asking him for the favor—especially since the show had a relatively low budget and could not begin to match his normal price, even if he made himself available. Leo asked and Sinatra replied:

"Is this for you, buddy?"

"Well, I guess you could say that. I was asked to get you, and it would be a feather in my cap if I could."

"All right," he said. "Done."

According to one report, Sinatra's agent was speechless when he heard what Sinatra had agreed to do—and for what price. Sinatra appeared on Shore's debut show on October 5, 1956, with Dizzy Dean, whom Durocher had also lined up. Suddenly, Leo had found his niche with NBC, and he told columnist Earl Wilson that he had never been as happy in his life as he was now.[6] Durocher spent the rest of the year announcing a minor golf tournament, making a guest appearance on a Bob Hope variety show, and doing color commentary for college football games.

More guest appearances and announcing jobs materialized in 1957–58. He cohosted NBC's Saturday afternoon baseball *Game of the Week* with Lindsey Nelson and was an immediate success because he was playing himself. Each game was aired on more than one hundred stations and drew an estimated eight to ten million viewers. He also did a five-minute daily radio commentary about baseball for NBC radio.

Durocher now presented himself as an even-tempered model of civility. He was president of the local Little League in which his stepson Chris played, and his marriage seemed as solid as any Hollywood marriage could be. In his role as a broadcaster, he was greeted warmly by all, including the umpires with whom he had once fought. Before one game, Tom Gorman invited him to come into the umpires' dressing room for a friendly chat.

Leo avoided controversy and made news by advocating more of what he called "window dressing" in ballparks—seats with cushions and backs, clean, well-lit ladies' rooms, and the like. He argued that baseball's declining attendance and lower revenue should be addressed by paying more attention to the family—not just the traditional single male fan.

In early 1958, Harry Paxton wrote a profile of Durocher as a broadcaster that appeared in the *Saturday Evening Post*. At the end of the article, Paxton posed the question: Was there anything left of the old Leo, who would stop at nothing to win a ballgame? He answered by recalling a tape-recorded Durocher quotation about which he explained: "I am giving it from memory since it was recorded, not my own visit with Leo, but by NBC technicians in the broadcasting booth one Saturday afternoon in Milwaukee.

This was during the early September slump which threatened to cost the Braves the pennant. The Braves lost again that day. Leo closed the broadcast with remarks to the effect that the Braves couldn't seem to get loose—that they needed some sort of lift. Then the program went off the air. The tape recorder played on. Durocher began talking to the people in the booth." Leo said: "If I was managing that club, you know what I'd do? I'd have the pitchers throw behind the hitters. Then the other club would get mad and start throwing at them. Then they'd get mad themselves. Maybe there'd be a fight. That would wake the whole ball club up!"[7]

From the end of 1957 through all of 1958, a series of published reports suggested teams—including the Cubs, Braves, Cardinals, and Indians— were trying to lure Durocher back into baseball. He turned them all down, because none of them offered partial ownership of the team in the form of stock. In 1957, Leo's federal tax rate was 62 percent, and if his income reached $100,000, the rate would climb to 75 percent. Leo wanted stock so he could take his money out later as capital gains at a much lower rate. Durocher was also rumored to be considering a return to the Dodgers or Giants, but only if he could land a stock deal.[8]

During 1958, Durocher appeared on several television variety shows, including *The Eddie Fisher Show*. He also hosted a full season of *Phillies Jackpot Bowling*, and he continued his role as a baseball announcer.* The year began and ended with Leo out of the headlines, off the sports pages, and all but gone from the gossip columns. He was on page five of the *Los Angeles Times* in January when he and actor Jeff Chandler were honored as the best-dressed men in America by the Men's Apparel Club of California. In terms of notice and notoriety, it was Leo's quietest year since he signed with the New York Yankees in 1925.[9]

IT WAS NOT long, however, before Durocher was back in the news, some of which involved personal losses. In January 1959 his older brother Clarence died at age sixty-two of a heart attack. And in April, David Redd, sixty-one, collapsed and died during a church service at the Bethel AME Church in Springfield, Massachusetts. Redd's obituary in the *Springfield Union* was headlined HELPED DUROCHER START IN BASEBALL.[10]

---

* The bowling show was sponsored by Phillies cigars, not by the Philadelphia baseball team.

During the All-Star break in July, rumors were rife that Durocher was returning to baseball. Leo confirmed that he was looking into possibilities, and evidence pointed to his interest in the Chicago White Sox, which were then owned by Bill Veeck and had Hank Greenberg as general manager. Rumors suggested that the Sox would replace the quiet Al Lopez with a flamboyant manager who would make some noise.

Then on September 17, Durocher was suddenly given his unconditional release from NBC, which was now paying him $65,000 a year. Whether he quit or was fired was a moot point: he was allowed to resign. Writer Richard Kaplan, who looked into the departure, was told by NBC insiders that Durocher left one step ahead of the axe. Earlier in the year Manie Sachs had died of leukemia and he had been Leo's protector.[11]

Durocher would later tell a more specific and melodramatic tale of why he left NBC: "When the president of NBC, Robert Kintner, who I despised, hollered at me in a restaurant to come over to his table, I said I told you once, twice and for the third and last time: I don't tablehop, I don't eat with drunken bums and as far as I'm concerned you should be eating out of the trough. That left me to live beyond my means while earning nothing."[12]

He immediately announced that he was returning to baseball as a manager, and that he was in negotiations with a team which he later confirmed was the Cleveland Indians. Joe Gordon, the manager of the Indians, had been fired after he said he probably would not be back the following season because of the criticism he was taking from Indians general manager Frank Lane. Two days later, Branch Rickey, who was in the process of forming a third league, the Continental League, offered Durocher the managership of any of the eight teams that would first take the field in 1961—an offer that would have kept Durocher without work for close to twenty months until the first games were played.

Five days after Leo left NBC, the Cleveland News reported that he had been hired by the Indians for three years at $65,000 per year plus a capital gains interest in the team. The Indians immediately denied the report, saying that it was still looking at two men: Durocher and an unnamed party.

On September 24, the Indians announced that Gordon had been renamed manager for two more years. It was stunning news, and the task of saying what happened was left up to Durocher, who finally talked about it almost a month later. Durocher told the Associated Press that he had the three-year contract in hand, but turned it down because the Indians had refused to come to terms with him on certain key points, including a larger ownership position than the Indians had offered him. Leo called Frank Lane to turn down the job, and Gordon was rehired the next morning.[13]

ABOUT THE TIME that Durocher was negotiating with the Indians, rumors began to circulate that Leo and Laraine were spending less and less time under the same roof and that their "ideal" marriage was in trouble.

What was not known at the time was that Leo had already moved out of the home he shared with Day and her children. He had been seeing a twenty-six-year-old dancer named Larri Thomas since the beginning of the year. He had already met with her parents on several occasions at their home in Wayne, Pennsylvania, and the parents had visited Leo and Larri in Hollywood. Thomas was married at the time to John Bromfield, who was the star of a television Western set in Arizona called *U.S. Marshal.*

In November, the *New York Daily Mirror* reported that Durocher's twelve-year marriage to Laraine Day was, according to sources in Hollywood, "all over but for the legal formalities." The story was picked up by the AP, which ran its story with Larri Thomas posing in a skirt that stopped at the top of her thigh and a full-length mink coat draped over her shoulders. The following day, Durocher, Day, and Thomas all denied the story.*[14]

Through the fall of 1959 into early 1960, the gossip columnists were filled with the rumors and with denials by both Leo and Laraine. In late January 1960, gossip columnist Dorothy Kilgallen reported that Leo had chosen to be with Frank Sinatra rather than return home, where Laraine awaited for "a discussion."[15]

The denials finally stopped on March 17, when the Durochers announced that they were separating, and a property agreement was signed on May 15 in Los Angeles. On June 14, Day obtained a Mexican divorce from Durocher on the basis of incompatibility. He was to provide $250 a month to support their two adopted children—Melina Michele, sixteen, and Chris Durocher, fifteen.

Durocher's life had changed radically by late 1960. He was out of work, and some of his Hollywood friends were losing interest in him—especially

---

* Director Morton DaCosta, who directed Thomas in a road company production of *The Music Man*, described her to the *Boston-American*: "She's so sexy even the birds and bees study her."

without Laraine. His lofty demands for a share of ownership as a condition of employment now sounded silly. But perhaps the most important change was that Leo was now out of the spotlight. As Dick Young wrote in December: "Durocher wants the spotlight for the nourishment it, in itself, gives his body. He sucks up attention. His ego must be fed more than his stomach, or he will perish."[16]

All during the autumn and into December, Durocher had hoped to be offered a job as the manager of the new American League franchise in Los Angeles (soon to be named the Angels). When it became clear that he was not going to get the job and it was being awarded to Bill Rigney, he told Mel Durslag of the *Los Angeles Examiner*, "I'm not too much concerned with losing the Los Angeles job as with the general pattern. Somebody has put in the knock for me and I don't seem to be wanted." He then added: "I can take the knocks—but I can't take a blackball when I'm trying to find a job."[17]

Sympathy for Durocher was in short supply, as columnists, including Red Sox announcer Curt Gowdy, reminded his readers that Leo had wanted more than a job; he wanted a piece of the ball club in the form of stock. Owners were loath to give up a slice of their pie, especially to somebody as volatile and unpredictable as Leo Durocher.[18]

At the very end of 1960, Durocher got two breaks. He was hired by the Mutual Network for a radio sports talk show that would air five nights a week. And on December 29, word leaked out through Red Smith of the *New York Herald Tribune* that Leo had been hired by the Los Angeles Dodgers as a coach under manager Walter Alston, a former schoolteacher who was as tranquil a man as could be found managing a baseball team, and whose team had slumped in 1960 after winning the 1959 World Series and therefore needed Leo.

Leo's connection with the Dodgers came about through a chance encounter with Walter O'Malley in a small restaurant in Los Angeles called Dominick's. The hiring was later described by O'Malley to Tex Maule of *Sports Illustrated*: "I was going there with some friends for dinner. We had an argument with another party about a parking place in front of the cafe and then, to save trouble, we let the other party have it. They came in and sat near us, and in a little while Leo joined them. He saw me and came over to say hello and ask me if he was really blackballed in baseball. I told him he wasn't. Then he said he would even take a job as a coach if it was with the right club. So the next day I got [General Manager Buzzie] Bavasi to talk to him, and we hired him."

Durocher gladly accepted: "After all, I'd been out of work for 15 months. I wanted to get back to work, especially in baseball." Durocher's role was to pump a little life into the club from his perch at third base. He was not brought aboard to challenge Alston. Bavasi told Durocher that Alston was still in complete command. He told him: "The first time there's any second-guessing, that's it." Leo got the Dodgers to give him his old number, 2.[19]

"O'Malley and Bavasi couldn't have been better to me," Durocher said. "When they offered me a contract I said the money doesn't matter. Just put the contract down, and I'll sign it. Well, some of the papers have said I'm getting $17,500, but that's not even close. I can't tell you any more than that without naming a figure, but that's not even close." The normal salary for a big league coach in 1961 was $15,000, but it was estimated by one writer that Durocher would earn in excess of $50,000 between what the Dodgers were paying him and the money he got for his daily radio show.[20]

The pairing of Durocher and Alston was an odd one, as they had little in common save for a desire to win. Many doubted the manager-coach relationship would work. Harold Kaese of *The Boston Globe* wrote, "Alston is sitting on top of a volcano named Durocher." Longtime Durocher watcher Bill Lee of the *Hartford Courant* observed: "If I were a betting guy, I'd lay all the 8–5 I could hustle that Durocher and Alston will never finish the 1961 season as coach and manager respectively of the L.A. Dodgers."[21]

But Alston and Bavasi knew exactly what they were getting with Durocher: one of the smartest minds in baseball, as well as a noisy, energetic competitor who would have a stimulating influence on the club.

News that the feud between Durocher and Jackie Robinson was over was now made public on the occasion of Leo's return to baseball. Robinson told Evelyn Cunningham of the *New Pittsburgh Courier*: "We didn't actually dislike each other. We were just too much alike. As a matter of fact, it was actually his wife Laraine who was responsible for us having problems. It started one day when I got hit hard on my elbow by a pitch. The pain was excruciating. On my way to first I was rubbing and swinging my arm to loosen it up and ease the pain. That night on her radio show, Laraine blasted me for feigning pain."

Sometime late in Durocher's time with the Giants, the two men met in Philadelphia. "He rushed up to me and hugged me and was genuinely warm and friendly," said Robinson. "I was so moved by the gesture that I wrote him a letter, telling him what it meant to me." In welcoming Leo back to baseball, Robinson added: "Leo will do OK."[22]

Monte Irvin, who was close to both men, reflected on why the feud had lasted for so long: "He and Jackie had their own ways and just couldn't get along—it was as simple as that."[23]

In early 1961, the gossip columns reported that Durocher's romance with Larri Thomas was over, and he was now dating Sheila Connolly, the estranged wife of actor Guy Madison. Thomas was now dating actor Van Johnson. Leo dated a lot of women during the 1961 season, including Marlon Brando's ex-wife Anna Kashi. Laraine Day remarried in early March in a three-hour Mormon ceremony. Her third husband, Mike Grilikhes, was a theater producer known for staging outsize theatrical productions.[24]

In early February, the Friars Club held a dinner in honor of Durocher in Los Angeles. It was a star-studded event during which comedian George Burns commented, "Baseball is baseball again with Leo Durocher back." Jim Murray wrote in his next column that it was the most glittering dinner ever held to honor a man for getting a job as a third-base coach.[25]

When Durocher arrived in Vero Beach for Spring Training, he displayed, as one writer put it, "the vitality of a teenager." Phil Collier of the *San Diego Union* followed Leo, noting that he doused himself freely with cologne, smoked cigarettes, and consumed cough drops in equally alarming rates, and admittedly preferred the Hollywood companionship of Frank Sinatra and others to the Spartan existence of Dodgertown.[26]

Durocher talked incessantly about his Hollywood friends, especially Sinatra and the Sinatra-led "Rat Pack." He also bragged about his new Italian Renaissance-style house in Trousdale Estates, a new and fashionable California development of elegant one-story homes. "From left to right, I have a view of the Pacific Ocean and all the San Fernando Valley. The Nixon house is spread below me, and I can drop a baseball down his chimney." Noting that Frank Sinatra lived across the canyon, Durocher said, "I can hardly wait to holler at him, 'Get up, you skinny bum!'"

Leo had arrived—at least in the Hollywood sense of the word. He was asking to be judged by where and how he lived. To get to Villa Leo, one drove up a long, dry, bony ridge, where half-acre lots started at $50,000, and where the neighbors, in addition to Richard Nixon, included Dinah Shore, Gypsy Rose Lee, Cornel Wilde, Vic Damone, and a number of executives, lawyers, and physicians. The centerpiece of the house was Leo's bed, which sported a gigantic headboard of carved chestnut that had once served as a fireplace in the Vanderbilt mansion in New York City. As Robert Cantwell wrote in *Sports Illustrated*: "The combination of his old hard-bitten baseball knowledge and experience and his new consciousness of himself as an authentic Hollywood celebrity makes this most recent phase of his career unique in the history of baseball."[27]

Even before the Dodgers left Vero Beach, the newspapers were filled with conjecture as to who would manage the new National League franchise awarded to New York City; the New York Mets were to play their first game on Opening Day 1962. On March 14, 1961, the Associated Press reported that Durocher was first in line to manage the new team. Buzzie Bavasi said that if the New York club wanted Leo, he would be available as early as July. On March 22, the *New York World-Telegram and Sun* reported that within forty-eight hours, Durocher would be named manager of the club. Durocher, who had the initial backing of owner Joan Payson, did not get the nod because it was believed by the brain trust behind the Mets that he would not do well with a starter team. The story was that Casey Stengel, now seventy, had refused the job.[28]

The regular season had hardly begun when Durocher got involved in one of the most memorable ejections of his baseball career. On April 16, 1961, in the fourth inning in a game against the Pittsburgh Pirates at the Coliseum in Los Angeles, Dodger first baseman Norm Larker hit a pop-up that landed in fair territory before bouncing foul. Before it went foul, Pirates catcher Hal Smith lunged for the ball while Larker made it to second base before home plate umpire Jocko Conlan called the ball foul. The Dodgers were fuming, arguing that the ball had been touched before it went foul, making it a hit. Durocher, who was not coaching at third that day, popped out of the dugout and pleaded his case with Conlan, but—unable to convince him to reverse his call—he headed for the dugout. While in the dugout, Durocher flung his towel in disgust. Conlan shouted: "You're out of the game!"

"You're ejecting me for throwing a towel in the dugout—our own dugout?" Leo asked in disbelief. "You can't throw towels," Conlan shouted back, insisting that the towel had landed on the field. "Oh, yeah? I can't do this, huh?" Durocher roared, and then flung a towel and a batting helmet onto the field and started charging at Conlan, incensed at being tossed for such a minor gesture. The two went eyeball to eyeball. Leo then started kicking dirt on Conlan, but he missed and his foot hit the umpire's shin instead. Conlan then kicked Durocher back in his shin, threw his face mask on the ground, removed his chest protector, and began clenching his fists as if he and the Dodgers manager were about to go a few rounds. The other umpires intervened before punches were exchanged, and pitcher Don Drysdale was able to restore order by grabbing Durocher by the collar. Vin Scully watched the event from the broadcast booth and told his radio listeners, "They're behaving like a couple of kids. It's as though they were saying, 'you kick me and I'll kick you.'" After the game, reporters tried to question Durocher, but all he would say was, "I got kicked twice; so did he."[29]

The screaming headline in the *Los Angeles Times* the next morning read: "LEO THE TOE" LOSES KICKING DUEL. Inside the paper, Frank Finch described the fracas: "They began dancing the Russian 'Kazotski,' standing up, their feet flying faster than did Bojangles Bill Robinson's educated puppies at the Palace." The next issue of *Life* magazine featured a series of photos detailing the confrontation.[30]

The next afternoon, National League president Warren Giles suspended Durocher three days and admonished Conlan for his part in the affair. There were those who felt Durocher had been provoked and that the punishment was too harsh, though some felt he deserved a much stiffer suspension. The Pirates, who flew back to Pittsburgh that night, discussed the penalty on the plane with Lester Biederman of the *Pittsburgh Press*. All the players agreed that Durocher would be lucky to get off with a thirty-day suspension. One player held out for a suspension of one year. Biederman called the actual penalty "absolutely ridiculous."[31]

Any hopes that Durocher might still be in the running for the New York Mets job came to an end on September 29, 1961, just before the start of the World Series, when Casey Stengel finally took the job.

After the season was over for the second-place Dodgers, Durocher spent a good portion of December in Australia, Hong Kong, and Japan with Frank Sinatra, who was on a tour that ended with him celebrating his forty-sixth birthday in Tokyo before heading home to film *The Manchurian Candidate*.

By the end of the year, former wife Laraine Day was generating more news than Leo. Among other things, Laraine was hosting the 384-voice Mormon Tabernacle Choir in a year-end television special and was giving interviews to promote the event. She spoke without rancor about Leo when asked about the failed marriage and admitted that she was still a Giants fan and would be for as long as Willie Mays was still on the team.[32]

WHILE LEO WAS with the Dodgers at Spring Training in 1962, a story broke that cast a new and unflattering light on Durocher during 1951 and on the

Bobby Thomson home run in particular. In this March 22 story, Joe Reichler, the highly respected Associated Press writer, claimed his source was "a former member of the New York Giants" currently with another major league team. The unidentified player claimed that the 1951 New York Giants under Durocher's orders had an electrician install a wire leading from the center field clubhouse to the dugout. As signals were stolen with the aid of high-powered binoculars, a button was pushed and a buzzer rang in the dugout—one buzz for a fastball and two for a breaking pitch. The information was then relayed to the batter from a bench coach who relayed the signal to the batter.

The story claimed that the Giants had used this "ingenious" system for the last three months of the season, during which time they had won thirty-six of their last forty-five games. The Dodgers had built a 13½-game lead over the Giants and then, in the most dramatic of all baseball collapses, lost their lead and, with the Thomson home run, the National League pennant. The informant insisted that Bobby Thomson was tipped off to the fateful pitch before hitting his pennant-winning home run. "You might say," said the anonymous informant, "that the shot heard 'round the world was set off by a buzzer." The story appeared atop sports pages across the country.[33]

Thomson's reaction was swift, denying in a follow-up AP story that he had gotten any signal before winning the famous game. "It was a high inside fastball and nobody called the pitch." Calling the charge "the most ridiculous thing I have ever heard of," he added, "If I'd been getting the signals, why wouldn't I have hit the first pitch? It was a fat one right down the middle." Branca backed up Thomson in the same story: "The first one was right down the pipe. On the second one, I tried to brush him back a bit but I didn't get the ball in tight enough. I always figured he just outguessed me."

Thomson challenged the man who had made the charge "to show some character" and to come out in the open. Others chimed in to dispute the charge that the historic homer came on a stolen sign. Whitey Lockman, the Giant on second base when the home run was hit, said "I couldn't even see [Dodgers catcher] Rube Walker's signal to Branca on that homer." Alvin Dark, then the current manager of the San Francisco Giants, along with Wes Westrum and Willie Mays, who were all members of the 1951 Giants, went on the record to say that the accusation against Thomson was completely baseless. Significantly, none of these players denied the spy operation, but they were specific about Thomson not getting the signal.[34]

Dark may have been the most emphatic: "Anybody who knows anything about baseball knows that with a runner on second base, no catcher in the business would give just one sign and stick with it. He flashes three or four phony signs. It would take either a genius or a very lucky man to select the legitimate sign and flash it to the hitter." Durocher was the only one to deny the sign-stealing system, declaring: "No, no, no. The man who dreamed up that story has been reading too much fiction. We never had anything like that. If we had signals, Bobby would have murdered that first pitch."[35]

The 1951 Dodgers reacted similarly to the accusations and were just as sure in their defense of Thomson. Gil Hodges and Duke Snider said that they had heard rumors of the sign-stealing operation during the latter days of the season, and Hodges had been told for sure after the playoff by "a fellow who had good information." Snider and others insisted that even if the Giants had such a system, it was not effective. "If the Giants were stealing the Dodger signs, why didn't they steal them the day before the Thomson homer?" The day before, they had lost to Clem Labine of the Dodgers, who shut them out 10–0.[36]

Branca insisted that a stolen sign had nothing to do with Thomson's home run. The Los Angeles Times quoted him: "The irony is that Rube Walker caught me that day (instead of Roy Campanella). Rube used a different series of signals. Thomson didn't get advance notice of that pitch, but the Giants did get quite a lot that season." Branca stated in another story that he learned from pitcher Ted Gray in 1953, when both men were at Detroit, that the 1951 Giants had stolen signs, and that it was confirmed in 1955 when he was a teammate of former San Francisco Giants pitchers Alex Konikowski and Al Worthington.[37]

Two days after Reichler's story broke, columnist Jack McDonald of the San Francisco News & Call Bulletin wrote, "No responsible wire service should dredge up a yarn after more than 10 years without pinning it on someone."[38]

The story died quickly over a long weekend and was quickly forgotten— at least for the moment. What seemed to kill the story was the logistics of picking up a coded signal from the outfield in the late afternoon gloaming, decoding it, and then getting it to the batter via the clubhouse in time to be of any use. During an interview in the mid-1970s by Thomas Kiernan for his book The Miracle of Coogan's Bluff, the issue was raised again with Rube Walker, who had replaced the injured Roy Campanella that day. Walker told him that his "steal-proof system" that year consisted of seven different finger-and-fist configurations flashed in sequence, that the "active" sign for the desired pitch was just one of the seven in the sequence, and that the active sign's number in the sequence was changed every few innings. Kiernan later asserted that when he had interviewed players for his book, the Dodger clubhouse was fully aware of Durocher's telescope and regarded it as a ploy designed to rattle opposing teams.[39]

But the issue was raised again in January 2001 in an article in *The Wall Street Journal* by Joshua Prager that gave the story new life. It reasserted what everyone had admitted in 1962: that the Giants, encouraged by Durocher, had been using an elaborate system to steal opponents' signs during the 1951 season and during the playoff against the Dodgers. All but one of the Giants still living again acknowledged the sign-stealing scheme, just as many Giants had never denied the fact in 1962, though they disputed that Bobby Thomson took the sign on his famous home run. In the *Journal* article, however, Giants bullpen catcher Sal Yvars maintained that he had given Thomson the sign from his position in the outfield bullpen, an admission he had been making for many years on the banquet circuit.[40]

The response to Prager's piece was without precedent for a modern baseball story, but in the end the assertion again seemed to wobble and weaken as testimony came from those on the field back in 1951. With Thomson at the plate, Whitey Lockman, the Giants runner on second, long maintained that he couldn't read Walker's signs. "I didn't recognize the sequence," Lockman, who was then seventy-four, told *The Wall Street Journal*, adding that he touched his belt buckle to let Thomson know he couldn't read the sign. Lockman consistently maintained that position, which supports Thomson's assertion that he didn't get the sign. If Lockman could not decode the sign from second, it is also hard to imagine that someone in the center-field clubhouse, even with a telescope, could have recognized the new sequence of signs and buzzed in the result to be relayed to Thomson in time.*[41]

In 2006 Joshua Praeger published *The Echoing Green: The Untold Story of Bobby Thomson, Ralph Branca and the Shot Heard Round the World*, a highly regarded book that focused more on the era and the remarkable relationship between Ralph Branca and Bobby Thomson. In a concluding

---

* Others, including a few Dodgers, were more amused than angry when they reacted to the story: "It doesn't surprise me. Leo Durocher would do almost anything to win a ball game," said Hall of Fame outfielder Duke Snider. "But it doesn't change anything. Everyone steals signs. It's part of the game. We were stealing signs," he said. "Still," he was reminded, "the Dodgers weren't using a spyglass in the clubhouse and a buzzer to the dugout and clubhouse to steal them, were they?"

"No," Snider added, then admitted: "But that's because we never thought of it."

author's note he added: "And I say that as regards the stealing of signs, my book is not about the debatable effects of a telescope on play but about the undeniable effects of a secret on two men."[42]

As THE 1962 season progressed, numerous articles discussed the threat Durocher posed to manager Walter Alston, and writers were always looking for new angles to this story. At the Polo Grounds on August 24, when the Dodgers were about to play a twi-night doubleheader against the Mets, Leo had a brush with his own mortality, and he gave Jerry Izenberg, a reporter for the *Newark Star-Ledger*, a lesson in how he always seemed to be able to steal the show.

"About an hour before the first game," Izenberg recalled, "the park was virtually empty. In the old center-field clubhouse, a man was talking to Leo when suddenly he [Leo] turned white and clutched his chest. The guy yelled for the trainer and they helped Leo onto a table. Subsequent events would show he was not having a heart attack as he suspected, but rather was suffering from a dose of penicillin to which he was allergic."

"Get Walter . . . get Walter," Leo croaked as he lay on the table.

The overweight Izenberg sprinted down the steps and across the length of the field to tell Alston that Leo had collapsed.

They ran back to Leo's side.

"Closer, Walter, come closer," Leo whispered, and Izenberg thought: "Well here it comes. The big deathbed confession. He's going to say he's sorry for trying to get Alston's job."

"Walter," Durocher said, "if I don't make it, tell the guys to win these games for me."

"The Mets were a team that would win only 40 of 160 games that year. Who says Leo didn't know how to pick his spots."*[43]

Leo did make it, thanks to a doctor who responded to an appeal on the public address system and gave Leo two shots of lifesaving adrenaline. He was back in uniform four nights later.[44]

In 1962, the Dodgers gave up a four-game lead over the Giants in the last two weeks of the season, ended in a tie, and lost to the Giants in a playoff series, two games to one. The loss was severely disappointing, and

---

* NL teams played 160 games in 1962 and the AL 162.

according to GM Buzzie Bavasi, the only time that owner Walter O'Malley considered replacing Alston. One possibility he mentioned was Durocher. Bavasi told O'Malley that if he fired Alston, he would have to fire him too.[45]

After the 1962 World Series, Bavasi got a call from Hank Greenberg, who had sat near Durocher in a restaurant and listened to him pop off about how he would have handled things differently. Greenberg said Leo was an embarrassment. The next evening, Bavasi confronted Durocher at a dinner at the Friars Club and told him: "Don't ever come near the ball club again. You're through. I don't ever want to have anything to do with you, you ungrateful SOB."

Leo claimed he had never said a word and Greenberg had been mistaken. The next morning, Bavasi called Alston and told him that he had fired Durocher.

"Don't do that," Alston replied. "I like Leo. I like having him around."

Bavasi rehired him.[46]

In the coming weeks, Durocher was given final absolution for his comments by none other than Dodgers owner Walter O'Malley, who said that people had to understand his social position. People like Sinatra, Danny Kaye, and Tony Martin were his friends, and he had to answer questions like "What would you have done in that situation?" O'Malley said: "He can't sit there like a dummy. He has to come up with answers."[47]

EVEN BEFORE HE left New York, Durocher would occasionally mention that such-and-such magazine or book publisher was talking to him about writing his memoirs but none could come up with the magazine collaboration fee or book advance he demanded. Then out of the blue, in May 1963, Durocher, with the help of a gifted collaborator named Ed Linn, published his "candid memoirs" in the *Saturday Evening Post*. Durocher was reputedly paid $50,000 for the mini-memoir, entitled "I Come to Kill You," which had been prepared the previous winter. The piece in the magazine ran thirty thousand words.

Durocher used the memoir to settle old scores, or as one columnist who reviewed the article put it, Durocher not only stepped on a lot of toes but "pulled on and laced up his spiked baseball shoes before stepping on those toes." Durocher ripped into Fred Haney of the Angels and Horace Stoneham of the Giants for "fouling" him up in 1961 by making it look like he had been offered—and declined—managing positions with both teams when he desperately wanted both jobs. He also revealed that Sinatra had been willing to put up $500,000 to buy stock in the club for Leo if he got the job with the Angels.

Durocher pulled out all the stops when it came to depicting Stoneham as a drunk. He even went so far as to recall a cleaned-up version of Danny Kaye's obscene skit targeting Stoneham. More than anything else, this was what upset others in baseball, including his staunchest allies who believed he had made himself unhirable. "Leo probably has ruined any chance he might have had to manage in the big leagues again," said Giants manager Alvin Dark. "Durocher can't publicly knock Stoneham for his drinking and expect another club owner to hire him."

Jack Murphy, a columnist for the *San Diego Union*, called the memoirs a strange, fascinating document that perfectly displayed Durocher's talent for saying the wrong thing at the wrong time. "As recently as two weeks ago," Murphy wrote, "it seemed almost certain Durocher would be the next manager of the wobbly Los Angeles Angels . . . Durocher was ready and eager to seize command. It was a situation requiring tact, patience and silence—virtues not usually associated with Durocher."[48]

The memoirs showed Durocher at his most revisionist, as his stories suddenly changed. For years, he had maintained that John Christian hurt himself when he tripped over a water trough, but now he had slipped on some wet cement. Inexplicably, Durocher felt compelled to bring up and deny the allegation that he had stolen Babe Ruth's watch. "I don't know of any other public figure that would feel compelled to defend himself against the charge of petty larceny," a puzzled Jack Murphy wrote, "yet Leo brings up the subject in his memoirs."

Some additional fallout from the *Saturday Evening Post* article came a few weeks later in the form of a tape recording that had been made with Ed Linn on which Durocher ripped into Walter Alston for a full five minutes. When the tape was recorded during the winter as research for the article, Durocher had stipulated that his attack on Alston could only be used if he were not still with the Dodgers for the season. After Durocher was rehired, the tape somehow ended up being played for Buzzie Bavasi, who was furious. As Dick Young noted, the tape was the reason why Durocher spent part of the summer exiled from the third-base coaching box and restricted to the dugout.[49]

The Dodgers had a remarkable 1963 season, which ended in the team winning the World Series in four games over the New York Yankees—with a key role played by Sandy Koufax, the man Durocher had let slip through his fingers back in Brooklyn. Still in the doghouse from his remarks about

Alston, he was all but invisible during the Series and its aftermath. As one columnist asked: "When was the last time you saw this anti-Alston coach pictured or mentioned in print?" His answer was that he had been "thoroughly squelched."[50]

On the other hand, 1963 was a particularly good year for Leo in show business. After he starred in an episode of *The Beverly Hillbillies*, he jumped straight to "Leo Durocher Meets Mister Ed." The season-four opener aired on September 29, 1963. Mr. Ed, the talking horse, like all Southern California residents, was a die-hard Dodgers fan. He had some problems with the team's play, and in the show, took to the field to show them a thing or two about hitting and base running. Ed then batted a few and slid into bases himself at Dodger Stadium. Half the team was on the show (including John Roseboro, Sandy Koufax, Willie Davis, and "Moose" Skowron), as well as the voice of Vin Scully. Durocher was at the heart of the story, the man who asked Ed to show up to help get the Dodgers in shape.

The third entry in his 1963 trifecta was a sophisticated set with Judy Garland on *The Judy Garland Show* on October 23, where the two performed like long-lost siblings genuinely pleased to be with one another. They sang "Take Me Out to the Ball Game" as a duet.[51]

While not rehearsing television appearances, Durocher spent much of his off-season as a paid public speaker. He was a big draw, especially in New England where he was regarded as a native son. On January 13, 1964, while staying at the Middlebury Inn in Middlebury, Vermont, and preparing to speak before an American Legion fund-raising dinner, he was served with a writ, putting him under arrest and forcing him to post an immediate $30,000 bail that was raised by a group of local citizens. Durocher stood accused of "alienation of affection" by a bricklayer named Rene Morin who was convinced that Durocher was having an affair with his fifty-one-year-old wife, Anna. Morin sought $150,000 in damages and demanded a jury trial. Durocher was allowed to leave the state, and before he did, he hired a top lawyer—Vermont's attorney general.

In early July 1964, Durocher was back in Vermont to face the alienation-of-affection lawsuit. Morin testified that Durocher—to whom he constantly referred as "that guy down on third base"—had made him so angry that he could bend a horseshoe like a pretzel. He alleged that Leo had bedded his wife, and that she in turn put her affections for Morin in the deep freeze. "Sleeping with her, like sleeping with an iceberg."

According to Ron Cohen, the UPI reporter who was the first to pick up the story for the national media, the most dramatic moment in the trial came when Durocher revealed that he was not in love with Anna but rather her twenty-six-year-old daughter, Carolyn. At this point, Carolyn, a tall attractive brunette, rose from her seat in the courtroom and declared her affection for Durocher. Then she revealed that Durocher had once asked her to marry him and she had refused, but she said, "If the invitation were still open, I might reconsider, because he's so wonderful."

The declaration took Leo by surprise. As he lurched forward in his seat, a loud clap of thunder shook the courtroom. "The one-two-three combination of the testimony, Durocher's reaction, and the thunderbolt caused the courtroom spectators to burst into laughter," Ron Cohen reported. "It took three minutes to restore order."[52]

The jury of six men and six women deliberated for two hours and fifteen minutes before finding Durocher not liable. Cohen's dispatches from Vermont on the trial appeared on the front pages of major newspapers, including *The Boston Globe* and the *New York Herald Tribune*. For Durocher, it was a jolly escapade contributing to his reputation as a rogue. *The Sporting News* called the episode "Leo's Heart-Balm Suit" in a headline.

Durocher flew from Burlington to Chicago where he rejoined the Dodgers, but the story of the bricklayer's daughter did not rest easily, as it gave those who liked to heckle Durocher some fresh material. On August 27, Durocher was hit with a new $200,000 lawsuit from Robert Hallsworth, twenty-nine, a heckler and autograph seeker whom Leo had slugged outside Dodger Stadium after a game on August 16. The trouble began when Leo heard a man in the crowd outside the stadium ask in a loud voice: "How's your girlfriend? Are you going with the mother or the daughter?" Leo paid no attention, but when he got in his car, he heard the same man call him a "dirty rat son of a bitch." Durocher then backed up, got out of his car, and addressed the crowd.

"Does the person who made that remark have guts enough to say it to my face?"

Hallsworth stepped forward and said, "I did."

"I saw his hand move. I thought he was going to hit me, so I slugged him first" was Leo's defense. Leo's confession came in court, where Hallsworth claimed, "If I had known he was going to hit me, I'd have kept my mouth shut."[53] Criminal charges were dropped by Hallsworth in favor of a $200,000 civil suit, which was finally settled in February 1969 with Durocher paying a reported $3,500.[54]

By his own admission Durocher had a hard time holding on to money during his Hollywood years, as one of his established daily rituals was to play golf in the morning and then head over to the Friars Club for lunch and gambling. "Some days I win maybe $600–$700 at gin," he later confessed. "But some days maybe I lose $600. Now, when I lose $600, I go to the bank and write a check for $600 and give the guy cash, right? Okay. So, when I win $600, what happens? Well he gives me cash, and it goes into my pocket and I spend it but I never put the $600 back in the bank. So you figure out what happens to your bank account?"[55]

The 1964 Dodgers finished with an 80–82 record, thirteen games behind the St. Louis Cardinals and tied for sixth place with the Pittsburgh Pirates. As the Dodgers stumbled, it became clear to many that Leo had been hired simply to improve box office receipts. Jim Murray pointed out that when Alston and Durocher squabbled it made page one coast to coast. He added: "If Alston had words with his first base coach, it would never make *The Sporting News*. If Kansas City's Mel McGaha had words with his coach, it wouldn't have made the *Kansas City Star*." The growing consensus seemed to be that Leo's value to the team as a publicity asset was now diminished and agreed with Murray that it was time for him to manage again—a point that got no opposition from Durocher.[56]

In 1964, Durocher squeezed in appearances on two more prime-time television programs—*The Donna Reed Show* and *Mr. Novak*. John Novak, played by James Franciscus, was an idealistic young teacher at Jefferson High School in Los Angeles who was dedicated to molding young students. Durocher, springing to the casting agent's mind as an anti-Novak, was cast in the episode "Boy Under Glass" as himself. The *Donna Reed Show* episode "Play Ball" features Leo, Don Drysdale, and Willie Mays. Paul Petersen, who played Donna Reed's son, was catching for Drysdale while Mays was hitting. "Then, on one pitch, Mays didn't swing 'cause the pitch was too low," remembers Petersen, "and I, mesmerized by the previous ten pitches, didn't get down for it and the ball skipped under me and hit Leo Durocher on his unprotected shin. Needless to say I got a ream-job from Durocher of epic proportions . . . and was called 'Donkey' the rest of the show." Being berated by a crotchety old manager didn't diminish the experience for the teenage Petersen. "Looking back, it was hilarious . . . but Lordy, could Durocher get hot. Mays and Drysdale would laugh every time I'd see them after that."[57]

Despite his success in show business, it was no secret that Leo was looking to become a manager again. As columnist Jim Murray said: "You can always tell when Leo Durocher is getting ready to get back in baseball when he (a) slugs a fan, (b) gets kicked out of a game and (c) gets sued for stealing some guy's wife."[58]

Leo was restless, ready, and talking to at least one major league team, the St. Louis Cardinals, discussing with owner Gussie Busch his taking over from current manager Johnny Keane, who on August 23 had fallen eleven games out of first place. Busch decided that he wanted Durocher while hearing him on the radio giving an interview on August 28 to Harry Caray, then a Cardinal broadcaster. After the show Busch called Caray to tell him he wanted to meet with Durocher the next morning at 10 A.M. at his estate. Busch told Leo that he wanted him to be his new manager, but no formal agreement was made.

On October 1, Durocher obtained his formal release from the Dodgers so that he could accept an offer to manage the Cardinals. The Dodgers were happy to oblige. But the next day, Busch decided to retain Keane. Not only was Keane winning, but the team went on to take the pennant on the last day of the season and then beat the New York Yankees in the World Series. After winning the Series, Keane immediately resigned, presenting Busch with a letter of resignation he had written before the team had won the pennant: when he had heard of the plan to hire Durocher in early September he had decided to quit despite his thirty-five years in the Cardinal organization. Busch was now caught in the middle, and his name was mud because of his plan to replace Keane with Durocher. With Keane gone, he quickly appointed the very popular Red Schoendienst as manager, and Leo was left out in the cold. Keane was hired by the New York Yankees to replace their manager, Yogi Berra.* [59]

Within days of leaving the Dodgers, Durocher signed with the American Broadcasting Company, where he had both a radio deal and a job as a commentator with the ABC-TV *Game of the Week*. In a column celebrating Leo's remarkable ability to land on his feet, Mel Durslag wrote, "Now 58, Leo is often asked whether he will ever come back to baseball, which, of course is a slight transposition, because it is more a matter of whether baseball will come back to Leo." Durslag concluded that it was just a matter of time and added: "Nobody is going to destroy Leo, because, as we say, he is inextinguishable . . . Geared superbly to the age in which he lives, he must flourish forever."[60]

Durocher headed off to Spring Training in 1965 not as a coach but as an

---

* Schoendienst wound up managing the Cardinals for fourteen seasons, with two pennants and one World Series title.

actor playing himself in *The Munsters*, a sitcom based on a family of monsters adapted to the wholesome, happy family televison fare popular at the time. In the episode Durocher discovers Herman Munster who has an explosively powerful arm and signs him as a prospect. The matriarch of the family, a vampire named Lily Munster, watches the two at play and comments: "I think this whole thing is ridiculous! Imagine, Herman, a grown man 150 years old, playing baseball with young men of 55 and 60."

Even as a sportscaster, Durocher found a way to make waves and grab headlines. On May 8, 1965, Vice President Hubert Humphrey attended the first game in Washington covered by Durocher and was invited to join Leo in the broadcast booth. Durocher decided that this would be the perfect moment to start stealing signs and calling pitches before they were thrown. With the aid of dugout cameras placed by ABC, he gave the vice president a quick lesson in how to pick up signs. Humphrey was clearly nervous about being put in this position as an accomplice and observed flatly that there were no secrets anymore. Durocher and ABC were rebuked by the commissioner's office for both the cameras and the live larceny.

The game also showed Durocher's style in the booth, which included curt and frank assessments of the men on the field. When beefy Bob Chance of the Washington Senators came to the plate, Durocher informed his audience, "They call this guy Fat Chance." When Chance failed to get on base, Leo added: "Now you see why."[61]

Meanwhile, the Cardinals got off to a horrendous start with their new manager, going 8–28, and the rumor mill positioned Leo as their next manager. Both St. Louis daily newspapers carried stories about Cardinals players holding a locked-door "truth" meeting without the manager and coaches in an attempt to get the team back on track. The team slowly improved, finishing 80–81, which was enough to quash the rumors of Durocher taking over.[62]

During the third game of the 1965 World Series between the Dodgers and the Minnesota Twins, Durocher began talking with John Holland, vice president of player personnel for the Chicago Cubs, about becoming their new manager to replace one of the oddest managerial schemes in the history of the game. For five years, the Chicago Cubs had operated not with one manager but rather with an unwieldy "college of coaches." The key was that the coaches would alternately serve time in various positions throughout the *entire* organization. In the words of Holland, "[A member of the college] could spend the first month of the season as the head coach of the Cubs.

The next month he may manage at San Antonio, and the month after he might manage our farm team at Wenatchee. Then he could come back to the Cubs in July or August merely as a coach."*

Holland and Durocher talked on several occasions and hammered out a three-year deal that did not involve stock ownership. On October 25, 1965, the Cubs made headlines by announcing the hiring of Leo Durocher. Standing at the podium in the Wrigley Field pressroom (dubbed "the Pink Poodle" because of its odd color scheme), Durocher put to rest any doubts. "If no announcement has been made of what my title is, I'm making it here and now," he boomed. "I'm the manager. I'm not a head coach. *I'm the manager.* You can't have two or three coaches running a ball club. One man has to be in complete authority. There can be only one boss." When asked why he picked Durocher, Cubs owner Phil Wrigley replied, "The primary reason is that he's a take-charge guy."[63]

Before the end of the year, the Chicago White Sox announced that they too had a new manager—the combative Eddie Stanky, one of the ten other managers in baseball who could be considered, or considered themselves, a disciple of Durocher. These managers had collectively been given the nickname "Leo's Young Lions" and were doing well for themselves. In 1962, Alvin Dark had won the National League pennant for the Giants, and Bill Rigney and Gene Mauch had since been named Associated Press managers of the year for the Angels and Phillies respectively. Rounding out the group, Bobby Bragan with Atlanta, Herman Franks in San Francisco, Wes Westrum with the Mets, and Babe Herman in Boston all had ties to Leo. As Durocher's first biographer, Gerald Eskenazi, put it: "This might have been the finest testament to Leo's talents running a show."[64]

With Stanky on the other side of town, Durocher now had somebody to spar with. "If he dares to step into my territory," he announced, "I'll have him tossed into the Chicago River wearing a new concrete kimono."

A new era of Chicago baseball was set to begin with two managers promising to keep their respective ballfields in an uproar. Bill Gleason of the *Chicago American* was quick to point out that the private Stanky had little in common with Durocher. "Stanky is a family man," he wrote. "Durocher belongs to the world."[65]

---

* *The Baseball Encyclopedia* lists Bob Kennedy as manager in 1963 and 1964 before being replaced by Lou Klein midway through the 1965 season. It is accurate that they were part of the college of coaches system.

CHAPTER 13

The Contentious Cub

THE CHICAGO CUBS HADN'T finished higher than fifth place for twenty years, and Leo was determined to quickly change their prospects. He got rid of marginally talented players and expressed his determination to purge the club of any trace of lethargy. He also declared that the Cubs—even in the state they were in when he got them—were not an eighth-place club.

"We are primed to make our move," he wrote to Leo Fischer, sports editor of the *Chicago American*, before Spring Training began. "We don't believe the Cubs are a second-division club. When the season opens in April we intend to show the rest of the league just how much better we are."[1]

Only five starters from the 1965 club—Glenn Beckert, Don Kessinger Ron Santo, Billy Williams, and Ernie Banks—were on the roster for the 1966 Opening Day. These men were all popular among the fans in Chicago, but none more so than first baseman Ernie Banks, now in his thirteenth season on the team, who had already earned and proudly bore the sobriquet "Mr. Cub."

Durocher, who was proclaimed the dean of managers with sixteen seasons of experience, predicted he would win with a new and improved team of young, enthusiastic players.

Leo tried a number of things in the 1966 season, during which forty-nine men played for the team. The Cubs started out by losing eight of their first nine games and quickly plunged to the cellar, where—with the exception of three days in ninth place—they ended the season, allowing the expansion New York Mets their first escape from the National League basement since their inception in 1962. Leo was right in the wrong way about the Cubs not being an eighth-place club, suffering through his worst year as a manager with a record of 59–103, finishing a distant thirty-six games out of first place.

On the plus side, the Cubs debuted a group of future stars during the season, namely catcher Randy Hundley and pitchers Bill Hands, Ferguson Jenkins, and Ken Holtzman. Holtzman was signed directly from the University of Illinois. At 11–16, he had the best record of any Cubs pitcher for the season, which reflects how bad the team was. But as George Castle wrote in *The Million-to-One Team*, his history of the Cubs: "The '66 Cubs were probably the most promising 103-defeat team in modern history."[2]

Besides the miserable win-loss record, the season cost Leo the loyalty of Ernie Banks's most ardent fans and caused friction between Leo and some members of the press who felt Leo wanted to get rid of Banks as part of his purging of the past. In late April, Banks was benched by Durocher, who even prevented him from taking batting practice on an off day. Banks was batting under .200 when he was taken out of the lineup, but Leo made matters worse by what he said the next day to Dick Young of the *New York Daily News*. Young had asked Durocher if Banks was through, and Leo blithely suggested that it might be the end of the road for the thirty-five-year-old. "I don't know," he said to Young, "but I do know this. He is doing things I have never seen him do before, things that make you wonder." He then said that Banks had developed a hitch in his swing and was no longer whipping his bat around. He also charged Banks with bailing out of the batter's box on inside pitches.[3]

Banks was perplexed. "I can't break out sitting down" was his comment on May 7 after more than a week on the bench. He was back in the lineup the next day as a replacement for an injured infielder and hit a double. Banks pulled out of his slump and batted .272 for the year, but the damage had been done.

Worse still for Banks were the lashings he took from Durocher in clubhouse meetings, where he became Leo's whipping boy. "I can trade you if I like. And don't be surprised if your black ass is moving out one of these days," he told Banks early in the season.[4]

Durocher never seemed to know what to do about Banks, whom he regarded as a problem. "He was a great player in his time," Durocher wrote in his memoir, *Nice Guys Finish Last*. "Unfortunately, his time wasn't my time."[5]

Banks's defense against Durocher was unusual. He went to his mother for advice and according to Banks she said, "'Ernie, kill 'em with kindness.' And that's what I did. I'd sit by him in the dugout, on the plane, in the dressing room. I was always around."[6]

Soon after Durocher took over the Cubs, it was clear that he was not going to cooperate with the local reporters on anything more than a quick comment before or after a game. "My story has been written a thousand times. Writers talk to me, but they add a few words or take a few out and it all comes out the way they wanted to in the first place. I've even had them come up to me and say, 'I'm sorry Leo, but I had to write it that way. You're controversial.' One guy even said it with tears in his eyes. 'Leo, I love you, but I gotta knock you.' Now, what kind of sense is that?"[7]

After going through several generations of sportswriters, Durocher had concluded that they were a bad lot out to do him more harm than good. Anything mildly critical written about him he termed a hatchet job, and he was soon feuding with several reporters. During his first Spring Training with the Cubs in Long Beach, California, Ray Sons, a Cubs beat reporter for the *Chicago Daily News,* introduced himself as Durocher was sorting through mail in his office. Leo hardly looked up at him. Sons said, "He gave me the most limp handshake I ever got from a human being." Sons got along with everybody except Leo. "I couldn't stand the fellow," Sons told sportswriter George Castle: "He was the most selfish, arrogant guy I ever knew. He was totally self-centered and impossibly arrogant."[8]

Bill Christine, who covered Durocher while working for two newspapers, recalled what it was like talking to Leo as Cubs manager: "If Leo ever had a New England accent, he had lost it long before I knew him. If anything, his voice sounded more midwestern. Nasally. But gravelly. And he had that *look.* If you asked a question that he thought was impertinent, the look was withering. Then he might answer anyway, or he might just flip you off by saying, 'Next question.' He was in control of everything he said, and would have made a good lawyer—he was always one question ahead of the questioner." Christine then added: "Leo had more to say after a loss than a win—particularly a tough loss. I never dreaded going into his office after a loss, because you always knew he would say something, many times controversial."[9]

Durocher was still good copy even when his team was not. In 1966, he engaged in a well-publicized war with the Astrodome in Houston, Texas. Leo took over the Cubs the same year the Houston Astros installed the artificial turf in the Astrodome. Durocher hated the place from the start. He called the dome "a million-dollar stadium with a 10-cent infield." He also wasn't a fan of the graphics features on the scoreboard, which were created by an Astros public relations man. It was used to taunt opposing teams and players, especially Durocher, who was an easy caricature. What got to Durocher was when it was aimed at an injured player. "They do this bit about the pitcher going to the showers when the visiting pitcher gets knocked out. My man has this spasm in his back and is in pain and has to be helped off the field and they start that cartoon."[10]

What really got to Durocher, however, was the plastic grass, which he claimed made the field feel like a pool table. The season began with only the infield covered with AstroTurf, but then, during the All-Star break, the outfield was stripped of grass and replaced with plastic turf. Leo bellowed his objections, and the Astros retaliated by sending Durocher the last divot of natural grass removed from the field with the suggestion that he use it to "cover his dome."[11]

In June 1966, Durocher had yanked a phone out of the visitors' dugout and tossed it onto the field. He did so again in August after being mocked by the electronic scoreboard. The second time, Leo denied having thrown the phone, but a hidden camera proved the opposite. Pictures of Leo in the act were sent to the *Chicago Tribune*, where they were published under the headline DUROCHER FALLS VICTIM TO "HIDDEN CAMERA" RUSE.

The battle raged on. The Cubs were in Houston for a final three-game series against the Astros and were swept. During the final game when it was raining outside, Leo called Bill Giles, who controlled the scoreboard, and said, "Giles, why don't you put it on the scoreboard that the roof leaks in this eighth wonder of the world? Why don't you admit your mistake?" A few moments later, a message appeared on the scoreboard: "OK, Leo, we admit the roof leaks, but in any other park today the game would have been called off." At the end of the game, a final message flashed across the scoreboard:

"Baseball's a fun game, Leo!"[12]

But in 1966 it wasn't a fun game for Durocher. Beyond the loss of more than a hundred games, the Cubs had flopped at the box office, drawing only 635,000 fans—a number close to what the New York Mets would draw in a couple of home stands. "The year 1966 was, for Leo, like a long stay in stir," Doc Young wrote in the *Defender*. "Accustomed as he was to the higher echelons, this was a disgrace."*[13]

---

* Stir = slang for solitary confinement.

For Durocher, one of the few highlights of 1966 was a near no-hitter by
Ken Holtzman against the Dodgers on September 25 that Dick Schofield
broke up with one out in the ninth inning. This caused Durocher to suggest
that this performance could very well be the beginning of another Koufax.[14]

Leo had gone through most of the 1966 season thinking that Ernie
Banks was finished and that he would need a new first baseman in 1967,
but he had to be careful about the replacement because of Banks's popularity. On January 12, Leo held a news conference and tried to put a halt to
any thoughts that he might be getting rid of Banks: "Whatever games Ernie
Banks plays this year will be for the Chicago Cubs."[15]

Banks's future as a Cub was a major issue in Chicago, because he was
already known far and wide for his cheerful and upbeat approach to the
game and was a fan favorite not just in Chicago but throughout the league.
When the Cubs arrived in Scottsdale, Arizona, in February, the thirty-
seven-year-old Banks was named a player-coach. He would instruct rookies,
but, according to Leo, would have to fight to keep his job at first base.
Durocher said that he wanted John Boccabella to get a shot at first base in
1967. "Boccabella will have to beat Banks out for the job, and vice versa."[16]

Boccabella was not the man for the job, nor were other candidates tried
by Durocher. Before the team headed back to Chicago, Banks was his only
option. As Jim Enright wrote in the *Chicago American*, "It was Banks whose
spirited and solid all-around play made Durocher change his tune and feel
as though [Banks] had discovered a new fountain of youth."[17]

Durocher's tiffs with umpires had subsided during his first year with the
Cubs, but they came alive again during Spring Training in 1967. In an exhibition game against the Angels in Palm Springs in early March, Leo got
into a heated argument with umpire Ed Runge that would have gotten him
ejected in a regular-season game, but Runge let him rave on. Former president Dwight D. Eisenhower, sitting in a front-row box with his brothers
Milton and Edgar, enjoyed Leo's tantrum. Ike's enjoyment of Leo's antics
raised the question of whether or not Durocher was really disputing the
play or putting on a show for a distinguished fan.* [18]

On May 19, Durocher showed a quixotic willingness to test the limits of
the rules of the game, which had nothing to do with his stewardship of the

---

* Sid Ziff of the *Los Angeles Times* reported that Eisenhower demonstrated his dedication to
the game by staying through the whole game, even though a cold wind whipped through the
park and the game went into extra innings.

Cubs but everything to do with his ego. Early in the year, a rule was established stating that a pitcher must be in contact with the pitching rubber when he is receiving a sign from the catcher. Durocher immediately deemed the rule to be "silly" because, in his words, "there's no penalty to it." So in the fifth inning of a Cubs game against the Dodgers, rookie Cub pitcher Joe Niekro forgot about the rule, and umpire Augie Donatelli told Niekro he must be on the rubber when getting his sign. Durocher then shouted to Niekro from the dugout that he didn't have to obey the umpire before running out of the dugout to argue his point and was thrown out of the game, which the Cubs went on to lose 8–0. After the game, Donatelli had harsh words for Durocher, whom he said was defying the umpires, the game, and everybody in general. "This game is bigger than one man." Donatelli said, "What does he think he's going to do, run the game?"[19]

On the field, the Cubs were doing much better than they had in years. During one stretch from mid-June into early July, the Cubs won seventeen of nineteen games, and on July 3 were 46–29, tied with Cardinals for first place in the National League and leading the majors in runs scored by a significant margin. It was the high point in the season, because they lost their next seven games.

Still, the season was becoming a major success, vastly beyond anyone's wildest expectations. The crowds and the excitement were returning to Wrigley Field, and "Cub Power" became the rallying cry among the fans. Durocher could sit in his office and hear the fans chant "We're number one!"—even after they had dropped out of first place.

Ron Santo and Banks were on fire. After one game-winning homer by Banks, second baseman Glenn Beckert asked Ernie in jest: "Let me check your arms for pinholes. Anybody as lively as you are at your age just has to be taking dope in one form or another. Be a pal, and give me a prescription."[20]

Despite this—or perhaps because of it—Durocher's attitude toward Banks, in the words of Jerome Holtzman of the *Sun-Times*, "approached the absurd." He mocked Banks for not taking long leads and embarrassed him in front of his teammates by offering to give him $100 each time he was picked off. "Mr. Cub, my ass" was how he referred to him. After one August win against Philadelphia in which Banks hit two rooftop home runs and drove in five of the team's six runs, Durocher was asked about the feat: "Beckert had a helluva game." Beckert had done nothing exceptional that day. Others could see what Durocher refused to see: "The one reason why the Cubs are first in the division," Dodgers manager Walter Alston said during the 1967 season, "is Ernie Banks." Banks, on the other hand, was always shrewdly generous to Durocher, calling him on several occasions "the greatest manager I've ever seen."[21]

In August, with the team now in second place, Durocher was given a new contract and a raise that would keep him as manager of the Cubs through 1969. The Cubs ended the season 87–74 in third place, fourteen games out of first. Home attendance was up over a million for the first time since 1952. The fans had many players to cheer for, but none more than Banks, who batted a solid .296, made the All-Star team, and ranked fourteenth in the Most Valuable Player voting. Because he had lifted the Cubs from tenth to third place, Leo was named National League Manager of the Year as the choice of thirteen of the twenty-four experts who participated in the United Press International's annual postseason survey. He finished second for the same award given by the Associated Press.

The Cubs were on the move, and the praise was almost always laid at the feet of Durocher.

After the 1967 season, Jack Zanger wrote of the Cubs in his annual *Major League Baseball 1968*: "There is no better catalyst in baseball than Leo Durocher. Pour Leo into any company and the resulting chemical reaction will be highly combustible. His latest lab is Chicago, where in two years he shook up the Cubs so well that he has transformed them from a cellar club to a pennant contender . . . [T]hat's Leo the Lion and the effect he can have on a ball club . . . what a manager he has become." Zanger, who had predicted a seventh-place finish for the 1967 Cubs, picked the team to win the 1968 pennant.[22]

ON THE PERSONAL side, Leo was seen constantly with Lynne Walker Goldblatt, and he was spending more of his time in Chicago. Leo had met Lynne during the 1966 season and during the 1966 World Series. Herb Lyon revealed in his "Tower Ticker" column in the *Chicago Tribune* that Leo and Lynne Walker Goldblatt were dating and it was "world serious." By the end of the month, Lyon was suggesting they were considering marriage. Goldblatt was an attractive television personality with custody of three children from her previous marriage to Chicago businessman Joel Goldblatt.[23]

Leo missed the 1967 All-Star Game in favor of taking Lynne and her children to a Frank Sinatra concert. Lynne and Leo spent Christmas at Frank Sinatra's home in Acapulco.

For the time being, Leo was spending less time in California. In September 1967, Durocher put his showplace home in the Trousdale Estates section of Beverly Hills up for sale. "I've got $220,000 in it," he explained. "The problem is that it costs me $2,500 a month to keep the place up. I have a maid and a gardener there and they've got to eat whether I'm there or not. I've been able to use the house only 11 days since February."[24]

FOR LEO, 1968 was another year in which many of the headlines he generated were off the sports pages. In April he sued Hungarian-born actress Zsa Zsa Gabor for a million dollars because she invoked his name in a television commercial for the AAMCO chain of transmission shops. "Tell 'em Leo sent you" was the offending line. It worked because there was only one Leo out there who mattered. Durocher's damages were measured, according to his lawsuit, in "mental pain," and he demanded a jury trial. Gabor was threatened with jail if she did not show up for a hearing in Chicago in September, but the charge was finally dismissed. Durocher finally dropped his charges against Gabor when he realized that she was completely indemnified, but continued his suit against AAMCO. The company and the advertising agency behind the ad settled out of court, but typical of Durocher, the suit was hashed out on Johnny Carson's *Tonight Show*, where both Gabor and Durocher were regular guests. Gabor got the last laugh when the *Chicago Tribune* published her deposition, and she said that even after the lawsuit, she still liked Leo.*[25]

Before 1968 Spring Training was over and for the second time in less than a year, Durocher decided that he would take on the rules of the game. The game was changing, and Leo did not like the new spitball rule, which declared that anytime a pitcher touched his fingers to his lips while on the field, the batter would be issued an automatic ball in the count. In an exhibition game on March 23, Leo twice instructed his pitchers to walk batters by licking their fingers four times in a row. When a member of the rules committee recommended that Durocher be fined $1,000 for making a

---

* The best line in the deposition had to do with her lack of concern over the lawsuit: "I don't listen about lawsuits. Who the hell cares? I listen about love affairs."

mockery of the rule, Leo responded: "The spitball thing is ridiculous. The best thing the rules committee could do about it can be summarized in two words—legalize it." Before giving up this battle, Leo was thrown out of a game on April 27 for arguing that one of his pitchers did not violate the rule because he was on the grass, not the mound, when he touched his lips.[26]

In a second challenge to the rules, Leo closed his clubhouse to the press for forty-five minutes after the game on May 1 and forty minutes after the game on May 2. On May 3, an order came down from the commissioner that a manager had to inform the press during the game if he was going to hold a closed postgame meeting. Durocher then declared that his club-house would be closed for twenty minutes after all games—soon changed to fifteen minutes—and he told the press in advance that the clubhouse was closed—win or lose—after every game.

Closing the clubhouse showed that Durocher clearly had no interest in improving his relationship with the local press. In the middle of the 1968 season, Robert Markus of the *Chicago Tribune* noted that Leo still did not know the names of some of the Cubs' beat reporters. Durocher tended to give his occasional in-depth interviews to men on either coast, like Dick Young of the *New York Daily News* and Mel Durslag of the *Los Angeles Herald-Examiner.*[27]

As his team won, Durocher seemed to go out of his way to defy rules. On June 16, the Cubs were in Pittsburgh when Jim Bunning was pitching for the Pirates. Durocher used two pinch hitters, both reserve catchers who he brought in from the bullpen. One of them didn't step up to the plate for five minutes while Bunning stood on the mound and fumed. A league directive specifically said that pinch hitters had to be on the dugout bench at the time they entered the game. Bill Christine, who was covering the game for the *Pittsburgh Press*, recalled: "Afterwards, I played Leo and Bunning off one another and got a lively story. Bunning accused Leo of deliberately stalling, interrupting his rhythm. A veteran, he had seen many of Leo's win-at-all-costs ploys. Biting his lip, withholding what he really thought, Bunning said: 'Leo's not a nice man.'"[28]

By the All-Star break, there was even talk of Leo repeating his 1951 Giants miracle with the Cubs. The team had gone from ninth place at the time of the All-Star break to second place on August 3 after a 17–7 run but was still fourteen games behind the Cardinals.

On September 24, the Cubs were in fourth place with a record of 80–78. Leo was asked by Edward Prell of the *Chicago Tribune* if he had any thoughts on the ebbing season or on the team's prospects for 1969. Leo replied: "I'd say my big disappointment has been Ron Santo, this hasn't been a good year for him. I think he has been trying too hard and knows it." Santo would end the year with twenty-six home runs and ninety-eight runs batted in and a .246 batting average. He was awarded a Gold Glove award for his defensive work.[29]

Then with four games to go, Leo had a rare club meeting and told his team it could finish anywhere from third to sixth, and that he wanted to finish third. The team won the last four games, and the Cubs ended the season in third place with an 84–78 record, thirteen games behind the National League pennant–winning St. Louis Cardinals. Second baseman Glenn Beckert had a great year, which included a twenty-seven-game hitting streak. Banks led the team with thirty-two home runs, and Ferguson Jenkins (20–15) became the first Cub pitcher in decades to post back-to-back twenty-win seasons. Leo seemed content at the end of the season and went out of his way to praise his coaching staff, calling it the best he had ever been associated with. He placed second—albeit a distant second—to Red Schoedienst in polling among the writers for National League Manager of the Year.

The 1969 season marked the beginning of baseball's second century. The majors expanded to twenty-four teams, and each league was now split into two divisions. The Cubs were in the National League East, along with the New York Mets, Pittsburgh Pirates, St. Louis Cardinals, Philadelphia Phillies, and Montreal Expos.

On January 25, Leo was sent a new contract that kept him through the 1970 season. At the signing, Durocher extolled the Cubs operation, calling it first-class from top to bottom. He said that neither Phil Wrigley nor John Holland had ever questioned any of his decisions. After the signing, Durocher spent the rest of the winter in Acapulco; from there he sent a letter about the upcoming season that was published in the *Chicago American*. Among other statements, he wrote, "It figures to be a mighty interesting season, and I wouldn't be surprised if the Cubs are the ones who make it just that."[30]

At the end of January, Ernie Banks turned thirty-eight and spent his usual two weeks at the Buckhorn Spa near Mesa, Arizona, before reporting for Spring Training. Despite three years of trying, Durocher had been unable to replace Banks, mistakenly presuming that he was in the twilight of his career. Banks had hit thirty-two home runs in 1968 and performed well in the field. Arthur Daley of *The New York Times* wrote: "The Banks contributions to the upsurge of the Cubs to contention are not confined to the physical, however. He is also an inspirational force because he has as sunny a disposition as is to be found in either league. Ernie is a delight." Such notices did not cheer Durocher, whose attitude toward Banks was well-known and more and more being ascribed to simple jealousy.[31]

WITH 40,876 IN attendance, the 1969 Cubs drew the largest Opening Day crowd since 1929. Banks hit two homers and drove in five runs as the Cubs beat the Phillies 7–6 on a pinch-hit home run by Billy Williams in the eleventh inning.

The team won eleven of its first twelve games, and fans could see that the 1969 Cubs were a truly exciting team. A number of young players— second baseman Glenn Beckert, catcher Randy Hundley, pitcher Ken Holtzman, and shortstop Don Kessinger—were now coming into their own, and the old standbys—Banks, Santo, and Billy Williams—were, as *Sports Illustrated* predicted early in the season, on their way to knocking in one hundred runs apiece. The starting pitching was stellar and the bullpen of Ted Abernathy, Phil Regan, and Hank Aguirre was among the best in baseball.

An added factor at work at Wrigley Field in 1969 was the full emergence of a raucous delegation of Cub fans, about three hundred strong, known as the Left Field Bleacher Bums. Tommy Agee of the Mets called them the harshest group of fans he had ever encountered, and they got louder. They brutally insulted visiting players. The treatment given to Jesus Alou of the Astros was typical. When he came onto the field early in the season, he was met with cries of "Hey, Carlos! Rico! Roberto! Felipe! Manny! Matty! Chico!" "The volley of Latin names thundered down in such volume that Alou turned and glared up at the bleachers with eyes of menace. For about a second, there was silence, and then Foghorn Ralph, one of the Bums, bellowed down, 'Don't even know your own name, ya dumdum!'"[32]

The Bums also had songs to fit all occasions. "Give Me That Old Time Durocher" was a favorite, and there was even one sung to bedevil the Cardinal announcer: "Harry Caray, Quite Contrary, How Does Your Ego Grow?"*

---

* The Bums established a new custom when they threw back any homer an opposing player hit into the bleachers. Returning a souvenir eventually spread to other ballparks and is still done today.

Despite the rosy outlook for the team and this band of brazen, beer-fueled cheerleaders, Durocher's connection with reporters was at a low ebb. His worst relationship was with James Enright of the *Chicago American*, which had just been renamed *Chicago Today*. "I remember, when I was a mere lad at *Chicago Today*," recalls Bill Hageman, "how Jimmy Enright hated Leo, and vice versa. My God. Enright was the nicest of people, but if Leo's name came up, he'd get red-faced and let it rip. I suspect it was because Jim was very close to Ernie Banks, whom Leo tried to phase out (or drive from the game, depending on your outlook)." Adding to Durocher's woes was Rick Talley, who had come from the *Rockford Morning Star and Register-Republic* to become sports editor of the *Chicago American* in 1969 and seemed to pick up where Enright left off in his disdain for Durocher, which was mutual.* [33]

If anything, Durocher's treatment of the press seemed to get worse as his team settled into first place. On May 20, he got into a major tussle with Jerome Holtzman of the *Sun-Times*. When Leo changed starting pitchers without telling the press, Holtzman exploded: "You crossed me up. You're bush—a liar."

"Are you running this club?" Leo shot back. "What difference does it make what I tell you? You're going to write what you want anyhow."

"Damn right, I'll write what I want," was Holtzman's reply.

Durocher replied: "You see where my hands are! See where my hands are! Want to sue me don't you? You want me to hit you so you can sue me. I made that mistake once but not this time. I've got the plenty of witnesses this time."

The confrontation moved to the clubhouse, where Durocher had Holtzman expelled.

Journalist Bill Christine recalled a conversation with Leo when the Cubs were in Pittsburgh: "One day, during batting practice at Forbes Field, I was on one side of the field, chatting with Leo, and Jerry Holtzman was gathering material across the way.

"Do you know that man?" Leo said, pointing toward Holtzman.

---

* Besides his life as a reporter, Enright was a top-notch basketball official whose credits included the NCAA Final Four, the NBA, and the Olympics. He was elected to the Basketball Hall of Fame in 1979. One of his many books, *March Madness, The Story of High School Basketball in Illinois*, made March Madess so nationally recognizable that it was eventually affixed to the NCAA tournament.

I said that I did.

"Well, let me tell you something. If you and he are ever inter-viewing me at the same time, and he asks a question and I give an answer, I wouldn't necessarily write it down."

"Why is that?"

"Because it won't necessarily be the truth."

His rudeness to reporters, especially young ones, guaranteed him the bad press he now seemed to thrive on. He called George Langford, a promising young reporter for the *Chicago Tribune*, "stupid." When rookie sports reporter Lynda Morstadt of *Chicago Today* was assigned to write a story about the Cubs in June 1969, Durocher reacted quickly: "What? A broad covering sports? Some of the men are bad enough, especially that bleep-bleep-bleep. Tell her to get off the field. I don't want her distracting my ball players."* [34]

It was as if Durocher were trying to establish an us-versus-them conflict when it came to the press in order to help motivate his team. Jack Brickhouse, the Cubs telecaster whom Leo had called "a mental midget," told Tom Fitzpatrick of the *Sun-Times*, who quoted him anyhow, "You can't quote me but I think he's the most unprincipled man in all of sports. If I had my way I'd like to see the Cubs win three straight in the World Series and fire Durocher that night and not even give him the chance to buy a ticket for the fourth game." [35]

During the season, Durocher filmed a series of commercials for Schlitz beer in which he sat around discussing baseball with a group of newspa-permen. "Of course," Dick Young noted sarcastically, "they're *make-believe* newspapermen."

In Leo's personal life, he and Lynne Goldblatt were preparing for their wedding. Some were surprised that Leo was about to tie the knot for the fourth time. In January 1968, Herb Lyon had called Durocher and Goldblatt "inseparable, but marriage? No, no, no." But in June, Goldblatt announced

---

* Morstadt paid Leo back in bad ink, which was not difficult, as she somehow managed to be around when Durocher was on his worst behavior, such as at a sports banquet where he made a fool of himself. In another article published later in the same month, he insulted her, and she dug deep to find stories of Durocher out of control. In 1939, for example, with help from a yellowing news clipping in the newspaper's morgue, she told a new generation how Durocher was almost fired as Dodgers manager for slugging his caddie on a golf course in Hot Springs, Arkansas.

that she had made a new alimony arrangement that would allow her to remarry without financial penalty. Leo and Lynne were now preparing for their wedding, which would take place during the season. The couple had originally planned to get married in October, but pushed the date forward to June 19, when Leo had a day off. Upon hearing the news, Buzzie Bavasi, now president of the San Diego Padres, announced a special ladies' night in Durocher's honor at which female fans were asked to wear black mourning bands to express their "grief" over the loss of the eligible Leo.[36]

Shortly after dawn on June 18, with the Cubs 43–22, Durocher slipped out of his hotel in Pittsburgh and flew to Chicago unannounced to attend a high-society bachelor reception on the eve of his marriage to Lynne. His coaches had not been informed, nor had his players or the press. John Holland reported that he had no idea where Leo had gone: "If he isn't with the club I don't know where he is, because he hasn't checked in here." When the team arrived at Forbes Field, Durocher was still missing, and Coach Pete Reiser took over. The Cubs lost the game in extra innings— their fourth loss in a row. "I don't like the way Leo walked away from the team without saying anything in advance," Phil Wrigley said, "but we'll just have to forgive him this time."[37]

The wedding, which was held at the Ambassador West Hotel, was probably better known for those who could not make it (Sinatra and rest of the Hollywood crew) and those not invited, including Cubs announcers Jack Brickhouse and Lou Boudreau. The team was there save for shortstop Don Kessinger who was increasingly unhappy with Durocher as a leader.

As the season progressed the behavior of the Bleacher Bums became more violent. With apparent tacit consent from Leo, they threw dry-cell batteries, ball bearings, marbles, fruit, and other solid objects at opposition players. In late June, after being struck in the mouth with a hard rubber handball while autographing a baseball for one of the bleacherites, Jim "Mudcat" Grant of the Cardinals retaliated by throwing the autographed baseball hard against the bleacher wall to get the Bums to scramble. Cardinal center fielder Curt Flood told *Jet* magazine that he had been the target of apples and ball bearings, and that the Cubs should be forced to forfeit games if this did not stop. "I have five kids to feed," he said, "If I got hit in my eyes, I'd be through." In early July, Cardinals manager Red Schoedienst demanded that the umpires start forcing the Cubs to forfeit games if the throwing did not stop. The umpires said they were powerless.[38]

The Cubs went to Shea Stadium and sustained two quick losses. But on

July 10, the Cubs beat the Mets 6–2. The Mets looked horrible—like the laughable team they once were. "Are these the real Cubs?" a writer asked after the game. "No," said Leo, "but you saw the real Mets."

The Cubs hit a low ebb five days later when they lost two games in their second successive three-game series with the Mets. This gave the Mets four victories in six head-to-head matches with the Cubs in nine days and sliced the Chicago lead to 3.5 games.

In first place at the All-Star break, which lasted from July 21 to 24, the Cubs relished the break in the season. Not only was it a moment of honor for the long-suffering team and fans as the entire infield plus catcher Hundley made the All-Star squad, but it gave the team a moment to catch its breath. "We're really exhausted, all of us," explained Hundley before the game. "I look for us to come back and get our second wind." Banks, now playing in his thirteenth All-Star Game, put a positive spin on the fact that the team was running out of gas: "When we go back to playing again it's going to be like a breath of spring. It's going to be like starting the season all over again."

Leo had not been platooning. As Banks told Jerome Holtzman at the All-Star break, "Actually, what some people don't realize is the same players start every day. It's been that way since Spring Training."[39]

On the Cubs' first day back from the break, they played a nationally televised game against the Dodgers in Wrigley Field. In the third inning, an announcement was made in the press box that Durocher had left the ballpark because of illness. The Cubs went on to win the game 3–2 in eleven innings, under fill-in manager Pete Reiser. During the game, Cubs physician Dr. Jacob Suker called Durocher's home, but there was no answer.

Durocher had taken a charter flight along with his wife, Lynne, to Camp Ojibwa, a boys' camp near Eagle River, Wisconsin, to visit his twelve-year-old stepson and sometime Cubs bat boy Joel Goldblatt.* Durocher had attempted to make his visit as anonymous as possible, but at Ojibwa he was greeted with a huge WELCOME LEO DUROCHER banner. Jim Enright had a good friend who had a son at the camp and was there for the weekend.

---

* Camp Ojibwa was the inspiration for the 1963 hit recording *Hello Muddah, Hello Faddah*, composed and performed by Allan Sherman, who was an Ojibwa staff man in the 1940s. In the song, a young summer camper described all the horrors of camp and begs his parents to let him come home after only one day. Ojibwa became "Camp Grenada" because it rhymed with *Faddah*.

Durocher arrived when the friend noted that the Cubs game, which had gone into extra innings, was still in progress. He called Enright. The story appeared in *Chicago Today* the next morning and soon became the big story in Chicago while Durocher was still absent. He had planned to return the following morning for the next afternoon's game, but bad weather kept his plane grounded. The Dodgers beat the Cubs 6–2.

When Phil Wrigley, at his summer home in Lake Geneva, Wisconsin, was told the real reason for Durocher's absence, he was livid. What if, he asked, a player pulled a similar stunt? "I was told Leo was sick," Wrigley said. "I had no idea he wasn't confined to his home . . . I feel he owes an apology to management, the players and fans. You can't run a ship without a rudder."

Wrigley was furious with Durocher and Durocher was furious with Enright, whom he would henceforth call a policeman masquerading as a newspaper reporter.

Wrigley and Durocher then met two days later. Leo came out of the meeting without having to issue an apology, and with Wrigley now siding with Durocher in claiming that the press had a vendetta against him. Leo later described his glee. "Now I have all of those jackals who thought they had me on the run grinding their teeth. Especially the Unholy Six led by one big Jack Brickhouse who got together to run me out of Chicago. Up yours, Brickhouse, screw you, Enright."[40]

But Leo was still stuck with fact that he had gone AWOL. As Edgar Munzel reported the story in *The Sporting News*, Leo had been taken to the woodshed by Wrigley; but even though it turned out to be a slap on the wrist instead of a sound paddling, there was no question that the usually mild-mannered and tolerant Wrigley was irritated by his manager abandoning the team at a time when it was fighting for a pennant.[41]

In treating the Ojibwa incident as a win for him in his war with the press, Durocher ensured that his coverage got worse at the same time as fan adoration of and affection for the team grew. If Durocher was hoping for an "us-versus-them" battle to motivate his players, it was destined to fail, as the battle was not with the team but with its manager. Robert Markus of *The Chicago Tribune* gave Durocher a tongue-in-cheek pass on the trip and the falsehood used to cover it up: "Durocher could set the Cubs on automatic pilot and spend the rest of the season in Wisconsin if he chooses without affecting the course of destiny."[42]

On August 16, the Cubs were 75–44, and after Ken Holtzman's no-hitter on August 19, the Cubs led the division by 6.5 games over the Mets.

Reporters and fans had been asking for weeks and now began to ask more frequently and more pointedly whether Durocher was making a mistake by not relieving his starters earlier in games: they were showing signs of fatigue and age. The offensive production of Santo, Kessinger, and Banks was dropping, but nobody was getting a day off—even for an exhibition game against the White Sox on August 18. Banks, now thirty-eight, was playing both ends of doubleheaders and would end the season starting in 153 games. Another factor at play as the summer got hotter was that the Cubs still played all their home games during daylight hours. The hottest day of 1969 was June 26, with a high temperature of 96°F, a day the Cubs played at home. It was also in July 1969 that the phrase "Let's Play Two" was attributed to Banks. The Cubs were to play a game in 100-degree heat and Banks, looking to inspire his teammates, uttered the phrase. Sportswriter Jimmy Enright reported it and credited Ernie.[43]

After the no-hitter by Ken Holtzman, the Cubs lost three games in a row at home, dropping their division lead from eight games to six. After the third loss on August 22, Dick Dozer of the *Tribune* asked Durocher: "Is anybody tired on the ball club? Do you plan to make any changes, give anybody a rest?"

Outraged, Leo, who was shaving when asked the question, put down his razor, led all of the writers out of his office into the cramped clubhouse, and ordered all of his players out of the shower.

"Now ask them what you asked me," Durocher bid the writer.

The writer obliged. "Not one ballplayer stood up and said he was tired," wrote Jack Griffin in the *Chicago Sun-Times* the next day. Leo turned triumphantly and went back to finish shaving.[44]

Ferguson Jenkins, in his 1973 book *Like Nobody Else: The Fergie Jenkins Story*, said of Durocher as the team went into the stretch in 1969: "If a man had a slight injury or was just plain tired Leo did not even want to hear about it. Leo just rubbed the man's nose in the dirt and sent him back out there. You played until you dropped."[45]

Without a change in the starting lineup, the Cubs won two and then dropped four more. During that fourth loss, Durocher ramped up his attack on umpires, his behavior reaching its nadir when he danced around Shag Crawford yelling "Dummy! Dummy! Dummy!" Crawford was so mad, he offered to fight Durocher on the spot. Durocher dared him to hit him first and then, according to Durocher, kicked dirt on him. Crawford said Durocher kicked his foot. Durocher called him a liar. He was booted from the game and then told the Associated Press that there was a conspiracy against him by the National League umpires. After this, the Cubs began to get some bad calls. As William Barry Furlong concluded in his *Look* piece on Durocher: "Whether or not Leo ever united the Cubs against the umpires, he certainly united the umpires against the Cubs."[46]

Toward the end of August, Leo treated a group of reporters to an open discussion of his past gambling habits. Among those attending was Rick Talley of *Chicago Today*. He reported Leo's bragging about betting $1,000 on a fixed horse race in 1941 with Sleepout Louie, the gambler who once sent a messenger to tell Leo, "You'd better win this game because Sleepout stands to win $100,000." He talked about playing gin at the Friars Club and the fact that he had surrendered prodigious amounts at the racetrack, having lost $8,000 two days in a row. Talley's piece appeared at a time when rumors were circulating to the effect that Durocher was again gambling heavily.*[47]

Still in first place on August 28, the Cubs received permission to print playoff tickets. The next day, the Mets crept to within two games, the closest they had been since May 10. The Cubs revived and entered September with a six-game winning streak and an 84–52 record, and on September 2, their first-place margin was back to five games.

Then the Pirates came into Wrigley, blasted Ken Holtzman and Fergie Jenkins in the first two games, and captured the third game with two unearned runs in the eleventh following an error by Kessinger. The lead was now cut to 2.5 games right before a series with the Mets in New York.

One of Durocher's managerial tactics was to belittle and enrage players, especially pitchers, so that they played better. It worked some of the time, as it had with Sal Maglie of the New York Giants, but it was not working with the Cubs. Before departing for New York, Leo staged a dugout meeting, berated his team, and called Fergie Jenkins "a quitter." Jenkins later told a reporter, "He really laid me out."[48]

On Monday, September 8, the Cubs lost to the Mets 3–2. The following night, a black cat wandered across the Shea Stadium infield on its way to

---

* A modern homage to Louie was a hot singles bar on Second Street in Cincinnati named for him which thrived during the years Pete Rose played for the Reds. In Sleep Out Louie's in 1977, Rose met Carol Woliung, who was a bartender there. At the time he was married to his first wife, Karolyn, whom he divorced in 1980. While Rose was playing for the the Philadelphia Phillies (1979–83), he invited Woliung to join him there. They married on April 12, 1984, four months before he returned to the Reds as player-manager.

the Cubs' dugout, passing Ron Santo, who was in the on-deck circle. The photo became a famous picture: Santo on deck at Shea, bat on his shoulder, the cat slinking across his path. "At the time, I didn't think anything of it," Santo later reflected. "The cat wasn't scared; it just walked around me and went through the dugout, with Leo there. He looked right at Leo and went underneath the stands." Ernie Banks, in an interview shortly before his death, added: "Some of our guys did feel it was done intentionally . . . Especially Durocher who was a superstitious man."[49]

Then in the sixth inning with the Mets leading 6–1, fans along the first-base line burst into song. The melody was the same one that football Giants coach Allie Sherman had been hearing for years, with the lyric changed from "Goodbye, Allie" to "Goodbye, Leo." Red Smith was there: "The chorus swelled by tens of thousands of voices. On all four levels, the park blossomed with handkerchiefs fluttering in derision. Whistles and hoots arose. The voices were strident, unfriendly. It was extraordinary."

The Cubs' lead was cut to a half game on this date as Tom Seaver, backed by homers from Donn Clendenon and Art Shamsky, beat Ferguson Jenkins 7–1 in what will forever be known as "the Black Cat Game."

The Cubs were defeated again the following night, September 10, when the Phillies scored three in the eighth inning, bringing the losing streak to seven and ending the Cubs' 155-day stay in first place. Leo maintained his stony silence. He admitted newsmen to the clubhouse after his mandated fifteen-minute wait, then brushed them aside with no comment. Al Spangler, a Chicago utility outfielder, captured the tension: "Twelve reporters came in here single file, walked to the middle of the room and then stood in the circle interviewing one another."[50]

Before the game with the Phillies on September 11, Durocher met with Rick Talley in his hotel room. Durocher was cordial and at ease. He announced that he was proud of his team and that he had not yet thrown in the towel. "These players have great pride and determination. But we have to go out and help ourselves now. Just play hard and be the best we can." When he was informed that the Mets had drunk champagne in their club-house the night before, he replied, "That party could have been a little premature." Leo talked about the tension that his players were experiencing. He said he had considered lifting the 1:30 A.M. curfew and ordering his players to go out on a bender to relieve that tension.[51] The Cubs lost again after the interview, and the Mets now led by two games.[52]

On the eve of the 146th game, against the Cardinals on September 12,

Leo met with his club and imposed new rules on the team to help keep his players' minds on baseball after an eight-game losing streak. He banned card games in the clubhouse two hours before road games and one hour before home games. Leo, who was often involved in games of gin rummy until just before game time, would now be out on the field for batting practice. During these hectic card games, some of the players had skipped practice to stay in them with their manager. He also said all outsiders—business agents and other guests—had to be out of the clubhouse at 12:30 P.M. before games. In his scathing article about the 1969 Cubs that appeared in *Look* magazine, William Barry Furlong called the team's clubhouse a "hustler's paradise" where agents were a constant.

The final new rule was that Leo was going to start talking to the reporters who covered the Cubs instead of having players make all postgame comments.[53] The same day that Durocher established these rules, Dick Young's column in the *New York Daily News* entitled "Poor Leo, or It Couldn't Happen to a Nicer Guy" portrayed Leo as being so despised by other managers and players from other teams that they tried especially hard to beat the Cubs. Joe Brown, general manager of the Pittsburgh Pirates, asked, "Don't you think everybody is trying just a little bit harder to beat the Cubs? They all seem to want to beat Durocher."[54]

The increasing venality and violence of the Bleacher Bums, who had become more and more given to physical assaults, only enhanced this attitude. Late in the season, the Cardinals lined up to tell Dave Nightingale of the *Chicago Daily News* how bad it had gotten. "Here's the yellow hard hat they threw at me," said Mudcat Grant after he had thrown a ball at the bleacher wall in June. "And here's the four inch spike. And here are the batteries." Grant said the insults to players' families got so bad that players wanted to go up in the stands and wring their necks, but since one couldn't do that, one just beat the Cubs to beat them up.

Bob Gibson and Lou Brock told of the white mice the Bums threw in the outfield anytime the Cubs got a hit. Hatred of the Cubs was the main reason Gibson was willing to pitch out of sequence late in the season just to beat the Cubs, which he did.[55]

Even though Leo was now talking to the press, the hostility remained. *Life* magazine sent a crew to cover the Cubs versus the Cardinals in St. Louis. Before the first game of the series, photographer Mike Mauney tried to get a photograph of Leo swinging a bat. As he moved close to his subject, Durocher swung the bat and let go of it, sending it in the direction of Mauney and *Life* magazine's Chicago bureau chief, John Pekkanen. The two men jumped out of the way, and the bat landed at the photographer's feet. Mauney picked it up, handed it to Leo, and said: "I believe you dropped this." Leo laughed at Mauney's comeback, but really he had little to smile about.

On September 15, the Cubs staggered into Montreal, where they lost again—they had now lost thirteen of their last fourteen games. Then they won the next day, thanks in part to four runs batted in by Ernie Banks. When the Cubs returned home to play the Phillies, they found that their fans were deserting them—the two games with the Phillies drew fewer than twelve thousand. The Cubs split those and then split a four-game series with the Cardinals. The Bleacher Bums began to dwindle in number when the Cubs dropped out of first place, and shortly after the season was over, columnist Bob Smizik of the *Pittsburgh Press* observed that some National League players believed the collapse of the Cubs was due to a group known to others in the league as the "Bleacher Scums."[56]

On September 23 when the Cubs lost in Montreal, the Mets were assured of a tie for the division lead based on the number of games left. On the same day, the Cubs' season ticket holders received order forms in the mail to reserve playoff tickets. The next night the Mets won, eliminating the Cubs, who were now six games behind, and the celebration was on in New York. The Cubs ended the season 92–70, a full eight games out of first place. Wrote *Tribune* sports columnist Robert Markus: "My theory is that the Cubs simply had to shoulder their burden too long. It is impossible to endure the kind of pressure the Cubs were under for six months." Cubs broadcaster Vince Lloyd believed that tension got to the club and they choked—"It got to Leo first, he transferred it to the players. You know, Leo never did take into account that nowadays, with a longer season and travel problems because of the scheduling, players might get tired." Lloyd added: "He was still managing, still living, back when he played. When ballplayers rode the train and had whole days to rest. Listen, you don't just keep forcing a guy out on the field every day in August when it's obvious to a three-year-old he's dead tired."[57]

If there was salvation in the season for some fans it came to those who had over time come to admire—or in many cases adore—Ernie Banks for his undampable enthusiasm and love of life. Tom Boswell of *The Washington Post*, Banks's fan since childhood, wrote in his eulogy to Banks following his death in January 2015: "On the final day of the season, when manager Leo Durocher . . . was disengaged from his team and stuck with the disgrace of his defeat, Banks was still showing up—just to play baseball."

On that last day, Banks, the oldest man in the lineup, played his 155th game of the year and had a triple, homer, and drove in three runs to finish the season with 106 RBIs.[58]

Others blamed the collapse on Leo's fractious impact on a team that needed less tension, not more. "He brought us closer to a pennant than anyone had in a generation," said Ron Santo after the fact, "but he also brought disruption and chaos."[59]

Dick Young seemed to take special relish in comparing the Mets Miracle to Leo's Miracle: "You think the Giants' 1951 wipeout of the Dodgers 13½ game lead was the greatest rush in baseball history? Forget it. They were standing still compared to the amazing Mets' sweep past the confused Cubs this year. In 1951, it took the Giants from August 11 to September 28 to wipe up out those 13½. This year between August 13 and September 13 the Mets went from 9½ back to 3½ in front, a pickup of 13 lengths in a lot less time."[60]

The morning following the Mets defeat of the National League West champion Atlanta Braves in the first National League Championship Series, a travel article in the *Chicago Tribune* with an Eagle River dateline opened with: "Leo Durocher should have waited until now to make a visit to a boys' camp near here. By going in the middle of the baseball season as he did, the Lip not only created a rhubarb with Cubs' fans and the press but he missed some of the Midwest's most spectacular scenery."[61]

The Mets defeated the American League champion Baltimore Orioles in five games to win the World Series, earning the team the appropriate sobriquet "Miracle Mets," as they had enjoyed the first winning record in team history.

The gloomy autumn suffered by Cubs fans was a time for finger pointing, and most of those fingers were pointed at Leo Durocher. Ojibwa hung over everything as a symbol of Leo's lack of leadership. At Chicago's winter baseball dinner, the 260-pound Dave Condon of the *Chicago Tribune*, dressed as a Boy Scout in short pants, presented Leo with a "Camper of the Year Award"—a flag from Camp Ojibwa.

After the 1969 season and for many years to come, countless gallons of ink and many hours of radio and television broadcast time have been spent analyzing the miracle of the Mets and the collapse of the Cubs.[62] But for those who followed the team most closely, Jim Enright may have spoke for many when he wrote "The Epitaph on the tomb of the 1969 Cubs reads: 'Died from lack of leadership.' Ironically the man who failed to lead had once been regarded as the most daring of all baseball leaders. But in 1969 Leo (The Lion) Durocher had little but his roar left."[63]

CHAPTER 14

Endgame

D URING THE FALL OF 1969, Durocher took a lot of criticism for the
Cubs' collapse. It came from all levels, including umpires, who were
now free to express their opinions as after-dinner speakers. "The Cubs
really started to slide ... when Durocher got married and he played hooky
from the games," said veteran National League umpire Paul Pryor at a
sports banquet in Rockford, Illinois. "Then the difference became notice-
able." Jackie Robinson opined on a radio show that the Cubs collapsed because
of Leo's decision to visit Camp Ojibwa, which robbed the team of its desire.
Robinson saw a strong parallel to his 1951 Dodgers blowing a thirteen-and-a-
half-game lead in August.[1]

Durocher, however, had a much bigger problem than pokes and prods
about the collapse. A rumor had circulated late in the summer of 1969
that somebody from the *Chicago Tribune* went to the Federal Bureau of
Investigation to report rumors that Durocher had been seen in the company
of a syndicate crime figure and had been gambling heavily. The wildest
suspicion was that Leo had thrown a game to pay off a gambling debt.
Whether Leo knew about the FBI's involvement in his affairs or not, at the
end of the regular season an FBI agent, accompanied by a reporter and
photographer, showed up at the door of the Durocher's Lake Shore Drive
penthouse. Leo was in bed suffering from bronchitis, so Lynne refused to
let the trio into the apartment, but she did agree to show Durocher a photo
of the hoodlum in question.

"I never saw the guy in my life," Durocher said. At this point, the agency
had nothing to go on but rumors that were fed by the FBI to baseball

commissioner Bowie Kuhn and the Cubs organization. The Cubs went so far as the check over the records of each game played by the team in September. The conclusion was that the Cubs were not done in by their manager but by the Mets. Durocher was declared not guilty by the Cubs, but the commissioner's office continued to investigate through the winter.[2]

A clearly subdued Durocher was slow to say anything other than positive things about the 1969 team and was loath to suggest why they had come apart in September. In December, he told Max Kase of the *Boston Record American* that his biggest mistake of 1969 had been to let Randy Hundley catch 151 of 162 games. Leo pointed out that Hundley had blasted seventeen homers before the All-Star game but only one more for the rest of the season.[3]

For the second year in a row, Leo failed to show up for the Cubs' midwinter press briefing. Team officials were not willing to discuss why Durocher was missing, but a particularly pointed UPI dispatch on the briefing led with his visit to a boys' camp and ended with "there was no assurance that Leo would show up for Spring Training." The running gag was that Leo the Cub was in hibernation.[4]

Meanwhile, Durocher seemed to get into trouble for what he didn't do rather than for what he did. In late January, Lou Boudreau, who was Durocher's broadcast partner on the pregame radio show called *Durocher in the Dugout* was elected to the National Baseball Hall of Fame. A few weeks later, Rick Talley of *Chicago Today* noted that Boudreau had not received any congratulatory words from Durocher. "Boudreau got a wire from number one—President Richard M. Nixon—but nothing so far, not even a postage-due postcard, from the man who wears Number 2."[5]

Then, seemingly out of the blue, the March 10, 1970, issue of *Look* magazine appeared in the mailboxes of its seven million readers in late February containing William Barry Furlong's article entitled "How Durocher Blew the Pennant." It was as severe a skewering as Durocher had received since the 1942 Stanley Frank short story, and it appeared in a general-interest magazine known more for its photography than muckraking.

Furlong's point-by-point indictment was that Leo had deserted the team on several occasions when the heat was on and then lied about it. His clubhouse lacked discipline and was characterized by card games and the distraction of hustlers. He carried on a feud with the press that had the effect of demoralizing his athletes. He baited umpires so relentlessly that the Cubs obtained very little justice. He aroused the enmity of rival players and managers to such an extent that they performed with extra zeal against the Cubs.

Those who did not actually read the article got to read about it in the nation's newspapers, as many well-known sports columnists wrote about it, calling the article, among other things, "a snarling attack" and "spiteful." Chancy Durden, a longtime Durocher watcher, said that Furlong threw his typewriter right at Leo's head. What the columnists criticized was the unrelenting tone of the article, but not the allegations.[6]

Red Smith noted that responsible reporters like Furlong might be disposed to give another manager the benefit of the doubt, but that nobody was willing to give Leo that benefit. "It's been a gift of Leo's for alienating people. In his 64th year, his hand has never lost its skill."[7] Durocher claimed he did not read the article but in rebuttal claimed he had learned that Furlong had buck teeth and dirty fingernails.

As if there was not enough working against Durocher, in mid-February Detroit star pitcher Denny McLain was suspended for alleged involvement in a bookmaking operation. Many accounts of the McLain suspension ended with a note saying that the last person suspended for associating with gamblers was Durocher. In the wake of the suspension, Happy Chandler gave an interview drawing a direct parallel between what he had done to Leo and what Bowie Kuhn had done to McLain.[8]

In the wake of the *Look* article, Durocher and Cubs announcer Jack Brickhouse effected a reconciliation, and Leo was soon back to his old aggressive, cocksure form. Jack Murphy wrote of him: "[Leo] is not a broken old man, weighed down by his burdens. If he is bitter, it doesn't show. Durocher is still a formidable man . . . [H]e brims with vitality and energy."[9] What gave Durocher new strength was the realization that the 1970 Cubs were one of baseball's strongest teams. They were, according to the increasingly acerbic Rick Talley, "good enough to win despite Leo."[10]

On March 27, Bowie Kuhn went to Scottsdale, Arizona, where the Cubs were training. He stated he was making a routine visit to all the teams, but his prime mission in Scottsdale was to discuss the allegations still pending against Durocher. Armed with a dossier on Durocher, he met with Leo and Cubs general manager John Holland and asked Durocher numerous questions about his friends and his gambling. Leo explained that he gambled, but not on baseball. He explained that he made numerous trips to Las Vegas, especially when his old pals Frank Sinatra and Dean Martin were performing there. Leo told Kuhn that he had made several killings in the casino, the biggest being $25,000, which he had reported on his income tax. The talk then turned from gambling to Leo's associates and whether or not he hung out or associated with gamblers and gangsters. Leo explained that he talked to all sorts of people both on the streets and in restaurants, adding that strangers often sent drinks to his table when he was in a restaurant, and he had no idea who they were.[11]

Kuhn ended the meeting without resolving anything, but that night, Kuhn went to dinner with the Hollands, the Durochers, and Monte Irvin, who was then working for the commissioner as a public relations specialist. While they were dining, a tray of drinks was delivered to the table with a business card. Kuhn demanded to know who sent the drinks. Leo asked somebody else to look at the card because he didn't have his glasses with him and couldn't read it. The card had been sent from somebody nobody at the table knew—just a character wanting to treat the illustrious table to a round of drinks. Kuhn accepted the drinks and then advised Durocher not to take drinks from strangers in the future.[12]

At the end of the meal, the commissioner invited Leo and Lynne to have breakfast with him at the hotel in the morning. This, as Smith reported, may have been "a tactical error on the commissioner's part, because Mrs. Durocher always sleeps late, always." But because she was concerned about Leo and the effect on his reputation of an investigation based on rumors, she got up early the next morning. She and Leo slogged through the wet grass to meet Kuhn. "I wouldn't get up this early to watch George Washington crossing the Delaware and you got me walking through wet grass," she quipped, and then demanded to know if her husband was in the clear. Kuhn said something about the *Chicago Tribune* being behind the investigation, to which she then pointed out that she was the daughter of Chicago judge John J. Kelly and the former wife of department store owner Joel Goldblatt. She made it clear that she wasn't afraid of any newspaper pressure and that she had a few influential friends herself.

"Is the case still opened or is it closed?" she demanded.

"It's closed," said the commissioner.[13]

In 1999, Lynne Durocher told reporter George Castle, who was researching a book on the Cubs, that her then-husband could not have done anything but manage on the up-and-up. She said Leo wanted to win badly, perhaps in the case of 1969, too badly. Joe Amalfitano, then Durocher's first-base coach, seconded that notion. "I spent a lot of time with Leo privately before and after games [in 1969] when the media wasn't around,"

Amalfitano said. "There were two different Leos—the tough, hard guy the public saw and the other person I got to know. I felt sorry for him because I know how heartbroken he was."[14]

Lynne Durocher told Castle that the couple had taken great pains to avoid being seen with organized-crime types who were attracted to Leo and the folks he hung out with. She said notorious Mafioso Sam Giancana came up to a table the Durochers were sharing with Dean Martin and his wife, Jeanne, in Acapulco, Mexico. "Leo was at my right and Dean was on my left," Lynne said. "All of a sudden I felt Leo freeze . . . He gave Dean a real shot in the arm. Dean put his head down and he had his hand in a fist. Leo had no conversation with him, he wanted nothing to do with him. Leo told me later that this is how he got thrown out of baseball once."

Another time, the couple was on a California golf course. A gangster nodded to Durocher. "We tried to walk quickly off the green," Lynne said. "The gangster said hello. Leo felt really terrible about it . . . Never in my 10 years of marriage to Leo did he ever have a [gangland] connection."[15] Leo later claimed in his autobiography, *Nice Guys Finish Last*, that the investigations were a setup, with the *Chicago Tribune* seeking his hide in part because of the feud with Brickhouse.

With the allegations out of the way, Durocher seemed to have mellowed by the end of Spring Training. He was giving his regulars more time off and seemed to be going out of his way to understand his players and their problems. One player told Jim Enright: "Whoever wrote that magazine story about Leo did such a terrible hatchet job on him that he's emerged as a hero—and he's living the role to help especially when it comes to public relations." Another player noted, "He's substituted kindness and consideration for ruthlessness."[16]

The 1970 season opened with two losses, a win, a loss, and an eleven-game winning streak that catapulted the Cubs into first place, but they lost seven of the next eight. Leo's disdain for the Players Association manifested itself on May 28 when Durocher reprimanded his players for rejecting an offer of the major leagues and voting for the Players Association by a vote of 22–3. He said that the team had made a fine man, Phil Wrigley, feel bad by not siding with every other club except the Philadelphia Phillies by voting down the owners' first proposal. He argued that considering everything Mr. Wrigley had done for them, the Cubs should have given the man a vote of confidence. Upon hearing this, the Associated Press called Wrigley and reached him at his country home in Lake Geneva, Wisconsin. It reported what Leo had said. "When this thing first came up a year ago," said Wrigley, "I talked to some of our players. I told them, when the matter comes to a vote, they should go along with the interest of all the players." The club owner seemed irked as he added: "There was no call for Leo to say anything about it."[17]

Then an unidentified Cub was quoted by Jim Enright as saying: "I didn't know Leo had such a short memory when it comes to turning against Mr. Wrigley. None of us accompanied Leo on that camping trip last year. And Mr. Wrigley didn't ask us for an apology like he did of Leo."

A doubleheader loss to the Mets in early June dropped the Cubs into second place, and they never led again. In early July, after losing twelve of thirteen games, there were calls for Durocher's dismissal. Robert Markus of the *Tribune* jumped to his defense, claiming that above all, Leo was good copy and that the writers in New York would hock their typewriters to have Leo back. "Durocher has the amazing ability to create news. Durocher is news when he talks to you and is even more news when he doesn't talk to you. Leo is a troublemaker, no doubt about that. He's gross, obscene, deceitful and devious . . . a wonderful guy to write about."[18]

For the first time, Ernie Banks, now thirty-nine, was used primarily as a reserve. Even when he got the chance to play, Banks was disrespected by Durocher. Once the manager sent Jim Hickman, like Banks a right-handed batter, to pinch-hit for him against a southpaw. "Hickman told me later it was one of the toughest things he ever had to do," said Brickhouse.[19]

At the 1970 All-Star break in mid-July, the Cubs were in third place, five games behind the Pittsburgh Pirates. On July 26, Durocher was prepared for the first anniversary of the now-infamous excursion to Camp Ojibwa, and as he no doubt expected, was needled by Jim Enright, who in his anniversary story called the event one of the most bizarre in the history of the game.[20] But not expected on the same day was a story by John Justin Smith of the *Chicago Daily News* that revealed that Durocher was being investigated for "playing footsie with some Chicago hoodlums and had been gambling heavily" during the 1969 season, which had come to a fiery head with a confrontation between Kuhn and Mrs. Durocher.

The story was everywhere—either in the full version from the *Daily News* or extracted into an Associated Press wire story. In a quick follow-up story in the Associated Press, Leo declared that this was old news and that "everybody in the world" knew he was being investigated. He confirmed that he had won $25,000 in a short stay in Las Vegas and claimed that all gambling that he had done was legal. Kuhn confirmed that he had talked to Durocher about certain allegations but that there was no real investigation.[21]

The story disappeared quickly but it left more questions than it answered, especially as to who from the *Chicago Tribune* had gone to the FBI, and who was the syndicate member with whom Durocher was alleged to have been seen, not to mention the ease with which Durocher won $25,000 in one short trip to Las Vegas.

For Wrigley and the Cubs, Durocher's future with the team was never in doubt. On August 14, the Cubs signed Durocher for another year—at this point, the Cubs' record was 60–58. Soon after, Leo's relationship with Ron Santo was again strained when he dropped him to seventh place in the batting order without telling him of the lineup change. Santo immediately hit a home run, a pair of doubles, and a single in his first game in that position in the batting order, but fumed at the way he was treated. "He didn't say a word to me. Not one word. He's a funny man. I don't understand him anymore," Santo said.[22]

The Cubs made a strong bid again for the playoffs in 1970, trailing Pittsburgh by one and a half games on September 19. But a 4–7 record to close the year made them runners-up again with an 84–78 record. They were five games out of first and one game ahead of the Mets. When it became clear that the Cubs would not win the division, a story appeared on September 24 in *Chicago Today* under the title "Leo's the Reason Cubs Won't Win." Rick Talley quoted one Cub regular who estimated that Durocher cost the team eight to ten games in the season. The main charge coming from the players was that Leo didn't know his own team. They resented his managerial mistakes, and they believed he hadn't evaluated his own personnel enough to know which man to use in which situation. "Perhaps, the most offensive thing to the players was he was singling out individual players for losing individual games when in fact the games were lost by the team." After a 2–1 loss the night before the column appeared, another regular came to Talley and asked: "Who did Leo blame for this one?"[23]

At the beginning of the 1971 season, Happy Chandler co-authored a two-part piece on his years as commissioner for *Sports Illustrated* written with John Underwood, one of the magazine's star reporters. Chandler once again asserted that he had banished Durocher "to keep him from killing somebody" even though he had denied the idea in an earlier issue of the same magazine.[24]

On July 27, Leo turned sixty-five while the team was in Montreal. "Forget that 65th," he barked. "I'm a swinging 22." The birthday also made Leo the highest-paid manager in baseball, because besides his $70,000 salary from the Cubs, he began getting his pension checks from baseball. He had been in the system from the outset, so he received $1,945 a month, and $23,340 a year. Those numbers had been revealed to the *Chicago Tribune*'s Richard Dozer a few days earlier by Marvin Miller, executive director of the Major League Baseball Players Association. Miller also pointed out that Durocher received the maximum the system provided.[25]

Durocher had been outspoken in his criticism of Miller and the Players Association and was tired of being reminded that the pension system had been the brainchild of Happy Chandler. As if to create an extra layer of irony, many of Leo's contemporaries were not in the system because they were too old when it was started in 1946. Casey Stengel, for example, got nothing, because he was two years outside the original limit.

On August 23, the day after Cubs hurler Milt Pappas gave up an 0–2 checked-swing double to Doug Rader of the Houston Astros resulting in a second straight loss for the Cubs, Durocher called a clubhouse meeting in which he berated his players for their lack of effort and sloppy play. After first baseman Joe Pepitone came to Pappas's defense, Durocher turned on Santo and accused him of malingering and playing front-office politics. He claimed that "the only reason the Cubs were having a 'Ron Santo Day' was because Billy Williams and Ernie Banks had one and that Santo had asked John Holland for one as well."[26]

Santo lunged for Durocher and had to be restrained by Billy Williams and Jim Hickman. "I grabbed Leo and had him around the neck," Santo reminisced later. "I could have killed him."

Ken Holtzman added that Santo had Durocher by the throat and Leo's tongue was sticking out six inches before Santo was pulled off. Durocher had pushed a special button by attacking Santo's special day. Santo suffered from diabetes and had, in fact, helped to plan the day with General Manager Holland, during which all money raised would be given to the Juvenile Diabetes Foundation.[27]

After this outburst, Durocher announced that he was quitting. He left the clubhouse for his office, only to change his mind when an apologetic but still seething Santo approached him with a peace offering. As word of the confrontation filtered out in press accounts, Phil Wrigley felt compelled to react. He acknowledged what had happened and then blamed the press and the Players Association for the rebelliousness of the players. Wrigley asserted that every sportswriter was after Durocher's hide and that the players read the papers and thought they had to take up the same theme. He then turned his fire on Marvin Miller, whom he claimed was making the players believe "that the whole game belongs to them."[28]

Wrigley then took the unusual step of taking out a full-page ad on September 4 in each of Chicago's four daily newspapers to offer a public letter of endorsement of Durocher. The eight-paragraph letter concluded with a poke at the dissident players, saying, "Leo is the team manager and the 'Dump Durocher Clique' might as well give up. He is running the team, and if some of the players do not like it and lie down on the job, during the off-season we will see what we can do to find them happier homes." Wrigley then added a line that, intentionally or not, irked many on the team: "P.S. If only we could find more team players like Ernie Banks."[29]

Writing in the *Official Baseball Guide*, Edgar Munzel was one of many to point out the remarkable nature of the Wrigley open letter: "He backed Durocher and slapped down the players. As a matter of fact, one interpretation of the Wrigley statement was that it was the first time a major league owner ever actually threatened to fire a ball club and keep the manager."[30]

The letter did nothing to improve the situation, as the team lost nine of its next eleven games. Relations between Durocher and his players were at their lowest ebb. A prime example was Ken Holtzman, who had hardly even spoken to his manager during the second half of the 1971 season. Durocher had previously criticized Holtzman for not using his fastball often enough and relying too much on what the manager called a "lollipop" curve. Durocher also questioned Holtzman's effort. "I wasn't happy when Leo Durocher was quoted in the paper saying I wasn't trying," he later told Glenn Dickey of the *San Francisco Chronicle*. After Durocher publicly criticized Holtzman, the left-hander asked Holland to trade him. Holtzman claimed that Durocher's handling of the team, rather than his own relationship with the manager, prompted his trade request. "I didn't have any real trouble with Leo," Holtzman said to Dickey. "I got along all right with him. But I didn't like the way he'd criticize players sometimes in the papers, instead of confronting a player directly."[31]

Holtzman was being diplomatic in his assessment of Durocher. In reality, Holtzman suffered under the brutal management style of Durocher. According to Andrew Hazucha in his article in *Nine*, Durocher repeatedly made anti-Semitic slurs toward Holtzman, even calling him a "kike."

Durocher also resented Holtzman for being unavailable to pitch during certain Jewish holidays.[32]

Others were not deaf to Rich Bladt, a journeyman outfielder who was called up from the minors briefly in June of 1969 and played just ten games for the Cubs that summer and later told Rick Talley that his most memorable moment of the 1969 season was Durocher calling Holtzman a "gutless Jew" in front of his teammates. Durocher also showed his frustration with Holtzman for throwing too many curveballs and change-ups. "Kenny," Durocher would yell at him in the postgame clubhouse in the same way he had taunted Maglie, "why don't you forget that dinky change-up and start throwing hard. You were like an old woman out there tonight."[33]

The 1971 Cubs finished in third place in the National League East with an 83–79 record. Ernie Banks retired at the end of the season after nineteen seasons as a Cubs player and as the franchise's all-time leader in games played (2,528), at-bats (9,421), home runs (512), total bases (4,706), and extra-base hits (1,009).

On November 17, Phil Wrigley tendered Durocher a one-year contract for the 1972 season. He also appointed Ernie Banks to a position as the Cubs' new first-base coach, at the same time noting that Banks was "too nice a guy" to be named Cubs manager. A few days earlier Wrigley ended rumors that he would make Banks the first black manager. "Managing is a dirty job, it doesn't last long and it certainly isn't anything I would wish on Banks who was headed for baseball's Hall of Fame," Wrigley said, adding, "Furthermore, I think Banks wouldn't take a managerial job."[34]

As per his request, Holtzman was traded to the Oakland A's at the end of November.

Then, unexpectedly, during a winter press conference in January, Durocher went to the media with a plea to kiss and make up. He pleaded, "Come on fellows, let's start the new season all even." He lifted the ban on clubhouse photography and said that he would make himself available for both pregame and postgame interviews—free of charge.[35]

Now in his fiftieth year in the game, Leo was as chipper and dapper as ever and his old optimistic self in Spring Training, proclaiming that the 1972 Cubs were the best lot of players he had seen since coming to Chicago. Banks was marginalized as the Cubs new first-base coach, Holtzman was gone, and Santo made peace in Spring Training, vowing to put the past behind him. At best, there was an uneasy truce between Durocher and the rest of his players.

But even as his relationship with the press seemed to mellow, in part thanks to having his own public relations/player relations man in former Cubs pitcher Hank Aguirre, his relationship with the Cubs faithful seemed to be souring. Fans who had come to Scottsdale, Arizona, to watch their team were rudely surprised by a coarse old man who behaved as if they were pests rather than people who paid for seats at Wrigley Field. In a town where it was heresy to speak ill of the Cubs, an editorial in the *Scottsdale Daily Progress* called Durocher a bum and said in part: "Your rudeness to patrons at the ballpark is not necessary. Your cruelty to youngsters who ask for your autograph is totally unnecessary. These kids want to look up to ballplayers, but you growl at them, shoo them away and make them feel very small." The editorial headlined LEO, YOU'RE BUSH LEAGUE was reported verbatim in *Chicago Today* and was read aloud on local news shows in Chicago.

The first baseball players' strike in history occurred from April 1 to April 13 over the central issue of pension payments. Leo did not like what was happening to baseball and was especially negative when it came to the Players Association. "Jerry," he said in an on-air interview with Jerry Coleman, the former Yankee, who was now a broadcaster for the Padres, "you won't believe this, but I haven't had one clubhouse meeting all season because it's getting so you can't say anything to a player. The way the Players Association is going, a man soon will need permission to say hello to a player."[36]

Leo missed the delayed Opening Day because of strep throat, and the Cubs witnessed the lowest Opening Day crowd in more than a decade. The club lost ten of its first thirteen games—most of which Leo missed as the strep throat eventually put him in the hospital. They picked up in June and came up on the All-Star break with a 46–44 record.

Durocher was uncharacteristically subdued during the first half of the season, but he put on a full display of his old petulance in Atlanta in early July, where he became furious with the Braves grounds crew, whom he believed caused a rainout. When his protest was refused by the National League office, he retaliated by refusing to make his lineup cards available to the press or to the Braves for each game of a doubleheader on July 5. Asked if he was concerned with Durocher's lineup escapades, Phil Niekro, who won the first game for Atlanta, said that he did not care if he ever turned it in, because the batters still had to come up there and face him sooner or later. To make matters worse, Durocher unloaded on the National League office: "The powers that be in this league are horseshit, and you can quote me on that."[37]

On July 23, the Chicago newspapers carried a notice of a meeting between Durocher and Phil Wrigley to discuss the team and its prospects for the remainder of the season. As if Wrigley were unaware, Rick Talley pointed out that the Cubs were barely playing .500 baseball over their last 437 games; they were 220–217 since September 2, 1969—the beginning of the miracle collapse.[38]

Late in the evening of July 24, at a meeting at Wrigley's apartment at 1500 North Lake Shore Drive, Durocher was persuaded to step aside. John Holland called Cubs beat reporters one at a time and said that Leo was no longer the manager of the Chicago Cubs and Whitey Lockman had been named to succeed him. Lockman had been told that Leo had "stepped aside," and Wrigley was adamant in saying that he had not been fired and would remain with the team for the rest of the season as a consultant. But there was no question in anyone's mind at the time that Wrigley had finally asked him to leave. Talley summed it up in the next morning's paper: "He was the man who took the Cubs from oblivion to the brink of glory. But he couldn't take them over the top." He calculated that during his six and a half years, Durocher had gone through almost two hundred players. "No manager ever used so many players to win barely half his games."[39]

Leo had been replaced as manager during the All-Star Game festivities in Atlanta, and thus many sportswriters across the country were alerted to make a comment or devote their columns to his departure, which looked like the end his managerial career. Many of the comments were innocuous farewells to a man who had created tons of good copy, but a few had a bite. Wells Twombly of the *San Francisco Examiner* noted that life would be a lot less colorful without Durocher, but that he had become an anachronism, and modern athletes no longer responded to his "blood-spattered 1940 style." Jesse Outlar, sports editor of *The Atlanta Constitution*, commented coldly that Durocher had started in baseball when Calvin Coolidge was president, and had had his turn at bat.[40]

Two days after his removal, Durocher addressed the team in the club-house before their first game after the All-Star break. He praised Wrigley, recalled his own long career in the game, and maintained that he had resigned and had not been fired. He read from a telegram Randy Hundley sent him thanking him for giving him a chance.

Coach Ernie Banks sat and listened to the man who had tried to break him and whom—despite Wrigley's claims to the contrary—he had hoped to succeed as the manager of the Cubs. Banks was clearly disappointed that he was overlooked but was gracious in pledging support to Lockman, who had actually said he didn't want the job. It was clear that Banks wanted to manage. He told Russ White of the *Washington Star* that he wanted to step into that job sometime, adding that the time was ripe for a black manager and suggesting his top candidates—Frank Robinson, Maury Wills, and Junior Gilliam. "Each of them," he said, describing himself in the process, "has experience, charisma, toughness. Each has a following and knows the people in various cities. Each has a rapport with members of the press."[41]

After Durocher finished with the players, he stopped by the umpires' dressing room and bade them farewell. "He's not such a bad guy—in civilian clothes," commented Chris Pelecoudes. Then he spent an hour with the press, gracious and deferential. The reigning cliché of the day was that Leo, like the month of March, had come into Chicago like a lion and was now going out like a lamb. Enright watched in disbelief: "Had you not known the difference, you would've thought Leo just finished managing the Cubs in a pennant clinching victory."[42]

Perhaps the last word on Durocher from Wrigley Field came from a twenty-two-year-old hot dog vendor named Dave Klemp, who had been fired in early July because he had hoisted a banner that read, LEO MUST GO! His friends then hoisted a banner which read, HOLLAND MUST GO!, and Klemp was rehired. The day of Leo's farewell to the team, the vendor was interviewed and admitted that he was glad Durocher was gone. The hot dog man spoke for many when he said: "Durocher's a good manager but not for the team he had."

Later, with time to look back on Durocher's time in Chicago, Mel Durslag waxed eloquent: "Into 6½ years with the Cubs, he packed 100 years of turmoil, figuring in a lingering commotion that brought him the harshest press in the history of the game."[43]

Sports journalists were divided into two camps—those who said that Leo had resigned, and those who said that he was fired. It really didn't matter. Phil Wrigley had finally lost faith in Leo.

Rumors swirled that Durocher was going to New York to replace Ralph Houk as Yankees skipper. The Yankees were not contenders, and some argued that Leo was the man to shake up the team. Houk, according to the same rumor, was headed to Boston to pilot the Red Sox. Then, on Saturday morning, August 26, 1972, Maggie Daly, the gossip columnist for *Chicago*

Today, was awakened by a telephone call from Lynne Durocher. "Maggie, I wanted to call you in a hurry because we just received the news that Leo is going to Houston to manage the Astros." The deal, she said, had been hammered out between midnight and 2 A.M. that morning. Leo's first call had been to Phil Wrigley, who gave his blessing and released him from any remaining obligations to the Cubs. The Durochers were already packing and she promised they would be there for the game the next day.[44]

The Astros hired Leo to replace Harry Walker for the remainder of the 1972 season and all of 1973. It was only the second time that someone had managed two National League teams in a season. The first time was in 1948, when Durocher had managed the Dodgers and the Giants.

The Astros general manager, Spec Richardson, said he hired Durocher because Leo had fire, and that's what was needed to bring Houston the division title. The Astros were enjoying their first winning season in their history, but they were losing ground to the red-hot Cincinnati Reds, who now led them by nine games, and Durocher was brought in to catch them. Leo donned his Astros uniform when the team had a 68–54 record.*

The first reaction was disbelief, especially among those who understood the degree to which Durocher hated the Astrodome. He would now go to work in the place where he least liked to play. With demonstrable glee, Jim Enright put together a feature story collecting all of Leo's disparaging remarks in which he also posited a thesis for Leo's hatred of the dome. The expansion-born Astros had a 56–46 record against the Cubs during Leo's years as Chicago's manager, so Leo, Enright argued, decided to ridicule baseball's only indoor playpen: the $3.6 million air-conditioned 45,000-seat Astrodome.[45]

With Durocher as skipper, Houston reeled off five straight victories. He predicted that his Astros would catch the first-place Cincinnati Reds, but it didn't happen, and on September 22 the Reds defeated the Astros 4–3 to clinch the National League West Division. That same night, Durocher yanked Larry Dierker in the first inning after he gave up two earned runs. Dierker was visibly upset over his removal, which angered Durocher. After the game, Durocher said, "I told my players that I will not show them up on the field or in the dugout and that I expect the same of them."[46]

Durocher benched Dierker for the remainder of the season but claimed he would not hold this incident against him for the following season,

---

* In 1973, there were no wild-card spots for runners-up, so that the only road to the league championship was by winning the division.

though it was a claim he had a hard time selling. The two men were at odds. The Astros finished 16–15 under Durocher, a distant second place to the Reds. Still, the 84–69 strike-shortened record was the team's best to date, and second place was the best finish in their history.

On October 23, 1972, Jackie Robinson passed away and Durocher was immediately reached by a UPI reporter. Leo said he was very sad and called him a great competitor who could do it all. "He was a great player, a manager's dream, he played all over." Durocher focused on his great base running. "He upset a pitcher so bad he didn't know where he was half the time. He was an alert smart baseball player. The catcher had to have a great arm to get him when he stole."[47]

One evening during the winter, Durocher played cards with Frank Sinatra at Tamarisk Country Club in Palm Springs after a golf game and then got into his electric cart to drive home in the desert's darkness. "I know where every palm tree on the course is," Durocher told a reporter. "So, *wham*, I run head on into a big one and break three ribs."[48]

In early March, Leo was back with the club in Cocoa Beach, Florida. "Now, in sparkling Florida sunshine, he was attired with his usual impactability in the orange and gray of the Houston Astros," wrote Mel Durslag. "Soon to be 67, Leo looks wonderful. He hasn't aged in years. His baby blue eyes are clear and the face and body are rested from the winter in Palm Springs where he has just purchased a new home . . . Just five minutes from his pal Frank Sinatra."[49]

His difficulties with his players and more significantly with the Players Association continued and were similar to the battles he had started in Chicago. The contentious umpire-baiting style he helped to create was losing favor, and he could no longer win over young reporters and impress players by telling stories about flying off to Japan with Sinatra on a whim. Leo would say "Frank," and his players, who knew to whom he was referring, would say "Frank, who?" to get his goat.

Just as Durocher landed in Florida for Spring Training, Marvin Miller began visiting Spring Training sites to brief the players on the new three-year deal with the owners. These meetings were legally necessary in order to ratify the agreement. Spec Richardson was furious when he learned that Miller had scheduled the Astros' meeting on March 12 before a game with the Texas Rangers at Pompano Beach, 165 miles away.

The Astros arrived in Pompano around 10:45 A.M. and joined the Rangers, who were meeting with Miller in center field. The players had listened to

Miller for about thirty minutes when Durocher came out and broke up the gathering, saying, "Come on, let's go, it's 11:30. We hit in ten minutes." Leo ordered his team out of the meeting. Miller and his attorney, Dick Moss, were furious, saying the Astros had violated the agreement, which specified that each team be available for a ninety-minute meeting.[50]

Durocher's action drew the ire of National League president Chub Feeney, who fined him $250. Durocher said he would retire before paying the fine and threatened to sue the league. Miller immediately denounced Durocher as "childish" and, because of his nonsupport of the pension system, labeled him a "free-loader riding the backs of his fellow managers and players." Miller grew to hate Durocher more than any other man he dealt with, including Billy Martin. "He was a crude, crass individual," said Miller of Durocher. "This was a character that used to attempt to bully people at all times. He beat up more people—older people and smaller people—in parking lots than you can count. A bum. He was an earlier version of Billy Martin."

On the other hand, Richardson backed his manager. "Leo was right. Thirty-eight ballplayers, every man on our under-control roster, have said that they didn't want to meet with Marvin Miller—not in Pompano. That's a heckuva blow to him. I think his pride is hurt. I think Durocher is the only man in baseball with the guts to do this and I think he is right."[51]

Unaccustomed to covering labor matters, the baseball writers tended to cover the story carefully, but many of them were taken aback by Durocher's apparent duplicity as a pensioner. "Naturally, what burns Miller is that the one man getting the maximum player's pension—$2,000 a month—is the one who defied him," wrote Harold Kaese in *The Boston Globe*. "Durocher didn't bite the hand that helps feed him. He chewed it right off." Durocher went out of his way to belittle the pension, saying that he spent more than he was getting from the union in tips to washroom attendants.[52] In order to keep the peace—and his job—a check for the fine was sent to Feeney in time for Opening Day.

Perhaps the greatest contrast between old and new was the flawed relationship between Durocher and pitcher Larry Dierker. Smart and savvy, Dierker explained in his own memoir: "If I could have gotten Leo Durocher fired I would have done it in a heartbeat . . . Leo was a manipulator. He was pretty good at it but at that stage of his career he was getting old and couldn't remember what he had told various players. He was frequently caught lying. When Leo was young he was smart as a whip, he had a passion for victory, and he was a good strategist on the bench. But he lacked character. He played favorites, which made some guys like him and some hate him. In my opinion, he was unprofessional."[53]

Dierker would later tell the Associated Press what it was like playing for Durocher:

I did not say anything to the press or make any complaint about it. But frankly I was afraid of what that guy in there would do. You couldn't tell what he'd do. He might have given me the ball and told me to pitch and left me in there until my arm fell off. I know myself well enough to know that if he kept giving me the ball I'd take it. My arm had been hurt seriously a couple of times and I did not want to jeopardize my whole future in the hands of Durocher. I figured it would be better to sit and wait and hope he was fired or that I was traded.

One time, while I was on the disabled list, I threw a simulated game and performed well, without any pain. I was ready to be acti-vated so Leo called me into his office and told me he would put me back on the list just as soon as he could get rid of outfielder Bob Gallagher. He ripped Gallagher up one side and down the other. I didn't know if he knew that Bob was my roommate and one of my best friends on the team; maybe he said those things for precisely that reason. He didn't have to tell me what he thought of Gallagher. All he had to do was to tell me I was going to be activated. I didn't relay Leo's feelings to Bob, as it would have served no useful purpose. A few days later, we went to San Francisco and Bob's dad met him at the airport. Leo just happened to be nearby and Bob took the opportunity to introduce Leo to his father ... The two Gallaghers were beaming and I was right there to witness the exchange. Leo told Bob's father that he had raised a fine son and that he was thinking about using Bob as his regular right fielder. "You should be proud of Bob," he said. "He's a fine young man and a helluva ballplayer." I thought I was going to vomit. I'll never forget that scene. As much as any other single event, it taught me the importance of honesty.[54]

The season opened on a high note with the Astros beating the Dodgers 4–1 in Houston. But by April 20, their record was 7–8. On that day, Durocher was hospitalized with an intestinal infection. As a celebrity,

Durocher still had the remarkable ability to befriend and attract the best in any arena. He was in awe of Dr. Michael DeBakey, considered the world's most celebrated surgeon. When doctors finally decided that Durocher needed an operation for diverticulitis a few days after being hospitalized, he was able to get DeBakey to manage his case, and DeBakey moved Durocher to his hospital at Baylor University.

Dave Condon of the *Chicago Tribune* devoted a column to the relationship between Dr. DeBakey and Leo. "Though some picture Leo as a man in love only with himself, you should see the awe in his eyes, hear it in his voice, when he talks of someone above the ordinary mold in any particular field. The characters are as diverse as General Patton, Frank Sinatra, and Dr. DeBakey."[55]

While Leo was in the hospital, the Astros climbed into first place by winning fourteen of seventeen games. "The players went on a rampage," Astros coach Grady Hatton said. "We could hardly do anything wrong. In one game we had so many injuries that we had to let the pitcher Jim Ray hit in a crucial situation. We told him to strike out if he could, anything but hit into a double play. He said that was the first time he'd ever had both teams pulling against him at once. So wouldn't you know it, he got a base hit and won the game."[56]

Leo was back in the saddle on May 10. In his absence, Preston Gomez led the team effectively, but the Astros did not play as well over the next two months. On July 2, after losing a game to the San Diego Padres, the Astros had a record of 44–38. Durocher canceled batting practice for the remainder of the season, declaring, "Batting practice is nothing but a waste of time so we just won't bother with it anymore." The announcement was met with disbelief, and it was pointed out that nobody in the modern history of the game had ever suggested that batting practice was a worthless exercise. Others pointed out that if Durocher was right now, he had been wrong for the more than forty years he had been in the game.[57]

By midsummer, Durocher was being quoted widely on his disdain for high-priced talent and by extension his anger over unionization. "Give me fighters and scratchers, guys making $15,000 and want to make $20,000. You can keep the $100,000 players—give me the ones who want to win."[58]

As the 1973 season dwindled into September and it was clear that the Astros would not win the division, a rumor that had first cropped up in July—that Durocher might be in line to become the next manager of the New York Mets—got new footing. It was pure speculation but taken seriously after Yogi Berra was fired abruptly on August 5, 1975, and the team still managed to win the National League pennant. Durocher, it was argued, might be able to persuade Willie Mays—then in his final season—to stay in the game for an extra year. The rumor was just that, but it stole headlines for a few days and underscored the point that Durocher could still see his name in large type.[59]

The Astros won their last game of the season in Atlanta. The stadium was packed on September 30, because after a three-run blast against Jerry Reuss in the previous game, Hank Aaron was now one home run shy of Babe Ruth's career home run record of 714. The fact that Durocher and Ruth had been teammates was not lost in accounts of the game. Many VIPs, including Governor Jimmy Carter, came to see Aaron tie and maybe break baseball's most hallowed mark. Pitcher Dave Roberts, who had yielded number 712 in Houston eight days earlier, held Aaron to three singles, and Houston won, 5–3. After the game, Durocher had nothing but praise for Aaron, calling him the best right-handed hitter since Rogers Hornsby.

Durocher ended the season as a winner, with his club finishing 82–80, even though the team had slipped back to fourth place, seventeen games behind the Reds. Two days later, he resigned with a smile on his face and nothing but good words for the Astros, the local news media, and his replacement, Preston Gomez. The game had changed, Durocher said on his way out of Houston: "I understand it's a different era, I learned that the players do what they please nine times out of ten. It's a different breed. Give them an inch and they take six inches. Give them a foot and they take a yard."[60]

During his last job as a manager, he had to work in a building he couldn't stand. When he got to Houston, he found players such as Larry Dierker who would obey him but not put up with his effrontery. "Whatever happened to 'Sit down, shut up, and listen'?" he asked as the players began to assert themselves.

It was somehow fitting that Leo's obsession with success and the fact that he was "unappeasable" was compared to Captain Ahab by "Word" Smith, the narrator in Philip Roth's *Great American Novel,* which was published in 1973, Leo's last year in the game.[61]

CHAPTER 15

The Rocky Road to Cooperstown

I F LEO DUROCHER GAVE easy interviews to the daily press while he was in
Houston, it was just the opposite with magazine writers. "I don't talk to
magazine guys," Durocher told Edward Shrake of *Sports Illustrated*
midway through the 1973 season. "Why should I tell you anything about my
life? It'll all be in the book I'm writing. Irving Lazar is my agent for the
book. Best there is. Got $150,000 in front. Not too bad, is it? So how could
anybody hope to write something if I didn't tell you, which I won't, about
what happened between me and Mr. Rickey, or me and Horace Stoneham,
or me and Larry MacPhail, or me and Mr. Weil from Cincinnati? They ain't
gonna tell you, and neither am I."[1]

This was the second time Durocher announced he was going to produce
a "tell-all" in an autobiography since he landed with the Cubs. The first
time was during the 1967 season, and he indicated that he had a ghostwriter in mind—a fellow named Truman Capote. "I don't know him but
he's a friend of Frank's."[2]

Durocher held on to the idea of working with Capote, who met with him
and Lynne in November 1973 at the Durochers' Palm Springs home.
According to Lynne, Capote told Leo that the book should not be just about
sports but should capture the flavor of his colorful times. So, she pointed
out, Leo was taking Truman's advice. Capote, who was writing a book about
the very wealthy, eventually chose not to be Leo's collaborator.[3]

Durocher finally settled for talented freelancer Ed Linn, who had worked
with him on the *Saturday Evening Post* memoir almost ten years earlier. In
the interim, Linn was best known for two books he had written with Bill

Veeck: the best-selling *Veeck—As in Wreck*, and the iconoclastic *Hustler's Handbook*.

Nice Guys Finish Last, Leo's second autobiography, was published in April 1975. It featured a single gushing blurb from Frank Sinatra, who said, among other things, that without Leo the sunshine just wouldn't mean as much. The publisher used the book jacket to bill it as the baseball book of the century.*

In this book, as he did in 1948 with *The Dodgers and Me*, Durocher sought redemption by recasting sordid elements of his past either in a heroic light or by avoiding them altogether. As in the first book, shameful episodes, such as the player revolt of 1943, were not even mentioned. Unlike the first autobiography, his new one neglected to mention his marriage to Ruby Hartley in 1930 and the fathering of a child—what Bob Broeg reviewing the book in *The Sporting News* called his "lost" marriage and daughter.[4]

Durocher presented himself as a kindly man with, as Jonathan Yardley put it in his scathing review of the book in *Sports Illustrated*, "a heart of mush," and Jerome Holtzman called Leo a "revisionist historian" for portraying himself as a good guy. Dave Condon of the *Chicago Tribune*, noting Durocher's use of the book to attack others, suggested that it was so volatile it should be printed on asbestos.[5]

Just as he done earlier, Durocher took potshots at men who had played for him, as well as figures like Jack Brickhouse and Jim Enright with whom he had crossed swords. Durocher actually wrote, "Up yours, Brickhouse," as part of the text. Writers, reviewers, and fans reacted negatively, as they had with *The Dodgers and Me*. But this time, the reaction seemed worse as Leo aimed salvos at Ernie Banks and Ron Santo— arguably the two most beloved Cubs of the last half of the twentieth century. He implied Ron Santo was, among other things, an overrated dimwitted baby, but it was the attack on Banks that created the most ire. A full chapter in the book was spent taking down Banks, whom he called out as a phony. Jim Murray of the *Los Angeles Times* wrote: "The man who punched out

---

* When Durocher left Chicago in 1972, Jim Enright quoted an anonymous wag—who was probably following an old custom in journalism to make up a great line and attribute it to a wag—who said: "Leo will never write a book about his life because he hasn't got a friend he would trust long enough to dedicate it to." Leo got around the problem by dedicating *Nice Guys Finish Last* to his long-departed parents.

Babe Ruth has a whole chapter of sarcasm for Ernie Banks, a man of such mythic affection in Chicago that he occupies the same place there as Mickey Mouse does in Disney World." Other Cubs came in for Leo's ire. For example, in a tip of the hat to theology, Durocher suggested that Joe Pepitone was God's punishment for his own ill-tempered behavior as a player. He even suggested that Red Smith, the patron saint of sportswriters, was on the payroll of the baseball owners.[6]

Taken together, the two autobiographies shed more light on how Durocher wanted to be seen rather than who he actually was. *Nice Guys Finish Last* attained the number one position on *The New York Times* nonfiction bestseller list in 1975. It is still regarded as a primer for anyone looking to play the game in the Durocher manner. "If a man is sliding into second base and the ball goes into center field, what's the matter with falling on him accidentally so that he can't get up and go to third? I don't call that cheating; I call that heads-up baseball."*

In anticipation of the book tour and Leo's press-friendly visit, Rick Talley, who had moved from *Chicago Today* when it was shut down in 1974 to the *Chicago Tribune*, published a long list of incidents that Leo had left out of his biography but which "added to his charisma."

It was a brutal list, including the charge that he had refused to pay his rent for nine months in a Lake Shore apartment because he said the air-conditioning didn't work properly and that he had paid Joe Pepitone $50 to dump a salad in a certain writer's lap.

Talley then addressed the rumor that still hung in the air: "It is comforting to know, though, that Leo wasn't really linked with any hoodlums and wasn't really in their company in a North Side restaurant. I always wondered about that story, and the resulting investigation by Bowie Kuhn, but never knew the true facts. Now we know this because Leo denies it all in his book and nobody would lie in their own book, would they?"[7]

When Durocher headed out to publicize *Nice Guys Finish Last*, he drifted even further from the reality of his life. On Roy Leonard's show on WGN in Chicago, Leo claimed the reason he and Grace Dozier divorced was that she wanted him to give up baseball, and he refused. He said she wanted to keep him around the house. Leo claimed a deep and abiding friendship with

---

* A new edition of the book was published in 2009 by the University of Chicago Press with no caveat as to its shortcomings.

both Dozier and Laraine Day and said that he made a better friend than a husband.[8]

Hal Bock interviewed Durocher when he was on his book tour. "It was a great chameleon act. He suddenly turned himself into Mr. Sweetheart answering all questions politely and praising everybody." The stunner was Leo's line with which Bock led his Associated Press story: "You know umpires are the most underpaid men in baseball." Bock flashed back to some of Durocher's most provocative attacks on umpires' moves and turned it into the kind of interview that Durocher had refused up until the book's publication.

Durocher was not done with baseball despite the bridges he burned with the book. He was asked back by Wrigley in 1975 to be the Cubs general manager. The hitch was that Wrigley also wanted Jack Brickhouse to leave his WGN job to become Cubs president. Leo said he wanted no part of the general manager's job when he heard of the plan to make Brickhouse his boss. As one writer put it, this was yet another harebrained Wrigley idea that often involved recycling people he knew.[9]

In December, Durocher went to Houston for his annual physical with Dr. DeBakey, who he had retained as his general practitioner, who discovered two severely blocked arteries. Now seventy-one, Durocher went under the knife for five and a half hours on December 17. When he was leaving the hospital, DeBakey told him, "I just gave you twenty more years, now take care of them." Lynne returned to be at Durocher's side during this illness. After the surgery, Frank Sinatra sent his private plane to Houston to pick up Leo, Lynne, and DeBakey and his wife, Katrin. Leo would convalesce at Sinatra's house while the DeBakeys would also stay there for a week.[10]

While still convalescing in January 1976, the Japanese Pacific League Saitama Seibu Lions hired Leo to manage their club. Lions owner Nagoyashi Nakamura said the contract was in "six figures," making Durocher the highest paid baseball manager anywhere. A disdainful Vin Scully said of the move, "It took the U.S. 35 years to get revenge for Pearl Harbor." William Barry Furlong, who was now a columnist for *The Washington Post*, wrote that, by hiring Durocher, the Japanese were about to earn the wages of losing a war.[11]

Durocher said later: "I had the contract which was the best contract I ever had in baseball. I won't tell you the salary but it would have been twice as much as I ever made in the U.S. There would have been a chauffeured Cadillac waiting for me every night to take me wherever I wanted to go and a suite of rooms—all at no charge." He added: "On top of everything else, I love Japan." He pointed out that he had been there at least ten times since he first went with Danny Kaye in 1945—most often as a part of Frank Sinatra's entourage.*

However, after returning to California and while still recovering from surgery, Durocher suffered an infection. He then came down with pneumonia followed by hepatitis. As Maggie Daly wrote in her column in the *Chicago Tribune*, Durocher was a "very sick man."[12]

In April, Durocher informed Lions owner Nakamura that his departure for Japan would be delayed by five weeks because he needed time to recover. Nakamura canceled the contract, thereby ending Leo's baseball career. According to the English-language *Japan Times*, Leo was shocked when Nakamura decided he could not wait for Durocher to show up. The *Times* editorialized: "The sudden submerging of Durocher into the Japanese way of life, together with the task of running a ball club he had never seen before, is a lot in itself. Five weeks into the season, it would seem impossible."[13]

The hepatitis kept him in the hospital for ten weeks. He told Daley: "Don't ever get hepatitis. It is the worst disease in the world. If you got it, you can be sitting there in that chair and you can just fall over backwards— you are that weak. I suppose cancer is probably worse, but hepatitis is the worst thing I've ever had."[14]

In mid-March, Leo was elected to a Hall of Fame—the Black Athletes Hall of Fame, along with Ernie Banks and eighteen others. Durocher was the only white person in the group and was awarded the honor for helping to bring black players into the game. As if to second this nomination, a few weeks later Maury Wills, an African-American, published his memoir entitled *How to Steal a Pennant* and gave Durocher, whom he knew as a Dodgers coach, rave reviews in terms of his kindness and compassion toward young players and black players in particular. "Leo Durocher was surely one of the nice guys of baseball."[15]

On February 2, 1976, Durocher became eligible for induction into the National Baseball Hall of Fame in Cooperstown. Election by the Veterans Committee required approval by at least 75 percent of the members. Leading

---

* *The Sporting News* of January 3, 1976, listed Durocher's salary offer from the Taiheiyo Club Lions as $150,000. *The Sporting News* of April 3, 1976, noted the salary offer had risen to $220,000.

up to the vote, there was much discussion of Leo's suitability. In January, former *New York Herald Tribune* sportswriter Harold Rosenthal conducted a poll of noted baseball figures, asking, "Should Durocher make the Hall of Fame?" Of those polled, nine voted yes, seven no, and two replied maybe. Pee Wee Reese, Bill Veeck, journalist Heywood Hale Broun, Ralph Branca, Pete Reiser, Eddie Stanky, Dodger owner Walter O'Malley, Bobby Thomson, and Buzzie Bavasi were all in Leo's corner, with some of those arguing for induction because he brought color to the game. The "no" votes were from Carl Furillo, who said Leo was not good for young ballplayers; baseball statistician Allen Roth, who argued that Durocher's numbers did not merit selection; Ed Fitzgerald, former editor of *Sport* magazine, who deemed him not a serious candidate; Harold Parrott, who called Leo divisive as a manager; Rex Barney, who opposed managers in the Hall of Fame; Dick Young, who said Leo was very colorful but that this was not a criterion for selection; and Red Barber, who opposed Durocher because Larry MacPhail had still not been elected. Former Dodgers infielder and major league manager Billy Herman and former Dodgers coach under Durocher Clyde Sukeforth were uncertain.*[16]

On the eve of the actual vote, Rick Talley gave a historical argument in favor of Durocher's election: "Grab ANY baseball fan past his teens," he said, "and ask him to list the 10 most famous people in baseball history. Durocher would easily crack into the top 10. Maybe be number three behind Babe Ruth and Ty Cobb, or number four or five."[17]

However, Durocher was not elected in 1976.

Durocher's health steadily improved through the remainder of 1976. By June 1977, he declared that he would be on the next plane if given a managing job. "Never felt better in my life," he told UPI sports editor Milt Richman, pointing out that he was now walking six miles a day. But the phone did not ring for new work until the following spring, when Durocher was hired by the Gillette razor company to help promote fan voting for the All-Star Game and to promote the game itself. Leo gave interviews highlighting his ten appearances at the game as a player, coach, and manager. This gave him a chance to express his own thoughts on baseball as it was now played. "You know what I think of today's ballplayer. He's a prima

---

* The article was the cover story in *The American Way* magazine, the in-flight magazine of American Airlines. Its placement in a general-interest magazine indicated the degree to which people were still interested in Durocher.

donna, spoiled, coddled, lazy," he said in one interview published in the *Los Angeles Times*.[18]

DUROCHER WAS NOT in the Hall of Fame class of inductees in 1977 or 1978. Meanwhile, Larry MacPhail's contributions to the game earned him election to the Hall in 1978, three years after his death. Along with the disappointment of not getting into the Hall of Fame, Durocher lost the last of his brothers, Armand, in the fall of that year. The obituary in the *Springfield Union* said that he had worked for some years as a chef. No mention was made of his criminal record.[19]

Willie Mays was elected in 1979 and made a point of pushing for Durocher's enshrinement in his acceptance speech. Mays's lobbying had little or no effect, as Leo was again rejected in 1980 and 1981. The constant rejection had an effect. After the 1981 rejection, Leo "silenced himself" and refused to give interviews of any kind. Confronted by Phil Elderkin of *The Christian Science Monitor* in the lobby of the Sheraton Plaza Resort and Racquet Club in Palm Springs, Leo said: "I am retired. I am no longer in baseball, I have no opinions on anything, and I no longer give interviews. I'm at home here in the desert with my wife and friends and I don't need any publicity"—but the claim about his wife was untrue. Leo and Lynne had been living apart since 1977, and later, in 1981, they were divorced and had not spoken since. The event created no press and was handled quietly.[20]

In the meantime, Leo was seeing younger women and would continue to do so for as long as he was able. According to Gerald Eskenazi's 1993 biography *The Lip*, Leo received a penile implant in 1987 in a Brooklyn hospital where he was accompanied by a much younger woman named Jeannie. Eskenazi suggested that the procedure was paid for by Frank Sinatra.[21, 22]

Leo only spoke out on rare occasions. Some weeks after declaring himself a private man, he broke his silence to label the players' strike, then in progress, as "stupid, that's all, stupid."[23] Just before Thanksgiving, Leo showed up in Manhattan for the opening night of a play about Jackie Robinson called *The First*. According to *The New York Times*, Durocher got the biggest hand at the theater, bigger than some of the old Dodgers present, including Duke Snider and Ralph Branca. The *Times* noted that he lived in retirement in Palm Springs, California, but New York was always Durocher's town. In an interview after the play, he told a reporter that he really wanted a chance to work for George Steinbrenner, the owner of the

New York Yankees, who was probably as disliked by as many fans as Durocher was. It was not going to happen, but it got Leo ink in New York.[24]

A few months later Steinbrenner came to a point where he demanded Yankee managers who fought with umpires. "Don't tell me baiting umps doesn't do any good," he told Dick Young in April 1982 after he replaced the easygoing Bob Lemon with a more contentious Gene Michael. "All the winning managers are baiting managers." Young then commented: "That's George Steinbrenner—Leo Durocher with money."

IN 1982, DUROCHER was again left out of the Hall of Fame, but Happy Chandler was elected. It came as a complete surprise or, as Joe Durso of *The New York Times* put it, "in electing Chandler, the committee executed one of the more remarkable reversals since voting for the Hall of Fame began in 1936." Durocher began thinking more and more of his exclusion, feeling that he deserved induction.[25]

Leo's appearances on television became fewer and fewer in the 1980s, but when he did appear he could still generate sparks. In 1982, while appearing with NBC-TV broadcaster Bob Costas during a Cubs-Padres game, Durocher was in fine fettle when talk got around to the 1954 World Series and the heroics of the Giants' Dusty Rhodes. "That bum," Leo said. "I couldn't give him . . . away for $1. All I could think of was getting that drunken bum off my back."

After a commercial break, Durocher said, "I'm not allowed to say that on television, am I?"

"You already said it," Costas replied.

"Well, I worked for NBC before," Leo quipped. "That's why they fired me."[26]

Later that same year, Durocher consented to his first in-depth interview with a Chicago newspaper reporter in ten years—Michael Davis of the Field News Service. Leo said little that was new except that he had reunited with the Roman Catholic Church and was receiving weekly Communion. He admitted that his turn to religion was the most significant change in his life in recent years. He said that religion helped him to control his temper and taught him to walk away from confrontation.[27]

In the spring of 1983, Durocher was brought to Spring Training in Palm Springs by California Angels owner Gene Autry as an unofficial member of the club's coaching staff, or as Ross Newhan of the *Los Angeles Times* called him, "a coach without portfolio." The man who was actually behind the hiring of Durocher was Buzzie Bavasi, who felt that Leo was good for the game and had already become a prime advocate for induction into the Hall of Fame.[28]

Durocher's influence on baseball management was at an all-time high, as his style of management was evident in both major leagues. Scott Ostler of the *San Francisco Chronicle* called Leo's more demonstrative protégés the "volcano managers," and they included Earl Weaver, Billy Martin, Jim Fregosi, Gene Mauch, Lou Piniella, and Tommy Lasorda. Like Durocher, these men managed by intimidation, they fought with umpires, refused to talk with the younger reporters, and were death to water coolers and post-game buffet spreads, which they destroyed. As Ostler framed it: If Tommy Lasorda was the jolly version of Durocher, Earl Weaver was the brooding, chain-smoking clone (who picked up Leo's habit of kicking dirt on umpires), and Billy Martin was Durocher recast as a thug.[29]

In July 1983, the seventy-seven-year-old Durocher donned a Cubs uniform for what would prove to be one of the last times. He had been appointed to manage the National League Old Timers team which was to play the American League Old Timers on the eve of the All-Star Game at Comiskey Park in Chicago. He wore the same number 2 as he had for so many years. The uniform was new, as all of his original Cubs uniforms had been eaten by moths or given away to Hollywood pals—specifically Sinatra, Dean Martin, Jerry Lewis, and Jeff Chandler.

For Durocher, this was an event of reunions, regrets, and mea culpas. In an interview with Alan Goldstein of the *Baltimore Sun*, Durocher confirmed the old and oft-heard rumor that he almost became manager of the Baltimore Orioles following the 1961 season after the departure of manager Paul Richards. He told the reporter that he twice turned down the offer because he preferred to live and coach in California. "That was," he admitted, "one of the biggest mistakes of my life." The Orioles hired Billy Hitchcock, who had a short tenure before Hank Bauer replaced him. Bauer brought the Orioles their first championship in 1966, at the end of Leo's first season with the Cubs—the only team he ever managed that finished in last place.

For decades, the one name that could bring Durocher to the boiling point was Happy Chandler, who was on the field that night in Chicago. Now eighty-five, Chandler was a speaker and special guest commemorating the fiftieth anniversary of the first All-Star Game, which had been played in Chicago. At one point, both men were on the field, and Durocher walked over to his old nemesis, who was standing on the third-base line, and shook his hand.

"I'm not a born-again Christian," Leo said, "but as far as I'm concerned, I'm willing to let bygones be bygones." Then, for the cameras, Leo pretended to kick dirt on former umpire Jocko Conlan, who made a fist and gestured at Durocher. Lou Boudreau narrated the pantomime.

After the three-inning old-timers game came to an end, Ernie Banks approached Durocher and in a stage whisper said, "Why don't we play till it's dark? We don't have any place else to go."[30]

Leo smiled and nodded his approval.

In the decade before his own death in 2015, Banks spent many hours with reporter and friend Ron Rapoport: "Ernie said the only time he became truly angry was when Durocher intimated that he was at fault for the Cubs' famous meltdown during the 1969 pennant race. The real problem, Ernie said, was that Durocher was jealous of his popularity. Leo thought he should be Mr. Cub."

Not until both men had retired and Durocher, sensing his mortality, embarked on a charm campaign was the bitterness truly healed. "Leo attended a reunion of the 1969 team many years later," Ernie said, "and stood up and said, 'The one thing I regret about that year is the way I treated Ernie.' That made me feel good."[31]

In 1985, legendary broadcaster Ernie Harwell published his memoir *Tuned to Baseball,* which once again presented Leo's dual nature. The book opened with an account of a fight Durocher had picked with him when Durocher managed the Giants and Harwell was one of the team's radio voices. The team was returning by train from Chicago, and after breakfast Harwell was reading a newspaper when Leo walked up to him and smashed his fist into the newspaper, pushing it into Harwell's face. Harwell jumped up and grabbed Leo in a bear hug. The two fell to the floor, huffing and puffing and trying to land punches but not really hurting one another. Eventually, the two ran out of steam and gave up.

"That was it," Harwell wrote. "No hard feelings, no recriminations. I broadcast four years with the Giants and neither of us ever referred to our fight again. I played golf often with Leo, attended parties with him, and we got along well." Harwell went on to praise Leo: "I believe that Durocher was one of the sharpest managers I've ever worked with. I'm sure he slipped later, but in his Dodger and Giant days he was innings ahead of his rivals. He knew the percentages but was not afraid to play on a hunch."[32]

In January 1987, Jim Murray of the *Los Angeles Times* visited "the old lion in winter at his lair in Palm Springs." He observed: "He's 81, the hair is gone and the eyes are fading but the voice is still piercing, the dugout growl intact. Leo still yells into a phone as if it were an umpire who just missed an easy call at second. The stomach is still flat, the tone firm. Leo doesn't need any shots from life. He still plays it from the back tees. A huge picture of Babe Ruth with his arm around him festoons Leo's den. There are pictures of Herbert Hoover, Will Rogers, Ernest Hemingway, Judge Landis. There are no pictures of former commissioner Albert B. (Happy) Chandler. Happy Chandler, you will recall, is the commissioner who once barred Leo from baseball for a year. The circumstances were the least bit blurry. Any store-front lawyer could have broken the judgment and maybe recovered damages today. But in 1947, baseball was a law unto itself."

On July 26, 1987, the day before Leo turned eighty-two, Billy Williams, Catfish Hunter, and Ray Dandridge were inducted into the Hall of Fame. Leo's rejection by the Veterans Committee was becoming more and more of an issue among sportswriters. "Durocher made a few enemies along the way, but time should have healed those wounds," wrote Steve Wulf in *Sports Illustrated*. "Each March, the veterans committee pretends he never existed."[33]

It would get worse, as Chandler was given a vote on the Veterans Committee. It was clear to Leo's friends that Chandler, now on the Veterans Committee, was settling old scores by blocking Leo's entry. After the 1988 meeting of the committee, when Durocher was again denied membership, Chandler, now ninety, was contacted by Buzzie Bavasi in reference to Durocher's election. Bavasi believed that if Chandler could be persuaded to signal his approval of Durocher, he could be elected. Enclosed with his appeal for Chandler's support was a photocopy of a letter from A. E. "Red" Patterson in which he confessed to have been the one who gave the tickets to Connie Immerman and Memphis Engleberg, proving that Durocher had nothing to do with either man in Havana in 1947. Bavasi then asked Chandler to clear Durocher's name so that he could be elected to the Hall of Fame.[34]

Chandler refused to do so and explained his position in a response to Bavasi that began with a friendly salutation:

> My Dear Buzzie:
>   Leo Durocher made me more trouble during my time as Commissioner than all the other Baseball players in both the

Major Leagues. I frequently talked with Rickey about him, and his need for discipline. Rickey promised me that he would take care of him, but after numerous failures on Rickey's part, I asked him to turn him over to me.

I do not think he is eligible for the Hall of Fame.

In a postscript to the letter, Chandler reminded Bavasi that Supreme Court justice Frank Murphy had said of Durocher, "Surely you can take some disciplinary action against this man."[35]

That same day, Chandler wrote to Pirates executive Joe L. Brown, who was also on the committee and also pushing for Durocher's induction, and made the simple request: "I sincerely hope that you do not elect Leo Durocher to the National Baseball Hall of Fame."[36]

As if Chandler's denial of Durocher needed a postscript dripping in irony, it came in early December when out of the blue Chandler let it be known that he supported efforts to clear the name of "Shoeless" Joe Jackson so that he could be considered for the Hall of Fame. Jackson had been accused of conspiring to throw the 1919 World Series and had been banned from the game in 1920 along with seven other members of the infamous Chicago White Sox team known as the "Chicago Black Sox."[37]

On February 17, 1989 Durocher was badly hurt in an automobile accident, suffering head lacerations when his car struck another vehicle that turned suddenly in front of him. He was hospitalized in serious condition at Desert Hospital in Palm Springs. As he recovered and was quickly upgraded to fair condition, several sportswriters gave him an excellent chance of making the Hall of Fame when the Veterans Committee met on the twenty-eighth.[38]

Durocher was again rejected.

Meanwhile, Chandler was not done with Durocher. Within days of the latest Hall of Fame rejection, the former commissioner published his autobiography, *Heroes, Plain Folks, and Skunks: The Life and Times of Happy Chandler: An Autobiography*. It was written with the help of Vance Trimble, a former editor of the *Kentucky Post* and a Pulitzer Prize winner, who had convinced Chandler to tell his story. "He just reeled it off and I think I was able to get his cadence and personality down," Trimble said in an interview when the book was published.[39]

The book, opened with a jolly introduction by Chandler's old friend Bob Hope, but immediately turned sour and spiteful as Chandler discussed his time as commissioner. He was still bitter about his treatment by the New York reporters, whom he now vilified in print. Dan Parker of the *Mirror* was a "blow-gut," Red Smith of the *Tribune* was "just a damn drunk," and Bill Corum of the *Journal American* was "as nasty as he could be." He dwelt on MacPhail's alcoholic dysfunctionality and general unreliability, added disturbing details to Branch Rickey's role in bringing Jackie Robinson to the majors, and went on for several pages on Robinson's inability to get along with umpires.

He also went after Durocher with renewed vigor. After reporting that Durocher changed his underwear twice a day, he said, "That didn't keep Durocher from being dirty and dangerous." He went on to state that Durocher was too ready to use his fists and that Chandler worried that he might kill somebody. He asserted that Leo's "chief pals" were gangsters such as Joe Adonis, citing "the newspapers" as his source, and called him "a skittish manager" who changed his pitchers and players every ten minutes.[40]

In retrospect, Chandler claimed his decision to ban Durocher from baseball had more to do with cleaning up the game and eradicating "the odor of sleaziness that had so strongly crept in" than any specific charge against or incident involving Durocher. The key ingredient in Chandler's decision was Judge Murphy's letter, which Chandler could not get out of his mind. "If little children couldn't go to the ball parks and look up to the players as their heroes and role models ... what was organized baseball coming to?" The incident with Engleberg and Immerman in Cuba was just one more item to tack onto Durocher's long list of other sins. "It had finally come time to crack down on him."[41]

Before the year was out, Pete Rose accepted a permanent ban from the major leagues after allegations that he gambled on games while he was a player-manager for the Cincinnati Reds. The Rose suspension brought up comparisons to Durocher's banishment. Many errors and exaggerations crept into the reporting of Leo's associations, and it was commonly asserted that he had associated with "gamblers and gangsters." According to one report, he had "gangster pals." As was true in 1947, the term *gangster* still referred to a member of a gang of violent criminals—hardly a description of Engleberg and Immerman, who were sometimes on the dark side of the law in terms of Prohibition and making book, but far short of Murder, Inc.

Irresponsibility and innuendo were the order of the day. George Kimble, a columnist for the *Boston Herald* with nary a hint at a source nor suggesting any evidence, stated: "While the specific charges against Durocher were never made public, a highly plausible scenario subsequently advanced had Durocher playing two parlay bets, the second half of which involved his team. If the first half of his parlay lost, the manager could then switch his own starting pitcher and thereby wipe out the whole bet." Kimble went on to assert that Chandler reportedly had the goods on Leo betting against his own team.[42]

LEO MISSED ELECTION to the Hall of Fame in 1989 by one vote because Red Barber, who was a supporter, was absent from the meeting. As if Durocher needed more negative publicity, in March a few days after the vote, Rick Talley's book *The Cubs of '69: Recollections of the Team That Should Have Been* hit the stores and reminded the world that Durocher had been a target of a gambling probe by then-commissioner Bowie Kuhn after the 1969 season.[43]

For his book Talley had interviewed Durocher in 1988 and found him living in a modest apartment in Palm Springs sustained on the $50,000 a year he got from the Players Association pension. The two men agreed to start out "even" despite their past and Leo told him that he was a regular churchgoer who went to confession once a week. "Sometimes when I go into confession the priest says, 'What are you doing here? You haven't done anything.' I say, 'Well, Father, if you want to go back a few years, I have done a few things.'"[44]

The book did contain the stunning discovery that Lynne had left him because of his heavy gambling. "I left because he started to gamble heavily. He told me when we married, 'I used to gamble, but I don't anymore.' But it was a disease with him."

Talley asked "What kind of gambling?"

"Rolling dice, playing gin at the country club. All he wanted to do was play cards."

Talley asked her if Leo bet on baseball games.

"I'd stake my life against it. I don't think he ever gave information to gamblers either. He had too much respect for the game. Leo was capable of almost anything, but he loved baseball too much. He was too much of a competitor. He had too much pride. It meant too much for him to win to take. If he'd been on the take he would have had money. But he never did."[45]

In February 1990, after five hours and three ballots, the members of the Veterans Committee were unable to elect anyone to the Hall of Fame and were sent home because four of the eighteen committee members were absent, and eleven votes were required for election. After the meeting, Durocher remarked that he believed the absence of Stan Musial, Birdie Tebbetts, Roy Campanella, and Red Barber hurt his chances. "It's entirely up to the committee," said Leo. "I have no control over it. I raised the question about proxy votes."[46]

Sometime later that year Durocher was approached by author Roger Kahn, who would later claim he confronted Durocher with the accusation that the real reason Durocher had been suspended by Chandler for the 1947 season was that he had fixed the 1946 pennant playoffs. Kahn claimed Alex "Shondor" Birns, a Cleveland racketeer, cleaned up, wagering against the Dodgers in their best-of-three tiebreaker series against the St. Louis Cardinals. Kahn reported that his source for the story was Bill Veeck, an acquaintance of Birns who he first met in 1946 shortly before he moved to Cleveland to take ownership of the Indians.

Kahn alleged that Birns and some other gamblers paid Leo to mishandle the Dodger pitching rotation. Birns said he personally made "a killing." For the opening game in Sportsman's Park, St. Louis, Eddie Dyer, the Cardinals manager, started with his twenty-one-game-winning ace Howie Pollet. As Kahn put it, "Durocher responded with a young right-hander, who in time would become famous as the worst pitcher in all the history of postseason playoffs, Ralph Branca." The Cards scored once in the first and two innings later knocked out Branca. Then, with the game slipping away, Durocher called on his own Kirby Higbe. Pollet stayed in command and the Cardinals won 4–2.

"Outrageous. Fucking outrageous," Durocher exploded. "You writers either say I tried to win too hard or that I didn't try to win at all. Double fucking outrageous, and you can print that anywhere you want."*[47]

In January 1991, Durocher made what would be his last trip east, where he was feted by the New York Baseball Writers at their annual dinner.

---

* To investigate Kahn's allegation, which concentrated on the selection of Branca over Higbe in the first game, which struck the author as tenuous at best and lacked any corroboration, I asked several acquaintances more well versed than I am in the analytics of the game to review Durocher's decision. Every response emphasized that the record would not support the claim of a fix.

The most persuasive response came from Alden Mead. "The Kahn accusation is certainly interesting, but personally I remain a bit skeptical. I decided to check on the Dodgers' results for the 1946 season. It's true that Higbe was one of their stalwarts (17–8, 3.03), while Branca was a

Looking frail, he was genuinely touched by being honored with the baseball writers' nostalgia award—and said as much in what was a moving, bittersweet "Thanks for the memories" farewell to New York and Brooklyn.

In February 1991, word came back to Durocher that he had again missed election to the National Baseball Hall of Fame—this time by two votes. Two members of the committee in Durocher's camp absent for the vote were Red Barber, who had missed a plane connection, and Roy Campanella, who was too ill to travel. The two men elected were owner Bill Veeck and Leo's fellow Yankee infielder Tony Lazzeri.

"It's a shame that Leo didn't make it. I think he's living just for this," said Monte Irvin, his most ardent supporter among the former players on the Veterans Committee. "There are a few guys on the committee who are prejudiced against Leo who aren't going to change their minds," Irvin added. "It's too bad, because Leo was one of the greatest managers who ever lived." That night, Irvin called Durocher: "I told him to just hold on and give us one more chance." To this day, Irvin believes that Durocher would have made it if Roy Campanella had not been absent when Leo lost by a single vote.[48]

A month after the 1991 vote, Bavasi again wrote a letter to Pirates executive Joe L. Brown. He noted that Durocher had been two votes shy of election and

---

lesser light used mostly in relief, record 3–1, 3.88. But, Durocher *may* have been influenced by their last series against the Cardinals in Brooklyn, September 12, 13, and 14. Higbe pitched the opener of that series, giving up 6 R, 5 ER, in 2 1/3 IP in a one-sided loss. Hig did better the next day, getting the save with 2 2/3 IP of runless and hitless ball. In the rubber game, Branca started and pitched a three-hit shutout for the win. Not bad! Higbe did have four days rest prior to the first playoff game, so could have gone, but in view of the above results, I don't think that starting the pitcher who had just blanked the enemy can be regarded as deliberately wanting to throw the game. Durocher may have just thought he was selecting the man with the hot hand." (E-mail from Alden Mead, September 12, 2014)

Ultimately if the "fix" was the real reason for the 1947 suspension, it would have been known to Happy Chandler, who suspended Leo. William Marshall, whose book *Baseball's Pivotal Era: 1945–1951* is essentially a biography of Happy Chandler, also recalled nothing in Chandler's papers regarding Kahn's suspicions that Durocher fixed the 1946 playoffs: "In my own interviews with Chandler he noted several reasons for suspending Durocher, but gave no hint whatsoever that it might include a suspected fix in 1946." He adds: "Chandler intensely disliked Durocher and I suspect would have been all over an issue that could have made him the second coming of Landis. Although at age twenty, Ralph Branca was a surprise starter, he already had logged two hundred major league innings and was 21–12, 2.67, the following year. In 1946 the Dodgers' 'big four' (Hatten, Higbe, Lombardi, and Behrman) were not really comparable to the Cardinal rotation. Moreover, I don't believe that Durocher's choice of Branca was 'out-of-character.'" (E-mail from William J. Marshall, September 13, 2014)

that some of the opposition had been unfair. "I can't believe that [Al] Lopez was serious when he said 'That S.O.B. beat me four straight.' Hell that's reason enough to put Leo in the Hall." He also mentioned Jack Brickhouse as another voter refusing to support Durocher. Brickhouse had based his refusal on the fact that Leo would not appear on his television show.

"I hate to think of an old man living alone, thinking about what could have been."

Happy Chandler died on June 15, one month shy of his ninety-third birthday. Almost every published obituary mentioned his suspension of Durocher in 1947, and many incorrectly stated that the cause was Leo's associations with gamblers—not for a more general charge. *The New York Times* had to print a correction to its first Chandler obit: "An obituary by the Associated Press in some editions on Sunday about A. B. (Happy) Chandler, the former baseball commissioner, misstated the reason he gave in 1947 for suspending Leo Durocher, the Brooklyn Dodgers' manager. It was 'the accumulation of unpleasant incidents' resulting in conduct detrimental to baseball, not association with gamblers." Widely noted in the obituaries was that Chandler had been the oldest living member of the National Baseball Hall of Fame.[49]

"It is pretty quiet around his condo in Palm Springs," John Hall wrote of Durocher in the *Orange County Register* on August 2, 1991. "He has not been well for a while. Not even a paragraph anywhere about him when he turned 86 on Saturday. He is frail and failing and forgotten, and it's a shame."[50]

Durocher's bitterness over the Hall of Fame rejection caused him to stop giving interviews. In early October, the documentary filmmaker Ken Burns called to invite him to appear in his forthcoming Public Broadcasting System series on baseball, but Durocher refused to take the call, believing Burns was a reporter. A day or so later, Steve Marcus of *Newsday* called Durocher for a fortieth anniversary piece on the Thomson home run on October 3. A doctor answered the phone, and Marcus asked for Durocher, who then got on the line. Marcus asked if he could ask him about the event:

"How much you paying?"

Marcus said he was not going to pay.

"Then I'm not doing it," Durocher declared as he handed the phone back to the doctor, who hung up the receiver. The exchange took place for a piece that ran on October 4. Durocher died three days later on October 7 at 1:20 P.M. Pacific Daylight Time of "natural causes" at Desert Hospital in Palm Springs. Laraine Day, who had remained friends with her former husband to the end, commented: "He had been so ill, for so long, that he died without too many friends around."[51]

One person who had stayed with him to the end was his old friend Buzzie Bavasi, who talked with Gordon Eades of *The Boston Globe* the night Durocher died. Bavasi said that two weeks earlier he had talked with Durocher, who had told him that he instructed his lawyer not to accept induction if he was elected to the Hall of Fame. "He was so mad at the world," said Bavasi, who had worked long and hard for Durocher's induction. "I think he said it in a fit of anger. I can't believe he meant it, but he said it."

Eades suggested at one point in the interview that perhaps Durocher's death might mean he would now get the votes needed for induction. "I hope not," Bavasi replied. "It'd kill me if he did. I worked so hard to get him in. I can't accept the old man had to die for people to see the light."[52]

In the days following his death, dozens of obituaries and columns were written about Durocher. The postmortems were diverse and far-flung. The *Times* of London called him "sort of a mercurial folk hero."[53] The writers who knew him the longest seemed to be the most ambivalent in their final assessment. To Shirley Povich, Durocher was "a sawed-off, umpire-baiting, loudmouthed tough guy" but also one of the game's finest managers. Joe Gergen referred in his obituary for *Newsday* to the "dichotomy of Durocher."

Bob Broeg of the *St. Louis Post-Dispatch* wrote that losing Leo Durocher was like losing either an old friend or an old enemy—you could take your pick.* Dick Young, sports editor for the *New York Daily News*, probably knew Durocher as well as any of the reporters who covered him. He wrote on Leo's passing: "You and Durocher are on a raft, a wave comes and knocks him into the ocean. You dive in and save his life. A shark comes and takes your leg. Next day, you and Leo start out even."[54]

On the other hand, those who modeled themselves after Durocher were the most effusive in their praise. Said Tommy Lasorda, who went as far as to manage with uniform number 2 in honor of Durocher: "He was brilliant, by far one of the greats. He was a gambling, aggressive manager. He didn't worry about people second-guessing him. He had an electrifying personality with an ability to motivate men."

---

* On the enemy side, Broeg went on to describe the two moments when he and Durocher nearly had fistfights—first when Broeg was a summer intern in 1939 working for the Cardinals public relations office, and in 1946 during the first year he covered sports for the *Post-Dispatch*.

Leo's funeral was held at the Old North Church at Forest Lawn in the Hollywood Hills. About forty family members and friends attended. "When he died," Laraine Day commented, "it was his ballplayers—not Hollywood— who showed up to say goodbye."

Bobby Bragan, now a Texas Rangers executive, but for four seasons in the 1940s a Brooklyn Dodgers catcher-infielder under Durocher, gave the eulogy. "Leo always had a keen sense of timing," Bragan began. "Wouldn't you know that he would swagger through the gates of God's hall of fame while the play-offs were going on." Bragan bemoaned the fact that Durocher, despite having been captain of the "Gashouse Gang" St. Louis Cardinals, and despite having won 2,008 games, was not in the National Baseball Hall of Fame. "He did step on some toes, [but] his accomplishments overshadowed the negatives."

Bragan recalled another side of Durocher: "I think the greatest thing about Leo is that he was as flamboyant and exciting off the field as he was on . . . He had as many friends in the entertainment field as in baseball. The players would go ape meeting those people—Mickey Rooney, Abbott and Costello, Milton Berle, Danny Kaye, Bob Hope, Carol Channing, Mary Martin, Tony Martin."

Bragan added: "He was a nice guy, compassionate. Two years ago when he came to the old timers' game in Texas, 40,000 fans were singing happy birthday to him, and tears were coming down this tough guy's cheeks. I've been in baseball 54 years and the highest honor I've ever been accorded is happening today, being asked to say a few words in honor of Leo. Before today, it was being one of Leo's boys, one of Mr. Rickey's boys."

Bragan shed tears for Leo as he ended his eulogy. So did the other main speaker, Willie Mays, who recalled his slow start with the Giants after he had been brought up from the minor leagues: "I went 0 for 12, I was crying, very disturbed. This man came to me, said, 'You're my center fielder. You don't have to hit, just be Willie Mays.' I can't stress the feeling that I have for this man. All I can say is that I have lost a dear father."

Tony Martin represented Hollywood at the service and paid his tribute by singing "You'll Never Walk Alone" and adding three spoken words at the end, "So long, Leo." As Leo's friends filed by the casket, organist Eileen Doria played a sad, slow tune, so solemn that at first it wasn't recognizable as "Take Me Out to the Ball Game" recast as a dirge. A short time later, at a plot not far from the church, Leo was lowered into the grave, where, as Joe Jares wrote in his *Los Angeles Daily News* account of the funeral, "all of us finish, nice guys and Durochers alike."[55]

The matter of Leo's election of to the Hall of Fame remained. Jim Murray of the *Los Angeles Times*—one of those Leo had told he would decline the election if finally offered—wrote that if put in posthumously, "don't be surprised if Leo comes down and kicks dirt all over it." Murray added: "If Leo Durocher doesn't belong in the Baseball Hall of Fame, neither does Ty Cobb. If Leo Durocher doesn't belong in the Hall of Fame, what are Joe McCarthy, Bill McKechnie, Bucky Harris and Larry MacPhail doing there?"

The next day, the *Los Angeles Times* backed up Murray with a rare sports page editorial which read in part: "Shame on the Baseball Hall of Fame Veterans Committee! To deny Leo Durocher's well-deserved entrance into the Hall of Fame before his passing is unforgivable."[56]

The committee met again in March 1992, and this time missed by a single vote. Bill Conlin commented a few days later in his column in the *Philadelphia Daily News*: "Durocher went to his grave unenshrined because of the illness of aging and infirmed members of a system that smells worse than the billions of clams that rotted on South Jersey beaches last winter."[57]

In 1993, *New York Times* sportswriter Gerald Eskenazi published his book entitled *The Lip: A Biography of Leo Durocher*, which made a strong case that Durocher belonged in the Hall of Fame. He argued that his winning percentage as a manager was .540, with 2,008 victories. Only five managers had won more games.

Finally, in 1994, Durocher got the votes needed to enter the Hall of Fame. The immediate question for those staging the event in Cooperstown was who would accept the honor at the induction. Laraine Day, who was now seventy-three years old and living near Hollywood with her husband, Mike Grilikhes, also a close friend of Durocher's, agreed to represent Leo. Day had retired from acting in 1986 and was now out of the limelight, and many younger baseball fans had no idea who she was and how she fit into baseball history.[58]

Day was a surprising choice for a number of reasons, not the least of which was that, at the time of her divorce from Leo, she had declared that she had never liked baseball. "When our relationship was over," she said "so was my relationship with baseball."[59]

"We were divorced in 1959," she told Sean Kirst of the Syracuse *Post-Standard* in a telephone interview a few days before the induction ceremony. "There was no bitterness. We had just become interested in different things and different people. But we always stayed friends." Day insisted that Leo's public savagery was self-created. "He was a very generous, kind, thoughtful person who put on a great show," Day said.

His favorite players, Day said, shared his kind of fire: Reese, Robinson, Mays, Sal Maglie, Alvin Dark, and Eddie Stanky. She remembered how Leo would weave yarns about his old teammate and later opponent the great Dizzy Dean—how Dean's wife would break things in the women's restroom whenever her husband lost, how Dean concocted wild new biographies for every new set of reporters.

Day admitted that she was feeling a few nerves about her presentation the following Sunday. "I'm afraid I won't know anyone," she said. "I'm afraid they'll all have grown old, or changed." But she had great faith in those whom she called "baseball people."[60]

Durocher's stepson Christopher opened for his mother and brought the crowd to its feet with a few emotion-choked words: "After my father's lifetime in baseball, he spent his days waiting for a phone call from the Hall of Fame. When we first got the call, I thought, 'What a shame.' But as I stand here today with my mother, I can only think that today, Leo Durocher got time off for good behavior to be here with us in spirit." In tears, Chris had to be led back to his seat.

Day's acceptance speech included a plea that Leo be reconsidered as the nice guy he mocked. It was a Hollywood ending that Leo would have appreciated, along with the fact that his plaque would hang on walls shared by some of the men who disliked him most. The plaque read:

COLORFUL, CONTROVERSIAL MANAGER FOR 24 SEASONS. WINNING 2,008 GAMES, 7TH ON ALL-TIME LIST. COMBATIVE, SWASH-BUCKLING STYLE. A CARRYOVER FROM 17 YEARS AS STRONG FIELDING SHORTSTOP FOR MURDERERS ROW YANKS, GASHOUSE GANG CARDS, REDS AND DODGERS. MANAGED CLUBS TO PENNANTS IN 1941 AND 1951 AND TO WORLD SERIES WIN IN 1954. 3-TIME SPORTING NEWS MANAGER OF THE YEAR.

"Leo Durocher must be livid someplace today," Jim Murray wrote in the *Los Angeles Times*. "Somewhere today, Durocher is looking for a helmet to throw, a water cooler to kick, an umpire to insult, a signal for his pitcher to hit somebody. I can hear him roaring, 'You can't do this to me!' It's too little, too late."[61]

Acknowledgments

Before I began working on this biography, I discussed Leo Durocher with fellow writer Ray Robinson. Now ninety-four, Ray's knowledge of baseball history is largely based on his own experience and friendship with players and managers, including Jackie Robinson and Bobby Thomson. Ray, who is both fascinated with and disdainful of Durocher because of the way he treated him, aimed a double-barreled question at me:

"Do you really want to spend two years with this guy? And do you think you have anything new to say about him?"

Ray's first question was loaded in that he was clearly implying that Durocher would prove increasingly despicable over time. The last time Ray had tried to speak to Durocher, which was for a piece in *The New York Times*, Durocher had told Ray to go "fuck himself." The message was actually relayed by his third wife, Laraine Day.

I thought about Ray's first question for a while, and as for spending two years with Durocher, the answer is yes—for reasons of age, temperament, investigative skills, and my enduring fascination with the era, I think I am the person to write about Durocher and his times. This was, more or less, what I told Ray.

I also explained to him that I grew up during this time with close associations with the game as it was played in New York and its environs, and Durocher seemed to work his way into just about every conversation about baseball in the city.

As for Ray's second question about saying something new, his point is well-taken. Durocher is one of the most oft-quoted figures in baseball history, wrote two autobiographies with the help of talented ghostwriters, and has been the subject of one biography written by Gerald Eskenazi twenty years before he was voted into the National Baseball Hall of Fame, but the author of this book believes he has said something new with the help of these folks listed in alphabetical order:

John Andrews OBE; Marty Appel.

Jack Bales; Allen Barra; Rick Bates; Edwin Bearss; Brad Beechen; Associated Press baseball writer Hal Bock; Professor Stephen Butler.

Terry Cannon; George Castle; Bill Christine; Ron Cohen, who covered the Durocher "alienation of affection" trial in Middlebury, Vermont, for UPI.

Nancy Dickson, as always.

Roberto González Echevarría; Chris Eckes, curator of the Cincinnati Reds Museum.

Dick Fischman; Jeffrey M. Flannery of the Manuscript Division of the Library of Congress; David Fletcher.

Dick Garten; Jim Gates; library director, National Baseball Hall of Fame and Museum; Stephen J. Gertz (cousin of "Sleepout Louie"); Neil P. Gillen; Peter Golenbock; as always, Joe Goulden; Jack Greiner; Robert Gruber.

Bill Hageman of the *Chicago Tribune*; Arnold Hano; Matthew Harris of the University of Kentucky Library; the late Dick Heller; Paul Hensler; Dr. Lawrence Hogan; John Horne; David Hubler.

The late Monte Irvin.

Gary Johnson of the Periodical Reading Room at the Library of Congress, Cooperstown, NY, mayor and fellow writer Jeff Katz; Dave Kelly; Ralph Keyes; Valerie Komar, director, Associated Press Corporate Archives; Karl J. Krayer, Ph.D., president of Creative Communication Network.

Cassiday Lent; Jon Leonoudakis; Bill Lucey; Bob Luke.

Skip McAfee, Cliff McCarthy of the Wood Museum of Springfield History in Springfield, MA; Bruce Marcusen; Jerry McCoy; Andy McCue; Diane Mallstrom, reference librarian, Public Library of Cincinnati & Hamilton County; Steven Marcus at *Newsday*; Alejandro Mayorkas; Alden Mead; Bill Mead; Vick Mickunas; Leigh Montville; Aly Mostel.

Andrew O'Toole.

John Pekkanen; Francesca Pitaro, Associated Press Corporate Archives; Bennett Price.

Ron Rabinowitz; Ron Rapoport, former sports columnist for the *Chicago Sun-Times* and the *Los Angeles Daily News*; Chris Rhodes; Ray Robinson.

Judy Sackett, University of Kentucky; Gary Sarnoff; John Schulian; Mike Shannon; Joe Simpich; Bob Skole; Brad Snyder; Jim Srodes.

Mary Frances Veeck; Bob Verdi of the *Chicago Tribune*; Dick Victory.

Russ White, formerly of the *Washington Star*; Andy Wirkmaa.

Dr. Richard B. Zamoff, director of the Jackie Robinson Project, George Washington University; Martin Zelnik.

In addition, thanks to The League of Distinguished Gentlemen and the Hamlet Group for aid and comfort during the preparation of this book.

Finally, many thanks to my agent, Deborah Grosvenor, and my editor, George Gibson, for making this book possible. Gratitude to my neighbor and friend Dan Marsh for his copyedit of the final manuscript and to old friend Bill Young for his many hours of editorial help. Thanks also to Skip McAfee for his special baseball fact check and to Sara Kitchen for her work producing the book itself.

Bibliography

If there was a single source that proved most important in getting to Durocher, it would have to be the writing and collected letters and papers of Arthur Mann (1901–1969). Mann considered himself a friend and critic of Durocher. He got to know Leo when he was a reporter for the *New York World* when Leo arrived for his 1925 cup of coffee with the New York Yankees. Mann's book *Baseball Confidential* was an account and a defense of Leo in the wake of his suspension, but also amounted to a Durocher biography. The thirteen boxes of Mann's papers ended up in the Manuscript Division of the Library of Congress—within feet of the papers of Jackie Robinson and Branch Rickey—allowing this author to gain insight that would have otherwise been denied. In addition the Rickey papers were invaluable, as they detail elements of his relationship with Durocher that are contained in memos marked confidential.

In the last few years key newspapers such as the old *New York Herald Tribune* have been digitized and made accessible through proprietary databases at the Library of Congress. The *Trib* sports department employed writers such as Red Smith, Roger Kahn, Bob Cooke, and Harold Rosenthal. Stanley Woodward and Jimmy Breslin covered the Giants and Dodgers like no others. In addition, other less widely circulated newspapers have been digitized. In terms of Durocher, a key addition to the digital world has been the full run of the *Brooklyn Eagle*, which includes the column bylined by Durocher but ghosted by Harold Parrott.

African-American newspapers are now machine searchable and invaluable in looking at things such as Durocher's fascination with Silvio Garcia. Durocher was a different man to black sports reporters, to whom he was civil and cooperative.

Other sources are still in an earlier format. I have worked with the microfilm records of the *Daily Worker* at the Tamiment Labor Archives at New York University to detail Durocher's early comments on race and the relationship of the Brooklyn Dodgers to the Communist Party.

In addition, there are scores of oral histories waiting to be tapped, including a number available from the National Baseball Library, the Society for American

Baseball Research (SABR), the A. B. "Happy" Chandler Oral History Collection at the University of Kentucky, and those collected by former commissioner Fay Vincent in 2003–04 that can be accessed through the Library of Congress. Durocher himself thwarted long interviews, using as his shield a demand to be paid exorbitantly—on one occasion $100,000.

I have been loaned envelopes on Durocher and Laraine Day filled with fragile clippings from a newspaper morgue that contains a wealth of material from the *Chicago American* (the paper of the "Front Page") but also included items from the *New York Journal American* and other newspapers whose pages will probably never be digitized or otherwise preserved. The glory of these thousands of clips is that they often lack the restraint of the "papers of record," such as *The New York Times*, *Washington Post*, and *Chicago Tribune*, whose archives are a keystroke away. The editor who loaned me these clippings—which were stored in a sub-basement of the *Chicago Tribune* after the *Chicago American* went out of business—told me that he doubted anybody had looked at them in more than thirty years.

The clips contain material that add color and zest to the book, including, for example, the account of Durocher flying with Greta Garbo to the West Coast when he advised her to avoid salads if she wanted to prevent airsickness. He also told her he advised his players to stay away from salad as it "softens the bones." Then there is the clip about a group of Harvard baseball players who wanted Durocher to take over their team in the wake of his 1947 suspension. These are examples of stories that did not make the major papers like *The New York Times*, *Chicago Tribune*, and *Los Angeles Times*. Admittedly the Garbo/Durocher plane ride and the Harvard story are trivial in isolation but not in the context of a biography.

In addition, here are the newspapers and magazines that I employed with the greatest regularity:

Atlanta Constitution	*New York Herald Tribune*
Baltimore Afro-American	*New York Times*
Baltimore Sun	*New York World*
Boston Globe	*Newsday*
Boston Herald	*Newsweek*
Boston Traveler	*St. Louis Post-Dispatch*
Chicago Tribune	*Sports Illustrated*
Christian Science Monitor	*Sporting News*
Daily Worker	*Springfield Republican*
Evening Star (Washington, D.C.)	*Springfield Union*
Hartford Courant	*Washington Post*
New York Amsterdam News	*Washington Star*

Adams, Caswell. "Has Suspension Ruined Durocher?" *Varsity: The Young Man's Magazine*, March 1948.

Algren, Nelson. *Nonconformity: Writing on Writing*. New York: Seven Stories Press, 1997.

Anderson, Dave. "Leo the Lip Was Baseball in New York." *The New York Times* (October 9, 1991): B11.

Arthur Mann Papers, Manuscript Division, Library of Congress, Washington, D.C.

Auker, Elden with Tom Keegan. *Sleeper Cars and Flannel Uniforms: a Lifetime of Memories from Striking Out the Babe to Teeing It Up with the President*. Chicago: Triumph Books, 2001.

Barber, Red. *1947: When All Hell Broke Loose in Baseball*. New York: Chelsea House, 1991.

Barney, Rex, with Norman L. Macht, *Rex Barney's Thank Youuuu for 50 Years in Baseball from Brooklyn to Baltimore*. Centreville, MD: Tidewater Publishers, 1991.

Barrow, Edward Grant, with James M. Kahn. *My Fifty Years in Baseball*. New York: Coward-McCann, 1951.

Barthel, Tom, "Ducky and the Lip in Italy." *The National Pastime: A Review of Baseball History*, Number 23. Cleveland: The Society for American Baseball Research, 2003.

Bavasi, Buzzie, and John Strege. *Off the Record*. Chicago: Contemporary Books, 1987.

Bryant, Howard. *Shut Out: A Story of Race and Baseball in Boston*, Boston, MA: Beacon Press, 2003.

Boston, Talmage, *1939, Baseball's Pivotal Year: From the Golden Age to the Modern Era*. Fort Worth, TX: The Summit Group, 1994.

Bouton, Jim, with Neil Offen. *I Managed Good, but Boy Did They Play Bad*. Chicago: Playboy Press, 1973.

Branca, Ralph. *A Moment in Time: An American Story of Baseball, Heartbreak, and Grace*. New York: Scribner, 2011.

Branch Rickey Papers, Manuscript Division, Library of Congress, Washington, D.C.

Brickhouse, Jack, with Jack Rosenberg and Ned Colletti, *Thanks for Listening*. South Bend, IN: Diamond Communications, Inc. 1986.

Broun, Heywood Hale. "Backtalk: The One Time Leo the Lip Kept It Buttoned." *The New York Times* (October 13, 1991).

Camerer, Dave. *The Best of Grantland Rice*. New York: Franklin Watts Inc., 1963.

Campanella, Roy. *It's Good to Be Alive*. Boston: Little, Brown & Co., 1959.

Castle, George. *The Million-to-One Team: Why the Chicago Cubs Haven't Won a Pennant Since 1945*. Boulder, CO: Taylor Trade Publishing, 2000.

Chandler, Albert B., with Vance H. Trimble. *Heroes, Plain Folks, and Skunks: The Life and Times of Happy Chandler.* Chicago: Bonus Books, 1989.

Claerbaut, David. *Durocher's Cubs: The Greatest Team That Didn't Win.* Dallas, TX: Taylor Publishing, 2000.

Cohen, Stanley. *A Magic Summer: The Amazing Story of the 1969 New York Mets.* New York: Skyhorse Publishing, 2009.

———. *Dodgers! The First One-Hundred Years.* New York: Carol Publishing Group, 1990.

Creamer, Robert W. *Babe: The Legend Comes to Life.* New York: Simon & Schuster, 1992.

D'Antonio, Michael. *Forever Blue: The True Story of Walter O'Malley, Baseball's Most Controversial Owner, and the Dodgers of Brooklyn and Los Angeles.* New York: Riverhead Books, 2009.

Daley, Arthur. *Times at Bat: A Half Century of Baseball.* New York, Random House, 1950.

Day, Laraine. *Day with the Giants.* Edited by Kyle Crichton. Garden City, New York: Doubleday & Co., 1952.

Desmond, Dan. "Baseball's Bad Boy." *Chicago Herald-American* (December 16, 1948).

———. "Durocher Right at Home with Gas House Gang." *Chicago Herald-American* (December 20, 1948).

Duin, Steve. "When Life Was a Breeze." *Portland Oregonian* (August 6, 1987): 17.

Durocher, Leo. *The Dodgers and Me: The Inside Story.* Chicago: Ziff-Davis, 1948.

Durocher, Leo, and Barney Kremenko, "As He Rose to the Majors, No One Who Saw Him Play Doubted He Would Be a Star." *The New York Times* (July 29, 1979).

Durocher, Leo, with Ed Linn. *Nice Guys Finish Last.* New York: Simon and Schuster, 1975, and Chicago: University of Chicago Press, 2009.

———. "The Candid Memoirs of Leo Durocher." *The Saturday Evening Post* (January 18, 1964).

Durocher, Leo, as told to Harry T. Paxton, "How I Watched a Ball Game." *The Saturday Evening Post* (August 7, 1954).

Eals, Clay. *Steve Goodman: Facing the Music.* Toronto: ECW Press, 2007.

Enright, James. "Look What Durocher Got for His Nickel." *Chicago Today* (September 24, 1972): 10.

Enright, Jim, *Baseball's Great Teams: Chicago Cubs.* New York: A Rutledge Book, Macmillan Publishing Co., 1975.

Eskenazi, Gerald. *The Lip: A Biography of Leo Durocher.* New York: William Morrow, 1993.

Feldmann, Doug. *Miracle Collapse: The 1969 Cubs.* Lincoln, NE: University of Nebraska Press, 2006.

Fitzgerald, Ed. "Leo Durocher—Man with Nine Lives." *Sport* (April 1951).

Fitzpatrick, Tom. *Fitz: All Together Now:* New York: David McKay Co., 1972.

Flavin, Harold. "Leo the Lip." *Springfield Journal* (March 26, 1998).

Frank, Stanley. "The Name of the Game." *The Saturday Evening Post* (May 23, 1942).

Frommer, Harvey. *Baseball's Greatest Managers.* New York: Chelsea House, 1991.

Gilbert, Bill. *They Also Served: Baseball and the Home Front, 1941–1945.* New York: Crown Publishers, 1992.

Gildea, William. "For Leo the Lip, Photos Recall Clear Images." *The Washington Post* (October 26, 1984): E-5.

Gold, Eddie, and Art Ahrens. *The New Era Cubs, 1941–1985.* Chicago: Bonus Books, 1985.

Gorman, Tom. *Three and Two: The Autobiography of Tom Gorman the Great Major League Umpire as Told to Jerome Holtzman.* New York, Charles Scribner, 1979.

Graham, Frank Jr., *The Brooklyn Dodgers: An Informal History.* Carbondale, IL: Southern Illinois University Press, 2003.

———, "The Durocher Story." *Chicago Herald American* (September 22, 1954).

———, *A Farewell to Heroes.* Carbondale, IL: Southern Illinois University Press, 2003.

———, *The New York Giants: An Informal History of a Great Baseball Club.* Carbondale, IL: Southern Illinois University Press, 2002.

Hano, Arnold. *A Day in the Bleachers.* New York: Thomas Y. Crowell, 1955.

Harwell, Ernie. *Tuned to Baseball.* South Bend, IN: Diamond Communications, 1985.

Hazucha, Andrew. "Leo Durocher's Last Stand: Anti-Semitism, Racism, and the Cubs Player Rebellion of 1971." *NINE: A Journal of Baseball History and Culture* 15: 1 (Fall 2006): 1–12.

Heidenry, John. *The Gashouse Gang: How Dizzy Dean, Leo Durocher, Branch Rickey, Pepper Martin, and Their Colorful, Come-from-Behind Ball Club Won the World Series and America's Heart During the Great Depression.* New York: Public Affairs, 2007.

Heller, Dick. "Durocher's Switch to Giants Was a Real Shocker in '48," *The Washington Times* (July 21, 2003).

Hirsch, James S., *Willie Mays: The Life, the Legend.* New York: Simon & Schuster, 2010.

Hogan, Lawrence D. *Shades of Glory: The Negro Leagues and the Story of African-American Baseball.* Washington, D.C.: National Geographic, 2006.

Holland, Gerald. "Mr. Rickey and the Game." *Sports Illustrated* (March 7, 1955).

Holmes, Tommy. *The Dodgers.* New York: Macmillan, 1975.

Holtzman, Jerome, and George Vass. *Baseball, Chicago Style*. Revised ed. Los Angeles: Taylor Trade Publishing, 2005.

Holway, John. *Josh and Satch: The Life and Times of Josh Gibson and Satchel Paige*. New York: Carroll & Graf Publishers/R. Gallen, 1992.

Honig, Donald. *The Man in the Dugout: Fifteen Big League Managers Speak Their Minds*. Lincoln, NE: University of Nebraska Press, 1995.

———. *The October Heroes: Great World Series Games Remembered by the Men Who Played Them*. Lincoln, NE: University of Nebraska Press, 1996.

Hynd, Noel. *The Giants of Polo Grounds: The Glorious Times of Baseball's New York Giants*. New York: Doubleday, 1988.

Isaacs, Neil D. *Batboys and the World of Baseball*. Studies in Popular Culture. Jackson, MS: University Press of Mississippi, 1995.

Jenkins, Ferguson. *Like Nobody Else: The Fergie Jenkins Story*. New York: NTC/Contemporary Publishing, 1973.

Kahn, Roger. *The Era, 1947–1957: When the Yankees, the Giants, and the Dodgers Ruled the World*. New York: Ticknor & Fields, 1993.

———. *Rickey and Robinson: The True, Untold Story of the Integration of Baseball*. Emmaus, PA: Rodale Books, 2014.

———, "They Ain't Getting No Maiden." *The Saturday Evening Post* (June 18, 1966).

Kaplan, Richard. "Leo Durocher, Headline Hustler Extraordinary." *Climax—Exciting Stories for Men* (June 1960).

Keenan, Jimmy. "From the Gashouse to the Glasshouse: Leo Durocher and the 1972–73 Houston Astros." *The National Pastime Annual* (2014).

Keyes, Ralph. *"Nice Guys Finish Seventh": False Phrases, Spurious Sayings and Familiar Misquotations*. New York: HarperCollins, 1992.

Kirst, Sean. "Baseball Makes Immortal a Man, a Romance an Era," *Syracuse Post-Standard* (July 28, 1994).

Koppett, Leonard. *The Man in the Dugout: Baseball's Top Managers and How They Got That Way*. Philadelphia: Temple University Press, 2000.

Koufax, Sandy, and Ed Linn. *Koufax*. New York: Viking, 1966.

Kram, Mark. "He's All About Sunshine." *Sports Illustrated* (November 28, 2013).

Lamb, Chris. *Blackout: The Untold Story of Jackie Robinson's First Spring Training*. Lincoln, NE: University of Nebraska Press, 2004.

———. *Conspiracy of Silence: Sportswriters and the Long Campaign to Desegregate Baseball*. Lincoln, NE: University of Nebraska Press, 2012.

Lanctot, Neil. *Negro League Baseball: The Rise and Ruin of a Black Institution*. Philadelphia: University of Pennsylvania Press, 2008.

Lewis, Lloyd. "It Takes All Kinds—Leo Durocher's Will to Win." *Chicago Sun-Times* (May 16, 1948).

MacPhail, Lee. *My 9 Innings: An Autobiography of 50 Years in Baseball.* Norwalk, CT: Mecklermedia, 1989.

Madden, Bill. *1954: The Year Willie Mays and the First Generation of Black Superstars Changed Major League Baseball Forever.* Boston: Da Capo Press, 2014.

Mandell, David. "The Suspension of Leo Durocher." *The National Pastime: A Review of Baseball History* 27 (2007): 101–104.

Mann, Arthur. *Baseball Confidential: Secret History of the War Among Chandler, Durocher, MacPhail, and Rickey.* New York: David McKay Company, 1951.

———, "Baseball's Ugly Duckling—Durable Durocher." *The Saturday Evening Post* (August 19, 1939): 14–15, 65–68.

Marlett, Jeffrey. "Durocher as Machiavelli: Bad Catholic, Good American." *The Cooperstown Symposium on Baseball and American Culture, 2007–2008,* Bill Simons, ed. Jefferson, NC: McFarland Press, 2009.

Marx, Groucho. "What's Wrong with the Giants?" *Collier's* (July 18, 1953): 13–15.

Maule, Tex. "The Return of Durocher." *Sports Illustrated* (March 6, 1961).

Mays, Willie, as told to Charles Einstein, *Willie Mays: My Life in and out of Baseball.* New York: E.P. Dutton & Co., 1966.

Mays, Willie, and Lou Sahadi. *Say Hey: The Autobiography of Willie Mays.* New York: Simon & Schuster, 1988.

Meany, Tom. "Brooklyn Must Win—or Else!" *Look* (June 3, 1941).

———. "Dr. Jekyll and Mr. Durocher." *Look* (July 11, 1944).

———. "Durocher: Always on the Spot." *Sport* (April 1947).

Millstein, Gilbert. "Durocher on Durocher et al.: The Manager of the Giants, at 45, Produces Some Apothegms Based on Experience with Ballplayers, Umpires and People." *The New York Times* (July 22, 1951), 131; reprinted in *The Fireside Book of Baseball.*

Murdock, Eugene. *Baseball Players and Their Times: Oral Histories of the Game, 1920–1940.* Westport, CT: Meckler, 1991.

Neft, David, and Richard Cohen, eds. *The Sports Encyclopedia: Baseball,* 16th ed. New York: St. Martin's Griffin, 1996.

Neyer, Rob. *Rob Neyer's Big Book of Baseball Legends: The Truth, the Lies, and Everything Else.* New York: Touchstone, 2008.

Parker, Clifton Blue. *Big and Little Poison: Paul and Lloyd Waner, Baseball Brothers.* Jefferson, NC: McFarland Press, 2003.

Parrott, Harold. "Leo the Lip." *This Week* (April 16, 1939), TW4.

———. *The Lords of Baseball: A Wry Look at a Side of the Game the Fan Seldom Sees, the Front Office.* 2nd ed. Atlanta: Longstreet Press, 2001.

Phalen, Rick. *Our Chicago Cubs.* South Bend, IN: Diamond Communications, 1992.

Pinelli, Babe. *Mr. Ump.* Philadelphia: Westminster Press, 1953.

Poe, Randall. "The Writing of Sports." *Esquire* (October 1974).

Polier, Dan. "Leo Durocher Almost Became a Marine Before He Bounced Back to Brooklyn on His 4-F Ear." *Yank* (March 26, 1943).

Polner, Murray. *Branch Rickey: A Biography.* New York: New American Library, 1982.

Powers, Jimmy. *Baseball Personalities.* New York: Rudolph Field, 1949.

Prager, Joshua. *The Echoing Green: The Untold Story of Bobby Thomson, Ralph Branca, and the Shot Heard Round the World.* New York: Pantheon, 2006.

Prince, Carl E. *Brooklyn's Dodgers: The Bums, the Borough, and the Best of Baseball, 1947–1957.* New York: Oxford University Press, 1996.

Rapoport, Ron. "The Last Days of Ernie Banks." *Chicago* (October 2015).

———. "Leo Durocher: The Spit Take and the Bow." *Chicago Sun-Times* (January 18, 1983).

Rhodes, Greg, and John Snyder. *Redleg Journal: Year by Year and Day by Day with the Cincinnati Reds Since 1866.* Cincinnati, OH: Road West Publishing Co., 2000.

Rice, Damon. *Seasons Past.* New York: Praeger, 1976.

Rust, Art, *Get That Nigger off the Field: An Oral History of Black Ballplayers from the Negro Leagues to the Present.* Los Angeles: Shadow Lawn Press, 1992.

Shapiro, Milton J. *The Willie Mays Story.* New York: Julian Messner, 1962.

Shatzkin, Mike, ed. *The Ballplayers: Baseball's Ultimate Biographical Reference.* New York: Arbor House, William Morrow, 1990.

Shrake, Edwin. "'I Talk Real Polite and Nice'—That Is the Leo Durocher Who Gets Cornered by Troublemakers, but at 67 He Can Still Flay a Hide When He Chooses To." *Sports Illustrated* (August 13, 1973).

Shaplen, Robert. "The Nine Lives of Leo Durocher." *Sports Illustrated.* Part I: Bridge to Yesterday, May 23, 1955. Part II: At the Gashouse, May 30, 1955. Part III: The Buttoned Lip, June 6, 1955. (This three-part series provides material from interviews with Sidney Weil, David Redd, Branch Rickey, and Leo himself, and is key to an understanding of Durocher.)

Silber, Irwin. *Press Box Red: The Story of Lester Rodney, the Communist Who Helped Break the Color Line in American Sports.* Philadelphia: Temple University Press, 2003.

Smith, Robert. *Baseball.* New York: Simon & Schuster, 1970.

Soderholm-Difatte, Bryan. "Durocher the Spymaster: How Much Did the Giants Prosper from Cheating in 1951?" *The Baseball Record Journal,* SABR 41: 2 (Fall 2012): 77–86.

Steadman, Joe. "Chin Music." *Baseball Digest* (September 2000), 50.

Stein, Fred. *Under Coogan's Bluff: A Fan's Recollections of the New York Giants Under Terry and Ott.* Glenshaw, PA: Chapter and Cask, 1981.

Steinberg, Steve, and Lyle Spatz. *The Colonel and Hug: The Partnership That Transformed the New York Yankees.* Lincoln, NE: University of Nebraska Press, 2015.

Stengel, Casey. *Casey at the Bat: The Story of My Life in Baseball,* as told to Harry T. Paxton. New York: Random House, 1962.

Talley, Rick. *The Cubs of '69: Recollections of the Team That Should Have Been.* Chicago: Contemporary Books, 1989.

———. "The Untamed Lion," five-part series in *Chicago Today* (July 5–10, 1970).

Thomson, Bobby, with Lee Heiman and Bill Gutman. *"The Giants Win the Pennant! The Giants Win the Pennant!"* New York: Zebra Books, 1991.

Thorn, John, Pete Palmer, and David Reuther, eds. *Total Baseball.* 2nd ed. New York: Warner Books, 1991.

Thorn, John, and Jules Tygiel. "The Signing of Jackie Robinson." *Sport* 79 (June 1988): 66, 69–70.

Time. "Again, Baseball" (April 15, 1929).

Time. "The Lip" (April 14, 1947).

Treder, Steve. "A Legacy of What-ifs: Horace Stoneham and the Integration of the Giants." *NINE: A Journal of Baseball History and Culture* 10, no. 2 (2002): 71–101.

Tygiel, Jules. *Baseball's Great Experiment: Jackie Robinson and His Legacy.* 25th anniversary edition. New York: Oxford University Press, 2008.

Vass, George. "Baseball's In-house Fights: Teammate Antagonisms Create Turmoil: Clubhouse Scraps Have Long Been a Part of the Game's History." *Baseball Digest* (September 2007).

Vecsey, George. "Sports of the Times: The Lion Roars a Little." *The New York Times* (May 24, 1987).

Veeck, Bill. "Durocher Comes to Win, Not Particular How." *Los Angeles Times* (October 31, 1965).

Vitti, Jim. *Brooklyn Dodgers in Cuba (Images of Baseball).* Charleston, SC: Arcadia Publishing, 2011.

Warfield, Don. *The Roaring Redhead: Larry MacPhail, Baseball's Great Innovator.* Boulder, CO: Taylor Trade Publishing, 1987.

Weil, Sidney. *The Memoirs of Sidney Weil.* Cincinnati and Evanston, IL: published by the Weil family, 1966.

Williams, Dick, and Bill Plaschke. *No More Mr. Nice Guy: A Life of Hardball.* San Diego: Harcourt, Brace Jovanovich, 1990.

Williams, Peter. "You *Can* Blame the Media: The Role of the Press in Creating Baseball Villains." *Cooperstown Symposium on Baseball and American Culture (1989).* Alvin L. Hall, ed. Westport, CT, and Oneonta, NY: Meckler Publishing and State University of New York, 1991, 343–60.

Wood, Gerald C., and Andrew Hazucha, *Northsiders: Essays on the History, and the Culture of the Chicago Cubs*. Jefferson, NC: McFarland Press, 2008.

Woodard, David E. "Durocher, Leo (1905–1991)." *St. James Encyclopedia of Popular Culture*. Thomas Riggs, ed. 2nd ed., vol. 2. Detroit: St. James Press, 2013.

Woodward, Stanley. "That Guy Durocher!" *The Saturday Evening Post* (June 3, 1950): 25–27.

Zachter, Mort. "If Gil Hodges Managed the Cubs and Leo Durocher the Mets in 1969, Whose 'Miracle' Would It Have Been?" *The National Pastime*, Society for American Baseball Research, 2015.

Notes

CHAPTER 1: PREGAME

1. *Chicago Herald-American*, April 10, 1947, p. 34.
2. Ibid., December 18, 1948, 11; *The Washington Post*, May 8, 1949, p. C-1.
3. Harold Parrott, *The Lords of Baseball: A Wry Look at a Side of the Game the Fan Seldom Sees, the Front Office*, 2nd ed. (Atlanta: Longstreet Press, 2001), p. 197; *Sports Illustrated*, June 6, 1955, p. 72.
4. Sean Kirst interview with Day, *Syracuse Post-Standard*. July 28, 1994.
5. *Newsday*, February 27, 1994, p. 26.
6. Interview with David Hubler, November 3, 2015.
7. Leo Durocher, with Ed Linn. *Nice Guys Finish Last*. (New York: Simon & Schuster, 1975), p. 26.
8. Neil D. Isaacs, *Batboys and the World of Baseball*, Studies in Popular Culture (Jackson, MS: University Press of Mississippi, 1995), p. 119.
9. Lawrence D. Hogan, *Shades of Glory: The Negro Leagues and the Story of African-American Baseball* (Washington, D.C.: National Geographic, 2006), p. 332.
10. Babe Pinelli, *Mr. Ump* (Philadelphia: Westminister, 1953), p. 138.
11. David Claerbaut, *Durocher's Cubs: The Greatest Team That Didn't Win* (Dallas, TX: Taylor Trade Publishing, 2000), pp. 21–22.
12. *St. Louis Post-Dispatch*, October 9, 1991, p. 14.

CHAPTER 2: ENFANT TERRIBLE

1. Mann, p. 4.
2. Tom Meany, "Durocher: Always on the Spot." *Sport* (April 1947), p. 65.
3. Flavin, Harold. "Leo the Lip." *Springfield Journal* (March 26, 1998), p. 1.
4. See, for example, http://www.newenglandhistoricalsociety.com/leo-durocher-springfield-boy/.
5. Flavin, Harold. "Leo the Lip." *Springfield Journal* (March 26, 1998), p. 6.
6. *Brooklyn Eagle* (August 20, 1928), p. 20; "Renew Rivalry Tomorrow at NL Park," *Springfield Republican* (October 7, 1928), p. 16. As for Maranville befriending young Leo and giving him a glove, there is not a single reference to such a relationship in the accounts of the many games he played opposite Maranville in the National League. This lifelong faux association with Maranville dated back as far as 1919 when he claimed that he learned from Maranville, who played semipro baseball with Leo's father in Springfield.

7. *The Boston Globe*, April 25, 1929.

8. *Springfield Republican*, July 4, 1922, p. 12; October 31, 1922, p. 5.

9. Ibid., October 5, 1941, p. 47.

10. Ibid., March 8, 1922, p. 4.

11. TK

12. *Baltimore Afro-American*, March 13, 1948, p. 7. This is an interview with Durocher by Sam Lacy. *Chicago American*, March 20, 1966, Chicago newspaper morgue.

13. *Sports Illustrated*, May 23, 1956, p. 67.

14. *Hartford Courant*, April 16, 1925, p. 10. Over time, however, Durocher chose not to accept this mundane version of his departure and cast it in vastly different terms in interviews with *Sports Illustrated* and other magazines and in an even more dramatic version in his own autobiography. Leo's version went like this: As his leave from Wico was nearing an end, he confronted O'Connor in his office and laid it out. "What about it? You haven't said a word since I got here. Am I good enough? Do I get the job?" According to Durocher, O'Connor replied with a noncommittal grunt and Leo "exploded in anger" and then he handed in his Hartford uniform and headed back to Springfield and the security of a regular job. At the very least, the Durocher version of his departure from Hartford seemed to display a need to frame his early life in terms of confrontation and anger. Quite simply and certainly, Leo was cut and O'Connor let him go while—as he later reported—keeping an eye on him with the idea that he could bring him back if needed. Hartford and Springfield are only thirty miles apart.

15. *Hartford Courant*, April 22, 1925, p. 14. This account and others about the Hartford team neglect to give Rose's first name.

16. *Bridgeport Post*, April 23, 1925, p. 10; *Bridgeport Times*, April 23, 1925, p. 6; *Hartford Courant*, April 23, 1925, p. 11; *Hartford Times*, April 23, 1925, p. 30.

17. *Hartford Courant*, April 25, 1925, p. 11; April 26, 1925, p. 28.

18. Ibid., May 21, 1925, p. 19; June 20, 1925, p. 12.

19. Ibid., June 21, 1925, p. B-9.

20. Ibid., July 13, 1925, p. 1.

21. *Springfield Republican*, July 18, 1925, p. 5, *Hartford Courant*, July 18, 1925, p. 11.

22. *New York Evening Journal*, August 31, 1925.

23. *Sports Illustrated*, May 23, 1955, p. 68.

24. The canceled $5,000 check sold at auction in 2014 for $711. http://www.robertedwardauctions.com/auction/2014_spring/1146.html#photos.

25. *Springfield Republican*, July 23, 1925, p. 10.

26. *Los Angeles Times*, July 23, 1925, p. 12. *Hartford Courant*, July 23, 1925, p. 10.

27. *Hartford Courant*, July 14, 1943, p. 13.

28. *The Boston Globe*, August 7, 1925, p. A11; *Hartford Courant*, July 24, 1925, p. 15; *Hartford Courant*, August 10, 1925, p. 8.

29. *Springfield Republican*, August 15, 1925, p. 8; *Idaho Statesman*, October 10, 1925, p. 6.

30. *Hartford Courant*, August 11, 1925, p. 11.

31. Casey Stengel, *Casey at the Bat: The Story of My Life in Baseball as Told to Harry T. Paxton* (New York: Random House, 1962), p. 139.

32. W. J. Lee, *Hartford Courant*, July 9, 1939, p. C2.

33. *Hartford Courant*, September 21, 1925, p. 9.

34. Casey Stengel, *Casey at the Bat*, p. 140.

35. *Spalding's Official Base Ball Guide*, 1926, pp. 206–11.

36. *Hartford Times*, October 3, 1925, p. 23.

37. *Atlanta Constitution*, August 4, 1926, p. 8; August 7, 1926, p. 12.

38. Patrick K. Thornton, Walter T. Champion, and Larry Ruddell, *Sports Ethics for Sports Management Professionals* (Sudbury, MA: Jones & Bartlett, 2012), pp. 119–122; *Atlanta Constitution*, August 29, 1927, p. 7.

39. *Nice Guys Finish Last*, p. 43.

40. Gene Schoor, *The Leo Durocher Story* (New York: Julian Messner, 1963), p. 56.

41. *Springfield Republican*, March 26, 1927, p. 5.

42. *Columbus State Journal*, August 7, 1933.

43. *Toledo Blade*, April 10, 1947, p. 22; *Springfield Republican*, May 12, 1927, p. 23.

44. Arthur Mann, "Baseball's Ugly Duckling—Durable Durocher," *The Saturday Evening Post*, August 19, 1939, p. 15.

45. Mann, *Baseball Confidential*, pp. 7–8.

46. Ibid., pp. 6–7.

47. *The Sporting News*, December 31, 1925, p. 8; *Springfield Republican*, December 6, 1925.

48. *New York Sun*, April 22, 1929.

CHAPTER 3: DAMNED YANKEE

1. Bennett was a young man with an abnormal curvature of the back caused by a childhood accident who became the mascot of the Chicago White Sox in 1919 at age fifteen, but he left the team in disgust as word filtered out that the team had been tainted by a fix in the most infamous scandal in the history of the game. Bennett then signed with the Brooklyn Dodgers, whom he mascoted to the 1921 pennant and two wins in the first three games of the World Series, which were played at home. But when it came time to board the train for Cleveland, Brooklyn manager Wilbert Robinson decided to leave him behind and the Dodgers lost four straight. Citing a "lack of trust," Bennett quit the Dodgers and signed with the 1921 New York Yankees. During his years with the Yankees the team won seven pennants and four world championships and many rituals were created by the Yankees to help harness his magic. The big hitters—Babe Ruth, Lou Gehrig, and Tony Lazzeri—took their bats only from Eddie's hands.

2. Tom Meany, "Durocher: Always on the Spot." *Sport*, April, 1947, p. 58.

3. *Springfield Republican*, March 5, 1928.

4. Steve Steinberg and Lyle Spatz, *The Colonel and Hug: The Partnership That Transformed the New York Yankees* (Lincoln: University of Nebraska Press, 2015), p. 269.

5. *The Babe Ruth Story*, p. 165. It was during the spring of 1928 that Ruth acquired the reputation as a worker of miracles—with an assist from Durocher. The story appeared in Fred Lieb's 1977 memoir *Baseball As I Have Known It*, which was published when he was eighty-nine years old. Lieb had been a sportswriter for seventy years, and carried the sobriquet "dean of sportswriters."

   During an exhibition game against the Cincinnati Reds at Phillips Field in Tampa, Florida, a large black car was parked along the right-field foul line. The players on the field and the reporters covering the game assumed it was a local dignitary. It did not move during the game and remained in place when the game ended.

   As Lieb, then with the *New York Press*, was leaving the field, his wife Mary ran up to him and said, "Leo Durocher just told me to tell you to look inside the car and you would have a whale of a story."

   What Lieb witnessed was something he called a miracle and likened to something right out of the New Testament. In the front seat of the car was a wildly excited man with tears running down his cheeks and in the backseat was a boy of about ten standing up and grinning. "This is the first time in two years that my boy has stood up," the man sobbed and smiled as he spoke. "You see him standing, don't you? I'm so happy I can hardly speak! It's two years since my boy could stand up!"

According to the father, when the boy had suddenly lost his ability to stand he was confined to his room, where he became a huge Babe Ruth fan, collecting all the pictures of the slugger his parents could find. When it was announced that Ruth would play in Tampa, the father got permission to park his car next to the field so that his son would be as close to his idol as possible.

6. AP, *Aberdeen (WA) Daily News*, April 6, 1928, p. 12.
7. *Chicago Tribune*, April 12, 1928, p. 19.
8. *The Springfield Republican*, March 25, 1938, p. 2.
9. Red Barber, interview with William Marshall, November 13, 1979, The A. B. Chandler Oral History Project, Special Collections and Archives, University of Kentucky Libraries.
10. Ty Cobb and Al Stump, *My Life in Baseball: The True Record*, p. 142. In an article in the June 1999 issue of *American History* magazine entitled "Cobb's Last Stand," the hip story is elevated to the status of a one-act play in which Durocher addressed Cobb, who was lying on the ground after being felled by the Lip's hip. Cobb started to say something, but Durocher interrupted. "Listen, Grandpa," he said in this fictional dialogue, "you're not going to cut off anybody's legs. You've gotten away with murder for a lot of years, but you're through, see? I'll give you the hip every time you come around my way, and if you try to cut me, I'll ram the ball right down your throat." The article adds: "Dizzy with rage, Cobb started after the loud-mouthed rookie, and the benches emptied. Cobb was eventually dragged from the bottom of the pile and ejected." This is all total nonsense.
11. *Brooklyn Eagle*, August 20, 1928, p. 20.
12. Durocher, *Nice Guys Finish Last*. This is also the same version he gave to Bill Gildea of *The Washington Post* in 1984 when he is seventy-nine (October 24, 1984, p. E-5).
13. Arthur Mann, "Baseball's Ugly Duckling—Durable Durocher," *The Saturday Evening Post*, August 19, 1939, p. 14.
14. *Springfield Republican* quoting Graham's column, May 29, 1928, p. 9.
15. *Springfield Republican*, May 29, 1928, p. 9; June 8, 1928, p. 23.
16. Frank Graham, *The New York Yankees: An Informal History*, Writing Baseball (Carbondale, IL: Southern Illinois University Press, 2002), p. 142.
17. *Springfield Republican*, May 30, 1928, p. 6.
18. "Lots of Nerve," *Los Angeles Times*, August 14, 1928, p. B-1.
19. *New York Sun*, June 12, 1928.
20. Marty Appel, *Pinstripe Empire: The New York Yankees from Before the Babe to After the Boss*, Reprint ed. New York: Bloomsbury USA, 2014, p. 57; Serialization of Raft's bio *I Can't Escape My Past*, from the *Boston Herald*, January 25, 1958, p. 4.
21. Leo Durocher with Ed Linn, *The Saturday Evening Post*, "I Come to Kill You: The Candid Memoirs of Leo Durocher," May 11, 1963, p. 26.
22. *Rockford Morning Star*, September 16, 1964, p. 18.
23. Mann's relationship with Leo is attested to in the recollections recorded in the file entitled "The Many Lives of Leo Durocher" in Arthur Mann Papers (1901–1969), Library of Congress, Manuscript Division, Box 3. This is an early draft of an article on Durocher that appears to have never been finished and published.
24. *Springfield Republican*, May 11, 1928, p. 16.
25. Mann, pp. 10–11. The Committee in Charge was typical of a Durocher clique and claque, even as a rookie. It included Lopez, the orchestra leader, and Abe April, Dinney Mahoney, Edward Rosenfield, George Pomerantz, Roy Psaty, Louis Russell, Connie Immerman, Mack

Goldberg, Gip Geizler, Irving Russell, and Max Klinkenstein, prominent nightclub opera-tors, and as Mann explained "an associate and employee of Lucky Luciano, a prominent witness at the Jimmy Hines policy-racket trial, and a key witness in the Lepke-Gurrah restaurant-racket scandal." *Brooklyn Daily Eagle*, August 17, 1953. p. 13. Also, Arthur Mann Papers (1901–1969), Library of Congress, Manuscript Division, Box 3.

26. *The Boston Globe*, June 24, 1928, p. A18, reported that the Springfield delegation claimed credit for the Yankees' "double demise" because of their rooting for the Red Sox.

27. *The New York Times*, June 4, 1928, p. S-1.

28. *New York Herald Tribune*, July 12, 1928, p. 23.

29. *The New York Times*, August 1, 1928, p. 15.

30. *Brooklyn Eagle*, April 29, 1929, p. 26.

31. *The Boston Globe*, "Durocher Rated as King of Goat-Getters on Diamond," February 9, 1930, p. A23; Leo Durocher, *Nice Guys Finish Last*, p. 52.

32. "Durocher Given Place with French Athletes, *Springfield Republican*, June 3, 1928, p. 20; *The Sporting News*, January 2, 1930, p. 5.

33. "The All-American Out," *New York Sun*, October 3, 1928.

34. John B. Keller, "Reserve Players Expected to Star," *Evening Star*, October 4, 1928, p. 33.

35. Arthur Mann, "Baseball's Ugly Duckling—Durable Durocher," *The Saturday Evening Post*, August 19, 1939, p. 64.

36. "Mr. Durocher Now with Yanks Does as Yankees," *State Times Advocate*, Baton Rouge, July 3, 1928, p. 9; Grantland Rice, *Hartford Courant*, March 25, 1938, p. 17.

37. *Springfield Republican*, October 11, 1928, p. 16; *Springfield Union*, July 12, 1953, p. 26.

38. *The Washington Post*, December 18, 1928, p. 16. It is hard to believe today but it took many weeks after the end of the season for statistics to be harvested, collated, double-checked, and released to the public.

39. "Free Speech to Continue for Leo Durocher," *Springfield Republican*, January 1, 1929, p. 7.

40. *Hartford Courant*, November 4, 1928, p. C-3.

41. *Springfield Republican*, January 10, 1939, p. 11; January 20, 1929, p. 24.

42. *Hartford Courant*, February 20, 1929; *Springfield Republican*, February 20, 1929, p. 7.

43. *New York Herald Tribune*, February 25, 1929, p. 21.

44. *Springfield Republican*, April 3, 1929, p. 9.

45. Mann, p. 18.

46. UP, *Trenton Evening Times*, March 30, 1929, p. 8; *Atlanta Constitution*, April 14, 1929, p. A-1.

47. *Seattle Daily Times*, April 9, 1929, p. 19.

48. "Again, Baseball," *Time*, April 15, 1929.

49. *Springfield Republican*, April 17, 1929, p. 6.

50. Combs cf #1, Koenig 3b #2, Ruth rf #3, Gehrig 1b #4, Meusel lf #5, Lazzeri 2b #6, Durocher ss #7, Grabowksi c #8. The remainder of the roster was apparently numbered as follows: The other two catchers were assigned #9 and #10; #11 through #21 were assigned to pitchers (except unlucky #13 wasn't used); and #22 through #28 were given to the remaining position players; then #29 and up were assigned to coaches.

51. *The Christian Science Monitor*, April 24, 1929. p. 16.

52. *The Washington Post*, April 30, 1929, p. 15.

53. Robert W. Creamer, *Babe: The Legend Comes to Life* (New York: Simon & Schuster, 1992).

54. Ibid., p. 1.

55. *New York Sun*, May 24, 1929.

56. *The Boston Globe*, June 27, 1929, p. 27.

57. *Brooklyn Eagle*, June 8, 1929.

58. *Ibid.*, July 3, 1929, p. 10.

59. Mann, p. 18. Durocher never denied this incident and even repeated it in *Nice Guys Finish Last.*

60. *Brooklyn Eagle*, February 9, 1930, p. 38.

61. *The Boston Globe*, August 21, 1929, p. 15.

62. Mann p. 18; also material in Arthur Mann Papers (1901–1969), Library of Congress, Manuscript Division, Box "scrap book"; Box OV-2.

63. *Huntingdon (PA) Daily News*, October 22, 1929.

CHAPTER 4: THE RED MENACE

1. Arthur Mann, "Baseball's Ugly Duckling—Durable Durocher," *The Saturday Evening Post*, August 19, 1939, p. 15.

2. UP, *Lexington Herald*, January 3, 1939, p. 10; AP *Springfield Republican*, January 22, 1930, p. 20.

3. *The New York Times*, April 13, 1930; San Diego Union, January 28, 1930, p. 15.

4. *Springfield Republican*, February 1, 1930, p. 13.

5. *Brooklyn Eagle*, February 6, 1930, p. 22; The two versions of this meeting are discussed in Rob Neyer, *Rob Neyer's Big Book of Baseball Legends: The Truth, the Lies, and Everything Else* (New York: Touchstone, 2008), p. 189.

6. Eugene Murdock, *Baseball Players and Their Times: Oral Histories of the Game, 1920–1940* (Westport, CT: Meckler, 1991), p. 34.

7. *Boston Herald*, February 6, 1930, p. 29.

8. Greg Rhodes and John Snyder, *Redleg Journal: Year by Year and Day by Day with the Cincinnati Reds Since 1866* (Cincinnati, OH: Road West Pub Co., 2000), pp. 239–40.

9. *The Repository*, Canton, Ohio, March 2, 1930, p. 45.

10. Bill Lee is one of those that alluded to this in the *Hartford Courant*, July 14, 1943, p. 13. "There is a story that Babe Ruth detested him so much that he practically rode Leo out of the American League."

11. Bob Broeg, "Happy Chandler Contests Durocher Claim," *The Sporting News*, August 2, 1975, p. 6. The column quotes extensively from a letter sent by Chandler to Broeg correcting some of the assertions made by Durocher in his biography *Nice Guys Finish Last.*

12. Bob Considine, "Ups and Downs of Leo the Lip," *Chicago Herald-American*, June 13, 1940.

13. Arthur Mann Papers (1901–1969), Library of Congress, Manuscript Division, Box OV-2; *New York World*, February 17, 1930.

14. *The Sporting News*, February 13, 1930, p. 8.

15. *Ibid.*, April 17, 1930, p. 4.

16. Sidney Weil, *The Memoirs of Sidney Weil* (Cincinnati and Evanston, IL: published by the Weil family, 1966); pp. 27–28. This is an exceedingly scarce work to find. I was able to get access to it with special thanks to Diane Mallstrom, reference librarian at the Public Library of Cincinnati & Hamilton County.

17. Frank Graham, *The Brooklyn Dodgers: An Informal History*, Writing Baseball (Carbondale, IL: Southern Illinois University Press, 2002), p. 148.

18. AP, *Baltimore Sun*, March 5, 1930, p. 10.

19. Robert Smith, *Baseball* (New York: Simon & Schuster, 1970), p. 275; Sidney Weil, *The Memoirs of Sidney Weil*, p. 27.

20. Sidney Weil. *The Memoirs of Sidney Weil*, p. 29.

21. Peter Glembock, *Bums*, p. 115.

22. *Springfield Republican*, August 14, 1971, p. 10.

23. *The Sporting News*, July 30, 1931, retrieved from National Baseball Library vertical file, not paginated.

24. UP, *Rockford (IL) Morning Star*, April 2, 1932, p. 11.

25. *Sports Illustrated*, May 23, 1955, p. 74.

26. Ibid.

27. *The New York Times*, July 27, 1972. Smith, now with the *Times*, recalls the story when Leo is forced to resign from the Cubs in 1972.

28. *Cincinnati Enquirer*, May 12, 1932, p. S-1. *The Washington Post*, May 13, 1932, p. 13.

29. *Boston Herald*, September 11, 1932, p. 22.

30. Ibid., August 15, 1932, p. 12.

31. *Brooklyn Eagle*, May 12, 1933, p. 21.

32. Weil, pp. 29–30; *Springfield Republican*, May 5, 1933, p. 19.

33. *Sports Illustrated*, May 23, 1955, p. 74.

34. Arthur Mann. *Baseball Confidential: Secret History of the War Among Chandler, Durocher, MacPhail, and Rickey*. (New York: David McKay Company, 1951), p. 22; Leo Durocher, with Ed Linn, *Nice Guys Finish Last* (New York: Simon & Schuster, 1975).

35. Arthur Mann, *Branch Rickey: American in Action* (Boston: Houghton Mifflin, 1957), p. 178.

36. *Cincinnati Enquirer*, May 8, 1933, p. 1.

37. *The Tampa Tribune*, March 5, 1933, p. 21.

38. *The Pittsburgh Press*, January 22, 1956, p. 47.

39. *Sports Illustrated*, May 23, 1955, p. 74.

CHAPTER 5: GASHOUSE TOUGH

1. *Boston Herald*, May 14, 1933, pp. 1, 36.

2. Greg Rhodes and John Snyder, *Redleg Journal: Year by Year and Day by Day with the Cincinnati Reds Since 1866* (Cincinnati: Road West Pub Co., 2000), pp. 267–70.

3. *The Sporting News* April 19, 1934, p. 7.

4. Charles C. Alexander, *Breaking the Slump: Baseball in the Depression Era* (New York: Columbia University Press, 2002), p. 126; *Sports Illustrated*, May 30, 1955, p. 35.

5. Arnold Hano, "Sport's Greatest Teams: The Gas House Gang," *Sport*, August 1962, p. 28.

6. Orsatti was hired as assistant property master on the comedy film *Sherlock, Jr.* (1924), since director Buster Keaton was a big baseball fan and insisted on playing baseball on the sets of all his films. Orsatti's two sons were both Hollywood stuntmen.

7. Durocher, *Nice Guys Finish Last*, p. 111.

8. J. Roy Stockton, *The Gashouse Gang and a Couple of Other Guys* (New York: A. S. Barnes, 1945), p. 85.

9. *The New York Times*, October 1, 1934, p. 22.

10. *The Sporting News*, September 27, 1934, p. 4; Columns from *The Chicago American* from the morgue files of that newspaper beginning with the column of October 2, 1934. *Springfield Republican*, October 3, 1934, p. 16. Durocher also told Graham: "This is our year, both for the pennant and the world championship."

11. Ray Robinson, *American Original: A Life of Will Rogers* (New York: Oxford University Press, 1996), p. 240.

12. *Springfield Republican*, October 4, 1934, p. 15; UP, *Trenton Evening Times*, February 24, 1937, p. 20.

13. *Boston Herald*, October 6, 1934, p. 6.

14. *Springfield Republican*, October 9, 1934, p. 13.

15. Leo used this story along with other tales of the Gashouse Gang as the basis for some of his best after-dinner speeches. *Brooklyn Eagle*, January 28, 1948, p. 15.

16. *Springfield Republican*, October 10, 1934, p. 15.

17. Ibid., October 12, 1934, p. 12.

18. *The Sporting News*, November 8, 1934, p. 4.

19. Arthur Mann was still reporting on Durocher, and he reported the conversation that ensued. Mann, *Baseball Confidential*, pp. 25–26.

20. UP, *Omaha World Herald*, April 29, 1935, p. 13; AP, *Illinois State Journal*, April 30, 1935, p. 12; AP, *Aberdeen (WA) Daily News*, May 19, 1935, p. 7; AP, *Omaha World Herald*, May 24, 1935, p. 24.

21. *Springfield Republican*, January 12, 1936, p. 28.

22. AP, *Springfield Republican*, November 20, 1935, p. 15.

23. *Brooklyn Eagle*, May 13, 1936, p. 20.

24. AP dispatch in the *Boston Herald*, May 13, 1936, p. 29; Scotty Reston, *Daily Illinois State Journal* (Springfield, IL), May 14, 1936, p. 14; John Lardner, NANA, *Springfield Republican*, May 14, 1936, p. 22.

25. AP, *The Washington Post*, August 12, 1936, p. X-16.

26. *Baltimore Sun*, May 12, 1937, p. 20.

27. Grantland Rice, *Hartford Courant*, March 25, 1938, p. 17.

28. Mann, *Branch Rickey*, pp. 178–9.

29. Leo Durocher in a bylined article for the *Chicago American*, September 11, 1966.

30. Argus editorial quoted in the *Baltimore Afro-American*, October 31, 1931, p. 14. Back to segregation at Sportsman's Park in St. Louis, according to the recollection of Bill Mead, who frequented Sportsman's Park before it was desegregated: "The right field pavilion, as it was called, was lower deck only. The right field wall was only 310 feet from home plate, so in the Ruth era, a screen was installed to avoid cheap home runs. That's where black fans sat. They were protected from the sun by a roof, but they had to view the game action thru a screen. Musial & Slaughter, both lh [left handed] batters, bounced lord knows how many doubles off that screen."

31. John Holway, *Josh and Satch: The Life and Times of Josh Gibson and Satchel Paige* (New York: Carroll & Graf Publishers/R. Gallen, 1992), p. 150; *Pittsburg Courier*, August 5, 1939, p. 1.

   In 1935, Judy Johnson got Durocher out on a decoy play at third during one of these games. Leo had reached third base and began dancing off the bag down the line to rattle the pitcher. Judy gave Josh Gibson "the whistle." "Durocher started in toward home," Johnson recalled to Negro league historian John B. Holway, "and I moved up with him. Then I just backed up, put my foot about two feet in front of the base. Josh had the best snap, wouldn't move to throw, just snapped the ball. I caught it. Here comes Durocher sliding in and the umpire says, 'You're out.'"

   Some twenty years later, Johnson and his wife were leaving Milwaukee County Stadium, where their son-in-law, Bill Bruton, had just finished playing a World Series game against the New York Yankees. In the crowd, they jostled against none other than Durocher. "Leo," Judy said, "do you remember playing a barnstorming game in Cincinnati back in 1934 or so?" Durocher stepped back and blinked. "Yes," he responded, "I remember you, Judy, damn your soul. That's the day you tricked me."

CHAPTER 6: THE ARTFUL DODGER

1. Robert Smith, *Baseball* (New York: Simon & Schuster, 1970), p. 1.

2. Leo Durocher, *The Dodgers and Me* (Chicago: Ziff-Davis, 1948), pp. 20–24.

3. Smith, *Baseball*, p. 278.

4. Frank Graham, *The Brooklyn Dodgers: An Informal History*, Writing Baseball (Carbondale, IL: Southern Illinois University Press, 2002), p. 164.

5. Pat Robertson, "Reds Rookie Writes Baseball History," *Daily Illinois State Journal* (Springfield, IL), June 16, 1938, p. 11.

6. Leo Durocher, *The Dodgers and Me: The Inside Story* (Chicago: Ziff-Davis, 1948), p. 28.

7. *The San Bernardino County Sun*, June 21, 1981, p. 1.

8. AP report from the *Chicago Tribune*, June 16, 1938, p. 1; John Kieran, "Thrills of a No-Hit Game," *The New York Times*, June 20, 1938, p. 20.

9. Leo Durocher, *The Dodgers and Me*, p. 29.

10. Ibid., p. 30.

11. AP, *San Francisco Chronicle*, June 20, 1938, p. 19.

12. George Kirksey, "Hiring of Ruth Aids Brooklyn Team at Gate," *Morning Star* (Rockford, IL), July 3, 1938, p. 21.

13. *Rockford (IL) Evening Star*, July 10, 1938, p. 20.

14. *The New York Times*, "Ruth Drives 430 feet," July 25, 1938, p. 9.

15. Smelser, Marshall. *The Life That Ruth Built* (New York: Quadrangle, The New York Times Book Co. 1985), pp. 520–521. The postscript to the Babe's inability to recall and understand signs took place in March of 1948, the year he died, when he made a trip to Spring Training and visited a Cardinals–Red Sox game in St. Petersburg. Ruth's old skipper, Joe McCarthy, was in his first year managing the Red Sox. In the middle of the exhibition game Ruth turned to Gerry Hern of the *Boston Post* and said, "McCarthy is still using the same old signs. How do you like that? Same old signs. He'll have to come up with some new ones when he plays the Yankees." McCarthy by all accounts was one of the canniest signers in the history of the game, known for his ability to constantly change his signs and his systems of sending them. Ruth may have recognized McCarthy's signs were the same, but their meaning had long since changed.

16. Leo Durocher, *The Dodgers and Me* (Chicago: Ziff-Davis, 1948), pp. 29–33.

17. Harold Parrott, *The Lords of Baseball: A Wry Look at a Side of the Game the Fan Seldom Sees, the Front Office*, 2nd ed. (Atlanta: Longstreet Press, 2001), p. 119. For the remainder of the season, writers alluded to the incident but without details, save for the fact that it had occurred at the Polo Grounds. The reports led to more questions than answers. A September report in the *Chicago Tribune* called it a "private but petty fight," while another writer called it "a spat."

18. George Springer, "Ruth Fails to Hit in Three Trips to the Plate," *Springfield Republican*, August 12, 1938, p. 17.

19. *Brooklyn Daily Eagle*, August 17, 1953, p. 13.

20. "Dodgers Dismiss Burleigh Grimes," INS, *Daily Illinois State Journal* (Springfield, IL), October 11, 1938, p. 9.

21. UP, *Morning Star* (Rockford, Illinois), October 15, 1938.

22. Arthur Mann, "Baseball's Ugly Duckling—Durable Durocher," *The Saturday Evening Post*, August 19, 1939, p. 66.

23. Frank Graham, *The Brooklyn Dodgers*, p. 179.

24. *The Sporting News*, March 16, 1939, p. 6.

25. UP, *State Times Advocate*, February 23, 1939, p. 77.

26. INS, *Repository* (Canton, OH), February 1, 1939, p. 8.

27. *The Milwaukee Journal*, February 23, 1939. p. 18. The Lardner column appeared in the *Rockford (IL) Evening Star*, February 28, 1939, p. 19.

28. *Time*, "The Lip," April 14, 1947. In this article Durocher spelled out the three categories of dispute: "When an umpire really calls one wrong, Leo strides out of his dugout menacingly, and patiently diagrams to him what happened. The fans see all the apparently angry pointing,

and imagine admiringly what is being said. Confesses Leo: 'Sometimes, the ump admits to me, "I missed that one," before I even start to tell him what a woodenhead son-of-a-bitch he is. But I keep on talking . . . maybe I'm telling him I'll buy him a beer after the game.'

"Where the umpire's decision was close but right, The Lip is apt to make far more noise . . .

"Sometimes one of his Dodgers gets too deep in debate with an umpire, and that calls for Technique No. 3. The trick is to take over the fight. He thrusts out his chin, wags a threatening finger under the ump's nose, and as a final insult kicks sand on the umpire's shoes. Says Durocher: 'Sure, I get bounced but my player stays in.'"

29. *Brooklyn Eagle*, July 3, 1939, p. 14; AP, *Los Angeles Times*, July 3, 1939, p. 5.

30. *The New York Times*, July 4, 1939, p. 21.

31. Frank Graham, *The Brooklyn Dodgers*, p. 177.

32. Durocher, *Nice Guys Finish Last*, p. 11.

33. *The Chicago Tribune, Chicago American, Chicago Daily Times, Chicago Herald Examiner*, July 30, 1938.

34. *The Pittsburgh Press*, August 4, 1938.

35. Al Monroe, "It's News to Me," *Chicago Defender*, October 1, 1938, p. 10.

36. *Pittsburgh Courier*, August 5, 1939; Irwin Silber, *Press Box Red* (Philadelphia: Temple University Press, 2003), p. 79.

37. Irwin Silber, *Press Box Red*, p. 70.

38. *Daily Worker*, September 13 and September 16, 1937, quoted in Rusinack, pp. 75–85; Lester Rodney, "White Dodgers, Black Dodgers," in Dorinson and Warmund, p. 92.

39. Interview with the *People's Weekly World* (New York) November 28, 2003, p. 10.

40. Quentin Reynolds, "The Pop-Off Kid," *Collier's*, August 5, 1939, pp. 14, 45–46.

41. Bob Considine, "Ups and Downs of Leo the Lip," *Chicago Herald-American*, June 13, 1940.

42. *Boston Herald*, October 6, 1940, p. 70; Louella O. Parsons column, *Sacramento Bee*, October 22, 1941, p 12.

43. Day, pp. 48–50; Jim Vitti, *Brooklyn Dodgers in Cuba*, Images of Baseball (Charleston, SC: Arcadia Publishing, 2011), p. 91.

44. *New York Herald Tribune*, September 8, 1941, p. 16.

45. The Lopez account appears in Donald Honig, *The Man in the Dugout: Fifteen Big League Managers Speak Their Minds* (Lincoln, NE: University of Nebraska Press, 1995), p. 190; AP, *Cleveland Plain Dealer*, September 18, 1941, p. 18

46. Frank Graham, *The Brooklyn Dodgers*, p. 179.

47. *Brooklyn Eagle*, September 20, 1941, p. 12.

48. Ibid., September 21, 1941, p. 21.

49. *Chicago Tribune*, August 27, 1969, p. 74.

50. Parrott, Harold. *The Lords of Baseball: A Wry Look at a Side of the Game the Fan Seldom Sees, the Front Office*, 2nd ed. (Atlanta: Longstreet Press, 2002), pp. 276–79; *Chicago Today*, August 27, 1969, p. 74; Gertz's blog, http://blog.seattlepi.com/bookpatrol/2009/09/21/on-the-road-with-minnesota-fats/.

51. *Washington Star*, July 17, 1948, p. A11.

52. Andy McCue, *Mover and Shaker: Walter O'Malley, the Dodgers, and Baseball's Westward Expansion* (Lincoln: University of Nebraska Press, 2014), p. 186.

53. *The Sporting News*, October 16, 1941, p. 8.

54. David Pietrusza, *Judge and Jury: The Life and Times of Judge Kenesaw Mountain Landis*, South Bend: Diamond Communications, p. 368.

55. Bex, October 13, 1941, p. 5.
56. *Brooklyn Eagle*, October 6, 1941, p. 15.
57. *New York Herald Tribune*, October 6, 1941, p. 18.
58. Medoff, Rafael, *The New York Jewish Week*, Oct 21, 2005, p. 23.
59. Gene Schoor, *The Leo Durocher Story* (New York: Julian Messner, 1963) p. 123.
60. "Owen's '41 Muff Doomed Dodgers," *The Washington Times* (Washington, D.C.), July 18, 2005.

CHAPTER 7: MUTINY IN FLATBUSH

1. Laraine Day, *Day with the Giants*, (Garden City, NY: Doubleday, 1932), p. 37.
2. *Brooklyn Eagle*, September 30, 1941, p. 7.
3. *The Sporting News*, November 13, 1941, p. 7.
4. *The Seattle Times*, November 9, 1941, p. 60.
5. Ruth Carson, "Designing Lady," *Collier's*, October 11, 1941, pp. 76–77.
6. INS, *Sacramento Bee*, December 9, 1941, p. 12.
7. *The Washington Post*, May 5, 1942, p. 18.
8. Bob Considine's syndicated column, *The Washington Post*, May 22, 1942, p. 28.
9. Neil Lanctot, *Negro League Baseball: The Rise and Ruin of a Black Institution* (Philadelphia: University of Pennsylvania Press, 2008), p. 168.
10. Richard Dozer, *Baseball Digest*, 1983.
11. Quoted in Tygiel, p. 30, *The Sporting News*, March 3, 1942; *Pittsburgh Courier*, July 25, 1942, pp. 16–17.
12. *Rockford (IL) Evening Star*, July 29, 1932, p. 44.
13. *Brooklyn Eagle*, December 28, 1948, p. 17; *Chicago Defender*, April 13, 1946, p. 11; Layton Revel and Louis Munoz, *Forgotten Heroes: Silvio Garcia*, Center for Negro League Baseball Research, 2014, http://www.cnlbr.org/Portals/0/Hero/Silvio-Garcia.pdf.
14. *The Saturday Evening Post*, March 23, 1942; Tom Meany, "Durocher: Always on the Spot," *Sport*, April 1947, p. 63.
15. Tom Meany, "Durocher: Always on the Spot," *Sport*, April 1947, p. 63.
16. *Baltimore Sun*, June 30, 1942, p. 13.
17. *Brooklyn Eagle*, June 30, 1942, p. L5.
18. Arthur Mann Papers (1901–1969), Library of Congress, Manuscript Division, Box 7.
19. *Chicago Tribune*, August 27, 1969, p. 74.
20. *Atlanta Constitution*, July 17, 1942, p. 21.
21. *Springfield Republican*, September 13, 1932, p. 6.
22. AP, *Greensboro Daily News*, September 14, 1942, p. 5.
23. UP, bylined piece by Jack Cuddy, *Register-Republic* (Rockford, IL), p. 13.
24. Mann, *Branch Rickey*, p. 39.
25. *Boston Herald*, November 19, 1942, p. 27.
26. Mann, *Branch Rickey*, p. 245.
27. *Trenton Evening Times*, September 24, 1943, p. 14.
28. UP, *The New York Times*, November 13, 1942, p. 31.
29. UP, *Chicago Sun-Times*, November 18, 1942; Durocher, *The Dodgers and Me*, p. 137; Frank Graham, *The Brooklyn Dodgers: An Informal History*, Writing Baseball (Carbondale, IL: Southern Illinois University Press), p. 200.
30. Harold Parrott's column in the *Brooklyn Eagle*, September 1, 1943, p. 15.
31. *Springfield Republican*, February 19, 1943, p. 4.

32. Dan Polier, *Yank* magazine, "Leo Durocher almost became a Marine before he bounced back to Brooklyn on his 4-F Ear," March 6, 1943, p. 23. This was the main source for the reporting on the whole day beginning with Durocher's waking up.

33. UP report in *Chicago American*, March 2, 1943.

34. *New York Herald Tribune*, March 2, 1943, p. 23.

35. Frank Graham, *The Brooklyn Dodgers*, p. 236.

36. *Evening Star*, June 19, 1943, p. 18.

37. Clifton Blue Parker, *Big and Little Poison: Paul and Lloyd Waner, Baseball Brothers* (Jefferson, NC: McFarland. 2003), pp. 173–74.

38. Frank Graham, *The Brooklyn Dodgers*, p. 241.

39. The verbatim comments come from Roscoe McGowen of the *The New York Times* (July 11, 1943, p. 1), who was in the room when the strike vote was taken. One of Vaughan's classmates in high school in Fullerton, California, was Richard Nixon. Years later, when he was president, Nixon put together all-time baseball teams for the American and National Leagues, and Vaughan was his all-time National League shortstop from 1925 to 1945. Nixon fondly recalled playing Pee Wee football with Vaughan.

40. *New York Herald Tribune*, July 11, 1943, p. 8.

41. Frank Graham, *The Brooklyn Dodgers*, 241–42.

42. *New York Herald Tribune*, July 15, 1943, p. 25.

43. AP, *Chicago American*, July 16, 1943.

44. *New York Herald Tribune*, September 21, 1943, p. 29.

45. *Atlanta Constitution*, August 14, 1944, p. 8.

46. *The American Weekly*, October 10, 1943.

47. *Brooklyn Eagle*, September 30, 1930, p. 13.

48. *Rockford (IL) Evening Star*, September 19, 1943, p. 26.

49. Ibid., October 28, 1943, p. 19.

50. Frank Graham, *The Brooklyn Dodgers*, p. 243; Mann, *Branch Rickey*, p. 245.

51. INS, Chicago morgue.

52. *Hartford Courant*, November 11, 1943, p. 13, and December 31, 1943, p. 11; *The New York Times*, March 4, 1944, p. S2.

53. Serialization of Raft's syndicated bio *I Can't Escape My Past* from the *Boston Herald*, January 25, 1958, p. 24

54. Harold Parrott, *The Lords of Baseball: A Wry Look at a Side of the Game the Fan Seldom Sees, the Front Office*, 2nd ed. (Atlanta: Longstreet Press, 2002), 194–96.

55. Ibid., p. 196.

56. *The Record* (Hackensack, NJ) October 9, 1991.

57. *New York Herald Tribune*, April 14, 1944, p. 19a.

58. Bill Gilbert, *They Also Served: Baseball and the Home Front, 1941–1945* (New York: Crown Publishers, 1992), p. 89.

59. AP, *Register-Republic* (Rockford, IL), May 13, 1944, p. 10.

60. UP, *Daily Illinois State Journal* (Springfield, IL), June 4, 1944, p. 22.

61. *Rockford (IL) Evening Star*, July 22, 1944, p. 10.

62. *Brooklyn Eagle*, August 20, 1944, p. 17.

63. *The New York Times*, August 20, 1944 p. S-1.

64. *Baltimore Sun*, October 3, 1944, p. 14.

65. *New York Herald Tribune*, September 29, 1944, p. 23.

66. *Springfield Republican*, October 12, 1944, p. 14.

67. AP, *New York Herald Tribune*, May 5, 1944, p. 21.

68. A. S. "Doc" Young, *Ebony* magazine, "A Few Hundred Words from the Front Office," January 1971, p. 48.

69. *Chicago Tribune*, November 15, 1944; November 16, 1944, p. 16; UP, *Atlanta Constitution*, November 16, 1944, p. 1, and November 17, 1944, p. 4.

70. For years, the story always has focused on the one game in which Shurin was victimized, but what else went on in other craps shooting sessions has long been a matter of speculation. In 2001, an old-time player named Elden Auker published a memoir in which he asserts that the player who had been taken in one of these rigged games was none other than Dizzy Trout, who gave up over $7,000, which Aucker claimed wiped Trout out. I mention it here because it lives on the Internet. It is one of those stories that lack a second source and must be regarded as suspicious.

71. *Chicago-Sun Times*, February 9, 1945.

72. *Chicago Herald-American*, January 18, 1945.

73. Frank Graham, *The Brooklyn Dodgers: An Informal History*, p. 248; Tom Meany, "Durocher: Always on the Spot," *Sport*, April 1947, p. 65.

74. Tom Meany, "Durocher: Always on the Spot," *Sport*, April 1947, p. 67. The Medwick story appears in Gary Stein's column in the *Rockford (IL) Morning Star* on June 30, 1971, p. 21.

75. Durocher, p. 205.

CHAPTER 8: GAME CHANGER

1. AP, *Springfield Republican*, April 7, 1945, p. 11.

2. *New York Herald Tribune*, April 7, 1945, p. 12.

3. Howard Bryant, *Shut Out: A Story of Race and Baseball in Boston* (Boston Beacon Press, 2003), pp. 36–39.

4. Jerome Holtzman, *Chicago Tribune*, "How Wendell Smith Helped Robinson's Career," March 31, 1997.

5. Ohio alone had two potential candidates: Senator John W. Bricker, a Republican, and Governor Frank J. Lausche, a Democrat. James A. Farley, for eight years FDR's postmaster general and chairman of the National Democratic Party, was under consideration, as was Robert Hannegan, President Truman's chair of the National Democratic Party and postmaster general. Even FBI director J. Edgar Hoover was considered.

6. AP, *Boston Traveler*, February 5, 1946, p. 36.

7. *Brooklyn Eagle*, June 11, 1945, p. 1/11.

8. Ibid., September 7, 1945, p. 3.

9. *Milwaukee Journal*, November 12, 1945, p. 36.

10. UP, *The Repository* (Canton, OH), October 15, 1945, p. 12.

11. *Brooklyn Eagle*, November 15, 1945, p. 19.

12. *San Francisco Chronicle*, October 26, 1945, p 13.

13. Mann, *Branch Rickey*, p. 225.

14. *The New York Times*, November 16, 1945, p. 26.

15. *San Francisco Chronicle*, November 15, 1945, p. 6.

16. *Sacramento Bee*, November 10, 1945, p. 12.

17. *Brooklyn Eagle*, December 3, 1945, p. 15.

18. AP, *Evansville Courier and Press*, March 3, 1946, p. 21; AP, *San Diego Union*, March 3, 1946, p. 27.

19. Chris Lamb, *Blackout: The Untold Story of Jackie Robinson's First Spring Training* (Lincoln: University of Nebraska Press, 2004), pp. 107–8. Lamb interviewed Rowe on March 10, 1993.

20. *Pittsburgh Courier*, March 23, 1946.

21. *Daytona Beach Evening News*, April 4, 1944.

22. *Brooklyn Eagle*, April 25, 1946, p. 1.

23. INS, *Chicago Herald-American*, April 24, 1946, unpaginated morgue clipping.

24. AP, *The Washington Post*, April 26, 1946, p. 12; *New York Herald Tribune*, April 29, 1946, p. 19.

25. AP, *Springfield Republican*, April 24, 1946, p. 14.

26. *The Washington Post*, April 25, 1946, p. 12.

27. UP, *Trenton Evening Times*, April 23, 1946, p. 12, and April 24, 1946, p. 21; AP, *Springfield Republican*, April 26, 1946, p. 14.

28. *New York Herald Tribune*, April 29, 1946, p. 19.

29. I am indebted to Ralph Keys, whose research findings first appeared in his 1992 work *Nice Guys Finish Seventh: False Phrases, Spurious Sayings and Familiar Misquotations*. Ralph left no stone unturned in his research, and his notes include interviews with Red Barber and Frank Graham Jr. Keys has this to say about the quotation: "Leo Durocher doesn't own that quotation; the quotation owns Leo Durocher, the way a parasite sometimes takes over the host organism. Quotations are in a perpetual struggle for survival. They want people to keep saying them. They don't want to die any more than the rest of us do. And so, whenever they can, they attach themselves to colorful or famous people. 'Nice guys finish last' profits by its association with a man whose nickname was the Lip, even if the Lip never said it." Also, Frank Graham Jr., *A Farewell to Heroes* (New York: The Viking Press, 1981), pp. 207–9.

30. Roger Kahn, *Rickey and Robinson: The True, Untold Story of the Integration of Baseball* (New York: Rodale Books, 2015), pp. 128–31.

31. *The Washington Post*, October 4, 1946, p. 14.

32. A. B. Chandler Papers, Box 162, University of Kentucky Library.

33. Day, *Day with the Dodgers*.

34. Mann, *Branch Rickey*, pp. 245–46.

35. Ibid., p. 246.

36. Pegler's columns of October 28–30, obtained through columns in the *Dallas Morning News* and *Chicago American*. Unpaginated morgue clipping.

37. Mann, *Baseball Confidential*.

38. Dan Daniel, *The Sporting News*, March 12, 1947, p. 8.

39. A. B. Chandler with Vance H. Trimble, *Heroes, Plain Folks, and Skunks: The Life and Times of Happy Chandler: An Autobiography* (Chicago: Bonus Books, 1989), p. 210.

40. *New York Herald Tribune*, May 7, 1947, p. 33.

41. Serialization of Raft's syndicated bio *I Can't Escape My Past* from the *Boston Herald*, January 25, 1958, p. 24.

42. *The Sporting News*, July 10, 1951.

43. Jack Hand, "Yanks Claim Assist on Leo's Deal," *The Washington Post*, November 27, 1946, p. 14.

44. AP, *Advocate*, December 5, 1946, p. 18.

45. AP, *Advocate*, December 9, 1946, p. 6.

46. *Chicago Herald-American*, December 12, 1946, unpaginated morgue clipping.

47. AP, *Boston Herald*, December 24, 1946, p. 11.

48. *Time*, April 21, 1947, p. 57.

49. A. B. Chandler with Vance H. Trimble, *Heroes, Plain Folks, and Skunks*, pp. 190, 211.

CHAPTER 9: EXILED

1. AP, *Baltimore Sun*, June 29, 1947, p. 1.

2. Maurice Zolotow, *Shooting Star: A Biography of John Wayne* (New York: Simon & Schuster, 1974), p. 214; Jeremy Arnold, "Tycoon," TCM Film Article, http://www.tcm.com/this-month/article/135970 0/Tycoon.html; Randy Roberts and James S. Olson, *John Wayne: American* (Lincoln: Bison Books, 1997), p. 228.

3. Damon Rice, *Seasons Past* (New York: Praeger, 1976), p. 337.

4. *Idaho Statesman*, January 17, 1947, p. 4.

5. *Brooklyn Eagle*, March 3, 1947, p. 5.

6. Dan Daniel, "Happy, Laraine Lead Lippy to Sawdust Trail," *The Sporting News*, March 12, 1947, p. 8.

7. Red Barber, interview with William Marshall, November 13, 1979, The A. B. Chandler Oral History Project, Special Collections and Archives, University of Kentucky Libraries.

8. The column also appeared in "MacPhail Added Blowhard Voice to My Critics-Lippy," *The Sporting News*, March 19, 1947, p. 5. Quoting from more of the column, Durocher (Parrott) wrote: "I want to beat the Yankees as badly as I do any team in the National League. And that certainly is saying plenty . . . I want to beat the Yankees because MacPhail knows in his heart that I love Brooklyn, always want to manage there and regard Branch Rickey as my father. He tried to drive a wedge between myself and all these things I hold dear. When MacPhail found I couldn't be induced to manage his Yankees for any of his inducements, he resolved to knock me, and to make life as hard as possible for me. He has added his blowhard voice to the criticism which I have been catching lately, trying to make it into a gale."

9. *San Jose Evening News*, March 1, 1947, p. 2.

10. *Brooklyn Eagle*, March 8, 1947, p. 6.

11. *The New York Times*, October 13, 1991.

12. *New York Sun*, February 28, 1947, retrieved from Chicago newspaper morgue, not paginated; *Brooklyn Eagle*, February 28, 1947, p. 17.

13. *Brooklyn Eagle*, March 17, 1947.

14. Parrott, p. 260. Leo Durocher with Ed Linn, "The Candid Memoirs of Leo Durocher," *The Saturday Evening Post*, January 18, 1964, p. 21.

15. *The Sporting News*, April 2, 1947, p. 6.

16. *Brooklyn Eagle*, March 22, 1947, p. 6.

17. Laraine Day, *Day with the Giants* (Garden City: Doubleday, 1952), pp. 46–47.

18. *Rockford (IL) Evening Star*, March 25, 1957, p. 15.

19. Day, *Day with the Giants*, p. 54.

20. Mann, *Baseball Confidential*, pp. 113–14

21. *Richmond Times Dispatch*, March 12, 1947, p. 18.

22. *Sports Illustrated*, June 6, 1955, pp. 35–36.

23. Goren's interview for the *Sun* was turned into an article for the April 2, 1947, *Sporting News* (p. 9) and ran under the headline "Robinson Refuses to Join Dodgers if Resentment Exists." The subhead read "Negro Star Declares Main Reason He Desires a Major Chance Is for Bigger Pay."

24. Bob Wolff presentation, Library of Congress, April 26, 2013, on the occasion of the donation of his papers and recordings to the Library. At the time of the presentation Wolff was ninety-two and still working for News 12 on Long Island.

25. UP, *Chicago Herald-American*, April 10, 1947. Retrieved from *Chicago American* morgue, not paginated.

26. *The Boston Globe*, April 14, 1947, p. 12.

27. *The Washington Post*, April 27, 1947, p. M-12.

28. Red Barber, interview with William Marshall, November 13, 1979, The A. B. Chandler Oral History Project, Special Collections and Archives, University of Kentucky Libraries.

29. *The New York Times*, April 10, 1947, p. 32.

30. Tamiment Library Manuscript Files, TAM 245, box number, folder number, Tamiment Library/Robert F. Wagner Labor Archives, New York University.

31. *New York Herald Tribune*, April 22, 1947, p. 28: *Time* magazine, April 21, 1947, p. 57.

32. Red Barber, interview with William Marshall, November 13, 1979, The A. B. Chandler Oral History Project, Special Collections and Archives, University of Kentucky Libraries.

33. Jules Tygiel, *Baseball's Great Experiment* (New York: Oxford University Press, 1983), p. 177.

34. *Chicago Tribune*, April 10, 1947, p. 31.

35. News clippings on MacPhail in Box 24, Branch Rickey Papers, Manuscript Division, Library of Congress, Washington, D.C.

36. *The Christian Science Monitor*, May 2, 1947, p. 14.

37. Interview with Frank Deford in *Sports Illustrated*, July 20, 1987.

38. *New York Herald Tribune*, May 7, 1947, p. 33.

39. *Brooklyn Eagle*, June 27, 1947, p. 13.

40. Ibid.

41. *Sports Illustrated*, June 6, 1955, p. 72.

42. Day, p. 59.

43. Ibid.

44. INS, *Omaha World Herald*, September 6, 1947, p. 9.

45. *The Christian Science Monitor*, August 1, 1947, p. 16.

46. Rob Edelman SABR bio of Shotton: http://sabr.org/bioproj/person/97735d3o.

47. Larry Moffi, *The Conscience of the Game: Baseball's Commissioners from Landis to Selig* (Lincoln: University of Nebraska Press, 2006), p. 125; A. B. Chandler with Vance H. Trimble, *Heroes, Plain Folks, and Skunks: The Life and Times of Happy Chandler: An Autobiography* (Chicago: Bonus Books, 1989).

48. Joseph Reichler, *The Baseball Encyclopedia*, 5th ed. (New York: Macmillan, 1982), p. 2155.

49. Jules Tygiel, *Past Time: Baseball as History* (New York: Oxford University Press, 2000), p. 114; Neil J. Sullivan, *The Diamond in the Bronx: Yankee Stadium and the Politics of New York* (New York: Oxford University Press, 2001), p. 79.

50. *New York Herald Tribune*, October 16, 1947.

51. Ibid., December 3, 1947, p. 35.

52. *Chicago Herald-American*, December 8, 1947, retrieved from *Chicago American* morgue, not paginated.

Chapter 10: Over the River

1. *The Washington Post*, February 4, 1948, p. 19.

2. *Brooklyn Eagle* January 20, 1948, p. 11, and July 17, 1948, p. 7; The most detailed recollection was in Bob Cooke's *New York Herald Tribune* column of July 17, 1948, p. 12.

3. TS Newsfeatures, Associated Press Archives, December 24, 1947.

4. Caswell Adams, "Has Suspension Ruined Leo Durocher?," *Varsity: The Young Man's Magazine*, March 1948, p. 50.

Adams is recalled today as the man who coined the term "Ivy League" for a group of eight northeastern universities that are regarded to be among the best in the United States. When

Adams coined the term in 1937 for the then-powerful eastern football conference, it included Army and Navy as well as the current members: Brown, Columbia, Cornell, Dartmouth, Harvard, Pennsylvania, Princeton, and Yale.

5. Day, *Day with the Dodgers* (Garden City, NY: Doubleday & Company, 1952), p. 66; *Los Angeles Times*, June 1, 1961, p. c-3. Durocher will retell this story often and almost always end with the comment, "Why Trujillo wanted those baseballs back, I'll never know."

6. *Brooklyn Eagle*, March 21, 1948, p. 30.

7. Box 24, Branch Rickey, Papers, Manuscript Division, Library of Congress, Washington, D.C.; The memo appears in the folder in the box labeled DUROCHER, LEO.

    The original copy of Rickey's memo is housed in Box 24 of the Rickey papers at the Library of Congress and is not referenced in any of four Rickey biographies or in any contemporary accounts of the relationship between Rickey and Durocher. Murray Polner mentions the gambling and the treatment of Blades in his 1982 Rickey biography (p. 209), but his information comes from Hal Parrott and others, not the memo. It is unknown whether the memo was for Rickey alone or whether it went to O'Malley and the board of directors. In any event, it appears to be a rare primary source that has not been cited before.

8. Peter Golenbock, *Bums: An Oral History of the Brooklyn Dodgers* (Mineola, NY: Dover Publications, 2010), p. 184.

9. Roy Campanella, *It's Good to Be Alive* (New York: Little Brown & Co, 1959), pp. 137–38.

10. Ibid., p. 138.

11. *The New York Times*, May 23, 1948, p. S-2; *Boston Traveler*, May 18, 1948, p. 43.

12. *The New York Times*, May 30, 1938, p. BR-10.

13. Ed Fitzgerald, "Leo Durocher—Man with Nine Lives," *Sport* magazine, April 1951, p. 27.

14. *Boston Herald*, June 2, 1948, p. 26.

15. *Brooklyn Eagle*, July 17, 1948, p. 7.

16. UP, *The New York Times*, July 18, 1948, p. S2; AP, *Evening Star*, July 17, 1948, p. 12.

17. Mann, *Baseball Confidential*, pp. 180–81.

18. *Sports Illlustrated*, June 6, 1965, p. 73.

19. Day, *Day with the Giants*.

20. Fred Stein, *Under Coogan's Bluff: A Fan's Recollections of the New York Giants Under Terry and Ott* (Glenshaw, PA: Chapter and Cask, 1981), p. 136; Mann, *Baseball Confidential*, pp. 182–83.

21. *Boston Herald*, July 17, 1948, p. 6.

22. "Durocher's Switch to Giants Was a Real Shocker in '48," *The Washington Times* (Washington, D.C.), July 21, 2003; Fred Stein, *Under Coogan's Bluff*, p. 133.

23. Telephone interview with Arnold Hano, October 1, 2015. Hano, ninety-three at the time of my interview, is best remembered for his handwritten account of Game 1 of the 1954 World Series, which would form the basis for his breakthrough book and classic of baseball literature, *A Day in the Bleachers*. He is also the star of Jon Leonoudakis's 2015 documentary film *Hano—A Century in the Bleachers*.

24. *The New York Times*, October 13, 1991. This was a piece written several days after Leo died, entitled "The One Time Leo the Lip Kept It Buttoned."

25. *The New York Times*, July 27, 1948, p. 20.

26. *Chicago Herald-American*, July 27, 1948, *Chicago Herald-American* morgue, not paginated.

27. *Afro-American*, October 13, 1951, p. 1. The Irvin quote is from: William C. Kashatus, *Jackie and Campy: The Untold Story of Their Rocky Relationship and the Breaking of Baseball's Color Line* (Lincoln: University of Nebraska Press, 2014).

28. *New York Herald Tribune*, December 15, 1948, p. 34.

29. My old friend and classmate Martin Zelnik was a frequent visitor to the Polo Grounds during the Durocher years and recalls: "In those days, fans were permitted to enter the ballfield at the Polo Grounds . . . and perhaps all stadiums . . . [T]here may have been a short time period where ushers stood at the gates to the field to hold back fans until the players *et al.* left. The Giants' clubhouse was about 480'+ away in dead center field . . . quite a walk."

30. Frank Graham, *The New York Giants: An Informal History of a Great Baseball Club*, p. 290.

31. Happy Chandler with Vance H. Trimble, *Heroes, Plain Folks, and Skunks: The Life and Times of Happy Chandler: An Autobiography* (Chicago: Bonus Books, 1989), p. 221.

32. AP, April 29, 1949, Chicago American Morgue, not paginated.

33. AP, *Chicago Tribune*, May 1, 1949. *Chicago American* morgue, not paginated.

34. INS,*Chicago Herald-American*, May 2, 1949. *Chicago American* morgue, not paginated.

35. Bob Considine in the *Chicago Herald-American*, April 30, 1949. *Chicago American* morgue, not paginated.

36. *New York Herald Tribune*, May 3, 1949, p. 20.

37. AP, *New York Herald Tribune*, May 3, 1949, p. 26.

38. *Sports Illustrated*, June 6, 1955, p. 73; Ed Fitzgerald, "Leo Durocher—Man with Nine Lives," *Sport* magazine, April 1951, p. 84.

39. Ruark's syndicated column, *Idaho Statesman*, June 16, 1949, p. 4.

40. *Chicago Herald-American*, August 3, 1949. *Chicago American* morgue, not paginated.

41. Frank Graham, *The New York Giants*, p. 29.

42. AP, *Chicago Herald-American*, March 7, 1950, retrieved from *Chicago American* morgue, not paginated; Frank Graham, *The New York Giants*, p. 294.

43. *The Washington Post*, April 30, 1950, p. C-1.

44. Telephone interview with Monte Irvin from Houston, Texas, September 25, 2015.

45. CNS, *Arkansas State Press*, June 30, 1950, p. 7.

46. Baltimore *Afro-American*, October 13, 1951, p. 1.

47. *The New York Times*, November 28, 1950, p. 52.

48. Ron Rapoport, *Chicago Sun-Times*, Jan. 18, 1983.

49. *Chicago Herald-American*, December 5, 1950.

CHAPTER 11: MIRACLE MAN

1. Gilbert Millstein, "Durocher on Durocher et al.: The Manager of the Giants, at 45, Produces Some Apothegms Based on Experience with Ball Players, Umpires and People." *The New York Times*, July 22, 1951, p. 131.

2. Ed Fitzgerald, "Leo Durocher—Man With Nine Lives," *Sport*. April, 1951, p. 24.

3. *The New York Times*, June 16, 1991.

4. *Chicago Defender*, April 21, 1951, p. 16.

5. *The Washington Post*, November 7, 1951, p. 17.

6. *Brooklyn Eagle*, May 25, 1951, p. 16.

7. Leo Durocher and Barney Kremenko, "As He Rose to the Majors, No One Who Saw Him Play Doubted He Would Be a Star," *The New York Times*, July 29, 1979, p. S2.

8. E-mail to the author, December 6, 2015. Gillen also recalled the logistics of being a vendor: "During my tenure from 1951 through 1954, I saw every major league team play and thoroughly enjoyed the job. It was hard work, hustling in the ball parks, but the pay was great: 11.5 percent commission. I never took home less than $10 and made as much as $60 in one day during the 1952 World Series between the Yanks and the Dodgers. Started selling hot chocolate in the bleachers in the early morning when the gates opened and by

midafternoon I was selling ice cream sandwiches. In fact we ran out of both hot chocolate and ice cream."

9. Arthur Mann Papers (1901–1969), Library of Congress, Manuscript Division, Box 3.

10. Dick Williams and Bill Plaschke, *No More Mr. Nice Guy: A Life of Hardball* (San Diego: Harcourt Brace Jovanovich, 1990), pp. 50–51.

11. Ibid., p. 1955.

12. Bobby Thomson, Lee Heiman, and Bill Gutman, *The Giants Win the Pennant! The Giants Win the Pennant!* (New York: Zebra Books, 1991), pp. 179–80.

13. Durocher, *Nice Guys Finish Last*, pp. 304–5.

14. *New York Herald Tribune*, October 4, 1951.

15. Donald Honig, *The October Heroes: Great World Series Games Remembered by the Men Who Played Them* (Lincoln: University of Nebraska Press, 1996), 71, *Springfield Republican*, December 21, 1951, p. 40; *Chicago Defender*, October 6, 1941, p. 1.

16. *The New York Times*, October 11, 1951, p. 63.

17. Donald Honig, *The October Heroes*, p. 71; telephone interview with Monte Irvin from Houston, Texas, September 25, 2014.

18. *The Washington Post*, November 7, 1951, p. 17.

19. David Eisenhower, *Going Home to Glory: A Memoir of Life with Dwight D. Eisenhower, 1961–1969.* (New York: Simon & Schuster, 2011), p. 29.

20. AP, *The Washington Post*, March 2, 1952, p. C3.

21. *Baltimore African-American*, March 17, 1952, p. 12.

22. *Jet*, July 24, 1952, p. 52.

23. *Springfield Union*, July 27, 1952, p. 21.

24. *Boston Traveler*, December 22, 1952, p. 4.

25. On his work with the Browns: "I will teach the players to talk to their arms, so he will feel more limber and strong: and talk to their legs, so they will feel more supple and swift" (*Los Angeles Times*, January 1, 1950, p. 15).

26. *Daily Illinois State Journal* (Springfield, IL), March 22, 1953, p. 20. The exercise was nonsensical in the sense that Tracy was working in the dark with faulty information and talked of Leo's dominating mother and older sister who browbeat him as fostering his need to dominate as "the sole man" in the family.

27. *Chicago American*, June 11, 1953, retrieved from *Chicago American* morgue, not paginated.

28. *Springfield Union*, July 23, 1953, p. 32.

29. Ted Reed, *Carl Furillo, Brooklyn Dodgers All-Star* (Jefferson, NC: McFarland, 2010), p. 97.

30. *The New York Times*, July 29, 1979, p. S-2.

31. AP, *Chicago American*, retrieved from *Chicago American* morgue, not paginated.

32. *Chicago American*, August 25, 1954, retrieved from *Chicago American* morgue, not paginated.

33. Sandy Koufax and Ed Linn, *Koufax* (New York: Viking Adult, 1966), p. 47. The glove that Koufax borrowed that day was from Johnny Antonelli, who always remembered Koufax from that one incident. "For years I couldn't meet Johnny in a ball park without him yelling, 'Hey, Lefty, have you got your glove with you?'"

34. Donald Honig, *The Man in the Dugout: Fifteen Big League Managers Speak Their Minds* (Lincoln: University of Nebraska Press, 1995), p. 197.

35. *The Christian Science Monitor*, June 19, 1985, p. 18.

36. James S. Hirsch, *Willie Mays: The Life, the Legend* (New York: Scribner, 2011), p. 236.

37. *New York Herald Tribune*, March 2, 1955, p. 24.

38. *Chicago Sun-Times*, April 10, 1955, retrieved from *Chicago Sun-Times* morgue, not paginated.

39. AP, *Chicago American*, retrieved from *Chicago American* newspaper morgue, not paginated.

40. *Chicago American*, reprint of Cannon's column, October 16, 1965, unpaginated clipping from *Chicago American* morgue.

41. Telephone interview with Monte Irvin from Houston, TX, September 25, 2015.

42. Willie Mays and Lou Sahadi, *Say Hey: The Autobiography of Willie Mays* (New York: Simon & Schuster, 1988), p. 145; James S. Hirsch, *Willie Mays: The Life, the Legend*, Reprint ed. (New York: Scribner, 2011), pp. 244–45.

43. Tex Maule, "The Return of Durocher," *Sports Illustrated*, March 6, 1961.

CHAPTER 12: HOLLYWOOD DODGER

1. *New York Herald Tribune*, November 6, 1955, p. B-5.

2. NEA, *Advocate* (Baton Rouge, LA), January 3, 1956, p. 2.

3. *Boston American*, January 27, 1956, p. 48,

4. *The New York Times*, February 6, 1956, p. 19.

5. *New York Herald Tribune*, March 17, 1956, p. B-1.

6. *The Saturday Evening Post*, May 11, 1963, p. 48; Earl Wilson's column, *Register-Republic* (Rockford, IL), September 7, 1956, p. 7.

7. "The Low-Down from Leo," *The Saturday Evening Post*, January 4, 1958, p. 49.

8. U.S. Federal Individual Income Tax Rates History, 1862–2013 (Nominal Dollars): http:// taxfoundation.org/article/us-federal-individual-income-tax-rates-history-1913-2013-nominal-and-inflation-adjusted-brackets; Harry T. Paxton, "The Low-Down from Leo," *The Saturday Evening Post*, January 4, 1958, p. 48.

9. *Los Angeles Times*, January 16, 1958 p. 5

10. *Springfield Union*, April 7, 1959, p. 2.

11. Richard, "Leo Durocher, Headline Hustler Extraordinary," *Climax—Exciting Stories for Men*, June, 1960. p. 78.

12. Leo Durocher, *Nice Guys Finish Last* (New York: Simon & Schuster, 1975), p. 69.

13. AP, *Christian Science Monitor*, October 15, 1959, p. 50.

14. AP, *The Washington Post*, November 14, 1959, p. A-11; *Los Angeles Times*, November 14, 1959, p. B-1.

15. *Rockford (IL) Morning Star*, January 24, 1960, p. 40.

16. *New York Daily News*, December 31, 1960, p. 11.

17. AP, *The Christian Science Monitor*, December 14, 1960, p. 11.

18. *Boston Record American*, December 25, 1960, p. 22.

19. *The Sporting News*, January 18, 1961; UPI, *The Jersey Journal*, January 10, 1961, p. 16.

20. Tex Maule, "The Return of Durocher," *Sports Illustrated*, March 6, 1961.

21. *Hartford Courant*, January 10, 1961, p. 21, *The Boston Globe*, January 11, 1961, p. S7.

22. *New Pittsburgh Courier*, January 21, 1961, p. 25.

23. Telephone interview with Monte Irvin from Houston, TX, September 25, 2015.

24. *Parade*, October 1, 1961, p. 1.

25. *Springfield Union*, February 19, 1961, p. 23.

26. *San Diego Union*, March 5, 1961, p. 119.

27. *Sports Illustrated*, February 18, 1963.

28. AP, *The Seattle Times*, March 14, 1961, p. 15; AP, *The Washington Post*, March 22, 1961.

29. *San Diego Union*, April 18, 1961, p. 29.

30. *The Sporting News*, April 26, 1961; *LIFE*, April 28, 1961, p. 31.

31. *Pittsburgh Press*, April 18, 1961, retrieved from National Baseball Library vertical file, not paginated.

32. *Dallas Morning News*, December 25, 1961, p. 8.

33. *Washington Star*, March 23, 1962, p. 10. When the story appeared the next day, *The Washington Post*'s headline for the Associated Press story put it directly: "Sign-Stealing with Binoculars Set Up Thomson's Flag Winning Homer." *The Washington Post*, March 23, 1967. The *New York Herald Tribune* headlined it: "Clubhouse Spy Helped Thomson Hit Homer in '51, Says Ex-Giant."

34. AP, *Boston Herald*, March 24, 1962, p. 16.

35. *Milwaukee Journal-Sentinel*, March 24, 1962, p. 13, *The New York Times*, March 24, 1962, p. 19.

36. Bob Hunter of the *Los Angeles Herald-Examiner* on March 23.

37. *Milwaukee Journal-Sentinal*, March 24, 1962, p. 13.

38. McDonald, Jack. "Signal Stealing Is an Overrated Trick." *San Francisco News Call Bulletin*, March 24, 1962.

39. *The New York Times*, October 14, 2001.

40. Joshua Prager, "Inside Baseball: Giants' 1951 Comeback, The Sport's Greatest, Wasn't All It Seemed," *The Wall Street Journal*, January 31, 2001, p. 1.

41. The story that appeared after Durocher had been admitted to the Hall of Fame had some calling for his de-enshrinement. Baseball moralists took the high ground a half century after the fact. Fumed the *Chicago Tribune*: "It's as if the Nazis made the D-Day invasion easier than it looked. As if the first moon landing was faked at some desert in New Mexico. As if Picasso secretly paid his landlady to sketch his best stuff." Some took Thomson at his word and declared that everyone in that era was trying to steal signs and that it was not really a story—especially since catchers from other teams had learned to encode their signs. Durocher had a well-earned reputation dating back to the 1930s as a master orchestrator of sign-stealing, often working in tandem with Coach Charlie Dressen. When Durocher and Dressen were removed from the 1947 Dodgers, it was noted that the team had lost its ability to steal signs.

42. Joshua Prager, *The Echoing Green: The Untold Story of Bobby Thomson, Ralph Branca, and the Shot Heard Round the World* (New York: Pantheon, 2006), p. 351.

43. *The Seattle Times*, October 13, 1991.

44. *Boston Record American*, August 28, 1962, p. 19.

45. *The Washington Post*, October 13, 1962, p. C-7.

46. Buzzie Bavasi and John Strege, *Off the Record* (Chicago: Contemporary Books, 1987), p. 59.

47. *Chicago American*, March 11, 1963, retrieved from *Chicago American* newspaper morgue, not paginated.

48. *San Diego Union*, May 12, 1963, p. S-2.

49. *New York Daily News*, September 16, 1963, retrieved from *Chicago American* morgue, not paginated.

50. *Omaha World Herald*, Tuesday, October 8, 1963, p. 19.

51. https://www.youtube.com/watch?v=gF2JLor2mvk.

52. *The Boston Globe*, July 11, 1964, p. 1.

53. *The Los Angeles Times*, August 27, 1964, p. B-1

54. UPI, *The Washington Post*, February 28, 1969, p. D-1.

55. *Chicago Today*, August 27, 1969, p. 74.

56. *Jersey Journal*, September 14, 1964, p. 19.

57. Paul Petersen e-mail to author Jeff Katz, February 7, 2007. Katz was extremely helpful to the author of this book in providing information on Durocher's role in television sitcoms.

58. *The Los Angeles Times*, September 16, 1964, p. 18.

59. North American Newspaper Alliance, *Omaha-World Herald*, October 19, 1964, p. 15.

60. Syndicated version, *Rockford (IL) Morning Star*, September 16, 1964, p. 18.

61. Dave Brady, "Leo Steals Show with Signal-Swiping on TV," *The Sporting News*, May 22, 1 965.

62. *Chicago American*, June 28, 1965, retrieved from *Chicago American* morgue, not paginated.

63. Scott Ferkovitz, *Hardball Times*, June 3, 2015, http://www.hardballtimes.com/p.k.-wrigley-and-the-college-of-coaches/.

64. Eskenazi, *The Lip: A Biography of Leo Durocher* (New York: William Morrow, 1993), p. 293.

65. *Chicago American*, January 12, 1966, retrieved from *Chicago American* morgue, not paginated.

CHAPTER 13: THE CONTENTIOUS CUB

1. *Chicago American*, February 6, 1966, unpaginated, from *Chicago American/Chicago Today* archives.

2. George Castle, *The Million-to-One Team* (South Bend, IN: Diamond Communications, 2000), p. 137.

3. *Chicago Tribune*, April 26, 1966, p. C1; *Chicago American*, April 27, 1966, unpaginated, from *Chicago American/Chicago Today* archives.

4. Jim Enright, *Baseball's Great Teams: Chicago Cubs* (New York: Rutledge, 1975), p. 160.

5. Durocher, *Nice Guys Finish Last*, pp. 365–66.

6. Interview with Richard Cohen published in *Sports Illustrated*, July 7, 2014, p. 49.

7. Leo Durocher in 1966 on why he had long refused to grant interviews, quoted by Charles Marr in the *Los Angeles Times*, July 27, 1971, p. 1.

8. Castle, *The Million-to-One Team*, p. 139.

9. E-mail from Christine, July 30, 2015.

10. *The New York Times*, June 26, 1966, p. S-2

11. *The Washington Post*, June 22, 1966, p. E-2.

12. *Chicago Tribune*, August 29, 1966, p. E-1.

13. *Chicago Defender*, April 19, 1967, p. 28.

14. chicagotribune.com/2008-08-19/sports/0808180927_1_no-hitter-ken-holtzman-three-run-homer/1.

15. *Chicago American*, January 13, 1977, unpaginated, from *Chicago American/Chicago Today* archives.

16. Ibid., February 28, 1967, unpaginated from *Chicago American/Chicago Today* archives.

17. Ibid., July 2, 1967.

18. *Los Angeles Times*, March 13, 1967, p. C-1

19. *Chicago American*, May 21, 1987, unpaginated, from *Chicago American/Chicago Today* archives.

20. Ibid., July 2, 1967, unpaginated, from *Chicago American/Chicago Today* archives.

21. Jerome Holtzman and George Vass, *Baseball, Chicago Style: A Tale of Two Teams, One City* (Chicago: Bonus Books, 2001), p. 140; Kram, Mark, "HE'S all about SUNSHINE," *Sports Illustrated*, November 28, 2013.

22. http://www.hardballtimes.com/the-williams-santo-cubs-1966–1969/.

23. *Chicago Tribune*, October 4, 1966, p. 16, and October 27, 1966, p. 20.

24. *The Los Angeles Times*, September 10, 1967, p. G-3.

25. *Chicago Tribune*, November 17, 1968, p. E1.

26. *Chicago American*, March 11, 1968, unpaginated, *Chicago Today* morgue clipping.

27. *Chicago Tribune*, July 10, 1968, p. C-3

28. *Pittsburgh Press*, June 17, 1969, p. 30; e-mail to the author from Jim Christine, July 15, 2015.

29. *Chicago Tribune*, September 25, 1968, p. C-2.

30. *Chicago American*, February 2, 1969, retrieved from *Chicago American* morgue, not paginated.

31. *The New York Times*, February 2, 1969, p. S-2.

32. Robert Boyle reporting in *Sports Illustrated*, June 30, 1967, p. 14.

33. Interview with Hageman, March 4, 2014.

34. *Chicago American*, August 15, 1969, unpaginated, *Chicago Today* morgue clipping.

35. Tom Fitzpatrick, *Fitz: All Together Now* (New York: David McKay, 1972), p. 197.

36. *Chicago Tribune*, January 11, 1968, p. 14; *Chicago American*, July 2, 1968, unpaginated from *Chicago American/Chicago Today* archives.

37. Enright, *Baseball's Great Teams*, p. 54.

38. *Jet*, July 17, 1969, p. 56.

39. *The Sporting News*, August 2, 1969, pp. 9–36.

40. Durocher, *Nice Guys Finish Last*, p. 359.

41. *The Sporting News* August 9, 1969, p. 24.

42. Doug Feldmann, *Miracle Collapse: The 1969 Chicago Cubs* (Lincoln: University of Nebraska Press, 2006), pp. 181–82.

43. Gerald C. Wood and Andrew Hazucha, *Northsiders: Essays on the History and Culture of the Chicago Cubs* (Jefferson, NC: McFarland & Company, 2008), p. 101. Also, Brad Beechen, a Chicagoan and longtime Cubs fan, suggested a note here to help non-Chicagoan readers understand why forgoing the White Sox exhibition game was not a possibility (rainout excepted). As he wrote to the author: "The Northside Cubs and the Southside White Sox have battled yearly for city bragging rights. If the teams are at all competitive, and maybe even if not, tens of thousands of tickets are sold long before the scheduled date (now dates, since the teams play a three-game series in both ball parks with the games counting in the standings). The Cubs, tired though they might have been, couldn't bow out of the game and would have been pilloried if they rested their regulars and maybe brought up players from their farm teams for a day in the Majors."

44. Castle, *The Million-to-One Team*, p. 147; Rick Phalen, *Our Chicago Cubs* (South Bend, IN: Diamond Communications, 1992), p. 103.

45. Ferguson, Jenkins, *Like Nobody Else: The Fergie Jenkins Story* (New York: NTC/ Contemporary Publishing, 1973), p. 132.

46. AP, *The Washington Post*, August 28, 1969, p. H-2; William Barry Furlong, "How Durocher Blew the Pennant," *Look*, March 10, 1970, p. 56.

47. *Chicago Today*, August 27, 1969, p. 74.

48. Furlong, "How Durocher Blew the Pennant," p. 55.

49. *Sports Illustrated*, July 7, 2014, p. 49.

50. *The Sporting News*, September 27, 1969, p. 38.

51. *Chicago Today*, September 12, 1969, unpaginated, *Chicago Today* morgue clipping.

52. Phone interview with John Pekkanen, August 18, 2015.

53. *Chicago Tribune*, September 13, 1969, p. A-2

54. *New York Daily News*, September 12, 1969.

55. *Pittsburgh Press*, Oct. 8, 1969.

56. Ibid., Oct. 8, 1969.

57. *Rockford (IL) Morning Star*, May 1, 1973, p. 25.

58. *The Washington Post*, January 24, 2015.

59. David Claerbaut, *Durocher's Cubs: The Greatest Team That Didn't Win* (Dallas: Taylor Publishing Company, 2000), p. 114.

60. *The Sporting News*, September 27, 1969, p. 14.

61. *Chicago Tribune*, October 7, 1969, p. 12.

62. See, for example, on the Cubs side of the equation, David Claerbaut, *Durocher's Cubs*; Rick Talley, *The Cubs of '69: Recollections of the Team That Should Have Been* (Chicago:

Contemporary Books, 1989); Doug Feldmann, *Miracle Collapse: The 1969 Chicago Cubs* (Lincoln: University of Nebraska Press, 2006); and George Castle, *The Million-to-One Team.*

63. Enright, *Baseball's Great Teams*, p. 54.

CHAPTER 14: ENDGAME

1. *Rockford (IL) Morning Star*, October 16, 1969, p. 23; *Boston Herald-American*, November 23, 1969.
2. *Baltimore Sun*, July 26, 1970, pp. 23–24.
3. *Boston Record American*, December 14, 1969, p. 135.
4. UPI, *Rockford (IL) Morning Star*, January 9, 1970, p. 24.
5. *Chicago Today*, February 6, 1970.
6. *Richmond Times Dispatch*, March 4, 1970, p. 28.
7. Syndicated column, *Evansville Courier*, March 1, 1970, p. 47.
8. *Sunday Washington Star*, March 1, 1970, p. 80.
9. *San Diego Union*, March 23, 1970, p. 19.
10. *Chicago Today*, March 26, *Chicago Today* newspaper morgue.
11. John Justin Smith, *New York Post*, July 27, 1970, p. 51.
12. George Castle, *The Million-to-One Team*, p. 150.
13. *The Boston Globe*, July 26, 1970, p. 34.
14. Castle, *The Million-to-One Team*, p. 170.
15. Telephone conversation with George Castle, September 2, 2015.
16. *Chicago Today*, April 6, 1970, *Chicago Today* newspaper morgue.
17. AP, *Daily Illini*, May 30, 1970, p. 17.
18. *Chicago Tribune*, July 8, 1970, p. E-3.
19. David Claerbaut, *The Greatest Team That Didn't Win*, p. 26.
20. *Chicago Today*, July 26, 1970.
21. *The Sporting News*, July 27, 1970, p. 51; *The Los Angeles Times*, July 26, 1970, p. C-3.
22. *Chicago Defender*, August 27, 1970, p. 30.
23. *Chicago Today*, September 24, 1970, *Chicago Today* newspaper morgue.
24. *Sports Illustrated*, May 3, 1971, p. 52.
25. *Chicago Tribune*, July 28, 1971, p. C-2.
26. Ron Santo and Randy Minkoff, *Ron Santo: For Love of Ivy* (Chicago: Bonus Books, 1993) p. 111.
27. *Guideposts* magazine, June 2003. In this piece Santo said of the day in question: "My life changed that day. I started spending more time in hospital pediatric units, visiting diabetic children. I urged them to remain positive and told them that they could accomplish anything they wanted despite their disease. Kids sent me letters; so did their parents." Jerome Holtzman and George Vass, *Baseball, Chicago Style*, Revised ed. (Los Angeles: Taylor Trade Publishing, 2004) p. 147.
28. AP, *Hartford Courant*, August 28, 1971, p. 21.
29. *Chicago Tribune*, September 4, 1971, Section 2, p. 1.
30. Steve Treder, *The Williams Santo Cubs*, http://www.hardballtimes.com/the-williams-santo-cubs-1970–1973/.
31. Bruce Marcus en writing in *Hardball Times*, http://www.hardballtimes.com/card-corner-1972-topps-ken-holtzman/.
32. Andrew Hazucha, "Leo Durocher's Last Stand: Anti-Semitism, Racism, and the Cubs Player Rebellion of 1971," *Nine* 15, no. 1 (Fall 2006).

33. Rick Talley, *The Cubs of '69: Recollections of the Team That Should Have Been* (Chicago: Contemporary Books), pp. 249–50; Claerbaut, *Durocher's Cubs*, p. 113.

34. *Charleston News and Courier*, November 11, 1971, p. 38.

35. *Chicago Today*, January 7, 1972, retrieved from *Chicago Today* newspaper morgue, not paginated.

36. Ibid., June 5, 1972, retrieved from *Chicago Today* newspaper morgue, not paginated.

37. AP, *Rockford (IL) Register-Republic*, July 6, 1972, p. 24. Newspapers replaced the *horseshit* with *blank-blank* lest they offend readers with one of Durocher's key words.

38. *Chicago Today*, July 22, 1972, retrieved from *Chicago Today* morgue, not paginated.

39. Ibid., July 25, 1972, retrieved from *Chicago Today* morgue, not paginated.

40. Ibid., July 26, 1972, retrieved from *Chicago Today* morgue, not paginated.

41. *Evening Star*, July 30, 1972, p. 61. Frank Robinson became the first black manager in 1975 for the Cleveland Indians.

42. *Chicago Today*, July 30, 1972, retrieved from *Chicago Today* morgue, not paginated.

43. *Boston Herald*, March 6, 1973, p. 22.

44. *Chicago Today*, August 28, 1972, p. 28.

45. Ibid., September 24, 1972, p. 10.

46. *The Sporting News*, October 14, 1972, p. 13.

47. UPI, *Boston Herald*, October 25, 1972, p. 28.

48. *Sports Illustrated*, August 13, 1973, *Sports Illustrated* online vault, not paginated.

49. *Boston Herald*, March 6, 1973, p. 22.

50. *The Sporting News*, March 31, 1973, p. 30.

51. Ibid.

52. *The Boston Globe*, March 15, 1973, 63.

53. Larry Dierker, *This Ain't Brain Surgery: How to Win the Pennant Without Losing Your Mind* (Lincoln: University of Nebraska Press, 2003), p. 117.

54. *The Sporting News*, February 23, 1973, p. 27.

55. *Chicago Tribune*, June 1, 1973, p. C-3.

56. *Sports Illustrated*, August 13, 1973, *Sports Illustrated* online vault, not paginated.

57. *Dallas Morning News*, July 3, 1973, p. 6.

58. *Boston Herald*, July 1, 1973, p. 28.

59. *The Los Angeles Times*, September 7, 1973, p. A-9. The earliest version of this rumor appeared in July under the byline of handicapper Jimmy the Greek in his syndicated column of July 13.

60. One of Durocher's lines from *Nice Guys Finish Last* that appeared in most of his obituaries, AP, Oct. 8, 1991.

61. This will not be the first nor the last time Durocher appears in American literature. He has a walk-on role in Ernest Hemingway's *Old Man and the Sea* and is central to Don DeLillo's *Pafko at the Wall*, the novella extracted from the 1996 novel *Underworld*. It was in Leo's box that J. Edgar Hoover and Toots Shor were witnesses to Jackie Gleason as he vomited on Frank Sinatra's lisle socks. Here is how DeLillo described Durocher: "Look at Durocher on the dugout steps, manager of the Giants, hard-rock Leo, the gashouse scrapper, a face straight from the Gallic Wars, and he says into his fist, 'Holy fuggin shit almighty.'"

CHAPTER 15: THE ROCKY ROAD TO COOPERSTOWN

1. *Sports Illustrated*, August 13, 1973, *Sports Illustrated* online vault, not paginated.

2. *Rockford (IL) Register-Republic*, June 23, 1967, p. 20.

3. *Chicago Today*, November 7, 1973, *Chicago Today* newspaper morgue, unpaginated.

4. *The Sporting News*, June 21, 1975, p. 6.

5. *Sports Illustrated*, June 16, 1975; *Chicago Tribune*, May 31, 1935, *Chicago Tribune* newspaper morgue.

6. *The Los Angeles Times*, June 22, 1975, p. 31.

7. *Chicago Tribune*, June 6, 1975, p. C-3.

8. http://wgnradio.com/2013/09/20/leo-durocher.

9. E-mail from George Castle, October 10, 2014.

10. Milton Richman, "Durocher's Heart Set on Managing," *The Los Angeles Times*, June 29, 1977, p. F2.

11. William Barry Furlong, "Durocher Goes on the Road," *The Washington Post*, January 6, 1976, p. D-1.

12. Maggie Daly, "Ill Durocher to Miss Japan," *Chicago Tribune*, March 24, 1976, p. B-13.

13. *Japan Times*, April 12, 1976, unpaginated clipping, National Baseball Library.

14. Neil Milbert, "Durocher Is Alive and Talking," *Chicago Tribune*, June 13, 1970, p. C1.

15. *The New York Times*, March 19, 1976, p. 57. *Chicago Tribune*, May 20, 1976, p. C-1.

16. *American Way*, January 1976, pp. 17–20.

17. *Chicago Tribune*, January 30, 1976, p. C-3.

18. *The Los Angeles Times*, June 21, 1978, *Chicago Today* newspaper morgue.

19. *Springfield Union*, September 2, 1978, p. 21.

20. *The Christian Science Monitor*, March 2, 1981, p. 13.

21. Gerald Eskenazi, *The Lip: A Biography of Leo Durocher* (New York: William Morrow, 1993), pp. 310–11.

22. David Claerbaut, *Durocher's Cubs: The Greatest Team That Didn't Win* (Dallas: Taylor Publishing Company, 2000), p. 22.

23. *The Christian Science Monitor*, March 2, 1981, p. 13.

24. *The New York Times*, November 19, 1981, p. B-11.

25. Ibid., March 11, 1982.

26. *Portland (OR) Scanner*, September 22, 1982, p. 15.

27. *The Oregonian*, September 5, 1982, p. 96.

28. Buzzie Bavasi and John Strege, *Off the Record* (Chicago: Contemporary Books, 1987), p. 59.

29. Scott Ostler, *San Francisco Chronicle*, February 20, 2014.

30. Alan Goldstein, "Durocher Said 'No' to Managing the Birds," *The Baltimore Sun*, July 7, 1983, p. C-2; Bill Center, "Herzog Likely to Call on Dravecky," *San Diego Union*, July 6, 1983, p. 27.

31. Ron Rapoport, "He Knew Ernie Banks as Thoughtful, Reflective, Complicated," *LAObserved*, January 25, 2015, http://www.laobserved.com/intell/2015/01/ernie_banks_was_a_thoughtful_r.php.

32. Ernie Harwell, *Tuned to Baseball* (South Bend, IN.: Diamond Communications, 1985), p. 3.

33. *Sports Illustrated*, August 10, 1987.

34. Letter from Bavasi to Chandler dated August 3, 1988, Legendary Auctions, February 27, 2015, auction lot 449, "Historic A. B. Happy Chandler Archive—Against Durocher going into HOF."

35. Letter from Chandler to Bavasi dated August 17, 1988, Legendary Auctions, February 27, 2015, auction lot 449 "Historic A. B. Happy Chandler Archive—Against Durocher going into HOF."

36. Letter from Chandler to Brown, dated August 17, 1988, Legendary Auctions, February 27, 2015, auction lot 449 "Historic A. B. Happy Chandler Archive—Against Durocher going into HOF."

37. *Marietta Journal*, December 3, 1988, p. 22.

38. *The New York Times*, February 18, 1989.

39. *Evansville (IN) Courier and Press*, February 29, 1989, p. 2.

40. A. B. Chandler with Vance H. Trimble, *Heroes, Plain Folks, and Skunks: The Life and Times of Happy Chandler: An Autobiography* (Chicago: Bonus Books, 1989), pp. 188–89.

41. Ibid., p. 216.

42. *Boston Herald*, June 21, 1989, p. 101.

43. *Chicago Tribune*, March 22, 1989, p. 9.

44. Ibid., March 22, 1989, p. B-9.

45. Rick Talley, *The Cubs of '69*, p. 301; *Chicago Tribune*, March 22, 1989, p. 9.

46. *USA Today*, February 28, 1990, p. 11C.

47. Roger Kahn, *Rickey and Robinson: The True, Untold Story of the Integration of Baseball* (New York: Rodale Books, 2015), pp. 128–31.

48. Telephone interview with Monte Irvin from Houston, TX, September 25, 2015.

49. *The New York Times*, June 16, 1991.

50. *Orange County Register*, August 2, 1991.

51. Interview with Marcus, April 15, 2015.

52. Gordon Eades, "Snub by Hall Irked Leo Durocher," *Augusta Chronicle*, October 9, 1991, p. 14.

53. *The New York Times*, October 15, 1991.

54. *Newsday*, October 8, 1991, p. 3.

55. Joe Jares, "Leo Is Laid to Rest," *Los Angeles Daily News*, October 12, 1991.

56. *Los Angeles Times*, October 18, 19, 1991.

57. *Philadelphia Daily News*, March 18, 1992, p. 79.

58. Her last appearance was in a two-part episode of *Murder, She Wrote*.

59. Quoted from her *New York Times* obituary, November 13, 2007.

60. Sean Kirst, "Baseball Makes Immortal a Man, a Romance an Era," *Syracuse Post-Standard*, July 28, 1994. Kirst appears to have been the only mainstream reporter to have interviewed Day before the induction.

61. *The Los Angeles Times*, August 2, 1994.

Index

Aaron, Hank, 287
ABC (American Broadcasting Company), 244–45
Adams, Earl "Sparky," 58
Adonis, Joe, 148, 149, 150, 203, 300
African-American fans, 74, 127
African-American players, 89–92, 134, 137–38, 160–62, 204, 211, 218, 292
    See also racial integration of baseball
Agee, Tommy, 257
Aguirre, Hank, 257, 279
Alexander, Grover Cleveland, 21
alien-of-affection law suit, 241–42
Allen, Artemus Ward "Nick," 21–22, 24
Alou, Jesus, 257
Alston, Walter, 230–31, 238–39, 240–41, 243
Amalfitano, Joe, 272–73
Anderson, Alf, 95
Angels in the Outfield (film), 212–13
Antonelli, Johnny, 219
Astrodome (Houston), 249–50, 282
Atlanta Baseball Co. v. Lawrence, 20n
Atlanta Braves, 268
Atlanta Crackers, 19–21
Autry, Gene, 295

Babe Ruth's Own Book of Baseball (Ruth), 27
Ballanfant, Lee, 126
Baltimore Orioles, 268, 296
Banks, Ernie, 247, 248–49, 251, 252–53, 256–57, 258, 261, 263, 265, 267–68, 274, 276, 277, 278, 280–81, 289–90, 292, 297
Barber, Red, 27, 76, 84, 87–88, 88n, 145, 151, 172, 190, 293, 301, 302, 303
Barlik, Al, 110
Barney, Rex, 293
Barrow, Ed, 16, 16n, 37, 46, 47, 48–49
Bartell, Dick, 55–56
baseball, 49, 50n, 57, 105n. *See also* racial integration of baseball; *specific team and player names*
Batista, Fulgencio, 93
Bauer, Hank, 212, 296
Bavasi, Buzzie, 230–31, 233, 238–39, 240, 260, 293, 295–96, 298–99, 303–4, 305
beanball, 3, 22, 29
Beckert, Glenn, 237, 252–53, 256, 257

Bell, Bert, 153
Benny, Jack, 103, 123, 220
Benton, Larry, 55
Berle, Milton, 123, 220, 306
Bermingham, Bishop, 156
Berra, Yogi, 159, 244, 287
Bevens, Bill, 178
Birns, Alex "Shondor," 302
Black Athletes Hall of Fame, 292
Bladt, Rich, 278
Bleacher Bums, 167, 257–58, 260, 266
Boccabella, John, 251
Bock, Hal, 291
Bonham, Ernie "Tiny," 101
Bonnibeau, Gene, 218
Bonura, Zeke, 86
Bostic, Joe, 131–32
Boston Braves (Bees), 43, 48, 54, 56, 57, 61, 70, 85, 98, 125, 134, 143, 183, 187, 192, 197, 206, 209
Boston Red Sox, 32, 38, 42, 43, 44–45, 74n, 112, 124, 133, 137, 199n, 281
Boswell, Tom, 267
Boudreau, Lou, 260, 270, 297
Boysen, Fred, 193, 194–95, 196
Bragan, Bobby, 116, 162, 169, 246, 306
Bramham, William, 138, 151–52
Branca, Ralph, 126, 146, 210, 235, 236, 237, 293, 294, 302, 302–3n
Brickhouse, Jack, 259, 260, 262, 271, 273, 274, 289, 291, 304
Broeg, Bob, 8, 289, 305, 305n
Brooklyn Brown Dodgers, 134
Brooklyn Dodgers, 1, 2, 3, 4, 54n, 57, 59, 71, 193, 207–11, 214, 215, 216, 218n, 235–37, 237n, 268
    Durocher traded to, 73–74
    1938 season, 75–83
    1939 season, 85–89
    1940 season, 92–93
    1941 season, 93–101
    1942 season, 104–11
    1943 season, 115–21
    1944 season, 121–26
    1945 season, 131–36
    1946 season, 142–47, 302
    1947 season, 160–79
    1948 season, 183–92, 282

Brooklyn Eagle, 27, 32, 43, 57, 82, 83, 96, 101, 107,
   135, 136, 142, 157, 160, 163, 175, 180, 182, 188,
   205
Broun, Heywood Hale, 159, 159n, 191–92, 293
Brown, Joe L., 266, 299, 303–4
Bryant, Clay, 81
Bucher, Jimmy, 73, 74, 74n
Bunning, Jim, 255
Burns, George, 220, 232
Burns, Ken, 304
Burr, Harold, 27, 57, 161, 163–64, 182
Busch, Gussie, 244

Cacchione, Peter V., 172
California Angels, 295–96
Camilli, Dolph, 93, 113, 119
Camp, Marcel, 46–47
Campanella, Roy, 134, 161, 163, 186–87, 199, 213,
   236, 302, 303
Camp Ojibwa, 261–62, 261n, 268, 269, 270, 274
Cannon, Jimmy, 62, 212, 222
Capote, Truman, 288
Caray, Harry, 244, 257
Carey, Max, 85
Carlton, James 'Tex,' 92
Carter, Jimmy, 287
Carver, Lawton, 120, 121, 177
Casey, Hugh, 94–95, 95n, 99, 182
Castle, George, 248, 249, 272–73
Chance, Bob, 245
Chandler, A. B. "Happy"
   Babe Ruth and, 49
   as commissioner replacing Landis, 133–34, 133n
   death of, 304
   disliked by sportswriters, 153–54, 157, 173–74, 178,
     193
   Durocher's assault trial and, 142
   as Durocher's old nemesis, 296–97, 298–300
   Durocher's second suspension by, 193–96,
     203–4, 271, 275
   Durocher's signing of Fitzsimmons and, 192–93
   Durocher's war with MacPhail and suspension
     by, 160, 164–65, 166, 167–68, 168n, 170, 171,
     172, 174n, 176–77, 176n, 181, 182, 298, 302,
     303n
   gambling and, 140–41, 151–52, 153, 154, 155
   Hall of Fame, elected to, 295
   Heroes, Plain Folks, and Skunks, 299–300
   integration and, 147
   on meeting Durocher, 54
   resignation of, 204
   Rickey's request to, 149–50
   warnings from, 200
   World Series (1947) money and, 179, 179n
Chapman, Ben, 46
Chicago Cubs, 2, 7, 15, 65, 70, 71–72, 79, 81, 125,
   178, 245–46, 291
   Durocher as manager of, 246–81, 297
Chicago White Sox, 141n, 228, 246, 263, 299
Christian, John, 135, 136, 140, 142–44, 145, 173, 182,
   187–88, 196, 240
Christine, Bill, 249, 255, 258
Cincinnati Reds, 33, 62, 65, 74, 76, 77, 78, 88, 92,
   108, 110, 187, 282–83, 300
   Durocher as player for, 48–60
Claerbaut, David, 7

Clark, Earl, 57
Cleveland Indians, 43, 192, 208, 219–20, 228–29
Cobb, Ty, 3, 27–29, 34, 37, 208, 293, 307
Cohane, Tim, 116, 117, 118, 119, 119n, 188
Cohen, Ron, 241–42
Collins, Rip, 63, 65, 80
Communist Party, American, 76, 91, 105, 107
Condon, Dave, 27, 268, 286, 289
Conlan, Jocko, 125, 185, 233–34, 297
Conlon, Charles M., 19
Connery, Bob, 22–23
Connolly, Sheila, 232
Considine, Bob, 80, 92, 126–27, 144, 219
Cooke, Bob, 93, 174, 225
Cooney, Johnny, 73, 74, 74n, 115
Corbitt, Claude, 104
Corriden, John "Red," 140, 169
Corum, Bill, 178, 190–91, 300
Costas, Bob, 295
Cox, Billy, 187, 208
Craft, Harry, 78
Crawford, Shag, 263–64
Creamer, Robert, 41
Critz, Hughie, 52
Cronk, George, 194
Crosby, Bing, 98, 138
Crosley, Powel, 62
Crump, Elijah, 194
The Cubs of '69 (Talley), 301
Cueller, Dick, 194
Cuyler, Kiki, 80

Daley, Arthur, 171, 187–88, 256–57
Daly, Maggie, 281–82, 292
Dark, Alvin, 197–98, 209, 215, 235–36, 240, 246,
   308
Davis, Curt, 140, 144, 145
Day, Laraine
   divorce from Hendricks, 155–57, 162, 174–75, 180
   Durocher's death and Hall of Fame induction,
     304–5, 306, 307–8
   Durocher's marriage to, 1, 182, 184, 190, 202,
     205, 212, 213, 219–20, 221, 226, 229–30,
     290–91
   Durocher's post-divorce relationship with, 4
   Durocher's romance with, 147, 150, 161, 162,
     165–66, 170, 176, 180
   at games, 5, 164
   as host of Giants pregame show, 198–99, 202
   Jackie Robinson and, 231
   meeting Durocher, 102
   memoir of, 177
   remarriage of, 232, 234
Dean, Dizzy, 61, 63, 64, 64n, 65–66, 67, 68, 71, 87,
   105n, 122, 226, 308
Dean, Paul, 63, 65–66, 67–68
DeBakey, Michael, 286, 291
Derringer, Paul, 58
Detroit Tigers, 65, 66–68, 74n, 178
Dickey, Bill, 80, 100
Dierker, Larry, 282–83, 284–85, 287
DiMaggio, Joe, 53, 80, 91, 99–100, 138–39, 178, 212
DiMaggio, Vince, 93–94, 95n
Dinah Shore Show, 225–26
Doby, Larry, 137, 197
Dockweiler, George A., 155–56

The Dodgers and Me (Durocher), 187–89, 289
Donatelli, Augie, 252
The Donna Reed Show, 243
Doyle, Jack, 15, 16
Dozer, Richard, 106, 263, 276
Dozier, Grace, 19–120, 64–65, 69, 88–89, 92–93, 102–4, 110, 111, 113, 156, 290–91
Dressen, Charlie (Chuck), 86, 94, 97, 110, 111, 112, 140, 143, 169, 173, 207, 210, 216
Dreyfus, Alfred, 207
Drysdale, Don, 233–34, 243
Duffy's Tavern (radio sit-com), 123
Dunbar, Bob, 48, 112
Dunn, Tom, 86–87, 93, 108
Durant, John, 188
Durocher, Leo
    as Brooklyn Dodgers manager, 180–90, 282
    as Brooklyn Dodgers player, 75–82
    as Brooklyn Dodgers player-manager, 82–101, 104–33
    as Chicago Cubs manager, 246–81, 297
    as Cincinnati Reds player, 48–58, 60
    criminal charges and trial, 135, 136, 140, 142–45
    death of, 304–6
    early life and career of, 9–24
    family of, 9–10, 12, 38, 50, 54, 63, 83, 222, 226, 227, 229, 261, 294, 308
    as Houston Astros manager, 282–87
    introduction to, 1–8
    as Los Angeles Dodgers coach, 230–44
    marriages of (*See* Day, Laraine; Dozier, Grace; Goldblatt, Lynne Walker; Hartley, Ruby)
    on National League All-Star team, 79–80
    at NBC, 223, 224–28
    as New York Giants manager, 190–223, 282, 297
    as New York Yankees player, 25–45, 46–48
    nicknames of, 1–2, 33, 34–35, 35n, 50, 66, 75
    as St. Louis Cardinals player, 59, 61–74
    suspension and reinstatement of, 168–80, 181, 207
Durocher's Cubs (Claerbaut), 7
Durslag, Mel, 230, 244, 255, 281, 283
Dyer, Eddie, 136, 302

The Echoing Green (Prager), 237–38
Einstein, Charles, 108n
Eisenhower, Dwight D., 213, 251, 251n
Engleberg, Memphis, 111, 112, 149, 159–60, 166–67, 298, 300
Enright, James, 251, 258, 258n, 261–62, 263, 268, 273, 274, 281, 282, 289, 289n
Eskenazi, Gerald, 246, 294, 307
Etten, Nick, 129, 168, 168n

Farley, James, 153
Feller, Bob, 104, 208
Filchock, Frank, 153
Finch, Bob, 131
The Fireside Book of Baseball (Einstein), 108n
Fitzgerald, Ed, 196, 203–4, 293
Fitzsimmons, Freddie, 87, 94, 99, 125, 192–93, 198, 206
Flavin, Harold, 11, 12
Flood, Curt, 260
Fonseca, Lew, 43
football, 36, 36n, 153
Ford, Hod, 52

Fothergill, Bob, 34
Foxx, Jimmie, 80
Frank, Stanley, 107–8, 108n, 270
Franks, Herman, 206, 208, 246
French-Canadian baseball players, 34, 34n
Frick, Ford, 27, 71, 72, 85, 86, 87, 95, 110–11, 133, 165, 173, 176n, 180, 189, 192, 193, 196, 204, 212
Frisch, Frankie, 62–63, 64n, 65–66, 68, 69, 70, 71, 72, 73, 192
Furillo, Carl, 3, 208, 216, 293
Furlong, William Barry, 264, 266, 270–71, 291

Gabor, Zsa Zsa, 4, 254, 254n
Galan, Augie, 116, 140
Gallagher, Bob, 285
Gamble, Lee, 77
gambling. *See also* Levinson, "Sleepout" Louie
    Chandler and, 140–41, 151–52, 153, 154, 155
    in the clubhouse, 109, 111–13
    Durocher and, 4, 8, 38–39, 41, 53–54, 85, 96–97, 109–10, 127–28, 157, 158, 161, 184, 269, 271–72, 274–75, 300–301
    Raft and, 89, 98, 122–23, 154
Game of the Week, 226
Garagiola, Joe, 146
Garbo, Greta, 201
Garcia, Silvio, 107, 127, 127n
Gardner, Billy, 218
Garfinkel, Jacob, 143
Garland, Judy, 241
Gehrig, Lou, 13, 15, 25, 26, 33, 44, 103, 136
Gehringer, Charlie, 67, 80
Gelbert, Charley, 57, 69, 70
Giancana, Sam, 273
Gibson, Josh, 74, 90, 106
Gilbert, Grant, 19
Giles, Bill, 250
Giles, Warren, 133, 216, 217, 234
Gillen, Neil, 206
Gilliam, Junior, 281
Gionfriddo, Al, 178
Goetz, Larry, 185, 214
Goldblatt, Lynne Walker, 253–54, 259–60, 261, 269, 272–73, 274, 281–82, 288, 291, 294, 301
Goldstein, Louis, 140, 144
Gomez, Preston, 286, 287
Gómez, Rubén, 216, 219
Goodman, Billy, 137
Gordon, Joe, 99, 100, 228–29
Gordon, Sid, 194, 197, 198
Goslin, Leon "Goose," 66, 67, 68
Gowdy, Hank, 29–30
Graham, Frank, 27, 29, 64, 77, 85, 115, 117, 118, 146, 197, 198
Graham, Walter, 66, 67–68
Grant, Jim "Mudcat," 260, 266
Gray, "Killer," 88–89, 89n, 138, 147, 148
Great Depression, 73, 74
Greenberg, Hank, 66, 138–39, 228, 239
Grilikhes, Mike, 232, 307
Grimes, Burleigh, 3, 76, 79, 81, 82, 90, 91
Guidotti, Major S. P., 114

Hallsworth, Robert, 242
Hand, Ed, 143
Hano, Arnold, 191

Hapes, Merle, 153
Harris, Bucky, 151
Harrison, James, 15, 32, 33
Hart, Bill, 143–44
Hartford Senators, 13–14, 14n, 15, 16–19
Hartley, Ruby, 53, 63, 64, 289
Harwell, Ernie, 216, 221, 297
Hatton, Grady, 286
Hawkins, Dick, 20, 21
Hearn, Jim, 200, 209
Heilmann, Harry, 35n, 52
Henrich, Tommy, 99, 101
Henshaw, Roy, 73, 74, 74n
Herman, Babe, 246
Herman, Billy, 53, 116, 293
Hickman, Jim, 274, 276
Higbe, Kirby, 161–62, 302, 302–3n
Hitler, Adolf, 100, 171
Hodges, Gil, 186, 209, 236
Hodges, Russ, 210
Hofman, Bobby, 218
Hogan, Frank S., 127–28
Hogan, Frank "Shanty," 57, 72
Holland, John, 245–46, 256, 260, 271–72, 276, 277, 280
Hollywood, 7, 103, 232–33
Holmes, Tommy, 32, 82, 83, 96, 107, 161, 163, 175–76, 182, 189, 205
Holtzman, Jerome, 252, 258–59, 261, 277–78, 289
Holtzman, Ken, 248, 251, 257, 262, 263, 276, 277–78
Hoover, J. Edgar, 167, 173–74
Hope, Bob, 220, 226, 306
Houston Astros, 249–50, 276, 282–87
Howley, Dan, 48, 50, 51, 55, 56
Hoyt, Waite, 32–33
Hubler, David, 5
Hudson, Johnny, 87
Huggins, Miller, 16, 22–23, 24, 26, 34, 36–37, 39, 40–41, 42, 43, 44–45, 59, 83, 92
Humphrey, Hubert, 245
Hundley, Randy, 248, 257, 261, 270, 280

"I Come to Kill You" (Durocher), 239–40
Immerman, Conrad (Connie), 32, 112, 149, 159, 166–67, 298, 300
Irvin, Monte, 6, 192, 197, 198, 199, 200, 205, 206, 207–8, 209, 211, 212, 214, 215, 218, 222, 232, 272, 303
Izenberg, Jerry, 238

Jackson, Corny, 4, 176
Jackson, "Shoeless" Joe, 299
Jansen, Larry, 200, 209
Japanese Pacific League, 291–92
Jarvis, Billy, 81
Jenkins, Ferguson, 248, 256, 263, 264
Jethroe, Sam, 132–33
Jim Crow policies, 74, 90, 91, 105, 127, 163
Jones, Mel, 163
Jorgensen, Spider, 187

Kaese, Harold, 231, 284
Kahn, Roger, 302, 302–3n
Kampouris, Alex, 121

Kashi, Anna, 232
Katz, Maxwell, 194–95
Kaye, Danny, 122, 136, 138, 140, 181, 220–21, 222, 239, 240, 292, 306
Keane, Albert, 37
Keller, Charlie, 100, 159
Kelly, Joe, 22
Kessinger, Don, 247, 257, 260, 263, 264
Kieran, John, 67, 78
Kilgallen, Dorothy, 112, 229
King, Pete, 67
Koenig, Mark, 16, 18, 21, 23, 26, 27, 29, 39
Koslo, Dave, 211
Koufax, Sandy, 218, 218n, 240, 241, 251
Koy, Ernie, 77, 78
Kremenko, Barney, 212
Krichell, Paul, 15, 16, 18
Kuhn, Bowie, 204, 269–70, 271–72, 274, 275, 290, 301

Labine, Clem, 236
labor union boycott, 69–70
Lacy, Sam, 163, 200, 206, 214
La Guardia, Fiorello, 139, 172
Landis, Kenesaw Mountain, 51–52, 55–56, 66, 70, 89, 98–99, 104, 105–7, 107n, 112, 115, 128, 134, 152–53, 196
Lane, Frank, 228–29
Laney, Al, 132
Lansky, Meyer, 54, 89
Lardner, John, 71, 75, 85, 107
Larker, Norm, 233
Lary, Lyn, 39, 40, 42, 46
Lasorda, Tommy, 2–3, 296, 305
Lavagetto, Harry "Cookie," 81, 104, 178
Lawrence, W. L., 20
Lazzeri, Tony, 18, 21, 23, 26–27, 29, 33, 35, 208, 303
Leibowitz, Samuel S., 135
Leo Durocher Day, 31–33, 112
Levinson, "Sleepout" Louie, 8, 54, 96–97, 97n, 109, 264, 264n
Life magazine, 135, 234, 266–67
Linn, Ed, 7, 239, 240, 288–89
The Lip (Eskenazi), 294, 307
Lloyd, Vince, 267
Lockman, Whitey, 205, 206, 209–10, 214, 217–18, 235, 237, 280, 281
Logan, Ella, 100
Lopat, Eddie, 211
Lopez, Al, 93–95, 95n, 219, 220, 228, 304
Los Angeles Dodgers, 6, 230–44, 261–62, 285
Lyon, Herb, 253, 259
Lyons, Leonard, 115–16, 121, 173–74

MacPhail, Leland Stanford "Larry"
    at anti-Hitler demonstration, 100
    in the Army, 110, 111, 121
    Chandler on, 300
    defense of Durocher, 173, 177
    end of career of, 179, 179n
    Hall of Fame and, 293, 294
    Leo's personal life and, 103, 110, 111
    as president of Brooklyn Dodgers, 73, 74, 78–79, 82, 83–84, 85, 86–87, 88, 93, 98
    as president of Cincinnati Reds, 62

as president of New York Yankees, 133, 134,
    139–40, 139n, 151
  racial integration of baseball and, 76, 139–40, 147
  war with Durocher, 158–60, 165, 166, 167–68
  on Webb and Siegel, 175
Magerkurth, George, 94, 95, 96
Maglie, Sal, 198, 200–201, 209, 210, 214, 219, 264,
    278, 308
Mann, Arthur, 9–10, 22–23, 23n, 27, 29, 31, 35,
    38–39, 41, 43–44, 45, 50, 68, 111–12, 147, 148,
    149, 165
  Baseball Confidential, 167n, 207
  as special assistant to Rickey, 166, 167, 168–69,
    168n, 173, 189
Mantle, Mickey, 205–6
Maranville, Walter "Rabbit," 11, 15, 35, 40, 48, 57, 61
Marion, Marty, 107, 125
Markus, Robert, 155, 262, 267, 274
Martin, Billy, 284, 296
Martin, Dean, 271, 273, 296
Martin, Tony, 98, 239, 306
Mauch, Gene, 124, 125, 185, 187, 246, 296
Mauney, Mike, 266–67
Mays, Willie, 5–6, 199, 199n, 204–6, 208, 211, 212,
    213, 215, 217, 218, 219, 221, 222–23, 234, 235,
    243, 287, 294, 306
McCormick, Frank, 80
McDougald, Gil, 212
McDuffie, Terris, 131, 132, 132n, 133
McGaha, Mel, 243
McGowan, Roscoe, 80, 142, 166
McLain, Denny, 271
McLaughlin, Hollis, 20, 20n
McLemore, Henry, 55, 66, 101, 171
Meany, Tom, 11, 25–26, 77n, 108, 129–30, 172
Medwick, Joe "Ducky," 63, 113, 119, 129, 130
Meier, Ted, 95–96
Miller, Marvin, 276, 277, 283–84
Minneapolis Millers, 204, 205, 222
"Miracle of Coogan's Bluff," 2, 211, 236–37
Mister Ed (TV show), 5
Mitchell, Jerry, 96
Monroe, Al, 90
Montreal Expos, 267
Montreal Royals, 137, 160, 161, 162–63, 166, 168,
    169, 169n
Moore, Joseph, 135, 140, 142–43, 144
Moore, Terry, 195
Moran, Duke, 95
Morin, Rene, Anna, and Carolyn, 241–42
Morris, Ed, 38
Morstadt, Lynda, 259, 259n
Moss, Dick, 284
Mr. Ed, 241
Mr. Novak (TV show), 243
Muchnick, Isadore, 132
Mueller, Don, 205, 208–10, 209n, 211
Mulbry, Walter, 168, 168n, 176–77, 180
The Munsters (TV show), 244–45
Munzel, Edgar, 262, 277
Murder Incorporated, 54, 89, 144, 300
Murphy, Frank, 154, 167, 299, 300
Murphy, Jack, 240, 271
Murphy, Johnny, 100
Murray, Jim, 31, 232, 243–44, 289–90, 298, 307,
    308

Musial, Stan, 214, 302
Myer, Buddy, 16

Nakamura, Nagoyashi, 291, 292
"The Name of the Game" (Frank), 107–8, 108n
National Baseball Hall of Fame, 2, 5, 6, 16n, 128,
    176n, 179n, 270, 304
  Durocher and, 292–308
NBC (National Broadcasting Company), 223,
    224–28, 295
Negro leagues, 74, 131, 132n, 134, 140, 140n, 160, 193,
    197, 199
Nelson, Lindsey, 6–7, 226
Newcombe, Don, 161, 209, 210, 214
Newsom, Bobo, 116, 117, 118, 121, 122
New York Giants, 2, 3, 5, 17n, 52, 58, 65, 70, 71, 72,
    77, 85–87, 93, 119, 142, 145–46, 238
  Durocher as manager of, 190–223, 282, 297
  1948 season, 189–92, 282
  1949 season, 193–97
  1950 season, 198–200
  1951 season, 204–12, 234–37, 268
  1952 season, 215
  1953 season, 215–16
  1954 season, 217–20
  1955 season, 221–23
New York Highlanders, 30–31, 89
New York Mets, 2, 233, 234, 238, 247–48, 250,
    260–61, 262, 264–65, 267, 268, 269, 274,
    275, 286–87
New York Yankees, 11, 13, 15, 16, 17, 18, 19, 21, 23–24,
    23n, 70, 74n, 281, 294–95
  Durocher sold by, 46–48
  Jake Powell affair, 89–90
  MacPhail as president of, 133, 134, 139–40, 139n,
    151
  "Murderers' Row," 1, 23
  1928 season, 25–37
  1929 season, 37–45
  1941 World Series, 99–101
  1947 season, 158–59, 166–67, 168–69, 177,
    178–79
  1951 World Series, 211–12
  1953 World Series, 216
Nice Guys Finish Last (Durocher), 5, 7, 11–12, 14n,
    168n, 248, 273, 289, 289n, 290–91, 290n
Niekro, Joe, 252, 279
Nieman, Butch, 134
Nixon, Richard M., 232, 270

O'Connor, Paddy, 13, 14, 17, 18–19
O'Hara, Jack, 13–14, 14n
Olmo, Luis, 188
O'Malley, Walter, 127, 156, 157, 165, 167, 168, 170, 183,
    230–31, 238–39, 293
Orsatti, Ernie "Showboat," 63, 64–65
Orwoll, Ossie, 29
Ott, Mel, 104, 142, 146, 188, 189, 191, 197
Owen, Mickey, 99, 100, 125
Owens, Jesse, 77, 77n

Packard automobile, 35, 35n, 41
Page, Joe, 178–79
Paige, Satchel, 90, 91
Pappas, Milt, 276
Parker, Dan, 109, 120, 172, 300

Parrott, Harold (Hal), 4, 54n, 82, 97, 124, 131, 158, 160, 161–62, 168, 172–73, 181, 187, 189, 293
Patterson, Arthur "Red," 100, 119, 119n, 166, 169, 298
Paxton, Harry, 226–27
Pegler, Westbrook, 26, 90, 90n, 147–49, 152–53, 157, 166, 172, 173, 175
Pekkanen, John, 266–67
Pepitone, Joe, 276, 290
Perini, Lou, 189
Petersen, Paul, 243
Philadelphia Athletics, 19, 24, 26–28
Philadelphia Phillies, 55–56, 124, 143, 168n, 257, 267
Pinelli, Babe, 6, 126, 198
Pittsburgh Pirates, 24, 65, 93–95, 117, 233–34, 243, 255, 264, 274, 275
Pius XII, Pope, 130
platoon system, 217–18
pocket billiards, 46–47
Pollet, Howie, 302
"The Pop-Off Kid" (in Collier's), 91
Povich, Shirley, 3, 173, 205, 213, 214, 305
Powell, Jake, 89–90, 90n
Powell, Vincent J., 156, 157–58
Prager, Joshua, 237–38
Pride of the Yankees (film), 103–4
Prohibition, 30, 31, 32
Pryor, Paul, 269

racial integration of baseball. See also Robinson, Jackie
    Brooklyn Dodgers and, 216–17
    Communist Party and, 105–6
    Durocher's role in, 5–6, 90–91, 127, 151
    MacPhail and, 76, 139–40, 147
    New York Giants and, 197, 200, 205, 216–17
    opposition to, 139–40
    Rickey and, 74, 131–33, 161, 164, 168, 168n, 169–70, 171, 172–73, 300
    sportswriters and, 90
racism, 74, 89–90, 135, 141, 169
Rader, Doug, 276
Raft, George, 1, 30–31, 66, 88–89, 92–93, 96, 98–99, 103, 122–23, 128, 138, 147, 148–49, 150, 152, 153, 154, 175, 187, 203
Rapoport, Ron, 200, 297
Raschi, Vic, 211
Ray, Jim, 286
Reardon, Beans, 56
Redd, David, 13, 91–92, 211n, 227
Reese, Jimmie, 46
Reese, Pee Wee, 92, 99, 111, 113, 115, 125, 164, 198–99, 199n, 222, 293, 308
Reiser, Pete, 92, 113, 115, 170, 186, 260, 261, 293
Rennie, Rud, 38, 221
Reston, James "Scotty," Jr., 71, 71n
Reuss, Jerry, 287
Rhodes, Dusty, 217–18, 219, 220, 295
Rice, Grantland, 27, 35, 72, 73, 125, 172
Richardson, Spec, 282, 283, 284
Rickey, Branch
    as Cardinals business manager, 57–58, 59, 69, 70, 72, 73
    on Durocher, 5, 63
    Durocher's Continental League offer from, 228

Durocher's reinstatement and, 183–86, 187, 189–91
Durocher's suspension and, 173, 174, 176, 177, 182
Grace Dozier and, 64, 65
as Leo's friend and benefactor, 92, 220
Leo's friendship with Raft and, 147, 148–49, 150
Leo's personal life and, 156
MacPhail and, 179
Mann's biography of, 165
as president of Dodgers, 111–15, 117–24, 126–27, 131–35, 137–38, 142, 144, 149, 151, 157–58, 160, 164–67, 183, 299
    racial integration and, 74, 131–33, 161, 164, 168, 168n, 169–70, 171, 172–73, 300
    Shotton and, 170–71, 180
Rickey, Branch, Jr. (Twig), 124, 189
Rigney, Bill, 222, 223, 230, 246
Rizzuto, Phil, 159
Roberts, Dave, 287
Robinson, Bill "Bojangles," 193–94
Robinson, Frank, 281
Robinson, Jackie
    Chandler on, 300
    Chicago White Sox and, 141, 141n
    death of, 283
    Durocher and acceptance of, 5–6, 137, 149, 151, 169
    on Durocher as Cubs manager, 269
    Durocher at odds with, 183, 186, 192, 200, 208, 209, 214–15, 231–32
    as favorite of Durocher, 308
    first season as Dodgers player (1947), 169–70, 169n, 171, 172–73, 179–80
    as Montreal Royals player, 137, 141–42, 160–64, 168, 168n, 169
    as MVP (1949), 199
    play about, 294
    signed by Dodgers, 137–38
Rodney, Lester, 90–91, 105, 106
Rose, Pete, 264n, 300
Rosen, Al, 219
Rosenthal, Harold, 293
Roth, Allen, 293
Rowe, Schoolboy, 67
Ruffing, Red, 99
Runge, Ed, 251
Runyon, Damon, 31, 66, 68, 109, 112
Ruppert, Jacob, 18, 37, 62
Russo, Marius, 99
Ruth, Babe, 15, 33, 62, 78, 136
    Babe Ruth's Own Book of Baseball, 27
    Durocher compared to, 293
    Durocher's photo with, 298
    Durocher's strained relationship with, 3, 49, 49n, 79, 81–82, 203, 207, 240, 289–90
    in fictional story, 107–8
    hired by Dodgers, 78–79, 80–83
    home run record, 287
    infield shift for, 57
    nickname for Durocher, 1–2, 34–35, 35n
    in 1928 season, 25, 26, 28, 34–35
    in 1929 season, 41–42
    in 1935 season, 70
    uniform sold at auction, 83n
Ryder, Jack, 51, 56, 60

Sachs, Emmanuel "Manie," 223, 228
San Diego Padres, 260, 279, 286
Santo, Ron, 247, 252, 256, 257, 263, 264–65, 268, 275, 276, 278, 289
Schoendienst, Red, 244, 244n, 256, 260
Schofield, Dick, 251
Schuble, Henry "Heine," 63
Schumacher, Garry, 25–26, 191, 196, 211
Schumacher, Hal, 86
Scott, Everett, 15–16
Scully, Vin, 234, 241, 291
Shaplen, Robert, 60, 174n, 211n
Shawkey, Bob, 46, 47–48
Shellenback, Frank, 218
Sherman, Allan, 261n, 265
"Shot Heard 'Round the World," 2, 210–11, 234–35
Shotton, Burt, 170–71, 177, 178, 180, 181–82, 183, 186, 189, 191, 207
Shurin, Martin, Jr., 128, 148, 150
Siegel, Benjamin "Bugsy," 89, 148, 149–50, 166, 175–76, 203
Silvers, Phil, 225
Sinatra, Frank, 1, 124–25, 138, 220, 225–26, 229, 232, 234, 239–40, 254, 260, 271, 283, 289, 291, 292, 294, 296
Slaughter, Enos, 146
Smith, Hal, 233
Smith, Red, 55, 170, 172, 180, 195, 211, 230, 265, 271, 290, 300
Smith, Robert, 52–53, 76
Smith, Wendell, 91, 132–33, 141, 142, 197
Snider, Duke, 236, 237n, 294
Spahn, Warren, 206
Spangler, Al, 265
Speaker, Tris, 28
spitball rule, 254–55
Stanky, Eddie, 178, 183, 186, 197–98, 199, 209, 210, 246, 293, 308
Steinbrenner, George, 294–95
Stengel, Casey, 16n, 18, 19, 22, 23, 71, 85, 213, 233, 234, 276
Stewart, Bill, 72
St. Louis Browns, 48, 50, 118, 197, 215
St. Louis Cardinals, 1, 17n, 21, 40, 80, 97, 108, 110, 111, 146–47, 178, 243, 252, 256, 265–67, 302
   Bleacher Bums and, 260
   Communist Party and, 105n
   Durocher sold to, and traded from, 57–59, 73–74
   Durocher's tricks while playing for, 87
   Durocher's withdrawn offer from, 244, 245
   "Gashouse Gang," 1, 64, 64n, 70, 71, 72, 306
   1933 season, 61–62
   1934 season, 62–69
   1935 season, 69–70
   1936 season, 70–72
   1937 season, 72–74
   union boycott of, 69–70
   vote for Durocher, 195
   in World Series (1928), 35
Stock Market Crash (1929), 47, 48, 62
Stoneham, Horace, 175–76, 189, 190, 191, 195–96, 204–5, 220–21, 222, 223, 239–40
Stout, Allyn, 58

St. Paul Saints, 21–23, 24
Stripp, "Jersey Joe," 73, 74, 74n
Sukeforth, Clyde, 124, 170, 186, 293
Sullivan, Ed, 224, 225

"Take Me Out to the Ball Game," 241, 306
Talley, Rick, 258, 264, 265, 270, 271, 275, 278, 280, 290, 293, 301
Taylor, Harry, 178
Terry, Bill, 70, 71, 73, 85, 191
Texas Rangers, 283–84
Thomas, Dave "Showboat," 131, 132, 132n, 133
Thomas, Larri, 229, 229n, 232
Thompson, Henry (Hank), 6, 197, 211, 217–18
Thomson, Bobby, 2, 206, 208–9, 210–11, 214, 234–36, 237, 293, 304
Toledo Mud Hens, 22, 23
Tracy, David, 215–16
Trauschke, Bunny and Eddie, 13
Troy, Jack, 110, 119, 139n
Trujillo, Rafael, 183
Tuned to Baseball (Harwell), 297

Ughetta, Henry L., 173

Vander Meer, Johnny, 77–78, 77n
Vaughan, Arky, 113, 116, 117, 118, 122
Veeck, Bill, 60, 192, 228, 288–89, 293, 302, 303
Vernon, Mickey, 137, 137n

Wakefield, Dick, 140–41
Walker, Dixie, 87, 95, 113, 117, 118, 120, 121, 122, 126, 138, 162, 169, 170
Walker, Rube, 236–37
Walsh, Christy, 79
Wanninger, Pee-Wee, 15–16
Washington Senators, 16, 29, 118, 137
Wayne, John, 156, 162
Weaver, Earl, 296
Webb, Del, 175–76, 176n, 179
Weil, Sidney, 48–49, 50–54, 55, 56, 58–59, 60, 62, 92, 121, 140
Wertz, Vic, 219
Westrum, Wes, 235, 246
Williams, Billy, 247, 257, 276, 298
Williams, Dick, 207, 208
Williams, Marvin, 132–33
Williams, Ted, 140–41
Wills, Maury, 6, 281, 292
Wilson, Artie, 204, 205
Wilson, Hack, 57
Woods, Arthur, 46
World's Fair (1939), 83, 88
World War II, 7, 104, 110, 112, 113–16, 117–18, 122, 124, 125, 129–30, 135, 136–37, 138, 173–74, 197
Wrigley, Philip, 133, 147, 246, 256, 260, 262, 273–74, 275, 276–77, 278, 280–81, 282, 291
Wyatt, Whitlow, 87, 99, 113
Wynn, Early, 219

Young, Dick, 159, 159n, 170, 230, 240, 248, 255, 259, 266, 267, 293, 295, 305
Yvar, Sal, 212, 237

A Note on the Author

Paul Dickson was born in 1939 in Yonkers, New York, where as a young baseball fan he spent many hours reading about the antics and achievements of Leo Durocher in Brooklyn and New York City. Dickson has written more than sixty-five nonfiction books and numerous newspaper and magazine articles, mostly about those things that intrigue him, which translates to a concentration on writing about the American language, baseball, and twentieth-century American history. His first biography, *Bill Veeck: Baseball's Greatest Maverick*, published in 2012, was awarded the Jerome Holtzman Award from the Chicago Baseball Museum, the Reader's Choice Award for the best baseball book of 2012 from the Special Libraries Association, and the Casey Award from *Spitball* magazine, also for the best baseball book of 2012.

Dickson has also been awarded the Tony Salin Memorial Award from the Baseball Reliquary in 2011 for his role in preserving baseball history, and his *Dickson Baseball Dictionary* was named by the New York Public Library as one of the best reference books of 2009. In 2010 *The Wall Street Journal* called the third edition of the *Dickson Baseball Dictionary* one of the six best baseball books ever published. In 2013 he was awarded the Henry Chadwick Award by the Society for American Baseball Research, which honors "baseball's great researchers for their invaluable contributions to making baseball the game that links America's present with its past." Among Dickson's other major works are the classic narrative history *Sputnik: The Shock of the Century* and *The Bonus Army: An American Epic*, which he coauthored with Thomas B. Allen. He lives in Garrett Park, Maryland, with his wife, Nancy.